GUARDIAN YEARS

GUARDIAN YEARS

Alastair Hetherington

CHATTO & WINDUS · LONDON · 1981

Published by Chatto & Windus Ltd
40 William IV Street, London WC2N 4DF

British Library Cataloguing in Publication Data
Hetherington, Alastair
Guardian years.
1. Journalism – Great Britain – Biography
I. Title
070.4'1'09224   PN4874.HY

ISBN 0 7011 2552 7

Printed in Great Britain by
Butler & Tanner Ltd, Frome and London

Contents

Illustrations

Foreword

By Fleet Street standards, nearly twenty years is a long tenure for the editor of a national newspaper. From the autumn of 1956 to the spring of 1975 I was editor of the *Guardian* (or *Manchester Guardian* as it was until 1959). This book is about those years.

It is an account of what was happening in one office. Each newspaper has its own character and philosophy, influenced by its owners, its staff, and its commercial purposes. I hope to illuminate the political, financial, and personal pressures on the *Guardian*'s editor and his senior staff – and to give insight more generally on the interplay of newspapers, politics, and politicians.

Only one instruction is given to the editor of the *Guardian* on his appointment. It is to 'carry on the paper in the same spirit as before' – a gloriously liberal directive, leaving the editor great freedom. It is derived from the deed which established the Scott Trust in 1936, in keeping with the intentions of C. P. Scott, who had been editor of the paper from 1871 to 1929 and principal proprietor from 1907 until his death in 1932. It was delivered to me by Laurence Scott, a grandson of C.P. and company chairman, as we walked round his garden at Alderley Edge in October 1956.

To the Scott family, the *Guardian* owes it character and survival. The family transferred to the Trust the whole ordinary shareholding in the company (the *Manchester Guardian* and *Evening News* Ltd, or latterly the *Guardian* and *Manchester Evening News* Ltd). The family divested themselves of all beneficial interest in the shares, and accepted thereafter only what some earned as salaried members of the staff. The Trust deed prevents the return of any shareholding to them. Creation of the Trust was an act of extraordinary generosity and public spirit, designed to perpetuate the *Guardian*.

Until 1961 the *Guardian* was printed only in Manchester, and until 1964 the editorial headquarters remained there. The company headquarters is still there, though the *Guardian*'s senior management are now all in London.

As for myself, I was brought up in an academic household in Scotland, my father having been a professor of philosophy and later Principal of Glasgow University from 1936 to 1961. I went to Gresham's School, in Norfolk, and then to Corpus Christi College, Oxford. After six years in the Army (including service in a tank regiment in Normandy and as a staff officer in Germany), I worked for the *Glasgow Herald* from 1946 to 1950, when I joined the *Guardian* as a leader writer and defence correspondent. I became foreign editor in 1953, continuing also as defence correspondent, and that was my position when the Suez events opened in the summer of 1956. That is where the book begins.

Alastair Hetherington
February 1981

1 Suez, 1956

The last time Britain went to war was at Suez, in October 1956. At that time, probably a majority in this country supported the Eden Government's action. Soon afterwards, most people had come to see that it was a mistake. From the start, Sir Anthony Eden's conviction that force must be used against Egypt was strongly opposed by the *Manchester Guardian* on moral and practical grounds. Among the national newspapers, only the *Observer* took a comparable stand. The Labour party in Parliament, led by Hugh Gaitskell, came round to the *MG*'s view only gradually – though in the end Gaitskell became a powerful and outspoken opponent of the Suez venture. There was nothing pre-determined about the *Guardian*'s view. It grew out of a belief in the rule of law, internationally as well as nationally, and out of the facts as reported by the *Guardian*'s own staff at home and overseas.

'Hit Nasser hard'

British forces had been withdrawn from the Suez Canal Zone in June 1956, following agreement with the Egyptian Revolutionary Government. Nasser, replacing General Neguib, had been in power as President for just over two years. Among Nasser's most cherished projects for pulling his backward countrymen into the twentieth century was the Aswan High Dam, which was to have been financed by the British and American Governments and by the World Bank. It was to provide water to irrigate the Nile valley and electricity for industry. But on July 19, 1956, Nasser returned to Cairo from Brioni, on the Adriatic, where he had been meeting President Tito of Yugoslavia and Pandit Nehru, Prime Minister of India – and was greeted with the news that the American Government had withdrawn its offer to help finance the high dam, and that the British Government had decided to follow the American lead. The World Bank's offer, three-quarters of the total sum, had been contingent on the US and British contributions and therefore lapsed. It was a bitter blow for Nasser.

The American decision appears to have been mainly because of Congressional opposition. Nasser had lately recognised Mao's China and had done a deal with Russia on the sale of Egyptian cotton; he was, in addition, believed to be in discussion with the Soviet Union on a big arms deal. In the end, as it turned out, Nasser not only got his arms from Russia but got finance for the Aswan High Dam – but that was still more than a year away. (The dam was eventually completed in 1970.)

Nasser replied publicly one week later: first with a speech flaying the Americans for saying that Egypt's economy was not strong enough to warrant the dam, and then, on Thursday, July 26, with another speech in Alexandria declaring that Egypt was nationalising the Suez Canal and freezing all the assets in Egypt of the international company which owned the canal. Egyptian troops moved into the canal company's offices and control centres while Nasser was speaking, but the canal remained open to shipping. Nasser promised that the canal's revenues would be used to build the high dam.

At the hour when Nasser was exciting his audience in Alexandria, Sir Anthony Eden and some of his Cabinet were holding a dinner at 10 Downing Street for the King and the Prime Minister of Iraq, Faisal and Nuri es-Said (both of whom were murdered in Baghdad two years later). The news of Nasser's speech was broken towards the end of the dinner, and according to Selwyn Lloyd, then the Foreign Secretary, Nuri said that 'we should hit Nasser hard and quickly'.[1] The Iraqi guests retired early, while the British Ministers adjourned to the Cabinet room where they were joined by the Chiefs of Staff and by American and French representatives. There are differing versions of what was said, but Eden himself indicates in his Memoirs published in 1960 that from the beginning he believed that force must be used if necessary to safeguard the canal. A dictator such as Nasser could not be allowed to 'have his thumb on our windpipe', and even if Her Majesty's Government had to act alone they could not stop short of using force to protect their position.[2]

While the Cabinet were in emergency session at Downing Street, in full evening dress, a rapid gathering of *Guardian* editorial staff was taking place in shirtsleeves at Cross Street, Manchester. It began, for me, in the corridor outside the sub-editors' room. As foreign editor I was on my way there to catch up on the latest copy. Out of the room came an animated colleague – John Anderson,* an assistant editor and a man with great knowledge of the oil industry. He was holding the first Reuter 'rush' message about Nasser's nationalisation decree. I was interested but at first not too excited, whereas he took the view that this was a momentous event. The first edition had already gone to press: but for later editions the *MG* carried, unusually, a three-decker headline and a double-column introduction to its front-page lead story. Editorial comment was reserved until next day.

In the House of Commons at midday next day (Friday 27th) Eden made a statement deploring the Egyptian action but saying little more. Hugh Gaitskell as leader of the Opposition also objected to Nasser's 'high-handed action'. (He had been at the Downing Street dinner the previous evening but had since discussed the situation with some of his

1 Selwyn Lloyd, *Suez 1956*, p. 74.
2 Eden, *Full Circle*, pp. 422–27.
* This and all future asterisks in the text indicate biographical notes about *Guardian* staff; please see pp. 368–73.

Shadow Cabinet.)³ Captain Waterhouse, a Conservative backbencher, demanded the placing of British warships at either end of the canal. Julian Amery said that public opinion would support any step, 'however grave'. The Prime Minister replied that the situation must be handled 'with firmness and care'. The public exchanges ended there. But we now know from Eden's Memoirs that that afternoon the Chiefs of Staff were told to prepare 'a plan and timetable for an operation designed to occupy and secure the canal, should other methods fail'. He also sent a telegram to President Eisenhower – then just preparing to campaign for re-election – saying that a firm stand was essential. We also know from William Clark, then the Prime Minister's press secretary, that from the beginning 'Eden was determined to overthrow Nasser'.⁴

In Manchester, in addition to a full Parliamentary report and much other material, we prepared a leading article. It was mostly written by John Anderson, after consultation with Guy Wint, a Cambridge scholar who contributed on Asian and Middle Eastern affairs. It was cool, beginning:

It would be a mistake either to lose our heads with vexation over Colonel Nasser's latest move or to underestimate its adroitness. . . . The withdrawal by the United States and Britain of the offer to finance in part the building of the Aswan high dam made it inevitable that Colonel Nasser should respond with some dramatic defiance – military dictators live by prestige, and in order to survive he had to strike out in a spectacular way . . .

The main interest of the Western countries in the Middle East is to be able to purchase and transport oil. The West can hardly use military power as a means of guaranteeing the oil supply. Any retaliatory measures which led to the closing of the canal would defeat the very end which Western policy should aim at securing. It is just silly to talk of withdrawing the canal's technicians. But, looking ahead, we should certainly examine any chance of making ourselves less dependent on transit through the canal.

It went on to recommend the building of supertankers (the biggest then being about 50,000 tons, a fraction of the size of VLCCs today) and to discuss the value of a pipeline from Eilat on the Gulf of Akaba to Haifa on the Mediterranean. This was a practical commentary: we still had no concept of what was in Eden's mind.

By the middle of the next week, the atmosphere was very much more tense. On Tuesday 31st five of the *MG*'s seven front-page columns were taken up with Suez, together with much space inside the paper; on Wednesday the front page reported 'precautionary' moves of troops and naval vessels to the East Mediterranean, including the aircraft carriers *Ocean* and *Bulwark* being prepared to leave Devonport and Plymouth; and on Thursday there was a long leader, 'Military Action', warning the Government against premature use of force – though also on the front

3 Philip Williams, *Hugh Gaitskell*, p. 419.
4 William Clark, in the *Listener*, November 22, 1979.

page was a report that the P & O liner *Himalaya*, homeward bound from Australia, had passed through the Suez Canal without incident.

The origin of the leader 'Military Action' is significant. Late on Tuesday evening, a private message reached me from our Washington correspondent, Max Freedman. Max was a meticulous journalist, with excellent contacts in the US State Department. He had ready access to the Secretary of State, John Foster Dulles. Max was a Canadian, from Winnipeg, but with an encyclopaedic knowledge of British history and British foreign policy. That Tuesday night he filed a message about the coming Presidential election and another reporting that Mr Dulles, though just back from Peru, was coming straight on to London to meet British Ministers and the French Foreign Minister, Christian Pineau. Tacked on to the end of these despatches was a private message, not for publication, addressed to me as foreign editor and to Richard Scott, our diplomatic correspondent in London. It ran approximately as follows (I say 'approximately' because it is the only one of Max's private messages of that period which was not preserved, but I have a contemporary note of it):

> From Max Freedman. Strictly private and not for publication. For Mr Hetherington and Mr Scott. Robert Murphy has reported to Mr Dulles and the President that the British Government is preparing for military action to seize the Suez Canal without delay. Mr Dulles has been instructed by the President to urge caution and to give preference to negotiation.

In Manchester that message jolted us. Murphy was Eisenhower's special envoy, newly sent to London. Until then we had thought it almost inconceivable that our Government would try to use force immediately. If traffic through the canal had been hindered or stopped by the Egyptians, it would be a different matter, but with traffic moving there could be no legal pretext. Also, because I worked as defence correspondent as well as foreign editor, I well knew that Britain had neither amphibious forces capable of quick deployment in the East Mediterranean nor airborne units strong enough to take and hold the canal by themselves. Further, the British forces had come out of the Canal Zone partly because of the difficulty of fending off attacks by Egyptian irregulars and rioters. (And when the assault on Suez was eventually launched, three months later, how ponderously slow it proved to be.)

Next morning, there was a disturbing leader in the *Times*. Its editor, Sir William Haley, was believed to be close to Eden. Years later, Sir Anthony quoted extensively from that leading article in his Memoirs, and in one passage the phrasing coincides with Eden's in his Friday telegram to Eisenhower. The leader compared Nasser's action with Hitler's march into the Rhineland in 1936 – a recurrent theme in Eden's own statements. This, it said, was a 'hinge of history'. Nasser's seizure of the canal must be resisted. 'Quibbling over whether or not he was "legally entitled" to make the grab will delight the finicky and comfort the fainthearted, but entirely misses the real issues.' The real issues, it said, were that the canal must be in 'friendly and trustworthy hands', which Nasser's were not, and that if Nasser were not stopped then other extremist demands would be made against oilfields in the Middle East.

The *Guardian*'s editor, A. P. Wadsworth, was at that time seriously ill with what proved to be a terminal debilitation of his body – but his mind was still sharp, and on the Wednesday morning a few of us gathered round his bedside at his home in Didsbury. That morning Wadsworth suffered the longest editorial conference of his career, 'unable to break it up as he liked to do by moving away'.[5] It lasted only forty minutes, but Wadsworth hated conferences and for him that was a long time. Afterwards, I was asked to write the leader 'Military Action', analysing the choice before Britain. Because it set the line for much of our later comment, and because that line was abhorrent to our many critics, let me quote its opening:

> The Government is right to be prepared for military action at Suez. If Colonel Nasser were to close the canal – but only in that event – British troops should move in. At present there is no possible warrant for using force. Colonel Nasser has not broken the 1888 convention nor do any of the later undertakings appear to have been breached. The 1888 convention provided for free passage of international shipping but said nothing about the ownership of the canal. The treaties of 1936 and 1954 did not alter the position on these points. It is hard, then, to see how Colonel Nasser can be said to have acted against international law. If the British Government has reasons for saying that he did, it should state them plainly today.
>
> What Colonel Nasser has done may be awkward, commercially damaging to the West, and perhaps even part of a plan for creating a new Arab Empire based on the Nile. But it is not ground for armed action – unless he closes the canal, or seizes the British maintenance bases there, or turns against his neighbours. We must be ready for action, but we must not launch it without cause.
>
> The *Times* argued yesterday that 'it would have been better to have had a foot in the door first' – which is a polite way of saying that our troops ought to be at Suez now – and that 'quibbling' about legal issues was unimportant. Such advice, if adopted, would destroy whatever claim Britain has to be an upholder of international law and morality. It would destroy the United Nations in a day, and it would land Britain in an appalling embroilment with at least three-fifths of the world ranged against her.

The following day, on the front page, the *MG* carried as full a summary as we could muster of the British and French military preparations – including three aircraft carriers being made ready to leave that weekend, other naval vessels being taken out of mothballs, the recall of army reservists, and advice to British and French nationals to leave Egypt. We had to be careful, for a D Notice had been issued advising against publication of specific designations of units or their destinations (other

5 David Ayerst, *Guardian: Biography of a Newspaper*, p. 620.

than Mediterranean') or strengths.[6] I had rung Admiral Thomson, who looked after the D Notices, to ask for clearance on one point and had received a courteous but cautionary answer. We did not want to flout the system needlessly, but we tried to indicate the extent of British military activity.

That day, Friday, August 3, the paper also reported the first results of Mr Dulles's visit – a joint invitation by the United States, Britain and France to interested nations (including Egypt) to a conference on an international administration for the Suez canal. And the Commons' first full debate on the crisis was reported, with the Prime Minister's announcement of the intention to take precautionary military measures, together with Hugh Gaitskell's broad support for the Government's approach. Gaitskell fiercely denounced Nasser's Arab expansionism, but he reminded the Government that Britain had signed the United Nations Charter and must not breach international law. It seemed clear that he did not suspect the Government of preparing to use force unilaterally – and indeed he indicated some time later that he had been misled by Eden in a private conversation at the House of Commons earlier that day.[7]

The pattern was repeated over the next few days. On Saturday Mr Dulles went back to Washington, saying that the West must not meet violence with violence; and shortly afterwards Max Freedman made one point more explicit in a despatch for publication.

When Mr Dulles went to London, he faced this dilemma. There would be war in 24 or 48 hours unless there could be an immediate conference on British terms. So Mr Dulles decided to play for time by accepting the British terms for the London conference.

On August 6, not for publication, Max sent another private message reporting that the British Ambassador in Washington had been asked by the Secretary of State again to transmit 'the most urgent warning' to go slow in taking military measures against Egypt. There was a further such message on August 10 and another on August 12. Parallel information was coming in to us from Richard Scott, who had good sources in the Foreign Office. A couple of short extracts from Max's message of August 10, in its own shorthand style, may give its flavour:

Dulles says no press conference because matter so critical and dangerous. Little doubt of determination of Britain and France not to accept situation where their economic life is at the mercy of someone as fanatical and irresponsible as Nasser. America very sympathetic with that general viewpoint. But situation does not call at present stage for military action. Such action was being planned by British and French, which Dulles learned Tuesday morning and thus went to London. Felt case would not be understood in world. Morally indefensible. Would destroy

6 Further discussion of D Notices in Chapter 11.
7 Philip Williams, *Hugh Gaitskell*, pp. 421-22.

United Nations if armed intervention. But did have good case if properly presented. . . .

We (US) are not engaging in combined military planning with Britain and France. They have basic plan and have not suspended it. Can Britain and France back down? There is complete determination not to acquiesce. They will fight rather than accept control by Egypt. A very very grave situation. We are trying to find peaceful solution.

With this stream of private advice coming in – advice that was in tune with our own thinking – the *MG* in leaders almost every day maintained support for 'negotiations first'. We said that there could be no justification for violent action against Egypt while the canal remained open, and that force simply would not succeed in keeping it open.

By mid-August Ministers had become seriously concerned (as we were hearing through our political and diplomatic staff) over the *Manchester Guardian*'s critical commentary and by its persistence in reporting that President Eisenhower and Mr Dulles did not share its view of the crisis. Eden in his Memoirs complains that the Americans did not behave 'in the spirit of an ally', but the Prime Minister consciously or unconsciously was blinding himself to the strength of American objections to the Anglo-French course. The reticence of the *Times*, *Telegraph*, and other papers on the American reaction was extraordinary, too, for it was clearly enough stated in the *New York Times*, *Washington Post*, and *Herald Tribune*.

The *MG*'s comments on Eden's television broadcast to the nation on the evening of August 8 seem to have particularly upset him, for we had pointed to the lack of a true parallel between Hitler in 1938 and Nasser in 1956 and to the importance of seeking the widest possible international support for diplomatic pressure on Egypt to reach an acceptable agreement on operation of the canal. Nearly all the other papers remained acquiescent or on the side of the Government – with only the *Daily Mirror* and the *Scottish Daily Record* among the major papers expressing many reservations.

On Monday morning, August 13, the Defence Ministry telephoned to ask if I would call next day on Sir Walter Monckton, the Defence Minister. I took the opportunity of being in London to call also on William Clark, the Prime Minister's press adviser at Downing Street. I knew and respected Monckton, and William Clark was an old friend. Monckton said, straightforwardly, that although our forces were being brought to readiness in the Mediterranean there was no decision to launch any operation. 'I am certainly not a party to it,' he said (according to a note I made immediately afterwards, not realising that Eden was now working with an inner Cabinet which at times excluded the Defence Minister). William Clark told me much the same story – while admitting that the invitation to meet Monckton had come because of the PM's concern over the *Guardian*'s line. So far as he knew the Government had never intended to start military action unless Nasser triggered it off. He

still believed that there was no intention to launch our forces unless
Nasser closed the canal to our ships or did something of the kind.

Retrospectively, of course, it is significant that Monckton was eased
out of his post as Defence Minister in mid-October, shortly before
hostilities began. And William Clark, having been on leave in the critical
fortnight before the war began at the end of October, quietly resigned his
Downing Street post on November 7 because, as he said twelve years later,
Sir Anthony's actions had required him to depart from telling the truth.[8]

On the train back to Manchester I wrote a note to Wadsworth enclosing
copies of my private memoranda on the conversations with Monckton
and Clark, and expressing some puzzlement over the different versions
that we were hearing. On the road home I popped it through his letterbox
about midnight, and about midday on Wednesday there was another
short editorial conference round his bedside. He was perturbed by some
of the letters the paper was receiving (and printing) from loyal readers
who wanted a tougher line with Nasser. He was perturbed also by some
that were coming to him at home – such as one from Lady Violet Bonham
Carter, an old friend of his and of Churchill's, who had written to say
that the *MG*'s staff must be out of their minds if they thought that 'dear
Anthony' would launch a war. Nevertheless Wadsworth agreed that we
ought to stick to our line, and that night I wrote another leader on the
opening of the London conference (which Egypt and Greece had declined
to attend). We said that there were signs that the Government was having
the 'second thoughts' for which President Eisenhower had hoped, and
that if British conduct in the conference were now to be moderate and
conciliatory we could win general support for international pressure on
Egypt.

The London conference led to the mission to Cairo by the Australian
Prime Minister, Mr Robert Menzies. But no sooner was he on the way
to Cairo, in the last week of August, than we received in Manchester yet
another indication from Washington that the French and British were
back on their old tracks. (We now know from General Beaufre's brisk
book that the commanders-in-chief meeting in Whitehall on August 24
agreed on a timetable by which naval forces would concentrate at Malta
in early September, a final decision would be made by the two Governments on September 10, the air assault on Egypt would start on September
15 and the landings on September 17.)[9] At any rate, on August 30 and 31
the paper returned to a stronger line with leaders headed 'A sabre rattled'
– about the well-publicised movement of French paratroops to British
bases in Cyprus – and 'To war?' On August 31 the *MG* also carried a
long interview with Hugh Gaitskell, which Wadsworth had asked our
labour correspondent Mark Arnold-Forster to secure. In this Gaitskell
insisted on the need for the Menzies mission to proceed. Echoing our

8 The *Guardian*, March 25, 1968.
9 André Beaufre, *The Suez Expedition*, 1956, pp. 43–44.

own words, he hoped that the Eden Government would not indulge in more sabre-rattling. 'In spite of rumours,' he said, 'I cannot believe that they can be seriously contemplating the use of force "to impose a solution" on Egypt.' In any event, Britain must go to the United Nations before there was any attempt at force.

Wadsworth was by now failing fast, but on September 10 he made his last contribution to the leader columns and to the *MG*, apart from one short book review. It was also his first direct contribution on the Suez issue, and it scolded the Sunday newspapers for suggesting that the Government had been the victim of a wicked press campaign, particularly in the *MG*. He curiously echoed Lady Violet's words, reversing their sense:

With leading newspapers advocating the use of force, it is not surprising that people abroad thought the British were out of their minds. Our friends have blenched – as has been plain in despatches from places as differing as Washington, Stockholm, and Singapore – and our critics have suddenly found their worst words come true. Probably the belligerence of these newspapers would not have mattered if the Government's position had been unequivocal. But it confirmed what little was known of the Government's attitude. Now the Prime Minister will obviously present himself as a man of peace and may believe it. Yet at the same time he may have adopted a policy – from the most worthy of motives – which if pressed would lead to highly dangerous courses. It seems right to point this out. The Prime Minister has only himself to blame if he finds that he has been so vague that he has left many doubts on where he really stands. He may be determined to work steadfastly for peace; equally he may be giving himself too much room for manoeuvre.

The essence of the British position today, as most people understand it, is that we do not want to go to war unless a war is forced on us. We want above all things to avoid a war in which the initiative is taken by us. And – if there should be no hope of agreement on international control of the canal – we are ready to refer the dispute to the United Nations rather than take the law into our own hands. That is the policy to follow.

It was typical of Wadsworth that he wanted to be as charitable as he could towards the Prime Minister and yet to try to make clear to him the error of his ways, and no less typical that he was sensitive to the opinions of our allies and of the third world. Through me, he had encouraged our correspondents abroad to report fully on reactions to the Anglo-French policy, with messages from Vernon Bartlett in Singapore, Taya Zinkin in India, Philips Price and Michael Adams in the Middle East, and our Swedish correspondent in Stockholm. Max Freedman, of course, had been reporting occasionally on Canadian as well as American opinion through visits to Ottawa and Winnipeg; and Alistair Cooke* was contributing from the United Nations in New York. Wadsworth finished his leader with these words:

We shall probably be told ... that the fears were all ignoble newspaper errors and that the Prime Minister has been the victim of heartless newspaper misre-presentation. That, however, is not the case. The vagueness has been his; it has been deliberate. It frightened Mr Dulles. It frightened the members of the (London) conference. The fears were acute. They are still alive. The onus of proof lies on the Prime Minister. We cannot feel safe until the United Nations is invoked. It is not enough to have peace or war at the mercy of the Prime Minister and his personal policy.

Parliament reassembled for three days on September 12. Hugh Gaitskell tried hard to secure a specific pledge that the British would not use force without first going to the United Nations. He secured it from Eden only in the closing minutes of the debate, and then only in the form of a qualified undertaking to go to the Security Council if Egypt refused to work with the Canal Users' Association. The debate had been tense and rowdy, and Labour's censure motion was lost by 321 votes to 251. But there had been some anxious speeches from the Conservative side, including one from the well-liked former Attorney-General, Sir Lionel Heald, who was among those wanting a pledge that force would not be used in breach of the UN Charter. There was virtual unanimity, too, on the Labour side. It is not my conclusion but that of the *Guardian*'s historian, David Ayerst, that our reporting and our advocacy in the previous six weeks had had a marked effect.[10] We had secured a firm stand by Labour, had alerted some Conservatives to the direction Eden was taking, and had told the Commonwealth that in Britain there was strong opposition to a warlike course.

A lull followed – or so we thought, mistakenly. We knew nothing at that time of the Israelis' secret negotiations with the French and the later involvement of the British; nor did any other newspaper. At the end of September I went on holiday to Scotland, having just become engaged and taking my future wife, Miranda, to meet my mother and father in Glasgow. We had a few days walking in the Highlands. A couple of days before we left Manchester Laurence Scott called me in to his office and said, to my surprise and delight, that the Trustees and Board had agreed that I should be the next editor.[11] I was to succeed Wadsworth at the end

10 Ayerst, *Guardian: Biography of a Newspaper*, p. 623. The *MG Weekly*'s overseas sale also contributed to the effect.

11 Somewhat later Laurence told me that four names had been considered. They were, first, Richard Scott – diplomatic correspondent and son of Ted Scott, editor from 1929 to 1932; but Richard lacked executive experience and anyway did not want the job. He was already a Trustee and became chairman of the Trust on Wadsworth's death. Second, Paddy Monkhouse – deputy editor and obviously a strong candidate; older than me and more experienced, but in some ways less resilient. Third, John Pringle – deputy editor before Paddy (from 1944 to 1948) and now editor of the *Sydney Morning Herald*; an excellent journalist but of uncertain health, and Laurence said that there were doubts about someone who had left the *Guardian* for the *Times* as he did. Finally, much the youngest, myself – and beyond question the summer's events had helped to clinch the choice. Laurence said also that, determined as he was to bring about the printing of the *Guardian* in London, he had to have someone decisive enough and fit enough to withstand the strain. I became a director of the company, in place of Wadsworth; Paddy was invited to join the Trust.

of October, though because of A.P.'s illness, Laurence said, I would effectively take over on the day of the announcement in mid-October. At the age of thirty-six it was a great responsibility, and I was painfully aware of my lack of experience in home politics. I kept the news very much to myself until a few days before the announcement, but I had three or four weeks in which to think how I would handle the paper. It was a happy holiday in Scotland.

There was an odd episode in Cyprus in early October. The paper of October 4 was the first in more than two months that had nothing directly about the Suez crisis on its front page, but it had a brief report from Famagusta that twenty-one soldiers had been arrested after 'a noisy and undisciplined meeting' on a hotel roof. A few days earlier the War Office in London had said that there was no possibility that the army reservists recalled because of the canal crisis could be released or 'stood down'. The noisy soldiers on the hotel roof – including a number of women reservists – were making an impromptu protest. A few were placed under close arrest, pending court martial, while the rest were returned to duty. The War Office tried to relieve frustration by announcing a week's leave for those reservists in the UK or Germany, but not for those in Malta or Cyprus.

The Prime Minister, even before that incident, was already exercised about the effect on troops in the Mediterranean of hearing about Gaitskell's statements in Parliament and the comments in *Manchester Guardian* leading articles. Eden attempted to prevent the broadcasting on the overseas services of reports of what Gaitskell and the *Guardian* were saying. This we later learned through Harman Grisewood – then chief assistant to the Director General of the BBC.[12] He had heard in conversations with William Clark at Downing Street that Eden had instructed the Lord Chancellor, Lord Kilmuir, to prepare an instrument which would take over the BBC altogether, putting it under Government control. This was to exclude individuals such as our own Richard Scott from taking part in discussion programmes. According to Grisewood, Eden found Kilmuir's draft inadequate; luckily the stronger version for which Eden asked was still not ready when the Suez landings took place in November. Eden himself makes no reference whatever to this in his Memoirs, but it was confirmed by William Clark when he spoke in 1968.

Ultimatum and assault

Something else happened at the end of October to push Suez off the front pages. Rebellion broke out in Hungary, with fighting in Budapest. Russian tanks came into open conflict with student insurgents in the streets, and the people of Hungary showed their hatred of the 'popular' regime. On October 28 Khrushchev ordered the Russian troops to withdraw from Budapest, and it looked as if, for once, the people had triumphed. The

12 Harman Grisewood, *One Thing at a Time*, pp. 197–201.

MG's front page on October 30 was split between two big stories – 'Israel invades Egypt' (columns 1 and 2) and 'Hungarian rebels asked to disarm' (columns 4 to 7). Although we did not know it, the orders for the British invasion fleet to sail that night from Malta had been given forty-eight hours earlier. By the end of the week, under cover of the war in the Middle East, the Russians were back in Budapest in full force. The rebels fought on, but not for long; Imre Nagy's coalition of Communists and non-Communists was crushed.

News of the Israelis' lightning attack across the Sinai peninsula took us by surprise at Cross Street, Manchester. We did not then suspect any pre-arrangement with the British and French, and we took at face value the first reports that Israeli forces had crossed the Egyptian frontier to destroy commando bases in Sinai, though it quickly became clear that this was much more than a shallow raid. But the 'rush' messages from the House of Commons next afternoon took us even more by surprise, showing that we had not fully measured Eden's secret purposes. For that afternoon he told the House that an ultimatum (though he did not use the word) had just been handed to the Egyptian ambassador, and that a similar communication was being handed to the Israeli chargé d'affaires.

These communications required the Egyptians and Israelis to 'stop all warlike action by land, sea, and air forthwith'. They were to withdraw their forces to a distance of ten miles from the canal (which Dayan's spearheads were still nowhere near). Eden's statement to the House went on: 'Further, in order to separate the belligerents and to guarantee freedom of transit through the canal by ships of all nations, we have asked the Egyptian Government to agree that Anglo-French forces shall move temporarily into key positions at Port Said, Ismailia, and Suez.' The Governments of Egypt and Israel were asked to reply within twelve hours, and if they did not comply, 'British and French forces will intervene in whatever strength it may be necessary to secure compliance'.

By now I was established in the editor's room at Cross Street, although formally my appointment took effect only next day. With the agency messages from Parliament in front of us, there was the usual brief consultation with colleagues. From the way the Prime Minister had phrased his announcement, we judged that by some extraordinary means at least part of the British assault force would be in a position to land next day – though the reality was much nearer to our earlier calculations, and although the first ships were already sailing from Malta the invasion fleet was not to reach Port Said for eight days. We also judged, and in this were closer to the truth, that the Israeli forces could not yet be much further than half way across Sinai and might not intend to go much further.

It took me only a few minutes to make up my mind. The ultimatum was consistent with all that we already knew of Eden's policy. He was

seizing the opportunity to make war on Egypt. He wanted to dislodge
Nasser. Whether or not he was justified – and I was convinced that he
was not – it seemed highly unlikely that he could succeed. The reasons
were those we had given again and again, especially in August and mid-
September. The United States was bound to be against us; Asia and
the third world were bound to be against us; even Canada and Australia
might stand aside. The Arabs would unite behind Nasser, however reluctantly. Our oil supplies would not be assured, nor was the canal likely
to be kept open. Our forces, being mainly 500 or 800 miles away, were not
organised or poised for the kind of rapier thrust that a Rommel or
Montgomery made in North Africa on other occasions. It was a breach
of international law, with possibly ruinous effects for the United Nations.
I settled down to write that night's leader on those lines, leaving the chief
sub-editor, John Putz, to plan the first edition front page.

It is worth recording the speed of decision at Cross Street, because I
had expected a swift reaction from the Opposition in the Commons and
from the *Daily Mirror* and *Daily Herald*. To my astonishment it did not
come for another twenty-four hours in the Commons and for forty-eight
hours from the other papers which I thought would share our view. Hugh
Gaitskell was given fifteen minutes' advance notice of Eden's statement,
but his response was muted. Denis Healey was more outspoken later that
evening. Not until next day did Gaitskell condemn the British action,
though he was forceful and effective then. The *Mirror* carried no comment
whatever next day – which perhaps should not have surprised me since
it had taken a fortnight to react in August and had then relapsed almost
completely into silence – but by November 2 was in full cry against the
Government. The *Daily Herald* and the *News Chronicle* were also afflicted
by indecision. (The *Observer*, being a Sunday paper, could not comment
until November 4.) The *Times*, after its belligerence in early August, had
withdrawn to a more detached position. Its editor, Sir William Haley,
had been in the United States in the autumn and had revised his judgment
– or so it was thought at the time, though he himself has a different
view.[13] At any rate, while admitting that 'boldness often pays', the *Times*
now saw grave risks in the Government's course.

There were few such hesitations among the main pro-Suez papers.
The *Telegraph*, in spite of having had reservations twenty-four hours
earlier about Israel's challenge to Nasser, now gave the Government its
fullest backing. It hoped the Americans would have the good sense to
support Britain and France, and that the United Nations would act

13 Sir William Haley, in a letter to me on May 30, 1980, says this: 'I was in the United
States during September and October 1956. The visit had no influence on my views about
Suez. I continued to abominate what I considered to be Dulles's double-dealing with Eden.
A talk with Eisenhower at the White House left me as unimpressed as I had long been with
him. My meetings with New York and other journalists convinced me that I knew much
more about Suez than they did.'

against both Egypt and Israel. 'But if it [the UN] cannot and will not, Britain must act the policeman as best she can.' Beaverbrook's *Daily Express* gave Eden and the ultimatum an imperial blessing and showed no reservations. Rothermere's *Daily Mail* was slower to react and rather more cautious, for it was unhappy that the Americans were not directly involved along with us. It was unsure about the legal sound-ness of our action, though by next day it had largely overcome its doubts.[14]

My leading article in the *MG* ran to nearly one thousand words. It acknowledged that the Israelis had good reason to make a counter-attack against the fedayeen (or commando) bases in Sinai, which had been used for repeated raids on israel. That, however, came towards the end of the article. The beginning was addressed directly to Britain and the British action:

The Anglo-French ultimatum to Egypt is an act of folly, without justification in any terms but brief expediency. It pours petrol on a growing fire. There is no knowing what kind of explosion will follow. There is admittedly, about one chance in twenty that it will put out the fire. By sheer weight it might extinguish the flames, temporarily at least. [The tenses in these two sentences were changed in later editions, after news of Egypt's rejection of the ultimatum.] But it is far more likely to lead Britain into direct war with Egypt, and perhaps with the whole Arab world. What is more, countless other nations will consider Britain and France to be in the wrong....

The Prime Minister sought to justify the ultimatum by saying that we must protect our shipping, our citizens, and 'vital international rights'. But what possible right have we to attack another country? The British and French military action threatened in the ultimatum, if carried out, will be flagrant aggression....

The leader went on to say that nothing in the United Nations Charter permitted such armed intervention. The proper course was to call on Israel, through the Security Council, to withdraw its forces – and at the same time to remind both sides of the tripartite declaration of 1950, under which the United States, France, and Britain had undertaken to prevent

14 The ultimate line-up among the nationals and London evenings was *Express, Mail, Sketch, Evening News, Evening Standard,* and *Telegraph* pro-Suez; *Mirror, News Chronicle, Star,* and *MG* anti-Suez; with the *Times* switching to a detached position. Among Sundays the *Empire News, Dispatch, Express, Graphic,* and *Sunday Times* were pro-Suez; while the *People, Reynolds News, Pictorial,* and *Observer* were anti-Suez, and the *News of the World* did not take sides. Among the major provincials, so far as I know, all except the *Scottish Daily Record* were pro-Suez (including the *Glasgow Herald, Scotsman,* and *Manchester Evening News*); but the neutrals included the *Glasgow Evening Times, Sheffield Star,* and *Newcastle Evening Chronicle.* Of great importance, however, was the *Economist* – which on Friday November 2 came out against the Government in the plainest terms. The *New Statesman* was no less anti-Suez, while the *Spectator* thought the Government's action untimely. In aggregate circulations, the pro-Suez papers were ahead but not by a large margin.

violations of the armistice lines between the Arabs and Israel. (Remember that in 1956, only eleven years after the creation of the United Nations, some of us were still intent on trying to see that it did not go the way of the League of Nations – and at that time the 1950 'uniting for peace' procedure was still effective in circumventing a veto.)

Almost the whole front page next morning – Wednesday, October 31 – was taken up with aspects of the Suez crisis, under the seven-column headline 'Egypt rejects Anglo-French ultimatum'. Inside the paper, pages 4 and 5 were taken up with affectionate tributes from both sides of the Atlantic to A. P. Wadsworth, on the occasion of his retirement, though unhappily Wadsworth himself was in no condition to enjoy them. I knew that these were his last days, for I had not been allowed to see him for a week. He died on November 4, aged sixty-five.

That Wednesday afternoon in the Commons, Gaitskell's reaction was no longer muted. His words, indeed, appeared to echo the opening of our leader, condemning the British course as 'an act of folly whose tragic consequences we shall regret for years'. Gaitskell's anger was directed not only at the ultimatum but at the use of the British veto – for the first time ever – late the previous night at the Security Council in New York. The United States had put forward a resolution demanding an immediate cease-fire in Sinai and withdrawal of Israeli forces, and urging all UN members to refrain from the use or threat of force in the area. Because the latter part of the resolution was plainly directed against the British and French, our veto was applied. Gaitskell had by now accepted the logic of the analysis that we had made immediately, in Manchester the previous afternoon. He said that no others would believe the 'transparent excuse' for a long-planned policy of force, and he went further than we had done: he asked outright whether there had been collusion with Israel. The Foreign Secretary, Selwyn Lloyd, replied later that the British Government had not 'incited' Israel – and added, misleadingly, that 'there was no prior agreement between us about it'.

While the exchanges were taking place in the Commons, at 1615 GMT the first British bombs fell on four Egyptian airfields – two near Cairo and two in the Canal Zone. The attacks were made by Valiant and Canberra bombers based in Cyprus. They continued with the aid of flares during the night, and were reported on the front page of Thursday's *Guardian*, as on the front pages of all other papers. The commander-in-chief, General Sir Charles Keightley, records in his despatch published a year later that there was 'an anxious moment' that afternoon when he was instructed not to attack Cairo West airfield, which was to have been among the first targets. The bombers were already on their way, but someone in London had discovered that American civilians were being evacuated to Alexandria by the desert road which ran right past the airfield. Since Cairo West was the main base of the Russian-built Iluyshin bombers, 'its sudden reprieve was a matter of concern'. General Keightley records, however, that the Egyptians only used the reprieve to remove their IL-28s to Luxor, far up the Nile.[15]

One section of the initial British air attack was a failure. The Egyptians were known to have prepared blockships to obstruct the canal, and some had been identified by air reconnaissance. The RAF were supposed to sink them before they could be moved into position. In practice most of the blockships were in position and sunk before this movement could be prevented, and the Egyptians went in for what General Keightley calls 'an orgy of sinking' to make sure that nobody could use their canal. 'We cannot afford to see the canal closed,' the Prime Minister had told the House. Within twenty-four hours it was closed, and was to remain closed for the next six months.

In addition to the bombing raids and the sinking of an Egyptian frigate in the Gulf of Suez, Thursday's *MG* (November 1) also reported the storm in the House of Commons and the 'intense anger' of the American Administration. A minor item from Max Freedman mentioned US gratitude for a statement by the Canadian Minister for External Affairs, Lester Pearson, regretting the Anglo-French action. And the *Guardian*'s Cairo correspondent, Michael Adams, filed the last message that he was able to send for nearly a month; like other correspondents, he was detained in house arrest in Cairo and then deported at the end of November. A further small item, from Reuter in Budapest, said that all Russian troops had now left the city and Cardinal Mindszenty had been freed after eight years in detainment. That was a flowering soon to wither.

The climax was still to come. On the war front at Port Said it was reached only with the airborne landings five days later and the seaborne assault on November 6. In the House of Commons it came sooner, with unruly scenes at the start of a censure debate on November 1; while in the United Nations General Assembly Mr Dulles in person moved a resolution calling on Britain and France to desist from their action. In the *Guardian*'s news columns all these events were chronicled as fully as possible, while the daily bombardment of the Government through our leaders was maintained.

Did it matter that there was open opposition to the Government, in the press as in Parliament? Ought all criticism to have been withheld once British troops were on their way to war? In my view it mattered a great deal that the opposition was heard and seen, not only in Britain but abroad, and from the earliest moment. It mattered that Eden and his

15 Eden's Memoirs record a curiosity at this juncture. On the 30th (before the ultimatum) a dawn reconnaissance had been ordered by four Canberras, flying at a great height, to establish exactly where the Israeli and Egyptian forces were. In spite of their altitude all four were intercepted over Egypt and some were fired on. 'The interception was a brilliant piece of work by any standards,' Eden says, 'and when it was reported to me next day it gave me grim cause for thought.' The unstated implication is that the MIG fighters were piloted by Russians.

colleagues were known not to be speaking for the whole British people. When the time came to restore relations afterwards – with the Americans and Canadians, as with others in Europe, Asia, and Africa – it was more readily possible because within the United Kingdom there had been a vigorous and vocal resistance to the Government's aggressive action. The following year I was in India for three weeks and was told plainly by the Prime Minister, Pandit Nehru, and by others in Delhi that they had welcomed the *Manchester Guardian*'s outspoken words. The BBC's broadcasting of those words – impartially along with comments favourable to the Government – was in the end of benefit to Eden's successors even though he had tried to prevent it.

Hugh Gaitskell's biographer, Philip Williams, notes a British MP on a visit to Beirut reporting that diplomats there saw the opposition as redeeming Britain's ruined reputation. Another Labour MP, in India and Pakistan, 'was told everywhere that only [Hugh's] broadcast had kept those countries in the Commonwealth'. Even the Irish were impressed.[16] Lord Attlee, returning from India and Pakistan on November 9, had said that it was 'the disunity of this country which is saving the Commonwealth.'

Another element of British opinion was making itself felt. Many individuals and organisations with no political or party alignment were speaking out. Letters to the editor were reaching every newspaper, taking strong positions on each side. The news columns reported also the abhorrence of the British Council of Churches, groups of academics, and some women's organisations towards the Suez action. In the House of Lords, the Archbishop of Canterbury said that Christian opinion was 'terribly uneasy and unhappy', and he urged the Government not to go into Egypt. He harrassed the Lord Chancellor with a succession of questions.

It remains my view that the *Guardian*, *Mirror*, *Economist*, and others were important in giving early warning of what was at stake and in helping to focus minds on the immorality and likely failure of British policy. Many people believed that we should have kept silent once British troops were on their way to battle, but I saw stronger counter-arguments. It was part of our job as a newspaper, we thought, to bring all possible pressure on the British Government to comply with the UN requirement. And three days before the first landings at Port Said the General Assembly had passed the Dulles resolution by 65 votes to 4, with 6 abstentions. If Britain had complied, British troops would not have gone into action and the crisis would have ended sooner.

The RAF, admittedly, were already flying over Egypt and the Navy had been in action in the Gulf of Suez. But strangely, it was not certain that Britain was at war. The worst storm in the House of Commons on November 1, which forced the Speaker to suspend the sitting for half an hour, was sparked off by the fact that neither the new Defence Minister

16 Philip Williams, *Hugh Gaitskell*, p. 435.

nor the Foreign Secretary could say whether Britain was now at war. The point of the question was to discover whether aircrew shot down over the Nile Valley would be protected by the Geneva Convention and Ministers apparently did not know. It is a side issue, but it illustrates the lack of clarity at the time – and some lack of responsibility towards British aircrew.

The *MG*'s letters' columns of November 2 may give a taste of public feeling, though on this day it was more representative of anti-Suez than of pro-Suez opinion. The first letter was from Bertrand Russell, still alert at over eighty:

Sir, The criminal lunacy of the British and French Governments' action against Egypt fills me with deep shame for my country. I endorse every word of Mr Gaitskell's indictment and of your leading article of November 1. Only one hope remains, that the United States will use its power to stop the fighting and so save us from the worst consequences of our Government's insanity. – yours, etc.

Contrarily, Mr Richard Parkes of Hadfield, Manchester, held that the *MG*'s legal and moral approach was mistaken.

I cannot help but feel that the old 'gunboat diplomacy' would have had far more immediate and satisfactory results. If Britain, France, and America had acted together with force at the time when Nasser grabbed the canal we should probably have been at peace now. A budding dictator has no respect for law, morals, or the United Nations for he knows that he has much to gain by ignoring them. Surely, therefore, your attitude should be modified accordingly.

Four students at Bristol University Union wrote to support the anti-Suez view, as did a don at Balliol College, Oxford. A cable from a group of German journalists in Bonn said 'Thank you for today's leader restoring our faith in Britain'. But a reader in Altrincham, Cheshire, wrote of the *Guardian*'s 'defeatist whine' – and there were many other reactions.

Alongside these letters were press comments from around the world – the great majority being hostile to the British action, many employing language stronger than we had used. On a more homely level, our own Norman Shrapnel* reported from a snack bar in Oldham:

A man with a pipe and a reliable face is explaining things in a corner, with a false reasonableness learned from the wireless. 'Ay, it's a gamble, lad,' he is saying. 'Better wait and see. Mebbe it'll come off, lad. Then again, mebbe it won't. That'll be a bit of a ——.' One loyally retains his actual word, which in Oldham speech rhymes with 'sugar', because it is the only one he uses that lifts him out of the world of Wilfred Pickles.

There was also a private letter from Lady Violet Bonham Carter, wishing 'to retract any and every critical thought' about the *MG*'s outspoken words on Suez. The *Guardian* had been 'vindicated by these stupefying events', and never since Munich had she felt 'such horror or such humiliation'. There was need, she said, for some great national gesture of repudiation transcending party boundaries.

Less cheerful was the news coming to me from the *MG*'s circulation manager. Cancellations of orders for the paper were beginning to be felt, particularly in some of its traditionally strong sales areas in the north. But it was a few days yet before the pattern became at all clear.

Max Freedman was still maintaining his flow from Washington, though now almost all for publication. An open message on November 1 conveyed the 'black anger' of President Eisenhower and his Administration. Not only had there been no consultation over the ultimatum, but 'there was something approaching deliberate deceit'. The American Ambassador had seen Mr Selwyn Lloyd on the Sunday evening and had been assured that British efforts were wholly devoted towards peaceful solutions and the avoidance of force. There were those in Washington, he reported, who believed that the wool had been deliberately pulled over the Ambassador's eyes just when Britain was about to go to war to topple the Egyptian President Nasser.

On Sunday, November 4, there was a big demonstration in Trafalgar Square, on the theme 'Law, not war'. Over the weekend both the Prime Minister and Mr Gaitskell had spoken in radio and television broadcasts, though the Labour leader's took place only after the BBC had overruled objections from the Conservative chief whip, Edward Heath. The *MG*'s front page on Monday morning led not with Suez but with Hungary under the headline 'Soviet tanks crush resistance'. Two Soviet divisions were thought to have been used in Budapest, and casualties in the city were put at fifty thousand. On the leader page, the main leader for once was spread across two columns. It said that Sir Anthony's policy over Suez, however sincerely intended, had been 'hideously miscalculated and utterly immoral'. A complete change of Government was essential. 'In no other way can the world be convinced that Britain repudiates the policy of the past week.' In no other way, it continued, could the authority of the United Nations be restored and a beginning made towards meeting the Hungarian catastrophe. Since no landings had yet taken place, we said, it was clear that when requested to do so by the United Nations four and three days earlier the Government could still have called a halt. But it had simply refused to accede to the UN resolutions. For Britain the past few days had been the blackest since Munich in 1938, we concluded, and blacker ones might lie immediately ahead.

Though we did not yet know it, the Cabinet's resolution that weekend was beginning to crack. The pressure of world opinion, American opinion, and British internal opposition was having an effect. The first parachute landings took place around Port Said at dawn that Monday morning, to be followed by second and third waves later in the day. The Cabinet on Sunday discussed postponement of the main landings but decided that it was not practicable. But when the Cabinet met again early on Tuesday, a new threat had appeared. The Chancellor of the Exchequer had to tell his colleagues that there was critical speculation against sterling, largely in the American market or on American account.[17] With the Americans not prepared to bail us out, Macmillan knew the game was up. Or, as William Clark has put it: 'he was the man who really pushed us over the edge into Suez and failed to see whether the money box was full, and it wasn't'.[18] On the other hand Macmillan was one of the quickest to learn the lessons and to try, with remarkable success, to make good the damage afterwards.

The rest of the Suez story is well enough known. The seaborne assault took place at dawn on Tuesday 6th. That same morning, the Secretary-General of the United Nations heard from Cairo that the Egyptians were now ready to accept a UN force on the canal and in Sinai. For Eden this was a face-saving way out, and in the afternoon orders were sent from London that there must be a cease-fire at 2359 GMT. By then the leading forces were some twenty-three miles south of Port Said, at El Cap. The first units of the UN force arrived ten days later, and Norwegian soldiers began to take over from the French and British in Port Said. The handover extended until just before Christmas. Petrol rationing was introduced in Britain on November 20 and in most European countries at about the same time. Sir Anthony Eden, now troubled with recurrent fever, went on holiday to Jamaica on November 23 and never fully returned to duty. His doctors advised him to retire, and on January 8 he resigned. Mr R. A. Butler had been acting Prime Minister but was not chosen to succeed him: that duty went to Mr Harold Macmillan. Mr Dulles, too, was struck down with cancer but later returned to work. On April 10 the canal itself was reopened to shipping, after an international clearing operation in which British salvage engineers took part – and remained open until the June war in 1967, when the Israeli onslaught again brought it into the front line.

The week of the cease-fire was a busy one for newspapers. The fighting was over, but the political debate intensified. If the cease-fire had been delayed for a further day, could the whole canal have been occupied? Would the main Egyptian armour, still in reserve near Cairo, ever have become engaged? Could Nasser have been toppled, and what would have followed? What was to happen about our oil supplies, with the canal closed and the Arabs angry? And what would happen to the alliance, after the severe strains of the past four months? Hungary was beyond retrieving, but could anything be done to restore the authority of the United Nations? In an exceptionally long leader on November 14, I set out positive lines for reconstruction, though concluding that while Eden remained Prime Minister it would be hard to convince the world that British policy had taken a new direction.

17 Eden, *Full Circle*, pp. 556–57.
18 William Clark, the *Listener*, November 22, 1979.

The evidence of collusion

For one bitter post-Suez controversy, the *Manchester Guardian* provided the first facts. At the outbreak of hostilities we had been caught without a staff correspondent in Israel – a misfortune that we avoided in every later Middle Eastern war – but James Morris* arrived in Tel Aviv at the beginning of November. On November 20, after James had flown out to Cyprus with his story which the censors would not pass, we led the front page with 'French collusion with Israel'. Until then, apart from Gaitskell's question to Eden at the start, collusion had been no more than a dark suspicion in some people's minds. Now the secret story began to emerge.

James Morris's report, sent from Nicosia, began in this way:

French aircraft flown by French pilots in French uniform played an important, possibly even a decisive, part in the recent Israeli offensive in the Sinai desert. The Israeli censorship has stifled this startling fact, and General Moshe Dayan, the Israeli chief of staff, flatly denied it when questioned at a recent press conference. There is, however, no doubt at all that French fighter pilots took part in the battle, and it is suggested that the accuracy of their napalm bombing was one of the most important factors in the rout of the Egyptian army.

Until a few days ago a line of Mystère jet fighters bearing French markings could be seen tucked away in a corner of Lydda airfield, near Tel Aviv. It is said, however, that the French markings were covered on the French Mystères which went into action. One French officer in uniform told me: 'There was very little opposition except flak. Most of our aircraft came back with a few flak holes in them but for myself I saw only four MIGs and they ran away.'

This was before the British and French had attacked Egyptian airfields, he said, and he could not understand why the Egyptians had not put up a better fight.

Anybody who has wandered about the Sinai battlefield during the past week or two must have been struck by the vast numbers of Egyptian lorries, tanks, and half-tracks disintegrated by the impact of napalm bombs. More often than not bombs seem to have struck them smack in the middle, pulverising everything combustible. It is possible that the Israelis themselves have supplies of napalm bombs, but it is said that most of this ghastly accuracy was the work of French fliers.

It was common knowledge, Morris said, that the French had been supplying Mystère fighters to Israel beyond the published numbers. He concluded that it was 'difficult to disbelieve' that the French Government knew of Israel's plans all along and perhaps even provided their inspiration. The British Embassy had denied all knowledge: 'but probably its staff shares with the censorship department the old philosophy of least said soonest mended'.

Alongside the message from James Morris it was reported that Sir Anthony Eden was suffering from overstrain and would have to rest. In a leader that morning we said that the evidence of complicity between the French and Israeli Governments was almost inescapable, and we asked about Britain's part, recalling the Foreign Secretary's reply in the House on October 31:

> It is quite wrong to state that Israel was incited to this action by Her Majesty's Government. There was no prior agreement between us about it.

Accepting that, we said that perhaps the collusion had been between France and Israel only. But, if so, 'were the British not informed in advance?' Was the Anglo-French ultimatum issued in ignorance of what the French had done? Was it likely that the joint operation to neutralise the Egyptian air force and seize the canal would have been launched so swiftly without prior knowledge of the Israeli plans? The Government, we said, ought to give a full explanation at once.

The leader went on to ask what had happened when the Prime Minister and Foreign Secretary flew unexpectedly to Paris on October 16. They had spent some hours in discussion with M. Mollet and M. Pineau, but the whole meeting had been shrouded in secrecy. Two days later Sir Walter Monckton had resigned and Mr Head had become Defence Minister. We drew attention to a recent report in the *Washington Post* that, at the Paris meeting, a 'conspiracy' between Britain, France, and Israel was arranged and that afterwards the British and French deliberately set out to mislead the United States. Were Ministers willing to explain?

We were coming fairly close to the truth – uncomfortably so, for the Government. But no light came from official sources. Because of the Prime Minister's illness, Mr Butler was answering questions in the House. The Foreign Secretary was at the United Nations, in New York. Rab replied blandly, 'I have no statement to make on the matter today.' It would have to wait until Selwyn Lloyd's return from New York. Our Parliamentary correspondent described him as listening to the questions and replying 'with an air of large detachment'.* In Paris a total but unspecific denial was issued by the French Ministry of National Defence: 'The Ministry issues the most formal denial that any French military personnel took part in any form in the Israeli operations.' The Ministry's spokesman would add nothing to this impersonal denial.

Our front page, however, now had more information. James Morris filed a further despatch from Nicosia saying that on October 29 – at the start of the Israeli action and before the ultimatum – an Israeli parachute force was dropped by French aircraft some thirty kilometres east of the canal in order to offer an immediate challenge to the Egyptians. He had also received information, which he considered reliable, that French aircraft were used to drop supplies in the Sinai desert at the start of the offensive. In addition there was a report by the *MG*'s London staff, based on conversations with a former *Guardian* man who had just returned from Tel Aviv. He was able to confirm that French fighter pilots had been in Israel and had flown in operational sorties against the Egyptians. He had tried as long ago as November 8 to send a telegram to this effect to the *MG* but had been prevented by the censor. He had described a victory celebration of the Israeli air force which he had attended with American and Canadian correspondents, meeting several French pilots. They were not Jewish and they were not volunteers, but had been on the reserve of the French air force and recalled to fly the Mystères for Israel. 'Their recall and despatch seems to have been hurried,' he had said.

That day the *New York Times* and the *Washington Post* also carried reports from correspondents lately in Israel that French aircraft had been used for supply dropping in Sinai before the ultimatum and that French fighters with French pilots had flown operational missions.

On November 22 Mr Butler was again questioned in the House and again had 'nothing to add'. Our Paris correspondent, Darsie Gillie,* had now obtained a further statement from the French Defence Ministry. It said that French air force members had been in Israel before, during, and since the fighting, looking after the maintenance of Mystère fighters delivered to Israel and teaching the Israeli pilots to fly them. If any French pilots had flown in operations, he was told, it would be insubordination and if it came to light it would be punished. The previous day *Le Monde* had reported that some French pilots now back at Dijon had talked to friends of operational sorties from bases in Israel. The French Secretary for Air had also been at Dijon to welcome pilots home and had said: 'the country has applauded your exploits but it will not know them all.' According to the official explanation, this was a reference to the strictness of French censorship. And on November 23, Reuter's correspondent in Tel Aviv was able to send a message previously stopped by the censors. It, too, said that he had been told by French pilots of flying 'patrols' and of 'strafing' Egyptian tank columns in Sinai. Others had told him of piloting French 'flying boxcars' in parachute and dropping operations. On November 24 Mr Selwyn Lloyd, still in New York, spoke again and adhered to the wording he had used on October 31. On November 29 *France Observateur* published further details of the use of French planes based on Cyprus for para drops of jeeps, mortars, arms, petrol, and water in Sinai on October 31 – hours before the ultimatum expired – and on later days. After the drop on October 31 the planes had landed behind the Israeli lines to take on Israeli jeeps, but these could not be dropped because they lacked the necessary attachments.

At the end of November Darsie Gillie sent me a long private analysis based on confidential Foreign Office and Defence Ministry sources in Paris. It referred to French exasperation at their inability to resolve the Algerian civil war and the view of one group of Ministers that a head-on collision with the Arabs must come. The young (forty-two) Defence Minister, Bourgès-Manoury – a former member of the Resistance – was the leader of this group. When the Suez crisis first arose they were ready to go ahead 'on a bold course' with Israel alone, believing Britain to be an unreliable ally. Bourgès-Manoury's staff, headed by Abel Thomas, had drafted a detailed plan for a Franco-Israeli operation leading to the occupation of Cairo. B-M put his plan in outline to the Cabinet at the beginning of August, but there was overwhelming preference for going ahead with England 'in spite of her drawbacks'. In the Bourgès plan Israel would have been the main base instead of Cyprus. 'Bourgès was bidding for the place of strong man with support from both right and left, with military glory to his credit, but without the drawback of being a military man.'

The rejection of his plan, Gillie wrote, led to the Franco-British plan for invading Egypt 'on about September 15'. Bourgès stepped up supplies to Israel, but Mollet as Prime Minister may not have known the full extent of what he did then and in the autumn. There was some conflict between French support for Israel and British commitments to Jordan. With the sudden visit of Eden and Lloyd to Paris on October 16, two alternative French policies (France and Israel or France and GB) came together, and Britain 'must have begun to come into the picture about Franco-Israeli relations'. One more piece was fitting into the jigsaw.

Two other private messages at that time were of interest. Philips Price, formerly a *Guardian* correspondent and now an MP, had been in Baghdad. According to the British Ambassador there, Nuri es-Said had been expecting tough action against Nasser; but Philips Price suggests that Iraqi opinion in general was hostile to the Suez action and that Nuri's views were personal. One of the Iraqi Ministers, Prince Zaim, had told the King that if the regime was to be saved Britain must be shut out of all activities in the Middle East while Eden remained Prime Minister. The other letter was from the military historian, Liddell Hart, an old friend. He had been talking to Ygal Allon, one of the Israeli Labour party leaders. Allon had told him that if the Israeli operation had not been halted, they had intended to cross the canal in order to destroy airfields but then to retire back across the canal before the Egyptians could recover and concentrate. They did not intend to occupy any area west of the canal. 'Their concept of speed and surprise is very different to ours,' he wrote, 'and they certainly did not intend to turn themselves into a stationary target on the populous west side of the canal.'

But back to collusion. It was right, I thought, both to publish the messages from James Morris and others, and to inquire further. It was important to know how far the most senior British Ministers had gone in deceiving Parliament, the electorate, and our allies (the Americans especially). We published a sharp letter from a Conservative backbencher, Sir John Smyth, VC, asking how we could doubt the veracity of Ministers. He said that we were basing our reports on 'the flimsiest evidence' and that it was 'inconceivable' that there had been collusion. His letter certainly represented the view of many loyal Conservatives, and it accounted for the fury over the *MG*'s evidence. But this was not the first time that the Whips had persuaded a respected backbencher, not fully in the know, to protest over criticism embarrassing to the Government. (It still goes on.)

Gradually, as some of the principal actors wrote their memoirs, more of the facts emerged – and corroboration came both for what James Morris had reported and for what, in the Manchester office, we had deduced.

General Sir Charles Keightley's despatch as commander-in-chief, published in September 1957, said that most of the invasion force embarked after the ultimatum was delivered and before it expired.[19] Seven years later a book by an artillery reservist, Major J. M. D. Clark, made evident that his unit embarked and sailed, with their orders, some hours before the ultimatum.[20] Bernard Levin, in the *Times* in 1980, quoted Lord Mountbatten as having said that the naval force commander's despatch was altered to conceal the fact that operational orders were given before the Israelis started their attack.[21]

Sir Anthony Eden's *Full Circle*, published in 1960, is fascinating to read but at key points gives nothing away. General Moshe Dayan's *Diary of the Sinai Campaign*, published in 1965, makes plain that Israeli planning was based on the assumption that the British and French forces were to launch their operations on October 31. The Israeli forces were therefore to go into action at dusk on the 29th. Sir Anthony Nutting's *No End of a Lesson*, published in 1967, gives details of the Chequers meeting with the French on October 14, the Paris meeting on October 16, the Cabinet meetings of October 18 and 25, and Selwyn Lloyd's 'torment' of doubts.

Even as these memoirs were being published, ten years after the event, there were still many Conservatives who believed that Eden's action had been an impartial police operation; the *Guardian* was still regarded by some as having behaved discreditably in doubting the word of Ministers. And that attitude was not confined to Conservatives. I came across it, as late as 1966, during a conversation at the Athenaeum with an otherwise friendly university vice-chancellor.

General André Beaufre's book, of 1969, adds more detail of the planning as well as being contemptuous of British delays in August and September.[22] Selwyn Lloyd's own version, published in 1978 after his death, indicates that until mid-October he had no precise knowledge of the extent of Franco-Israeli preparations. Like Brutus, Selwyn Lloyd was a most honourable man. He had had a gruelling three months, and Eden

19 Supplement to the *London Gazette*, September 12, 1957.

20 J. M. D. Clark in *Suez Touchdown*, a highly readable account of events and feelings from a soldier's point of view, and on the whole pro-Suez.

21 Bernard Levin, in the *Times* of November 5, 1980, quoting from the transcript of a television interview with Lord Mountbatten that was never broadcast.

22 General André Beaufre, *The Suez Expedition*, 1956.

was intent on bringing Nasser down. On their side the Israelis had had an infinitely difficult choice, and it was certain that they were now about to move. That they would not have been ready to move without at least an assurance of British neutrality and preferably with British support was no less certain. After the cease-fire Eden's illness removed him from the scene just when the acute questioning about collusion began – backed by the evidence first provided by the *MG*. Lloyd was left to answer and consistently held to the line that there had been no agreement with Israel. In a narrow sense that was true, for it was all done through the French. Yet every Minister present at the meetings of October 18 and 25 must have known precisely what was about to happen.

Looking back on the *Guardian*'s part, twenty-five years later, I have no regrets. We reported as fully and fairly as we could. We gave as much space and prominence to opponents as to friends. We reflected, I believe, a more balanced perspective of world reaction than did most other newspapers. We used the advocacy of our leader columns and occasional special articles to try to bring home to readers – and to the country's leaders – the mistaken and dangerous course of British policy. We succeeded perhaps better than at the time we knew.

It was a strenuous and anxious time for me, especially in the two weeks after the ultimatum. I was newly in the editor's chair. I worked an eighteen-hour day, and in the first week my short sleep was twice interrupted in the early morning by transatlantic telephone calls. It was the week when my much-loved predecessor, A. P. Wadsworth, died. Miranda, still a student at Cambridge, came home to Manchester the weekend after the ultimatum and did much to encourage me. But in spite of all the strain, there was also exhilaration. I had never expected to be editor of the *Guardian*.

For a short period, it looked as if the paper might pay a heavy price for being candid and outspoken. On Friday, November 10, after the cease-fire but with public controversy still hot and strong, I had a visit from the company's chairman and managing-director. Laurence Scott was a tall man, and he stood with his back to a bookcase across the room, declining to sit because I was busy and he was not going to stay long. 'You've heard what's happening?' he asked. I had indeed. The circulation manager had been to see me three times in the past eight days, and always with a long face. An uncomfortable number of cancellations had been coming in. 'Well,' Laurence said (the words may not be exact but the sense is), 'if you believe your policy is right, stick to it. Don't be put off. It may be economically painful for a time, but we shall have to live with that and you must not be influenced by it.' With that encouragement, I went on to write another leader looking at how Britain must try to recover its standing in the world.

A week later I wrote to my father, who also had been concerned about how the *MG* was faring under my control:

Last week because of our Suez policy we suffered severe cancellations. The worst were in the wealthy areas outside Manchester; in the Macclesfield, Wilmslow, Knutsford, Chester belt alone we lost between eight and nine thousand. This was economically the more hurtful because the profit margin is biggest where the distribution cost is lowest. It was also politically painful, because reports from retailers indicated that the *Daily Telegraph* was gaining all that we lost.

This week the gloom has been astonishingly dissipated. The orders have been coming in all week. There have also been some cancellations, but completely outweighed by the gains. The net effect remains a quite serious loss in the Manchester area. Obviously a large remnant of people who were reading because it was the *Manchester* Guardian have dropped out; and a number of old Liberals, now Conservative, have gone. The greatest gains have been in the London area. On Wednesday and Thursday, for the first time, we sold over fifty thousand copies in the London area alone. There have also been solid gains all over the country outside Lancashire and Cheshire; in places like Sheffield and Leicester there has been a tremendous jump, though in each city that means only a matter of hundreds.

On Wednesday and Thursday, for the first time, the gross print (including machine waste and staff copies) was over 200,000. The gross distribution was about 198,000. After deductions for unsold copies the net average for the week is likely to be about 180,000 or 181,000. Staggering.

Cautiously, I went on to say that we should not be too cock-a-hoop, for the gains might prove temporary. But mostly they were not. The circulation manager eventually reckoned that starting from a sale of 165,000 at the beginning of the crisis we had probably lost a little over 30,000 and gained about 46,000 or 47,000 gross. A remarkable turnround, and in the end a springboard towards printing the paper in London.

Most of all, though, I shall remember the support given by Laurence Scott. There can be few newspapers in the world where the management's response would be so unequivocal. Laurence Scott upheld the family tradition; and I was a happy editor.

2 Editorial imperatives

If Suez was a fiery baptism, there were many more crises to come – though none of the political intensity, within Britain, of the 1956 Suez affair. The rest of this book picks salient episodes, to illustrate the process of editorial decision. First, however, let me explain how the *Guardian* office worked in my time.

Setting the course

A cynic once said that the average *Guardian* reader must be a graduate unmarried mother living on a derelict farm in Wales. There was a time when some letters, particularly on the women's pages, gave that impression. Readership surveys in the mid-sixties provided perhaps a more accurate picture, though I never entirely trusted them. In southern England the average *Guardian* reader – if such a mythical person could be found – was in his thirties, a graduate, in a profession and doing well, mildly left-of-centre in politics, and interested in current affairs. But women readers were still no more than about 30 per cent, a proportion greatly improved by the early seventies. In the North the average age was over forty, the political outlook more conservative, and interests less international.

Happily the paper's navigation did not depend on any opinion polls or readership surveys. Those were always interesting, but of value to the promotion people and the advertisement department rather than to editorial decisions. The injunction to 'carry on the paper in the same spirit as before' meant, above all, treating readers as rational, intelligent, and capable of making up their own minds. Getting the news and presenting it as fairly and accurately as human fallibility allowed were therefore paramount. The 'page traffic' figures in the surveys were in fact an encouragement, for they showed that the *Guardian*'s news columns were heavily read, with features close behind. More than half the *Guardian*'s foremost story, the front-page lead, was generally read by a staggering 95 per cent of those who saw the paper. The first leader also enjoyed an exceptional following, with usually 88 per cent reading half or more of it, which was a tribute considering that it often ran to nine hundred or one thousand words. No other paper, so far as I know, had such close attention from readers to its main news and main leader.

We steered, nevertheless, by instinct and not by any pre-ordained formula. As editor, I depended heavily on the advice of my senior staff. But, especially in the years after the *Guardian*'s financial and managerial crisis in 1966 (reported in Chapter 7), the whole editorial staff had opportunities to put their views on the way the paper was run – more opportunities than probably on any other national newspaper. The final decisions had to be mine or the deputy editor's, or had to be taken by heads of departments on my behalf. Events move too fast for a newspaper to be run by a committee.

The *Guardian*'s editor was and is exceptionally fortunate in the freedom he enjoys. The *Guardian*'s writers, too, have customarily enjoyed greater freedom than is common in Fleet Street and have used it well. I was attracted to working for the *Guardian* because of its character and atmosphere, and that was long before I had the remotest thought of ever becoming its editor. I had read it while still at school, having luckily gone to a school which believed in making a wide range of newspapers available to the boys. (When I went back to speak there years later, only the *Telegraph* and the *Mail* were on offer, which told me a lot about how the school had changed.) Then while working at the *Glasgow Herald* I read the autobiography of Neville Cardus,* published in 1947, and loved his description of the 'austere but passionate Puritanism' that inspired the paper. I loved also his account of the paper's care for words, and his comment that the *MG* 'did not commit the blue-pencil brutalities which transformed the sub-editors' rooms of most newspapers into an abattoir'. That book reinforced my wish, already fed by daily reading of the *MG*'s columns, to become a member of its staff. From 1950 onwards I, too, enjoyed that freedom – though I knew that after printing in London began in 1961 the subs' room was sometimes an abattoir, to the fury of the reporters and specialist writers.

No formal instruction or written advice was given to new members of the staff, except during the period of extra recruitment just before and soon after the start of London printing. Usually newcomers were left to absorb the atmosphere and discover from daily practice what was expected of them. The 1961 'Advice to Staff' was intended only as an elementary guide to news judgements and priorities. It said that the *Guardian*'s first concern ought to be 'with government in the widest sense' – with the shaping of public policy, the events affecting it, and the influences on it. Within that priority there were these preferences:

1. Home policy and home politics (policy decisions, actions, and their consequences taking precedence over politics, or the process of influencing policymakers).
2. The international setting (including war, threats of war, peacemaking, and disarmament – though any direct threat to the UK would obviously take top place).
3. The economic, financial, and industrial aspects (with anything affecting jobs, earnings, and prosperity coming highest within that category).

Apart from these matters of primary concern, the document mentioned topics that had long been given special attention by the *Guardian*:

The social climate – care of old people, young people, slum clearance, new towns, changing social habits, and so on.

Books, the Arts, architecture, archaeology, and history.
Science, medicine, and meteorology; technology and invention.
Outdoor activity, the countryside, national parks, and conservation.

No precise place was given to fire, flood, and other man-made or natural calamities; but staff were asked to try to give as much priority to human achievements as to human failings. Variety was wanted on every page, for an unrelieved diet of 'government' was bound to become dull. Sports stories deserved a place on page one from time to time. 'Our lowest priority in news', that section ended, 'is the field of murder, sex, and scandal – except where an event has wider implications.'

Some more general advice was added. *Guardian* staff were encouraged to write as individuals, being neither exploited as 'personalities' (though their names might become well known) nor cut and trimmed like robots. Reporters would often find that bare facts were best given bare, but they should write like human beings, not recording machines. Wit and humour were always welcome, so long as they were not superficial. Reporters must not leave a trail of broken confidences or misused hospitality. Sub-editors, while performing their nightly miracle of sorting out the mass of incoming copy, deciding priorities, and writing headlines, ought to respect the knowledge and skill of our reporters. We were writing for an intelligent, alert, and literate audience; those were the qualities that we must employ ourselves.

The 'Advice' was indeed no more than a general guide. Day-to-day application was left to news editors, night editors, and everyone else on the staff. Each day's paper contributed to that 'slow deposit' of actions and ideals which created the climate within which we all worked. We assumed that readers shared our belief in parliamentary government and the rule of law, though they must often question the wisdom of Ministers, judges, and other public servants; that they valued tolerance and free speech, and that they shared a deep concern with diminishing the poverty, misfortune, and misery of others. Also that they enjoyed good writing and a bit of fun. Any newspaper must start from common ground with its readers and build on that; we were fortunate in having so many sensitive, conscientious, and at times irreverent readers.

Marxists and some non-Marxists may object that in making these assumptions about our readers and their beliefs we were guilty of a dangerous conservatism – that we were narrowing our own vision and theirs, perpetuating established values, and blighting our own reforming zeal. I do not believe it. The *Guardian*'s stand at Suez went directly against the convention of closing ranks in time of war, because we believed that the Government's action was both immoral and doomed to failure from the start. The paper's view on nuclear arms and disarmament, accepting NATO's need for a deterrent but rejecting Britain's independent role, followed no established line – and the 'non-nuclear club', to be described in the next chapter, was a piece of original *Guardian* thinking. Anyone who reads the rest of this book will, I trust, find plenty of examples of non-conformity, unblinkered reporting, and creative policy-making.

The three advisers on whom I leaned most heavily were the deputy editor, the news editor, and the night editor (later called production editor). In 1956 as deputy I inherited Paddy Monkhouse, a man of long experience and scholarly knowledge. He happened to share my enthusiasm for hill walking and introduced me to the Pennines when I first moved to Manchester in 1950; he also shared my moderate left-of-centre political leanings, though he was more firmly committed to the Labour party. Though disappointed at not becoming editor himself, he gave me every possible support. He was succeeded in 1963 by Harford Thomas, who had come to us two years previously from editing the *Oxford Mail* – in turn a good and friendly deputy, with energy and a liberal political instinct.

It is no diminution of Paddy or Harford, however, when I say that John Cole, deputy for my last six years, was the strongest in that post. He had come up in a hard school, through the *Belfast Telegraph* and general reporting on the *Guardian*; in 1957 I had appointed him labour correspondent, one of the most prized posts and one of the most arduous, and in 1963 he moved for six years to the news desk. He was a highly effective news editor, though some of the staff thought he drove them too hard; and his political instincts were acute. Between 1969 and 1975 he provided many of the *Guardian*'s initiatives in home policy and on the economic front. He was a wise guide on labour relations and on incomes policy; and in my view he did more than any other British journalist to dispel illusions about short-cuts to solutions in Ireland. We had one serious disagreement about Irish policy, but that will emerge later.

The news desk – controlling the reporters and coordinating the work of specialist writers – was run for much of my time by women. John Cole was preceded by Nesta Roberts,* the first news editor in London, from 1961 to 1963; and he was followed in 1969 by Jean Stead, a strong Yorkshirewoman who handled the newsgathering during my last six years as editor. Nesta was a skilful diplomatist, who had to weld together the previously somewhat independent London staff and those who moved south from Manchester; she was particularly good at schooling young reporters in *Guardian* ways, but after two years on the desk preferred to return to writing, first specialising in social welfare and then as Paris correspondent. Jean's six years included a major extension of investigative reporting, of which some account is given in Chapter 11; and she had to organise coverage of the IRA's London bombing campaign in 1973-74, with a special 'bomb shift' from 6 pm to 1 am nightly and with political cover through Irish contacts in London as well. (Her worst disappointment was in not uncovering as much as she wished of the London operations of BOSS – South Africa's Bureau of State Security.)

News editors exercised much influence through their choice of topics for assignments and through their choice of reporters for those assignments. Young men such as Harry Jackson, Adam Raphael, and Simon Hoggart – and my successor, Peter Preston – were tested on difficult stories, found good, and promoted. Harry Jackson* started as a messenger in the old *MG* office in Fleet Street but quickly earned himself a job as a journalist, and in 1968 won the award as Reporter of the Year for his work in Vietnam, Czechoslovakia, and elsewhere abroad – and by the time he won it he was carrying the heaviest share of the *Guardian*'s coverage in Northern Ireland. Adam Raphael* started as an all-round reporter but developed a special interest in the motor industry, working on his own rather than through the motoring correspondents' circle; he won his award as Journalist of the Year in 1973 deservedly, after his inquiry into the wages paid by British companies in South Africa, the most significant investigation undertaken during my time at the *Guardian*. The choice of individuals for political or welfare stories also made some differences to the way they were handled; and news editors exercised further influence by stimulating the specialists, making sure that they did not confine themselves too narrowly in their own expert fields.

The third of the top triumvirate was the night editor or production editor. He was the man who actually put the paper together at night, dealing with the final choice of news and the design of pages, determining the placing of pictures, and making sure that a lively diet was offered every morning. The night editor for more than twelve of my years was John Putz – someone almost unknown outside the office but carrying, night by night, probably the heaviest burden of anyone on the staff. Until the start of London printing he was simply called chief sub-editor, but when he moved to London in 1961 to establish the operation there we renamed him, more appropriately, night editor. A phlegmatic but cheerful character, with roots in East Anglia and Devonshire, he had in my view a pre-eminently sound judgement of news (apart from a lenient favouritism for the occasional royal story). He embodied *Guardian* values. Some of the reporters thought that, like John Cole on the news desk later, he was 'a hard man', for he was determined to get the best possible paper out, edition by edition, and to get it out on time; and, under pressure himself, he was an extremely fast worker.

John Putz, now at seventy-five the justly proud cultivator of a fine garden in Somerset, recalls only one occasion in all his years when the film writer's favourite order 'stop the presses' was actually given. That was when an obvious libel was spotted on the front page, because of careless headline writing in relation to a murder case, and five thousand copies had to be scrapped. But he recalls numerous other nights of intense activity, with major front-page stories changing for each edition. Suez in

1956 was one such time, and the Cuban missile crisis another; polling nights at general elections, although thoroughly planned in advance, always brought the unexpected and required rapid changes.

Such changes sometimes had their lighter side. John has kept his front pages of July 21, 1966, the morning after Harold Wilson had announced a package of stiff deflationary measures –

First edition (off stone 10 pm, which means front page complete by then, and printing at 10.25):

Mr Brown thinks again
about resignation

Premier rejects his decision
to leave Government

Second edition (off stone 11.15):

Mr Brown hands in
his resignation

No decision on acceptance:
three meetings with Premier

Third edition (off stone 12.30):

Mr Brown withdraws
his resignation

Persuaded by Premier: duty to
help make Britain strong

Final edition (off stone 2.15):

Mr Brown swallows
deflation dose

Resignation withdrawn after
three talks with Premier

The reports from the *Guardian*'s political and labour correspondents and its financial editor were, of course, bringing readers up to date edition by edition – not only with George Brown's protests but with analysis of those deflationary measures. (A by-product of the measures was the sharp decline in display advertising because companies became short of cash and advertisement budgets were easy to cut – and that decline finally unnerved the Astors at the *Times* and dismayed our own Laurence Scott, leading to the talks between the two on a merger and eventually to the sale of the *Times* to Roy Thomson.)

After John Putz retired, the title of night editor was superseded by that of production editor. Brian Jones, who took over in 1969, was in much the same mould – a fast worker, with excellent news judgement and an eye for harmonious page layouts, and a man who did not spare himself. He had joined the *Guardian* during the 1961 expansion but left us for a few years in the mid-sixties, to be editor of the *Bath and Wiltshire Chronicle*, returning in 1968; from 1972 to 1975 he was Northern editor, but then chose a more domestic life in Wiltshire (returning eventually to Fleet Street, to the *Financial Times*). The production editor from 1972 to 1975 was Peter Preston, who was a ripe thirty-three when appointed to the post, having served already as a political reporter, war correspondent in Cyprus and Pakistan, education correspondent, originator of Miscellany (much disliked by Harold Wilson and others), and as features editor. When I decided in 1975 that I ought to depart early rather than work myself to exhaustion in the editor's chair – as Wadsworth and Crozier had done before me – Peter was chosen to succeed me; an excellent choice, as the paper's performance since then has proved. Like me, he was thirty-six when he took over.

In addition to the triumvirate, the leader writers were a constant source of advice. Each had his areas of speciality, and all wrote much more than leaders. In Wadsworth's time we hardly ever met collectively – indeed the conferences round his bedside during the early stages of the Suez crisis are about the only ones I can remember. I continued his practice of individual consultation, dropping into separate rooms and chatting there, until 1960. Then one of the leader writers – Harold Griffiths,* trained like me at the *Glasgow Herald* – persuaded me to adopt the *Herald*'s amiable practice of a half-hour exchange of ideas in the early afternoon. It became a daily fixture, though I believe it has now been moved to before lunch.

The formal business of the office began with the news desk, which was manned from 10.30 onwards or earlier in times of crisis. (I did not come in to the office myself until midday, since I normally stayed until 12.30 or 1 am to see the main London and home counties edition away.)

Some telephoning took place from homes around 7.30 or 8.0, when reporters had to be briefed or despatched on long-distance assignments. Whenever possible, though, briefing took place the night before so that a reporter could read library cuttings and prepare his mind before setting off. Once London printing had begun in 1961, there was a pattern of regular conferences all on the loudspeaker telephone so that they could be shared between staff in London and Manchester.[1] (It took a little time to learn not to make jokes on the loudspeaker telephone; when the speaker's face was invisible, and a group were listening at the other end, what was meant as a joke could sound stinging.) The first was a planning conference at noon, mainly concerned with page layouts and advertisement allocations. At 4.30 there was a quick check on page layouts, again with ad. department people present.

1 The London printing operation is more fully described in Chapter 7, pp. 144-49.

At 6 pm came the main news conference, at which the news editors in London and Manchester and the foreign editor outlined the chief stories they were expecting. That meeting served effectively as the 'hand over' from day staff to night staff. It was the longest, lasting about fifteen minutes. At 8 pm the front-page conference followed, with the night editor (or later the production editor) in London proposing the plan and priorities for front and back pages. It was a compact meeting, with fewer people, and lasted only eight or ten minutes. We had all been seeing duplicates of the main stories as they came in. Usually I took an active part in that myself, and the news editor tended to stay for it in order to protect cherished projects.

At 10.15 or 10.30, as soon as the front page was 'off stone' – fully made up in the composing room, proofed, and sent to be stereotyped – there was a London–Manchester discussion of what to change for later editions. And at that point sparks often flew about stories that were late or had failed to turn up or were just not good enough. Thereafter the two night editors or their chief sub-editors kept in touch as necessary by telephone.

The gathering of leader writers, from 1960 onwards, was usually about 3.15 and informal. It was not held on the loudspeaker unless London–Manchester discussion was strictly necessary. Part of its value was in being more relaxed and discursive than other meetings, allowing ideas to flow. If I was writing a leader myself, which I generally did two or three times a week, I tried to start between 4.30 and 6.0; and the last pages had to be in the composing room by about 7.45, though changes could be made or new leaders written for later editions. In the sixties we regarded 7.45 pm as deplorably early; but today higher technology, which in theory ought to mean later deadlines, has in fact brought even earlier deadlines because of higher staff costs. I am horrified when I go into the *Guardian* office now and find leader writers, including Peter Preston, having to finish by 6.0 or 6.30 when much of the night's main news has still to come in.

Within the office, before and after the start of London printing, there was much debate and some unhappiness about the consequences of its technical requirements. Some of the staff felt that we had forced the paper into a straitjacket, with the sequence of conferences, the strict deadlines, and production limitations. We had, it was said, destroyed the happy Oxbridge collegiate atmosphere of the old *Guardian* office at Cross Street, Manchester; and that was true. But there was no other way at that time of securing a national distribution, and in the end there were great advantages from having our headquarters within easy reach of Westminster, Whitehall, and the City.

The physical and mental strain of a two-headed operation cost the *Guardian* some good staff. John Rosselli,* a gifted journalist whom Wadsworth had recruited from Cambridge in 1951, became features editor soon after the start of London printing. His department was split between London and Manchester, and because of production restrictions many of his pages had to be made up in Manchester a day ahead of printing and sent south as 'matts' (full-page impressions for making into metal in the machine room). Rosselli found the system crazy, unmanageable, and exhausting, though he worked extremely hard to make a success of his department. In the summer of 1964 he accepted an academic post at Sussex University, satisfying to him because of his interest in modern history, and he has stayed there ever since. Quite probably he would soon have moved to university life anyway, but the physical changes in the *Guardian* from 1961 contributed to his decision; and he believed that in trying to make itself more popular, to cover the costs of London printing, the paper was compromising its standards. David Marquand* also went to Sussex University at about the same time, not because he had been under great strain but because he wanted to move to the academic environment. He, too, expressed some anxiety lest physical requirements impaired the paper's quality. After John's departure, fortuitously, we were able to transfer more of the features department's work to London and ease the production restrictions. His successor, Christopher Driver,* was able to build on John's work.

Editors and proprietors

The *Guardian* editor's position is unusual because there is no proprietor above him and he has greater freedom of decision than most editors. The paper is owned by the Scott Trust, through the parent company (*G&MEN* Ltd), and the trustees are the ultimate authority. The trustees appoint the company's directors, and, jointly with the Board, appoint the editors of the *Guardian* and the *Manchester Evening News*. Once appointed, the *Guardian*'s editor is autonomous editorially – though he must work in close conjunction with the management in commercial and financial matters, and must keep within his budget.

At the time of my appointment the Scott Trust and the *MG&EN* Board were smaller than they are today. A. P. Wadsworth and Laurence Scott were members of both bodies, A.P. chairing the Trust and Laurence the Board, and altogether there were only four other trustees and four further directors. Richard became chairman of the Trust after A.P.'s death. Day to day he worked under me while still an active journalist, being diplomatic correspondent and then in Washington and finally in Paris until retirement in 1974; but the Trust's authority nevertheless stood above me. In 1956 Laurence really made the choice of new editor himself, because of A.P.'s illness, though after discussion with the other trustees and directors. By 1975 there were ten trustees, the limit under the Trust deed, and ten directors. My successor, Peter Preston, was chosen after more systematic consultation – mainly through a joint committee drawn from the Trust and Board, and with an advisory group formed from the editorial staff.

In general the core of the Trust lay in members of the Scott and

Montague families, the descendants of C.P., and the remainder were long-standing members of the staff or others who had a special association with the *Guardian*. I myself became a trustee in 1970 and remain one today (1981).

Laurence and Richard are both grandsons of C.P.; Laurence's father, John Scott, was manager under C.P. for more than twenty years and then continued as chairman and managing director of the company until he handed over to Laurence in 1947. It was he, effectively, who devised and created the Scott Trust. He did so after the deaths within a few months of each other, in 1932, of his brother Ted and of C.P. Ted Scott, Richard's father, had become editor on C.P.'s retirement in 1929 but was tragically drowned in Windermere in the spring of 1932. The Trust deed proved difficult to draw up, because of legal and tax problems, but it was completed in 1936. Its purpose was and is to secure continuity of the *Guardian*. Its terms, however, leave the trustees almost total discretion as to how they conduct their affairs and apply their funds. The overriding requirement is to carry on the company or companies 'as nearly as may be on the same principles as they have heretofore been conducted' and to run the papers 'on the same lines and in the same spirit as heretofore'.

Laurence was never a conventional proprietor or company chairman, but rather the head of the family. From an editor's point of view, he was generally a model manager with whom to work. He was shrewd on the business side and never interfered with editorial affairs. Only on a few occasions did he comment at all on editorial conduct, one being the Chatterley case in 1961 (covered in Chapter 6). C.P. had turned a small local newspaper into one with a national and international reputation; it was Laurence who, after the war, foresaw rightly that the paper could not maintain its status unless it became truly national in distribution through printing in London. He had the courage to put his vision into practice; but for a time in 1966–67, five years after the start of the London operation, its heavy cost undermined his confidence in the *Guardian*'s ability to survive. He proposed a merger with the *Times*. As will be explained in Chapter 7, he had good reasons for his proposal; but I disagreed with him profoundly. For many months relations were extremely strained. Years later, in his retirement speech, he gracefully admitted that he had been wrong and I had been right. The *Guardian* did not merge with the *Times*.

As a result of that episode, the *Guardian*'s management was overhauled and separated from the *MEN*'s. The combined load in London and Manchester had become too great for a single team to handle. Peter Gibbings was recruited from the *Observer* as the *Guardian*'s managing director, and later he took over from Laurence as group chairman. Looking back, I believe that I never did a better day's work for the *Guardian* than on the afternoon when I put the case to Peter for joining us. He in turn recruited Gerry Taylor, first as advertisement director and later as the *Guardian*'s managing director, when Peter himself became group chairman.

Relations between editor and proprietor or editor and management are never static in any newspaper. The conduct of Northcliffe, Beaverbrook, Roy Thomson, Cecil King, and others towards their editors varied at different times and is a rich field for study, but there is no room for it here.[2] C.P. had written in his centenary essay that between editor and business manager there should be 'a happy marriage', but with the proviso that the editor should be 'just an inch or two in advance'. For the second half of his life C.P. was effectively proprietor as well as editor, and much more than an inch or two ahead. At the time of my appointment, the sheer weight of Laurence's experience and his position as head of the family were bound to put him many yards ahead of me, but he never misused the position. With Peter Gibbings and Gerry Taylor, after they were installed at the head of the new *Guardian* management in 1967, there was a more equal relationship. Apart from the 1966–67 crisis, I was extremely fortunate in the managements with whom I had to work.

Relations between the *Guardian* and the *Manchester Evening News* were always delicate and called for tolerant understanding on both sides. The *MEN*, under separate ownership, had been printed on the same plant since the 1860s but was acquired by the Scotts between 1923 and 1930 as a support for the *Guardian*. From then onwards the *MEN* almost always made more money than the *Guardian*, though for a period before the start of London printing both papers paid, as the figures in Appendix 1 show. Some jealousies were unavoidable but some could have been averted. When I first went to Manchester in 1950, there was almost no social contact with *MEN* men and no interchange of staff. In 1959 I wanted to offer Harry Evans, then an assistant editor of the *MEN*, a post as assistant editor on the *Guardian*; Tom Henry, editor of the *MEN*, absolutely prohibited it, and Laurence took Tom's side. The barriers are now less rigid and the rivalries fewer, for on the whole the *MEN*'s staff are as well paid as the *Guardian*'s (and sometimes better). And although it might be disputed, I suspect that the *MEN* under the Scott Trust has been a better employer and has offered better conditions than it would have done in commercial ownership, with its profits milked off as part of a big international group.

The *Guardian* and its staff owe a great debt to the *MEN* for the security

2 In that connection, do not miss the report of the first Royal Commission on the Press, the Ross Commission, published in 1948, and particularly the evidence given by Lord Beaverbrook; also *Studies on the Press*, prepared for the third Royal Commission, the McGregor Commission, by Oliver Boyd-Barrett, Colin Seymour-Ure, and Jeremy Tunstall, published by HMSO in 1977. Also Colin R. Coote's *Editorial*, 1965; Charles Wintour's *Pressures on the Press*, 1972; Arthur Christiansen's *Headlines All My Life*; Michael Foot's *Debts of Honour*, 1980; John Whale's *The Politics of the Media*, 1977; and Russell Braddon's *Roy Thomson*.

that the partnership has offered and for the funds made available to the *Guardian* through *MEN* profits. The *Guardian* owes much also to others in the group – notably to the Rochdale papers and, since 1979, the *Surrey Advertiser* series.

The biggest debt, however, is owed to the Scott family and the Scott Trust. C. P. Scott set out to create a newspaper of the highest standards, and one that was a friendly place within which to work; the Trust has been the means of keeping his ideals alive.

Libel and worse

In my time, by far the worst and most embarrassing error of judgement, in news columns, was a front-page lead in 1964 saying that Egypt was acquiring her own nuclear weapons. The report came on a Sunday afternoon from a staff correspondent of good reputation, who was convinced of its accuracy. John Cole was off duty and his deputy on the news desk that night was short of good material and therefore doubly keen to see it used. I was off duty, too, and out walking with the children in Greenwich Park when a niece brought a telephone message from the office; so I went in to see the story. Unluckily our science correspondent, John Maddox, proved to be out of reach – for when he saw it in the paper next morning he said he knew at once that it must be wrong. I ought to have held it for twenty-four hours, even at the risk of losing an 'exclusive', but did not do so. That was an error I never made again; one such error undoes the benefit of twenty exclusives. Much later, when Jean Stead became news editor and organised some remarkable exclusives, she cursed my caution more than once when I insisted on waiting for more evidence. I now suspect that the Egyptian story was a deliberate and well-organised Israeli plant.

In leading articles, the most questionable judgements were over Vietnam in 1967, over the Arab–Israeli war also in that year, and over Rhodesia in 1968, two and a half years after UDI. All these are more fully discussed in Chapter 10; and of the three, as will emerge, only over Vietnam did I feel in the end that we had gone wrong. The most difficult of all policy decisions were over Northern Ireland, and ten years later I am still not sure whether we took the right course. Looking back one can say, 'If only British troops had not been committed to the streets of Belfast and Londonderry ...' or alternatively, 'If only we had set a date for withdrawal, after the events of Bloody Sunday, instead of imposing direct rule ...' But either course would most probably have led not to Irish unity, which was then unattainable, but to Protestant rule even tougher than before the civil rights marches of 1968 and 1969. The Irish dilemma is explored more fully in Chapter 12; here I am only saying that, over Ireland, it was desperately difficult to be sure of the best approach.

Libel was a lesser worry, but needed watching. During my time the *Guardian* was, I believe, the only Fleet Street paper with no resident lawyers reading copy or proofs.[3] Every reporter was supposed to seek advice if in doubt, and every sub-editor to watch out for hazards. Our solicitors – Lovell, White and King, from about 1959 onwards – had a rota of their people so that we could reach someone for advice any night at any time. The number of consultations grew as the years passed, so much so that in the last few years the Guardian has had a duty lawyer in the office every night.

The most troublesome action in my time, and by far the longest, was brought by Morgan Phillips, general secretary of the Labour party. It began in 1959 and ended in 1967, some years after his death. The writ covered not only defamation but breach of copyright of a Labour party document, conversion of the infringing copies, conspiracy, and breach of confidence – and because of the additional claims the case was able to continue after the death of Morgan Phillips. John Cole had written an exclusive report about a document on the overhaul of Transport House and its staff, prepared by Phillips, and had quoted extensively from it. He held that John's story implied that he was the source, which in our view it did not – nor was he. He sued, and after his death his executors continued the case. Hugh Gaitskell wanted to end it, but agreement on terms for a settlement could not be reached; for although, on advice, we were prepared to concede an infringement of copyright we were not prepared to concede anything else. The case was eventually allowed to lapse.

The *Guardian*'s legal files show the rising frequency of cases. Apart from a 'general' file for those cleared up quickly – either by an immediate apology or by rejecting the complaint and hearing no more about it, which was the most common experience – we had six substantial cases in 1961, three in 1962, and a gradually growing number reaching a peak of eighteen in 1972. The identities of the six files from 1965 are curious, and none was a case which came to court: they were Jack Dash (the trade union leader), Michael Melody, the London Symphony Orchestra, Oundle School, the Pit Ponies Protection Society, and the sixth case was one instituted by the *Guardian* against *Private Eye* leading to an apology on their side (in the terms that we required). The only expensive settlement in my years was over a book review, on the PQ 17 convoy to Murmansk in wartime. The convoy commander sued the publisher and author, and separately

3 In law libel is any statement which lowers the reputation of a man, woman, or group in the estimation of their fellows. There is an absolute defence of truth, but the onus of proving the truth of the statement lies on the newspaper, publisher, and author. It is no defence to show that someone else said it, unless it has been said at an open meeting of a public authority or other public body – and then the report must be shown to be fair and accurate, and not inspired by malice. A claim for libel ceases with the death of the plaintiff. That, in the simplest terms, is the nature of libel and defamation. Unlike some editors, I thought the law a necessary protection for individual citizens, though I should have welcomed some form of defence on grounds of public interest.

sued the *Guardian* and our reviewer. Since we had no primary evidence, having relied on the book, we had to follow the publisher's defence; but, when tested, the author's version crumbled.

The *Guardian*, like some but not all others, was insured against libel damages. The terms were that we paid any award below £4,000 or any excess over £80,000 or thereabouts, but the insurers could require us to settle if their lawyers thought the case too difficult to defend. Alternatively we could waive claims against them and carry the whole cost ourselves. We did that only once, in a case which eventually went our way. Because the insurance was expensive, there was much debate on whether or not to continue it.

Common sense was often as important as the exact law. With our lawyers we had to decide what the plaintiffs were really after, how a judge and jury might react, and what interest was served by defending a case. Frequently LW&K were consulted before publication; and sometimes, having advised that we were at risk, they agreed that because of the circumstances the risks were worth taking. They were never legalistic in their approach, and we were well served by them. Until the mid-sixties John Notcutt looked after editorial matters – libel, contempt, copyright, and so on – and Geoffrey Grimes thereafter, while other partners could be brought in for commercial and financial matters. Geoffrey rebelled only once, over an investigation into police corruption, but that comes into Chapter 11. In that and other cases Geoffrey made us think out beforehand how we would reply to inquiries from Scotland Yard or the Home Office or aggrieved authorities on the morning after publication. It was just as well that he did.

Advertisements were another occasional cause of headaches – through their presence, their absence, their political content, and in other ways. The advertisement department often wanted extra space on prime news pages, and as often we had to refuse this, in the paper's general interest, while trying not to discourage them. More than half the *Guardian*'s revenue used to come from advertisements – more than two-thirds, in fact, during the sixties before Fleet Street began to adopt more realistic pricing policies. (The *Guardian*'s selling price went up from 6d to 8d in February 1970, and then to 9d in October, and to 5p in September 1971: a doubling of the cover price in eighteen months, and strictly necessary to prevent undue dependence on advertisement revenue.) The paper could not survive without a fair volume of display, classified, and financial advertising – but an outspoken newspaper, left-of-centre, was one that commercial advertisers were liable to strike off their schedules. Certainly the *Guardian*'s advertisement department had a hard struggle to maintain revenue; and in some lucrative areas, such as 'company meetings' (the paid reports of annual meetings, with the company chairman's statements), the *Guardian* in the sixties and early seventies received only a shadow of the business that went to the *Times*, *FT*, and *Telegraph*.

Direct pressure from advertisers was rare. During the Suez crisis in 1956 two big companies cancelled advertising explicitly because of the paper's policy – one a merchant bank and the other a major steel company – but others, while simply withdrawing or not placing advertisements, said nothing. In 1968 over Rhodesia there was thought to be some effect but it could not be measured. In 1973–74, after the investigation of wages being paid by British companies in South Africa, there was undoubtedly a levelling off after a period of good growth in advertisement volume. But apart from a few dark hints to advertisement department representatives there was no hard evidence.

One interesting case, indicative of the delicacy of these matters, was in dealings with Marks and Spencer. In 1967 a 'special feature' was proposed in connection with the fiftieth anniversary of the Balfour Declaration, 'special features' being groups of extra pages, bringing substantial revenue through a high ratio of additional advertising, with articles written for the occasion. In 1917 the Foreign Secretary's letter declaring the British Government's support for a Jewish national home in Palestine was a milestone on the road to creating the state of Israel – and it was C. P. Scott who had introduced Chaim Weizmann to Lloyd George and A. J. Balfour, as well as giving strong support in the *MG*. The idea of a 'special feature' had come from the Israeli side, because of C.P.'s involvement.

Marks and Spencer rarely advertised, but a provisional booking had been made before the June war; and because of the Sieff family's prominence in Jewish affairs, other bookings had come. Articles had been commissioned, some from distinguished authors; but then, after the June war, most of the advertisers failed to confirm their bookings. They were entirely within their rights, for 'provisional' bookings are provisional until a set date before publication. After a discreet hint through our advertisement department, I went to see Lord Sieff – the only time in my years as editor when I undertook such a mission. He was reluctant to discuss the matter, but eventually said that he and others had disliked the way the *Guardian* reported the June war; and he made clear that, had I not pressed him, he would never have stated the reason behind M&S's action. We had a long conversation about the Middle East and about his early memories of Manchester. The special feature had to be scrapped, though we carried some of the articles in the paper because of their historic value.

Others among the Jewish community were more belligerent. Two Jewish publications campaigned for the withdrawal of all custom from the *Guardian* – myopically, in my view, for the paper had been impartial in its reporting and its leaders had been understanding of the reasons why Israel went to war (so understanding that this was part-cause of the resignation of one of my best leader writers, as will be explained in Chapter 10). A further irony was that we were taken to the Press Council three years later by a Jewish group of anti-Zionists because we refused to publish their advertisement, which said among other things that the Government of Israel 'on every possible occasion' had sought to heap humiliation on the Arabs and was 'a dire threat to world peace'. The Press Council rejected the complaint.

Much earlier, in 1962, there were problems over political advertising. Almost simultaneously requests came from South Africa House for space to state the South African Government's view on apartheid and from the Soviet Embassy for two whole pages with which to advertise extracts from Mr Khrushchev's 'de-Stalinisation' declaration to the Communist party congress. Our general principle was that we ought not to censor political advertising, however much we might disagree with its content, but that we ought not knowingly to carry any incorrect or misleading information. On that basis we sought and obtained some changes of wording in the South African advertisements; but Khrushchev's words were a different case, because these were the actual words of his speech. Apart from his denunciation of 'anti-party' groups within the party, he had made apparently extravagant claims about the Soviet ballistic missile programme and about possession of an anti-missile missile. Clearly there was no way of checking accuracy; but since his speech was of immense international interest, and we had given more than two news columns to it already, I decided that we should accept the advertisement.

It caused something of a sensation, for nothing of the kind had previously been seen in the West. It was the first of a number of such advertisements placed by the Soviet Government in Western newspapers, though at first there were many criticisms of the *Guardian* for having accepted it. The occasion had a certain piquancy, for five weeks previously a group of Soviet editors had visited Britain and some of them had been to the *Guardian* office. It happened on a day when a number of newspapers, including the *Guardian*, were carrying whole-page advertisements telling Britain to keep out of the Common Market – advertisements paid for by Lord Beaverbrook – and the Russians had questioned me on the reasons why we were ready to accept these when they were contrary to *Guardian* policy. I felt fairly certain that the idea of Soviet advertisements had immediately been carried back to Moscow, and that this was the result. Khrushchev's son-in-law (Aleksei Adzhubei) had been one of the Soviet party.

In 1974, after publishing one inflammatory advertisement, we retracted and apologised. It was by 'Free Palestine', and among its charges against Israel was that explosive toys had been dropped on refugee camps, leading to the death of two Arab children and injuries to others. The advertisement was illustrated by photographs which, we found before publishing them, had been issued internationally through Associated Press and published in a number of newspapers together with reports of Palestinian allegations of the use of booby-trapped dolls, teddy bears, and other toys during reprisal raids on the Lebanon on May 17. Therefore, though with much reluctance, it was decided that the advertisement should appear; I happened to be away, but afterwards agreed with the decision.

Publication brought an immediate protest from the Israeli embassy – followed by complaints from the Board of Deputies of British Jews and others, and renewed demands in the *Jewish Gazette* for a boycott on the *Guardian*. To the embassy I replied in detail, including an unpublished verbatim report from our Beirut correspondent of an interview with a boy apparently injured in a raid on May 17; that appeared to go some way towards confirming the Palestinian charge, though our correspondent said that there was no way of being precisely sure how the boy had lost an eye. After ten days the Israeli embassy came back with a list of the targets attacked on May 17, which looked to me authentic and did not include the boy's camp, and with copies of an Arabic leaflet (which we translated) on how to make booby-trapped toys. Therefore I published a statement saying that, while verification was not attainable, the *Guardian* thought it highly improbable that the Government of Israel had employed booby-trapped toys – and that we regretted publication of the original advertisement. That, of course, then brought Arab or pro-Arab complaints that we had yielded to Israeli pressure.

A prohibition on all political advertisements seems to me wrong; but checking their statements must often be impossible. After the 'Free Palestine' experience, we stopped all such Middle Eastern advertisements for some months; and, ironically, advertisements by Jewish groups were among the first to be barred. The pragmatic endeavour to be fair can prove painful.

Politics, sources, and politicians

Among younger readers, as among some of the staff, there was an expectation that the *Guardian* would always take the radical side. The weight of the British press – especially among the so-called 'heavy' dailies – tended to be conservative and conformist. The *Times*, the *Telegraph*, and the *Financial Times* were not noted for political support of the left (though the *Times* at the last minute in the 1966 election came out in full support of the Liberals). The *Guardian* caused double annoyance and disappointment, therefore, when it refrained from backing popular leftist causes – whether 'troops out' from Vietnam or Ulster or any other fashionable target. But it was a cardinal rule that we must examine the facts first.

Another cardinal rule was that reporting must never be coloured by the paper's opinion. Once at a senior staff meeting to discuss policy in the impending 1974 February election, I suggested seriously that perhaps we ought to support Ted Heath: I saw Ian Aitken's* jaw drop at this heresy, but I am certain that in his work as political correspondent he never let his Labour loyalties sway his reporting one way or the other. I had some sympathy with the complaint attributed to Roy Hattersley in that election: 'When I see the *Daily Excess*, the *Daily Hail*, the *Moon*, the *Daily*

Telephone, and even the *Eternity* prejudiced on the side of the Tories, I just want to see someone being corrupt and unfair on *my* side.'

For a short time in the early seventies there was a trend towards 'committed journalism' – the belief that every word you wrote should contribute to a campaign (preferably a campaign against a corrupt capitalist society). At that time one or two of our more ardent young reporters tried to write in that way, but they had to be stopped. Fortunately the infection did not reach any of our more experienced staff, who believed in the *Guardian*'s commitment to a rational and impartial approach.

What we did encourage was concentration on reforming topics – as in Ann Shearer's investigation of conditions in mental hospitals or Malcolm Dean's various series on child poverty, homelessness, and the payment of doctors or the Beaton–Maddox series on stopping the spread of nuclear weapons.[4] The feature pages and the women's pages were a frequent setting for insistent evidence on the need for social reform; and it was no coincidence that articles on these topics often brought a strong response from readers. The Disablement Incomes Group was the direct result of articles on the *Guardian*'s women's pages; and the series on the 'Permissive Society' not only caught the mood of the sixties but was probably an influence in shaping it.

We also encouraged the ingenuity of reporters in getting to places where events mattered – and in cultivating good contacts. Harry Jackson got back into Czechoslovakia on the night of the Soviet invasion in August 1968, when the frontier was supposed to be closed, by trying a succession of border posts until he found one where a dissident guard let him through. It was eight o'clock in the evening, and some fifteen kilometres up the road he ran into a Russian tank squadron moving down to seal the border. Fortunately they ignored his car. He drove on through the night to Prague, only to discover that there had been a shoot-to-kill curfew in force. Hella Pick,* in a less warlike setting, proved adept at getting information out of international bankers and civil servants. Her very accurate story the morning before the sterling devaluation in November 1967 was obtained through a few words with a senior OECD man, standing behind a pillar at the Rothschilds' former Château de la Muette, in Paris. There was a lot of skill, she said, in recognising from a few key words what was afoot and knowing the context of what was being discussed. A good specialist had to keep up to date all the time, meeting contacts even when there was nothing immediately to be obtained for publication, and creating confidence that information would be used with care.

Sources and contacts were often a difficulty, especially with Government departments. My relations with Harold Wilson were generally good, but I once caused him deep offence. In a public lecture at Stirling

4 For Beaton–Maddox on nuclear weapons, see the next chapter.

University in March 1970, when he was at Downing Street, I quoted something he had said in 1963 as Leader of the Opposition. On vital issues, he said, Parliament was being told less and less; and press comment was conditioned by official press conferences – particularly in the Foreign Office.

Nothing is said to Parliament by the Foreign Office, and diplomatic correspondents are reduced to utter dependence on a daily briefing at the Foreign Office. If the press exercises its undoubted right to criticise, then facilities dry up. Correspondents are demoted from the inner ring to the outer ring, and are denied information altogether by a system of administrative blackballing.... Whitehall spokesmen should recognise not only that facts are sacred but that comment must be free.

It was a great speech, I said, and it would have been greater still if Harold Wilson, in office, had applied its lessons. But it could be said with equal force in 1970. The methods by which much Government information was given to the press – Lobby meetings, private briefings, 'off the record' information, and so on – had not changed. Some of these methods were legitimate, some not.

My lecture was reported in a number of newspapers next morning and in the BBC's radio programme at breakfast-time. A despatch rider from Downing Street arrived at the *Guardian*'s London office about 11 am with a pained private letter on Harold's behalf from his press secretary; but by that time I was near the top of an ice-covered mountain in Perthshire with the *Guardian*'s Scottish correspondent, John Kerr, discussing the rise of the Scottish Nationalists. I talked it over with Harold after I returned to London.

But I had no cause to retract or modify anything. The Foreign Office was behaving as it always had done, and some other departments were not much better. The Lobby correspondents – the privileged group registered with the Sergeant at Arms and allowed to talk with MPs in the Inner Lobby – were being used as much as ever, so that no source was quoted and Government opinion was frequently given as fact. The Lobby system had many advantages, I said at Stirling: it allowed the background of Government policy to be explained, it allowed informal questioning, and it provided for continuity of knowledge. But it was being abused when information that ought to be provided with a source and attribution was provided 'off the record', and it had grown into a kind of semi-secret society. Dick Crossman, while a *Guardian* columnist in 1961–63, had offered to provide an almost verbatim account of what Rab Butler as Leader of the House was saying to the Lobby at his Thursday meetings with them simply by putting together the reports in the *Times*, *Guardian*, and *Telegraph* – and had once done it – but now Dick himself was a prince among Lobby briefers. In 1971 when Harold Wilson was out of office he told me that next time he was at Downing Street he would restrict the use of the Lobby, and to an extent he did; but the system survives today, and no single editor by himself can let his paper break away from it, since it is still the primary source of Government documents and Government briefings.

My objection to Foreign Office methods went back to early days in journalism. In 1948 the *Glasgow Herald* sent me to Germany, and there I obtained my first 'scoop' – the impending decision of the Western Powers to stop the policy of breaking up cartels in the Ruhr, particularly in the steel and coal industries, and to restore larger units for the sake of economic efficiency. I sent the story and the *Glasgow Herald* printed it as its lead; but it was an embarrassment to the Foreign Office. The FO's news department was then headed by Sir William Ridsdale, and one of his staff telephoned to the editor of the *Glasgow Herald*, Sir William Robieson. Who was this young man in Germany, he asked? The report was wrong and there was no truth in the story, he said. Robieson, a wise and experienced man, said he would wait to hear my side when I got back. Somewhat shaken when I heard, I told Robieson privately that the story had come – with the intention that I should use it – from another Glasgow man, Sir Cecil Weir, then head of the Iron and Steel section of the Control Commission. He had his own reasons for thinking that the news should be known. Six weeks later the change of policy was announced in the House of Commons. If Robieson had not been as shrewd as he was, my career might have been jeopardised.

It was no wonder that in the late forties the circle of diplomatic correspondents were known as 'Ridsdale's trained seals'. Yet, you may say, is there not a lack of logic in my readiness to take off-the-record information from someone like Sir Cecil Weir and still object to the Lobby system and the Foreign Office 'inner ring' briefings? I believe not: selective use of private information is well justified, both because of the insight it gives on policies and governmental decisions and because it is sometimes the only way to protect sources. Selection ought to be made according to a journalist's or newspaper's judgement of the honesty and reliability of the source, and the possible public interest of the information. Over the change of policy on Krupp, Thyssen, I. G. Farben, and other German combines, for example, I suspect that Sir Cecil Weir, while not against it, believed that public discussion of how far it should go would be beneficial before Anglo-American decisions became irrevocable.

My objection was and is to the constant use by Governments of the Lobby, the Foreign Office inner ring, and the like to put out information that can and ought to be on open public record – and to their use to put out misleading information.[5] A classic example of the absurdity of the first came at the end of the Chequers meeting on Northern Ireland in the

---

5 Ian Aitken held that stories given at Lobby briefings ought not to be relied on unless an independent source was available; Hella Pick took the same view of FO private briefings.

autumn of 1971, when the Prime Ministers of Northern Ireland and the Republic, Mr Brian Faulkner and Mr Jack Lynch, appeared at open press conferences and live on television while the British Prime Minister talked only to the Lobby and could not be quoted. On misleading information, at the time of my Stirling lecture there had been a succession of incidents in the previous nine months over the supply of British arms to Nigeria during the Biafran war and over interference with relief flights to Biafra. The information being given by the Foreign Office, in conflict with reports in the *Guardian* and *Sunday Times*, had been proved to be wrong.

On top of that, I had had a sharp disagreement with the Foreign Secretary, Michael Stewart, when he summoned me to his presence and demanded retraction of a *Guardian* report on the British attitude to Greek membership of the Council of Europe. I was willing to print anything that he or the FO would say officially, on the record, but he wanted the paper to retract on its own authority. Since I knew the story had come through the Whips' office at the Commons and had been reported in good faith, I refused. He tried to browbeat me; so I got up and walked out, the only time I have ever done such a thing to a Cabinet Minister. I would have liked to withdraw the *Guardian*'s diplomatic correspondent from the FO and its inner ring, but after discussion with others decided that it was not practicable. The facility of reading telegrams from ambassadors abroad, accorded to the inner ring, was at times valuable. In a situation such as the Czech crisis, we ought not to cut the paper off from that.

As editor, my own relations with Prime Ministers and Opposition Leaders were at times delicate. Contact with them began only gradually, with social invitations from Harold Macmillan and then with fairly frequent private discussion with Hugh Gaitskell. In June 1957, when newly married and on holiday in Skye, I had a telephone call one evening from Downing Street. Lady Dorothy Macmillan had seen our wedding photograph in the *Guardian*, where it had been published contrary to my instructions, and her secretary wanted to know whether we could both lunch at Downing Street a fortnight later. We did, and it was a happy lunch. Miranda, extremely good-looking and with a sharp mind, was a hit with Harold Macmillan and Sir Ralph Assheton (former chairman of the Conservative party). Suez was never mentioned.

After lunch the Prime Minister steered me to a window seat overlooking the Horseguards Parade, where we talked about the Persian Gulf. The ruler of Oman, faced with tribal turbulence which he believed was being backed from outside his territory, had asked for British help. Macmillan said that he had sat up late the previous night reading James Morris's book *Sultan in Oman*. Although the book did not bear directly on the present troubles, it had given him a sense of the country and its character which did not come from any official brief. That morning, therefore, he had ordered a dozen copies and sent them round to the Chiefs of Staff and the relevant Ministers, suggesting that they read the book quickly.

We went on to talk of Southern Africa, of which my knowledge was imperfect. I felt that I had done no better than a gamma minus, but it was a friendly interrogation.

Other invitations followed, about once every nine months. At first I thought twice about accepting them, lest political judgement was softened by hospitality. But the occasions were interesting and often informative. In 1958 I started keeping notes of political conversations, chiefly in order to circulate them privately among senior staff in the office. It proved a valuable device. It meant that within a day or two four or five others at the *Guardian* knew what had been said to me and what I had replied. It helped to prevent misunderstandings and to overcome anxiety lest Ministers or others influenced me too much. (Those notes have also helped greatly in the writing of this book.)

Social invitations came occasionally from Buckingham Palace. Again I had misgivings about accepting them, but never regretted it when I went. The first was to a small lunch in 1958 and included a graphic account by the Queen about Suez as seen from inside the Palace. She said that it had been a terrible time, with the Palace torn into factions. People had been 'clawing' at each other – she did a vigorous clawing gesture – and would not speak to each other. She hoped that there would never be anything like it again.

With Hugh Gaitskell I soon developed a friendly though often argumentative relationship, of which some account is given in the next two chapters. At the same time I was quite often seeing others – Maudling and Marples on the Conservative side, Crossman and Wilson from Labour, and most frequently Jo Grimond. After Gaitskell's death, meetings with Harold Wilson became more regular. He had a special interest in the *Guardian*, not only as the friendliest to Labour among the 'heavy' papers but for a more personal reason. Soon after we started to meet, he told me that he might well have been sitting in my chair as editor of the paper. It had been one of his early ambitions, and indeed he had applied for a post in 1937 and had been interviewed by the editor, W. P. Crozier. He was offered a place in the leader writers' 'corridor', but then he had won the Webb Medley Senior Scholarship and had also been offered the chance to work with Beveridge. So he had written to Crozier, who had sent a sympathetic reply accepting his decision to stay at Oxford. Except for that, he said, he would very likely have been editor of the *Guardian* by now – as indeed he might. In the files I found the correspondence, including Crozier's note of the interview, kept for his own use, in which he described Wilson as 'intelligent and unassuming', with not many ideas on topics about which he might write, but 'a promising candidate'.

My most fruitful contact with Harold Wilson was in 1964–65, particularly in his early months as Prime Minister. After visits to Washington and Bonn, I brought him information and advice which were of immediate concern in decisions he had to take – thereby providing him with a reaction and dimension not available to him through official channels. Such use of an editor or political journalist was unusual, but not without precedent.[6] For the paper it brought a number of stories on Anglo-American and Anglo-European affairs, either exclusive to the *Guardian* or exceptionally well informed. In addition it provided me and others of the paper's senior staff with extra insight on the way British policy was being formed – an insight sometimes very unfavourable, as over the economic measures of 1964 and 1966 – and therefore gave greater depth to our judgements and to what we wrote. Some of the information we gained we could use in the paper at once, as when Lyndon Johnson told me what he intended to say to Wilson, but some we had to keep to ourselves for a long time afterwards.

The objection to such close dealings with a Prime Minister is that the relationship can become too cosy. In my judgement that never happened, for there were always points of disagreement and dispute, and the paper retained a critical stance – much too critical, Wilson at times thought. After 1966 we were never again so close – partly because our first bright optimism over the change from Conservative to Labour leadership had become tarnished, partly because of the *Guardian*'s own crisis in the winter of 1966–67 (precipitated by Wilson's stiff deflation), and partly because I felt that the Prime Minister was becoming less ready to listen to dissenting voices. But I continued to see him frequently, and once or twice a year he came to lunch with two or three of the *Guardian*'s senior staff.

John Cole took a purist view of those occasions, saying that their sole purpose was to get what information we could from the Prime Minister (as from others to whom we gave occasional lunches). I took perhaps a broader view, valuing of course what we could learn – while savouring it with a long spoon – but believing also that it was good for Wilson and others to be exposed to a critical perspective. It was good for us, too, to have to meet his arguments.

Throughout those years Wilson must have been seeing people from the *Mirror* Group at least as often as he was seeing me – mainly John Beavan, a former editor of the *Manchester Evening News*, who was political adviser to the *Mirror* Group; and now Lord Ardwick. He frequently saw others as well, being always concerned about his relations with the press. He had a love-hate feeling for Roy Thomson and Thomson's *Times*, after the takeover in January 1967. At first he believed that it was the best thing that could have happened to the *Times* – and that he would receive

6 C. P. Scott's mission in October 1921 to the Irish leaders – Michael Collins and Arthur Griffith (founder of Sinn Fein) – is an obvious precedent, for he went at the behest of the Prime Minister and reported back at once to Lloyd George at Chequers. President Wilson's use of Walter Lippman in 1918 is another, though not an exact precedent since Lippman (editor of the *New Republic*) was seconded to US Government service. A study of the volumes of the *Times* history will surely produce further examples.

friendlier treatment from it – but his rose-tinted view of Denis Hamilton and William Rees-Mogg quickly turned dark purple. He admired the *Financial Times*, especially while Gordon Newton was editor, and generally he scorned the *Daily Telegraph*. But he kept a close watch on all the newspapers and talked about them constantly.

Heath I found prickly and hard to penetrate. It was said that Wilson woke up every morning, read the papers and found them unfair, and was hurt – whereas Heath woke up every morning, read the papers and found them unfair, and was pleased. Certainly he almost always behaved as if he felt the *Guardian* was hostile to him, which often it was not. (Actually, the story was not true anyway, because Wilson had the early editions delivered to Downing Street before he went to bed; Heath did not, or did not look at them.) Before Heath became Prime Minister, I used to try to see him two or three times a year, and after he reached Downing Street about twice a year. In fact he seemed more approachable after winning the 1970 election, and Donald Maitland, who came over from the Foreign Office to be his press adviser, was always a helpful intermediary. (Like Wilson, he came to lunch once every nine or twelve months with a small group of *Guardian* staff.) The *Guardian* supported Heath's 1970-72 endeavour to take Britain into the European Community, and warmly applauded his success; that was a change from 1961-62, when Heath was credited with having said in one moment of exasperation that Leonard Beaton's reporting in the *Guardian* was doing more damage than de Gaulle. In its later stages Heath's incomes policy also brought him *Guardian* goodwill. The Conservatives' tax policy, which in our view benefited the rich, was the strongest point of criticism; but we supported Heath against the miners, and he need not have felt so distanced from us. Perhaps at that time abrasion was in his blood.

There is not, so far as I know, any reliable way of knowing what political influence newspapers have. It is probably less than they sometimes like to think, but great nevertheless. Their primary influence lies not in policies they may advocate but simply in the information they supply. The greatest check on misuse of their power is through television and radio, which provide an alternative source of information, perhaps more superficial but reaching immediately and vividly into people's homes. Most newspapers are at their worst during general elections, as are most politicians; both groups go in for exaggeration, half-truths, and deception. A comparison of front-page headlines and of party claims in the last few days before polling is always revealing. In the closing days of the February election in 1974, Wilson said that Heath's Government was the most divisive in living memory, as if his own memory did not extend to Baldwin's or Chamberlain's; Alec Douglas-Home said that Labour would pull the British Army out of Northern Ireland; Roy Jenkins said that Barber was the most profligate Chancellor in living memory, and Barber said that Labour's programme would add a net

£4,000 millions a year to Government spending. The press at its worst could do no worse than that. Fortunately the voting public are not easily taken in.

A tally of circulations and loyalties at that election showed, typically, the weight of the press on the Conservative side. Among the 'heavies' the *Times* (then 360,000 daily), *Financial Times* (200,000), and *Telegraph* (1.5 million) were with the Conservatives; the *Guardian* alone (380,000) was, with reservations, Lib-Lab. Among the populars only the *Mirror* (at 4.2 million the highest sale) was with Labour; the *Express* (3.3 million) and the *Mail* (1.8 million) were strongly for Heath, and the *Sun* (3.4 million), while not notably political in that election, was pro-Heath. By 1979 the *Sun* was well ahead of the *Mirror* and hotly in the Thatcher camp.

In policy terms, outside election periods, the 'heavies' count disproportionately just because they are read by Ministers, MPs, senior civil servants, company chairmen, judges and lawyers, and party executive members. Regularly one can detect leaders in the *Times* or *Guardian* which are written with the effect on a particular Minister or Ministry in mind, or a particular parliamentary committee, though their message may be of much wider interest. While their influence cannot be measured exactly, it is real.

The choice of staff

For the choice of staff the *Guardian* had no such formal procedures as the BBC and some other large corporations use. Recruitment of reporters was initiated by the news editors, of sub-editors by the night editors, and of other staff by the relevant heads of department. There was a running file of applicants, kept up to date by news editors, night editors, and others. When a vacancy was imminent, cuttings or other examples of an applicant's work were sought, and three or four likely individuals were invited for interview. Some 'talent scouting' also went on, especially through the advice of people who had recently come from other papers. The interviews were conducted first by the head of department, along with someone else if he or she wished, and were as likely to take place in a neighbouring pub as in the office. The strongest candidate – or more than one – then came to me or the deputy editor or the Northern editor. It was all very informal, but it worked. Later experience of the BBC system convinced me that the *Guardian* found out much more about applicants and their abilities than the BBC did.

Although most of our staff came with experience and training on other papers, until 1968 the *Guardian* recruited one or two high-grade graduates each year. Michael Frayn was my own choice in my first year as editor; Neal Ascherson had come the previous year, though he had spent some time in Africa between university and coming to us. David Marquand, Ann Shearer, Benedict Nightingale, Dick Bourne, Martin Adeney, Victor Keegan, and Rosalind Morris were among those recruited that way, and although some later left us for academic life or authorship they brightened the *Guardian* scene while they were with us. From 1968 the scheme was killed by the refusal of the NUJ nationally to allow any further recruitment direct to Fleet Street papers, and the press has been the poorer as a result.

Promotion was determined informally as well, though vacancies in the higher posts were notified as often as possible through our weekly or fortnightly 'Editorial news', which appeared on notice boards and went out to specialists. On one occasion a head of department, about to go to a more plush job elsewhere, tried to dictate who should succeed him – telling me that his staff would accept nobody other than his nominee. I chose someone else, whom the department soon accepted and enjoyed as its head. But a sounding of departmental feelings was usually worthwhile, unless clearly it was time for a shake-up. It would be misleading to suggest that we always made the right choice; sometimes I had to extricate myself and the paper when staff were badly handled or semi-specialist functions were poorly performed, and that could be difficult. A sideways move, slightly downhill, was usually the answer.

The *Guardian*'s NUJ understood the importance of promotion, and in 1970 the London chapel (or union branch within the office) proposed a staff veto on senior appointments. I had to refuse, saying that the position of managers and editors would be untenable if their nominees for senior posts were to be the subject of a staff ballot. Confidential negotiation with someone from the *Times* or *Express* or BBC would be impossible if one could offer the job only 'subject to staff approval', and the paper had benefited from the infusion of fresh blood, as with the appointment of Ian Aitken or the return of Brian Jones. And, internally, what would be the position say of a chief sub-editor if his appointment to a higher post had been vetoed? His authority in his existing post would be undermined. I knew of no successful organisation run on these lines. The NUJ sensibly dropped the demand. I did, however, agree to advertise all vacancies internally except where there were special reasons against doing it. While that was already our practice, it became a more formal agreement. Of the *Guardian* NUJ's endeavour to gain more influence at the top – in many ways constructively – more will be told in the concluding chapter.

To involve the staff more fully in policy decisions, and to try to overcome the loss of the old collegiate atmosphere of Cross Street, Manchester, from 1963 to 1970 we held fortnightly or monthly open meetings for as many as could be squeezed into my room at Gray's Inn Road in London. That meant not more than thirty-five or thirty-six people, cramming them in, and we served a woefully inadequate sandwich lunch. The agenda was sometimes on editorial policy in terms of allocation of staff, news priorities, and other executive decisions, but more often on what we were saying or writing in the paper. These meetings were entertaining but diffuse: they produced occasionally sharp clashes among the specialists, but too often they failed to point to fresh conclusions. I therefore devised a tighter gathering, with never more than twelve present and a proper lunch – usually in a top-floor room at the Gay Hussar, in Soho, where no more than twelve could sit round the table. These were the real policy seminars of the senior staff between 1970 and 1975, and invaluable to me. (The proper lunch, let it be said, was in recognition of the fact that some of us would afterwards be working right through to 1.0 am or later without leaving the office, and it was a blessed relief after those dreadful sandwiches.)

Infrequently much larger gatherings continued, and about twice a year I made a report to all the staff who chose to come to general meetings in London and Manchester. Also, twice there were special Saturday sessions at LSE with fares paid from Manchester for those willing to sacrifice the day. We practised open and collective government as thoroughly as we could, though it was tiring at times. Twice in the last few years Miranda and I held huge staff parties, with wives and children – once, at great risk from wind and weather, in the garden of our house at Blackheath and overflowing on to the heath itself, with a football match that went on for hours; and once, more orderly but without children, in a marquee at Greenwich to celebrate the *Guardian*'s 150th birthday.

Though there were moments of painful tension with the NUJ, and still more at times with the printing unions, ours was a more harmonious office than most in Fleet Street. There was a common ideal, and it was felt most obviously at times such as the 1966 crisis. Without it, the *Guardian* with its slender resources could not have survived.

An editor's life

Editing a daily paper is extremely hard work. Wadsworth once told me that it took him five years to learn the job, and by the time he had mastered it he was too tired to do it properly – which was not strictly true, for he was a great editor until within a few months of his death, and wonderful to work for. He enjoyed a happy and secure home life, without which he could not have withstood the daily strain, and he frequently escaped for quiet weekends to a cottage in the Derbyshire dales. Miranda and our children provided the same kind of secure base for me, first in Manchester and later in Blackheath, and we too had a refuge at the old farm in Westmorland. The family, however, saw much less of me than they should have done. An editor's long and erratic hours bring their penalties.

In the office, the most memorable nights were those of sudden death – and it must be admitted, that I enjoyed coping with them. The night news came that Jack Kennedy had been shot dead in Dallas, only a year after steering the world to peace through the most tense and dangerous nuclear crisis yet experienced. Or the night of Bloody Sunday, in Londonderry, which was a turning point in the long Irish tragedy. Or the night Nasser died, struck down by a heart attack on return from a vital but exhausting mission to Amman.

Each of these was a night when the news broke late, with little or no warning and with only two hours or so before the *Guardian*'s first edition – with new front pages to be designed, new first leaders to be written, and new assessments to be prepared of the political implications. These were nights which tested editorial speed, skill, and judgement. The tone of the front-page headlines and the flavour of the paper's opening story must be right. The *Guardian*'s specialists and reporters must be given the space they needed to detail and explain events. And for later editions, on such nights, revision followed hourly as new material flooded in.

Almost always, I thoroughly enjoyed my work. But I needed time off, nevertheless. Scattered through this book you will find mention of days out on hills and mountains, winter and summer. They are not irrelevant, for they were essential to my editorial sanity. I found, too, that when I had an awkward editorial or managerial problem a day out walking or climbing could be invaluable to clear my thoughts. During the *Guardian*'s 1966 crisis I had a weekend in Westmorland with Tom, then aged seven, and it did much to steady my nerves and refresh me; also during parts of that troubled period, when there were few others to whom I could talk candidly, private discussion with Miranda was vital in maintaining a sensible perspective.

If the domestic side of life appears only infrequently in this book, its importance was nevertheless great.

3 Doomsday – the bomb and the banners

The 'non-nuclear club' was one of the most creative acts of journalism in my time. The *Guardian* devised it as a proposal to prevent the spread of nuclear weapons to fourth, fifth, sixth, and further nations. Its essence was that Britain should offer to give up its nuclear weapons on condition that the existing nuclear powers undertake not to supply weapons or technology to anyone else and that the nations next in line undertake not to build or acquire them. The Irish Government sponsored a resolution on these lines at the United Nations, and with the help of worldwide *Guardian* inquiries secured its adoption.[1] Although it never became British policy, it may have helped towards decisions by the Canadian and Swedish Governments – both of them capable of making nuclear weapons – to stay out of the nuclear arms race. Just possibly, it may have contributed to the West German decision (though a sense of war guilt and the proximity of the Russians were stronger influences).[2] The debate over the 'non-nuclear club' gave extra impetus towards the test ban treaty, which was achieved and has diminished nuclear pollution.

This chapter is about how and why the *Guardian* devised the 'non-nuclear club'. It concludes with the Cuban missile crisis – the nearest the world has yet come to nuclear disaster – and with President Kennedy's judgement of the *Guardian*'s treatment of the crisis.

Genesis of the 'non-nuclear club'

The paper's approach to nuclear disarmament evolved only gradually. It had consistently supported the American alliance, especially after the events of 1948 and 1949 – the coup in Czechoslovakia, the death of Jan Masaryk, the Berlin blockade, and the Soviet pressure on Tito. It approved of the North Atlantic Treaty and the appointment of Eisenhower as NATO's first supreme commander. It approved also of the rebuilding of Rhine Army and Bomber Command as two of Britain's major contributions to European defence. It was unhappy, however, about the duplication of American nuclear effort; and it was unhappy also to see scarce British scientific and industrial resources being spread too thinly over too many advanced projects.

The chief scientific adviser to the Defence Ministry in the mid-fifties was Sir Frederick Brundrett, and to the *MG* he was an extremely good source of unattributable information. Early in 1956, for example, he had

1 UN General Assembly, December 2, 1959; and again December 14, 1961.

2 Chancellor Erhard used the terms of the Irish resolution in the course of proposals, in March 1966, for the improvement of East-West relations.

told me that the Government was having to order both the Vulcan and the Victor, instead of concentrating more economically on one big bomber, because neither Avro nor Handley Page could tool up to provide adequate output and neither company had a design and development team strong enough to do its work properly. Much the same information came to me from Reggie Maudling, the youngish Minister of Supply with responsibility for equipping the armed forces. (The managing director of Avro, Sir Roy Dobson, made an apoplectic phone call to the *MG* when we published parts of this information.) In March 1956 I learned also – and published before any other paper – that the Cabinet had decided to go ahead with research and development of a supersonic bomber to follow the V-force, giving the main contract to Avro, while proceeding simultaneously with a ballistic missile with an intended range of 1,500 to 2,000 miles.

The V-bombers, the supersonic bomber, the Bluestreak missile, and Bluesteel 'stand-off bomb' were all intended to carry the new British nuclear weapons. It seemed clear that we were indeed hopelessly overloading limited research and production resources and that much of our nuclear weaponry would be obsolescent before going into service. Reggie Maudling, discussing this with me in private, on three occasions admitted to serious doubts but saw no practical alternative to proceeding with all the programmes. He agreed that we would be 'following in the US wake'. In the end, as it turned out, the thousands of millions spent on the Bluestreak and the TSR-2 supersonic bomber were almost wholly wasted, though the Vulcan was still in operational service, adapted both for low flying and for high altitude work. (Bluesteel was to have been replaced by the American Skybolt after 1960, but Skybolt in turn went wrong.)

Thus far it must seem that the *MG*'s approach was only practical and pragmatic. It was, I believe, rather more than that. Of course we were concerned with the waste of scarce resources and the unlikelihood of achieving through Bluestreak or the TSR-2 the security that people in Britain deserved; but we were also concerned to maintain an Atlantic alliance that would diminish the risk of another world war. In the mid-fifties it was only ten or eleven years since most of those writing at the *Guardian* had come out of uniform, thankful to be alive after, for some of us, battlefield or blitz experiences through which we had hardly dared hope to survive. For myself, I wanted to take part in the Normandy campaign and the freeing of France – though it terrified me at the time – and in the removal of fascism from Europe. We were still looking for the safest road to peace, and nothing else mattered so much.

Hardly a week went by without some comment on the nuclear issue. Thus in mid-February 1957 we argued that the deployment of tactical nuclear weapons with NATO's front-line forces (mobile rockets with a range of fifty to seventy miles giving an atomic blast of Hiroshima proportions) would be of no avail, because NATO's ground forces were too few to hold secure the bases from which the weapons could be fired. Russian tanks were always in a position to reach Hamburg, the Ruhr, and the Rhineland within five or six hours, and the Russians too could hit back with a series of nuclear counter-attacks. No route to greater security lay that way. The better course was to maintain the strength of Rhine Army and its RAF support and our naval force in the North Atlantic, leaving the nuclear side to the United States.

In mid-March, when Harold Macmillan as Prime Minister returned from his first meeting with President Eisenhower in Bermuda, he stated openly that Britain was five or six years behind the United States in its progress with guided missiles – so we argued that it would be best to scrap the British missile programme and rely on those with which the United States was now willing to supply us. In mid-April we returned to the issue of tactical weapons in Europe, saying it was wrong to reorganise Rhine Army so that it depended on them, for it would lead to the use of more and bigger weapons by each side. 'One cannot simply fire a few nuclear rockets at places where hostile troops might be and think that that would end the action.'

At the beginning of June 1957, six months before the founding of the CND, the Bishop of Manchester called on the Government to renounce hydrogen weapons. Dr Greer was neither left-wing nor notably radical. He was speaking to the Manchester diocesan conference, and he had given us advance warning of his intention. He saw British renunciation as a Christian step which, through promoting mutual trust, might lead to general disarmament. Dr Greer's was not the first such call. In 1955 Sir Richard Acland had resigned his seat in Parliament, intending to fight a by-election with a campaign against the bomb, but his brave protest had been submerged in the general election soon after Churchill's retirement. J. B. Priestley had written in the *New Statesman* calling on the British to renounce nuclear war. But Bishop Greer, as a senior figure in the Church of England, was a powerful voice from a new direction.

The *MG* next morning reported the sermon on its front page and commented in a long leader. We argued that unconditional renunciation stood at best one chance in ten of leading to general disarmament. More probably it would lead in a few years to the extension of Khrushchev's kind of socialism to all Western Europe and the British Isles. Nevertheless Dr Greer's appeal moved the *Guardian* to make its own proposal – that Britain should renounce tactical nuclear weapons, as a step towards stopping the nuclear arms race. 'It is a less dramatic step,' we said, 'but it is also less dangerous as a beginning.' Combined with an experimental zone of inspection in Central Europe, that renunciation ought to be Britain's immediate aim. The *Guardian* had taken its own next step towards the non-nuclear club.

Consultations followed in two directions. Lord Simon of Wythenshawe – Ernest Simon, a wealthy Manchester engineer and former chairman of the BBC – invited the Bishop and some others to an informal gathering at his house in Didsbury. I lived only a few hundred yards away and quite often visited Simon to talk about current controversies. He used to take out a little black notebook, to write down points that one had mentioned or make sure that he had covered all his own points properly. Dr Greer came to discuss his proposal, together with one or two people from Manchester University – among them Sir Bernard Lovell, director of the new Jodrell Bank space observatory, so far as I can recall. It was no more than a pre-lunch chat, in Simon's large drawing room, but it was the first of a number of nuclear sessions.

Soon afterwards Simon invited Bertrand Russell to come from North Wales to stay, and they spent many hours examining together ways to prevent nuclear war. The Campaign for Nuclear Disarmament was partly a result of these talks, and Simon contributed a substantial sum to it. Although he was one of the first members of the CND's executive, he was soon 'plagued with doubts'.[3] Eventually he left the CND and became a valued supporter of our non-nuclear club.

The other line of consultation was internal. The *MG* had acquired an exceptional pair as science correspondent and defence correspondent: John Maddox and Leonard Beaton. John had been a nuclear physicist at Manchester University and wanted to move to journalism. He was with the *Guardian* from 1955 to 1964 and became one of the best science correspondents in the business, but went on to the Nuffield Foundation of which he became director. Leonard was a Canadian from McGill with a post-graduate degree from Cambridge. Then from Reuter he had gone to the *Times* as naval correspondent. While the *MG*'s defence correspondent I had met him and had admired his writing, thinking, and integrity. I persuaded him to join the *Guardian* soon after I became editor, and he was an excellent colleague for about nine years, until he left to become assistant director of the Institute for Strategic Studies. He died untimely young, aged forty-two, in 1971. To these two the non-nuclear club owed much of its vigour. Together they wrote a book in 1962, *The Spread of Nuclear Weapons*.[4]

Our proposal to try to stop the spread of weapons did not emerge in full until February 1958. During the second half of the previous year there were frequent reports in the paper from Beaton and Maddox on weapons development and defence strategy, and frequent comments on the risks and hazards. That summer the Russians test-fired their first ballistic rocket – forerunner of the intercontinental missile – and in the autumn put their first sputnik into orbit. Jodrell Bank was ready just in time to track it, and John Maddox had to advise Bernard Lovell in calculating where to point the enormous radio telescope to find it on the

3 *Ernest Simon of Manchester*, by Mary Stocks, p. 146
4 *The Spread of Nuclear Weapons*, published by Chatto and Windus in 1962.

night it went up. Being by then more than ever concerned about Britain as a prime target for Soviet thermo-nuclear attack – because of the presence here of the American Air Force forward bases from which they could reach to the Urals and beyond, as well as our own V-bomber bases – we said that the West's deterrent missiles ought to be dispersed in ships and submarines. Leonard Beaton, at a private meeting with the US Defence Secretary in December, learned that in fact the Polaris submarine programme was being speeded up, so that the first vessels should be in service by 1959 or 1960, and that the Russians were reckoned to be well ahead of the United States in the development of long-range missiles. The Russian tests during the summer had been monitored by American radar for some weeks before they were announced triumphantly from Moscow.

In mid-January 1958, on the eve of a Lords' defence debate, we gave an indication of the way our thoughts were moving. Adapting the story of Nevil Shute's gruesomely hypnotic novel *On the Beach*, we pointed to the risk in the spread of nuclear weapons. Unidentified or accidental use of a bomb on Tel Aviv, we suggested, could lead to British and French demonstration flights over Cairo; and then to Egyptian nuclear attack on London and Washington, using planes with Soviet markings; and so onwards to Doomsday. We were astonished that Aneurin Bevan and George Brown, on behalf of the Shadow Cabinet, had virtually committed Labour to backing an independent British deterrent. We mentioned the view – from the Bishop of Manchester among others – that Britain should set an example by renouncing her weapons, but we concluded that renunciation unaccompanied by a British diplomatic initiative was not enough.

On February 14 we stated what that initiative should be. Britain ought to volunteer to abandon her separate weapons 'in return for agreement that nobody else will start making them'. As usual, the leader began with a recognition of the Government's reasoning – that having her own bombs must give Britain stronger influence over American policy and an insurance against an American withdrawal from Europe. On the question of influence we said that the most notable occasions when British advice had restrained the Americans were before Britain began to make its own nuclear weapons and when the advice itself was good enough to be persuasive; and on the question of insurance we said that the Americans were extremely unlikely to withdraw so long as liberal democracy in Western Europe remained vital enough to make its defence an American interest. But that was not all:

Because Britain is committed to having its own deterrent, it is prevented from taking the initiative to stop the spreading of nuclear weapons to half the nations of the world. This is an urgent task. ... The need to persuade the French, the Israelis, and a dozen others not to make bombs must weigh heavily. The French have decided to join the nuclear club. They have started to make their own bombs. They can, of course, put forward exactly the same arguments as the British, for they too want to influence Washington and to insure themselves. ... After France who will come next? It may be Sweden or Israel or Japan. And with each new entrant to the field the risk that these new weapons may be used increases. It is perhaps hurtful to say that French military commanders are not always completely under the control of French Governments, but it is true. With other nations the risk may be as large or larger.

This is the competition which ought to be stopped now. Britain, by volunteering to renounce her separate possession of nuclear weapons in return for an agreement that nobody else will start making them, could lead the way. Russia and the United States can stay outside such an agreement at present; plainly the process of negotiating nuclear disarmament for them will be long. But can the Government not seek a rapid treaty with all other nations? It seems a worthy object and worth pursuing vigorously. It could turn the tide away from the rising danger that, through misjudgment or inadvertence, we shall all be blown to pieces.

On the Sunday after that leader appeared – that Sunday being the eve of the Commons' annual defence debate – the CND held its first big rally in London, at the Central Hall, Westminster. Christopher Driver's history of the CND gives an account of the platform speeches, 'chosen to accommodate all tastes'.[5] Bertrand Russell thought it an 'even chance' whether any human beings would exist in forty years' time; Sir Stephen King-Hall put the case for non-violent resistance; and Michael Foot said that Britain had given rocket bases to America and received nothing in return. In the Commons debate the Prime Minister put reasoned arguments against the unilateralist case, rejecting the idea of a moral gesture which might have grievous practical consequences, and Hugh Gaitskell, as leader of the Opposition, broadly agreed with him. To the *Guardian*'s disappointment, neither addressed himself to the proposal of a British initiative using an offer to renounce our nuclear weapons in return for an agreement to stop the spread. So the paper restated its view, saying that the addition of one British bomb or missile to every ten American weapons made the Western deterrent no more effective. A week or two later the Labour party and the TUC issued a joint statement on disarmament and nuclear weapons which, we said, was the best yet to come from Government or Opposition but still 'insufficient'. The statement wanted a lead from Britain in suspending thermo-nuclear tests for a limited period and in seeking a scheme for controlled disarmament in a trial zone in Central Europe.

Within the statement there was one minor flaw, where emotion had overcome reason. While accepting the American bomber bases in East Anglia and the Cotswolds, it said that the aircraft must remain grounded except when they were not carrying bombs. In effect it wanted them to stay as sitting targets, totally vulnerable to surprise attack.

Throughout the summer and autumn of 1958 we kept up the flow of articles and comment – welcoming especially the Geneva agreement in August on the technical means of monitoring a ban on nuclear tests within

5 Christopher Driver, *The Disarmers*, published by Hodder and Stoughton in 1964.

December 1962

the earth's atmosphere. Scientists had been present with the delegations
of both sides, and in marked contrast to the general disarmament negotiations the Geneva meeting had been short and completely successful.
It had been preceded by the suspension of Soviet tests, and it was
immediately followed by an Anglo-American offer to maintain a standstill
on nuclear tests for one year while a test ban treaty was negotiated. The
offer was to take effect on October 31, and in the two months before that
both sides carried out a number of small tests. The French declined to
take part in the standstill, being about to explode their first nuclear device
in the Sahara. In the end the East-West diplomatic negotiations broke
down after the U-2 spy plane incident in 1960, for which Eisenhower, to
almost everyone's astonishment, accepted personal responsibility. (The
test ban treaty was not signed until August 1963, nine months after the
Cuban missile crisis.)

But in the autumn of 1958, after the summer's success at Geneva, the
outlook was promising. We were buoyed up in our determination to press
for the non-nuclear club. Leonard Beaton and I spent a happy day walking
in the Lake District – making a circuit of the Langdale Pikes, Bowfell,
and Crinkle Crags – and discussing what we should do next. The Cabinet

Minister then responsible for scientific matters, including the technical aspects of the test ban, was the Lord President, Lord Hailsham. He invited himself to dinner and pursued the argument over the non-nuclear club with much interest, while not accepting it. The Liberal party conference endorsed the proposal, as indeed Jo Grimond himself had done some months earlier. With the Labour leaders, however, we had initially no such success. Hugh Gaitskell was determined if possible to avoid dissension within his party and, since he might well be Prime Minister within a year, to refrain from commitments until fully informed in office on all the scientific and military implications. In talking privately to me he insisted that he must have *all* the facts before making a decision. Meanwhile, with Nye Bevan as the Shadow Cabinet and party executive spokesman, at the Scarborough conference a unilateralist motion was defeated by six to one (or 5,538,000 to 1,005,000 on a card vote). Gaitskell, winding up, said that the horror of the bomb was not removed by getting rid only of the British bomb. The non-nuclear club would be ineffective if the Americans and Russians did not join it; and, he said, conference must leave the leaders 'a free hand' until they had access to secret information. Eight months later Gaitskell and Labour were to endorse the non-nuclear club.

Enter the Irish

In December 1958, at the Government's request, Ernest Simon agreed to defer a motion due for debate in the House of Lords. We had worked together on the wording of the motion, which urged the Government

to negotiate with the leading non-nuclear powers with the aim of securing their agreement to renounce the manufacture, ownership, and use of nuclear weapons, and as part of the negotiation to offer ourselves to renounce any such weapons, and to endeavour to persuade the United States and the USSR jointly to sponsor a world-wide system of inspection under the auspices of the United Nations to enforce effectively any such agreement which may be arrived at; and to move for papers.

The request to Lord Simon was made because of the delicate state of the test ban negotiations in Geneva; but in February the motion was duly debated in the Lords. Simon proposed it, supported by Bertrand Russell (by then fully in agreement with it after further sessions at Didsbury). Lord Adrian, a distinguished scientist and former Vice-Chancellor of Cambridge University, also spoke in favour, as did three bishops and two other peers. Five or six peers spoke against, the only aggressive speech coming from a former permanent secretary at the Foreign Office, Lord Strang, who said that as many nations as possible should acquire hydrogen bombs so that the 'balance of terror' might be extended. Lord Home replied for the Government, effectively black-balling the non-nuclear club. He suggested that Britain, instead of being an American base, might be forced to become a Soviet rocket base; and he thought 'it was asking a bit much' to expect the Americans alone to provide the nuclear defence for the whole free world. He said further that the inspection system proposed by Lord Simon would let the Russians oversee our defences in Western Europe – not mentioning that it would equally let us oversee their defences in Eastern Europe. In the courteous way of the House of Lords, Simon withdrew his motion at the end of the afternoon.

Soon afterwards I had a letter from someone in the Irish Department of External Affairs in Dublin – Conor Cruise O'Brien – of whom I had never heard. He was then working as a civil servant for the Irish Foreign Minister, Frank Aiken. Conor later became much better known as the UN representative in Katanga, during the 1961 civil war, and later still as a writer, as an Irish Cabinet Minister, and most recently as editor-in-chief of the *Observer* in London. Were we aware, he asked, that Frank Aiken had been working at the United Nations on lines parallel to ours? We weren't, which was a lamentable admission. At the earliest convenient date I hastened across to Dublin to talk to Frank Aiken, Conor, and others – including the Prime Minister, Eamon de Valera.

What we had missed, for it had had no publicity apart from a paragraph or two in the Irish papers, was a significant Irish initiative at the UN. In the General Assembly's first committee Frank Aiken had put forward a resolution closely similar to Lord Simon's in the House of Lords, and it had received thirty-seven votes in favour and none against, with forty-four abstentions. Because it had coincided with the December disagreements at Geneva, it had been completely overshadowed. Frank Aiken had therefore withdrawn it, in order not to prejudice possible progress at the 1959 General Assembly. Before bringing his proposal to the vote for the first time, the Irish Foreign Minister had done some lobbying. Initially the Great Powers had not favoured it, but in the end none had voted against it. Sweden, although already considering the manufacture of her own weapons, had voted in favour. Canada, New Zealand, and Australia, while all abstaining, had spoken with sympathy towards it. Most of the Afro-Asian block and six of the Latin-Americans voted in favour. And in spite of an initially cold comment by the USSR's Mr Sobolev, the Soviet block (apart from Russia) eventually followed a Polish lead in voting for the resolution. It was a considerable achievement for the small delegation of a small country.

In 1921–22 Frank Aiken had been chief of staff of the IRA, fighting first the British Black and Tans and then in the civil war. At the UN he argued that where nuclear weapons were developed in smaller sizes, they might eventually get into the hands of revolutionary movements. 'All through history portable weapons which are the monopoly of Great Powers today become the weapons of smaller powers and revolutionary groups tomorrow', and 'the Hiroshima-type bomb, used by a small and desperate country to settle a local quarrel, could be the detonator for a world-wide thermo-nuclear war involving the destruction of our whole civilisation'.

When I went to Dublin that spring, Frank Aiken had not finally made up his mind whether to pursue the issue again at the Assembly in the autumn. Thanks partly to the publicity that the *Guardian* belatedly gave his previous efforts, thanks still more to inquiries we set going in a number of capitals about likely attitudes next autumn – and no doubt thanks to private urging from Conor Cruise O'Brien – Mr Aiken decided to maintain his effort.

From the Taosaich, Mr de Valera, I heard something of the domestic reasons for hesitation. He agreed that the Aiken initiative at the last Assembly had been of great importance; but it had cost his party, Fianna Fail, some support at home. There were those in Ireland, he said, who asked 'why should we prevent ourselves from getting these weapons to protect ourselves?' He had to think of his Government's parliamentary position. Much to my relief, he eventually indicated that no slackening of the Irish initiative was likely, but he said that it was not altogether easy at home.

Discussing this afterwards with Conor and with Jack White (then part-time correspondent for the *Guardian* in Dublin and recently one of the top people in RTE), I heard that there was some feeling in Ireland that at the UN Aiken had been too friendly to the Communists. He was thought to have been 'shaking the blood-stained hand' of the Soviet representatives, to which Aiken had replied that they must take every possible opportunity of talking to the Russians and of trying to persuade them to move towards the Irish views on disarmament. And Conor said that at the time of the vote on whether to put China's admission on the agenda, the Americans had wheeled in Cardinal Cushing and Archbishop Spellman to influence Aiken – but he was not going to be bulldozed by anyone.

Back in Manchester after the Dublin visit – which included a quick day out in the Wicklow mountains and a delightful afternoon at Conor's eyrie on Howth Head – I set about getting reactions to the Irish resolution. We cabled or spoke to our correspondents in Delhi, Tel Aviv, Cairo, Ottawa, The Hague, and other capitals. This was a ploy which worked well – since we not only secured initial reactions but caused the Foreign Ministries there to think twice about the Irish resolution. Among the initial replies Australia, New Zealand, India, and Burma were favourable; Cairo also was favourable, while the Israeli reply was reserved. Canada's reply was friendly but cautious. The Netherlands and Belgium both expressed warm sympathy for the proposal though the Belgians felt it likely that they would abstain. The Belgian Government wanted further information on the means of enforcing the agreement and added that 'in equity there are no grounds for refusing to other powers weapons which Britain has entered the race to obtain, however desirable such a restriction might be'. Belgium was worried by the French 'policy of greatness', which followed the British lead, and was felt to be taking France into isolation.

Cairo's reply was particularly concerned with the impending French tests in the Sahara. Nevertheless the United Arab Republic (as it then was) remained ready to support the Irish draft resolution – unless Israel were suddenly to acquire some form of nuclear weapon. From Tel Aviv the Israeli reply was that, while the problem raised by the Irish 'is certainly very real', the Government of Israel preferred to reserve its views until the Assembly met.

At the Assembly in the autumn Frank Aiken put his resolution again, and this time it went through the Political Committee to the full Assembly. Once more he used the known arguments, adding that even if full international control could not be obtained that did not vitiate the scheme. It was the plain self-interest of the Great Powers to keep the weapons to themselves because in parting with them they parted with a measure of their power and influence. He accepted that the French and Chinese might have become nuclear powers by the time an agreement could be negotiated, but held that that also would not vitiate it. This time the vote in the Political Committee was even better then in 1958: it was sixty-eight to none, with twelve abstentions – the abstainers including the three nuclear powers and France. (The Soviet delegate said the resolution was 'inadequate' and would not stop the supply of US nuclear weapons to NATO.) The Assembly accepted the resolution by acclamation, without a vote, remitting it to the Geneva disarmament negotiators.

At home the summer had brought a dramatic change in the Labour party's official position. In May Aneurin Bevan pledged the party, if returned to office, to 'stop all nuclear tests at once'. Hugh Gaitskell remained a little more guarded, leaving latitude for resumption of non-polluting tests (underground, for example) if after a period our lead had not been followed. But the big change came at the end of June, when a joint statement by the Labour party and the TUC unequivocally committed them to the non-nuclear club. After Gaitskell's previous coolness to the principle, it was a great conversion.

Having had private indications that opinion was shifting – they came through our labour correspondent, John Cole – we weighed in heavily with articles on three consecutive days at the beginning of the week when the joint Labour-TUC meetings were due to be held. And on the second day the *Guardian's* front page led with a Parliamentary staff report indicating what was likely to come: 'A Labour Government will actively promote the idea of a non-nuclear club.' We also reported a 'virtuoso performance' by Aneurin Bevan in putting the case to the TUC's international committee. When the official statement came, we welcomed it wholeheartedly.

Many other newspapers gave it an astonishingly good reception, not so much for its substance as because they saw in it a firm rebuff to those

union leaders now demanding unilateral disarmament. The *Times* spoke
of it as a 'great personal victory', proving Gaitskell's command over the
parliamentary party and the union leaders. Henry Fairlie in the *Daily
Mail* likened him to Wellington in the brilliance of his tactics, holding his
fire until he was ready to strike. Dick Crossman wrote in the *Daily Mirror*
of the merits of the non-nuclear club and of Gaitskell's maturity as party
leader. The *Daily Telegraph*, however, called it 'the biggest piece of
humbug' yet produced by socialist policy makers.

Gaitskell afterwards said that two factors in particular had moved him.
One was the growing evidence, from the Pugwash group of international
scientists and from others, that a number of countries would soon have
the capacity to make their own nuclear weapons – in the next five or ten
years, in fact. The other was that he had been impressed by the success
in negotiating the first stages of a test ban treaty, in marked contrast with
the failure to make any headway towards general disarmament.

The joint statement said candidly that there were stiff difficulties in
trying to apply the policy. 'Certain Governments' – the French were not
named – would resist. But there was a unique opportunity for Britain to
persuade others not in possession of the bomb to join in this effort. It
would undoubtedly be easier for other nations to give up the prospect of
nuclear weapons if Britain were willing to put herself on the same level.
And a fortnight after the joint statement, Gaitskell went over to the attack
on Cousins and the unilateralists in a tough speech at Workington in
Cumberland. The unilateralists, he said, were arguing that France and
China would not join an agreement with effective controls – yet they
assumed that if Britain renounced the bomb unconditionally others would
follow without such an agreement. They must decide whether or not they
intended Britain to stay in NATO, and if not, what the effect might be
on Soviet strategy. Gaitskell spoke with force and conviction – and the
election was drawing near.

The election result was a mortal blow to the non-nuclear club, though
we did not immediately admit it. The bomb had featured in the campaign,
though not prominently. At the start Mr Selwyn Lloyd and the Conservative Central Office launched an attack on the non-nuclear club as a
'non-starter'. The Prime Minister followed on, saying in Manchester on
September 22 that with a test ban treaty near 'it would be madness to
throw it away in pursuit of a will-o'-the wisp like the Socialist proposal
for a non-nuclear club, which has many drawbacks'. As Macmillan well
knew, the two were not alternatives but complementary, and one could
follow the other. But that is election campaigning – and Mr Macmillan's
new election slogan, coined that day, was 'Stick to the facts'.

The debate went on for three or four more years. In spite of much
advance publicity, the French did not explode their first bomb until well
into 1960. President de Gaulle had replied beforehand to a UN approach
by saying that if the Russians and the 'Anglo-Saxons' wanted to invite

France to abstain from nuclear tests while others possessed nuclear weapons 'there is no chance that France will accept the invitation'. Leonard Beaton remarked that the Russians and Americans, though they knew better than to say so openly, were not impressed by the odd bomb 'from a nation that they could wipe out to the last man without exhausting their stocks – indeed probably with obsolete weapons and delivery systems'. But, he said, one question we could not answer was whether the French would ever have started to produce operational weapons if Britain had not done so first. France, after all, did not take the decision to embark until eight years after Britain and three years after the first British test off the Australian coast.

Technically, Canada was ahead of France in the ability to produce nuclear weapons and a delivery system. But successive Canadian Governments took an opposite course. Not only was Canada sympathetic to the Irish in the UN, but in February 1959 the Prime Minister, Mr Diefenbaker, told Parliament in Ottawa that the policy of the Canadian Government was not to undertake the production of nuclear weapons. The Canadian chiefs of staff supported him in this view. Since then no Canadian Government has shown any inclination to alter the decision, although there was a Cabinet crisis over it in 1963, leading to the Defence Minister's resignation and a reaffirmation of the policy by Diefenbaker and a majority of his Ministers. It has never been challenged since. In that sense, the non-nuclear club has had a distinguished founder nation since 1959.

China, at least chronologically, has followed France. Her first atomic test came in 1964 and her first thermo-nuclear device in 1967. Sweden, Switzerland and Norway – all with the capability to arm themselves atomically – have followed the Canadian course. Japan and West Germany had or could have had the capacity, but each had special reasons for holding back – Japan as the first victims of the bomb, and Germany as the originator of the Second World War. About Israel we do not know for certain: a limited capacity exists, but there is no evidence that Israel has yet used it to make her own bombs. India, too, has the capacity but so far has preferred not to employ it, apart from one non-weapons experimental explosion. In Eastern Europe, so far as is known, the Soviet Union has not allowed Poland or Czechoslovakia or East Germany to develop any military use of nuclear energy. So, if not exactly by the route proposed by the *MG* in 1959, the non-nuclear club has grown more rapidly than the list of nuclear nations.

Questions remain. Had Gaitskell won the election, would the list today be any different? Probably not. Would Gaitskell have persisted with a separate British deterrent force? We shall never know, because he rightly said that he must be briefed before deciding. There is a fifty/fifty chance that he would not have sought the American Skybolt in 1960, as Macmillan did, and a stronger chance that when Skybolt failed he would not have gone ahead with the four Polaris submarines and their costly back-up systems. Would Britain have been less safe? No: there is nothing to suggest it. Would we have had any less say in NATO's handling of a nuclear crisis in Europe? Not really: for the process of decision must be swift, if front-line forces and airfields are not to be overwhelmed, and supreme commanders have time for the shortest of consultation only. Washington must be asked first, if there is time, and Bonn and London next. The British have never had any effective veto over the use of US nuclear forces based here, nor could they have, though the promise of consultation will stand irrespective of Britain's own nuclear strength.

Would a non-nuclear Britain have lost influence with the United States? I think not, for Presidents and Secretaries of State will listen if they are in a mood to listen and if they believe the advice is likely to be worth hearing. Canada, a small nation without nuclear weapons, has the ear of the White House as often as Britain. But that question – and the nerves of the whole world – came to be tested in the crisis of 1962.

The Cuban missile crisis, 1962

'We sat there within five minutes of destruction.' The words were Vice-President Lyndon Johnson's, telling me afterwards of his feelings as a member of the President's Executive Committee in the White House on the evening of Saturday, October 27, and the next morning. On October 22, six days after secretly receiving clear photographic evidence that Soviet offensive missiles were being installed in Cuba, Kennedy had imposed a blockade or 'quarantine' to try to prevent completion of the missile sites.[6] He told Khrushchev openly that the sites must be dismantled. One way or other, the Soviet missiles must be removed. It was known that alternative courses had been prepared – by pinpoint bombing of the sites, by a parachute assault, by a massive invasion of Cuba, or by a nuclear strike. No time limit had been set, but Khrushchev's first response had been angry and unclear. On the Sunday morning, just over five days after the blockade began, Khrushchev's answer came. The missiles were to be dismantled.

It was a near thing. On both sides, for the first time since each had built itself intercontinental missiles, there was a full alert. Lyndon Johnson, when we talked a month later, had on his desk a small silver plaque which he had received from the President with the initials 'JFK' and 'LBJ' engraved at the top and an ordinary calendar for October below but with the dates from October 16 to 29 set in heavy type.

For newspapers, the crisis came out of an almost blue sky. I had just returned from a weekend looking at hydro-electric schemes in Scotland – and from an excellent walk through Glen Affric to the west coast, with

6 The word 'quarantine' was used in official statements, because blockades were forbidden by international law.

auburn autumn at its richest. Monday morning's front page (October 22) carried a report from Max Freedman in which the White House denied that US marines were preparing to land in Cuba, though Max quoted the *Washington Post* as saying that the Cuban situation was 'tense'. He also quoted reports in the *Miami Herald* and the *Los Angeles Times* of naval and air force movements. About seven on the Monday evening we heard that Kennedy was to broadcast at midnight on a most urgent matter, so we held back as much of the *Guardian*'s print as we could. Alistair Cooke had filed an early message from New York saying that 'a hail of radio bulletins' during the day had frozen in their tracks the election campaign, the UN Assembly, and much else.

Our front page in the later editions next morning led with the imposition of the blockade, with the US Navy 'ready to sink Soviet ships if necessary to prevent offensive weapons reaching Cuba'. Max Freedman added some interpretation on page one, and the full text of Kennedy's calmly powerful speech was carried on an inside page. Our leader, which I wrote in haste between 12.20 and 12.45, noted that the United States had stopped short of invasion or total blockade and asked three questions: Will the blockade be effective? What will be the repercussions in Europe? And can the US justify its action before the UN? We drew the reverse parallel with Berlin, where the Americans had made no attempt to run armed convoys through to West Berlin because the airlift was possible, and we thought that the Russians might use long-range aircraft for a Cuban airlift. While unsure of Khrushchev's motives, we suggested that he was demonstrating to the US and the world the meaning of American bases close to Soviet territory. 'What is sauce for Cuba is sauce also for Turkey, Berlin, and other places.'

On the Tuesday I was due to spend the day in London – the *Guardian*'s editorial headquarters being still in Manchester – and I had an appointment with Hugh Gaitskell. That proved a useful consultation. He had been the previous night at a dinner for General Norstad, the North Atlantic supreme commander, and there Harold Macmillan had shown him Kennedy's message about the blockade. Gaitskell had urged the Prime Minister to go to Washington immediately, for he found that absence of consultation disturbing. Gaitskell, too, expected repercussions in Europe and especially over Berlin. He was to see the Prime Minister again an hour after our meeting and discussed what he should recommend. We were both perplexed about Soviet motives but hoped that some form of negotiation might cool the crisis.

I also saw Russell Wiggins, editor-in-chief of the *Washington Post* (and later US Ambassador to the UN). Wiggins drew a strong distinction between American bases in Europe and Russian bases in Cuba, for the Americans were invited in as the friends of governments under threat and could at any time be thrown out by the will of the people if their bases weren't wanted. He asked how we would feel if the Russians were building bases in Southern Ireland – a point which I relayed to Gaitskell, who used it in his lobby briefing later in the day.

On Wednesday morning virtually the whole front page was taken up with the Cuban crisis, including aerial pictures of a missile base. We found the pictures fairly convincing, though not conclusive, though the *Times* ran a front-page comment by its military correspondent saying that they could be a 'fabrication'. Also on the front page was Moscow's initial reply, saying that 'a most powerful retaliatory blow will follow if the US aggressors touch off war'. The US submarine depot ship *Proteus* was reported leaving its Holy Loch base on the Clyde, while in West Berlin British and American troops were at stand-by.

That front page had the *Guardian* team well in action – Max Freedman from Washington and Michael Wall from Berlin; Leonard Beaton in London, analysing the photographs but saying that they could provide no evidence of warheads (a point indeed made by the Defense Department in Washington); Richard Scott from the Foreign Office reporting the British accusation of deliberate Soviet 'deception'; and Victor Zorza,* our Soviet analyst, on the 'cool evasions' in Moscow statements and on Mr Khrushchev spending the evening at the Bolshoi Theatre along with other Kremlin leaders, to put a confident face on the crisis.

Alistair Cooke, on another page, wrote at length of the American nation's full backing for Kennedy. The United States, he said, had 'fallen in behind the President'. Max Freedman on the leader page contributed nearly three columns of analysis of the White House discussion that had led to the decision to impose a quarantine – an analysis which turned out, as we had hazily surmised on receiving it, to be precisely based on the papers and thoughts of the President's Executive Committee.

In our first leader that Wednesday morning we still believed that Khrushchev was trying to make a point about 'defensive' bases on both sides of the Atlantic, for if the Polaris installation on the Holy Loch was defensive in our eyes he was bound to press the defensive nature of his installations in the Caribbean. Though the situation was alarming, we were still hopeful that it would not get out of hand. We also carried a second leader on international law on freedom of the seas, noting that in 1812 the United States went to war with Britain in order to preserve her concept of free navigation and again in 1917 went to war with Imperial Germany for the same reason.

Thursday's paper carried the news that some of the Soviet ships had altered course to avoid contact with the US naval blockade, and a report that at the United Nations U Thant was working on a peace formula. Max Freedman from Washington said that ten bases were being built in Cuba, each to carry four rockets, and that thirty of the missiles were already there. Another front-page picture showed dismantled Ilyushin bombers on the deck of a freighter in the Atlantic, on their way to Cuba.

Friday brought more news of U Thant's mediation, with the outline of a standstill agreement provided there could be some way to make sure that no more weapons were getting through to Cuba. Without that, the Americans were not prepared to lift their blockade. They had, however, let a tanker through since it could not be carrying nuclear equipment. They also let through an East German passenger ship and a Greek freighter on charter. In the Commons, on prorogation day, the Prime Minister had insisted that the allies must stand shoulder to shoulder. This was no time 'to go into the niceties of international law or seek pedantically for precedents'. (Was he remembering Suez?) He preferred the UN initiative to any of his own. There was an angry little scene when Black Rod cut short the exchanges to summon the Commons to the Lords to hear the prorogation speech.

By Saturday morning the news was more menacing; according to the White House, work on the ballistic missile sites had been accelerated and there were pictures to prove it. A State Department spokesman had indicated that, in these circumstances, action beyond the blockade would be justified. Max Freedman, in his front-page report, said that there was talk of a nuclear attack to take out the missile sites. Alistair Cooke, from the United Nations, reported (more nearly verbatim than any other paper) a taut encounter between Adlai Stevenson and Russia's Valerian Zorin. Had the Russians bluffed and lied in saying that Cuba housed no offensive weapons of their construction? Stevenson put categorical questions to Zorin: 'Do you deny that the USSR has placed and is placing medium and intermediate range missiles and sites in Cuba? Yes or no?' Zorin, Cooke reported, remained smilingly silent. Stevenson: 'Don't wait for the interpretation. Yes or no?' Zorin, with a Pickwickian face: 'I am not in an American courtroom, sir, and therefore I do not wish to answer a question that is put to me in a fashion in which a prosecutor puts questions. In due course, sir, you will have your reply.' To which Stevenson retorted that he was ready to wait until hell froze over, but they would have the reply now. The evidence was in the pictures, he said, and he called for more large blow-ups to be brought in. Zorin kept his head down while all other eyes studied the photographs.

The tension was now mounting fast, and the Saturday morning leader – in the later editions only, after Max Freedman's warning had come in – reflected this. It was headed 'When to break ranks'. It acknowledged the acute danger if work on the sites was indeed going ahead fast, but said that if the authorities in Washington were contemplating a nuclear attack 'it would be madness'. The use of such force would be out of all proportion to the immediate danger to the United States. It would turn the whole civilised world against the Americans, however much sympathy there had been for them hitherto in meeting Russian duplicity and provocation.

It is one thing for Mr Macmillan to say that the allies must not waver or break ranks at a time when the United States has done nothing but impose the 'quarantine' on offensive weapons. Certainly America's allies should do their utmost to back her up in this tight corner. But matters will be very different if the United States takes to aggression.

The reason for breaking ranks at that point would not just be that an armed attack on Cuba is unjustified at a time when Cuba is not attacking anybody. The consequences would be great and might be highly dangerous. The Soviet Union has threatened to retaliate with nuclear weapons against an attack on Cuba. Whether it would make good its threat nobody can tell. Possibly the Soviet leaders themselves are not quite sure. But it is a tremendous risk to run in a cause which, if it came to bombing or invasion, would seem to most of the world to be as much a piece of aggression as the British and French attack at Suez. . . .

Monday's paper had a quite different tone, for on Sunday afternoon – just after I had arrived in the office with forebodings of another tense night – we heard that Khrushchev had accepted Kennedy's terms. So the front page led with Khrushchev's agreement that the missiles should go and Kennedy's astute welcome for a 'statesmanlike move' by Moscow. It reported, too, that U Thant was to fly to Havana next day to discuss means of verifying the dismantling. And, as Monday's first leader said, 'Profound thankfulness is the first and strongest reaction to yesterday's news: a grave and exceedingly dangerous crisis may now be solved without military action.'

The thankfulness of our Monday morning comment was tinged with concern that Krushchev should have so miscalculated as to bring the world close to a nuclear war. At least, though, he had shown himself capable of turning back from the brink. We thought it possible – and here I was relying heavily on advice from Victor Zorza – that Khrushchev might soon lose his place at the head of the Soviet Government, and if so we suspected that the new leaders might try other destructive tactics. That proved not too far from the mark, for less than two years later Khrushchev was removed from office and the second of seven charges against him was that he had 'committed grave errors of policy' by introducing missiles into Cuba. (The first charge was that he had reduced the conflict with Mao to a 'personal feud' and had underestimated the speed of Chinese progress towards nuclear weapons.)

It has been suggested that Khrushchev had been misled because, after Kennedy's hawkishness during the 1960 election campaign, the President proved softer when the two met in Vienna in June 1961. There is nothing in Khrushchev's memoirs to confirm this, for he speaks of Kennedy as a real President, unlike Truman, Eisenhower, and Nixon.[7] He explains the decision to deploy missiles in Cuba somewhat blandly, in terms of defending Castro, whereas he must have known that it was much more than that.

Mercifully, the memory of October 1962 has lived with statesmen of East and West ever since; and, nearly twenty years later, we can say with

7 *Khrushchev Remembers*, published in the West in 1971 and now generally regarded as authentic, pp. 360, 421, and 461-62 (Sphere Books edition).

October 1962   '... and then I said "To hell with you too".'

assurance that the world since then has never been so terrifyingly near to
a nuclear conflict. There have been other nuclear alerts, as during the
Yom Kippur war of 1973, but none of anything like such intensity. It is
perhaps no coincidence that the October crisis of 1962 came soon after
the two greatest powers acquired the ability to fire their weapons at each
other half way across the world. Both seem to have well learned restraint
in threatening to use them. But as the years pass, will the effect of the
experience wither?

One other lesson of the crisis preoccupied the *Guardian* then, and had
featured in my discussions with Hugh Gaitskell and others from 1957
onwards. Who, in the last resort, would take the decision about the use
of nuclear weapons on behalf of the Western Alliance? Plainly there had
been no consultation with the British Government during the October
events. That was clear from the Prime Minister's statements to the
Commons, though he said that there had always been 'the closest communication'. Apart from his Executive Committee, the only people whom
Kennedy had consulted were the Congressional leaders of both parties
and ex-President Eisenhower. At the same time ex-Secretary of State

Dean Acheson had been flown to Paris to brief de Gaulle while Ambassador Bruce in London briefed Harold Macmillan and Ambassador Dowling in Bonn briefed Chancellor Adenauer. Thereafter there were only a few telephone conversations. Macmillan in his memoirs records conversations with Kennedy towards midnight on the Monday, Wednesday, Thursday, and Friday nights, the Wednesday conversation being quoted almost verbatim.[8] But these did not constitute effective consultation.

In the *Guardian* we felt - and this derived from debate with Leonard Beaton, Richard Scott, John Rosselli, and David Marquand - that ultimately one man alone had to take the greatest decisions for the alliance and must be put in a position to take them quickly. But in return he must keep in touch with the British, French, and West German heads of Government and others in the front lines no less than with the Congressional leaders. If the alliance was to work, that mattered as much as American constitutional proprieties; and we said so in the paper.

A month after the missile crisis I went to Washington for a few days. There I was able to learn more about the October events and about the way the crisis had been handled; also about the implications for the future of the alliance. I began by talking to Max Freedman, who as usual knew much more than he had written in the paper, and he then took me to see Lyndon Johnson. Next was a meeting with Walt Rostow, head of the policy planning staff in the State Department, and a brief moment with Dean Rusk. Finally, there was a kind of relaxed and cheerful tutorial with the President himself in his study at the White House.

Max emphasised that Kennedy's strategy had succeeded, above all, because he had been careful to leave Khrushchev a line of retreat. In the days before the blockade was imposed White House security was effective, and the Kremlin could have had no premonition of what was coming. On the Thursday (18th) Gromyko had been to see the President and had lied, saying that the Soviet Union was putting no offensive weapons into Cuba; Kennedy had remained impassive, although the photographs and intelligence information were already in his hands. Once the blockade was imposed, there had been no wavering. But the President had insisted on keeping the navy and air force under close control. The navy wanted to go further out into the Atlantic to intercept the Soviet ships, but he had kept them back to the set line of which the Russians knew. If there was an encounter, the orders were to cripple a ship if necessary but not to sink it. He had let the tanker and the East German passenger ship through - for which he was criticised as 'soft' by some diehard Congressmen - because they could not be carrying missiles or bombers or vital equipment. When Khrushchev had asked for a pledge that the US would not attack Cuba, in return for dismantling the sites, he had been ready to give it.

Max mentioned also the confidential part played by another journalist,

8 Macmillan, *At the End of the Day*, pp. 190-212.

John Scali of ABC Television. He was known and respected both in the State Department and in the Soviet Embassy. Mid-week he had been approached by the Soviet Embassy's senior counsellor, Aleksandr Fomin, and had been asked discreetly to sound the White House about a solution on the lines eventually agreed. He had done so through Dean Rusk and then with direct access to the President, though at one point, after Khrushchev's second Saturday letter, he had felt that he was being double-crossed. He had had to take the decision, painful for a journalist, not to make direct use of his inner knowledge lest it jeopardise the negotiations.[9]

Lyndon Johnson gave me a graphic personal account of the events as seen from inside the White House, and of the working of the Executive Committee drawn from the National Security Council. He had been impressed by their brains and practical ability, and by the cool and thorough way they examined each possible course of action. He mentioned especially McNamara, McGeorge Bundy, Ted Sorensen, and Bobby Kennedy. One value of Bobby was that he stood up to the President and spoke freely, and at one point when Jack Kennedy had had to fulfil a campaign engagement in Chicago early in the crisis Bobby had been left to secure agreement in the Executive Committee on how they should proceed. (In fact Bobby Kennedy chaired many of the Executive Committee meetings, because the President felt that members might speak more openly in his absence.)[10]

From the beginning nobody had known what would happen; even those most knowledgeable about the Russians hadn't been able to tell, Johnson said. It had been a testing experience, especially in the 'five minutes from destruction' period towards the end. They had made clear to Khrushchev from the beginning that the missiles 'must be taken out' by negotiation or by other means, and there were a number of other means immediately available. Having gained their point, they now felt soberly that they could handle any crisis.

With Walt Rostow in the State Department I had a long discussion about the proposed multinational European deterrent force, which was valuable in shaping later *Guardian* policy, and also brought us to the question of crisis control. Rostow said that any European deterrent ought to be integrated with the American deterrent, with a common targeting system. In his view, which coincided with ours, there must be a single military commander in Europe. But what was to happen about political control? Rostow said that once again 'Whose finger on the button?' was the key question. For cold war planning one could get along with joint

9 For a fuller account of Scali's role, see Pierre Salinger's *With Kennedy*, pp. 271–80; Arthur Schlesinger's *A Thousand Days*, pp. 825–27; and Theodore Sorensen's *Kennedy*, p. 712.

10 Robert Kennedy, *13 days*, pp. 34–37.

committees (ministerial committees and official ones), but for nuclear decisions in a crisis there had to be a single man.

If the Europeans could not evolve political machinery so that one man was trusted with the power of decision, he said, then in emergencies they would have to leave control to the White House. There was much to be said for this, and the experience of October had reinforced it. Kennedy's headquarters had run with smoothness, speed, and efficiency. It was just like a 'regimental headquarters'.

And so finally to the White House, where Kennedy sat in his rocking chair while Max and I sat on sofas on either side of him. There, knowing from Max that Kennedy had read some of the *Guardian*'s comments, I began with an apology for having been too critical in the later stages of the crisis.[11] Kennedy laughed off the apology and said that perhaps our analysis hadn't been so far out, but there were three things that we had not fully understood. First, there was deliberate bad faith on the Russian side; Gromyko had told him categorically that no offensive weapons would be put in Cuba, and Ambassador Dobrynin and their man at the United Nations had said the same thing.[12] A personal message had been brought and read to Bobby Kennedy from a note taken in Khrushchev's presence, again saying that there would be no offensive missiles in Cuba. The most personal and private messages could not be trusted. Second, if America had accepted the presence of these missiles there would have been no future faith in the United States. None of its allies in Europe or Latin America would have relied on future American action, and that was more important than the military effect of the missiles. Thirdly, the Russians had tried to bring about an open alteration in the balance of power and that had to be resisted.

The most frightening thing, he said, was that the two sides were so far from understanding each other. US intelligence had said that the Russians would never put offensive missiles in Cuba because they would be too exposed. Theirs must have told Khrushchev that the Americans would not react. Such misunderstandings could easily lead to nuclear war. Can we, he asked, get through the next ten years without nuclear war? He was not sure; he thought that the European demand for a separate deterrent was no help in this connection. He mentioned also, as Rostow had done, that the Russians now had Polaris-type submarines off the Pacific coast – though they weren't such an open challenge as the placing of rockets in Cuba had been.

The greatest flaw in what the *Guardian* had written, he said, lay in our failure to realise that the Russians were still expansionist; they were still

11 When living in London before the war, he had known the *MG*, and he liked still to see it intermittently.

12 It has since been suggested that the Kremlin deliberately kept Dobrynin and Zorin in the dark - see Sorensen's *Kennedy*, p. 668, and Schlesinger's *Robert Kennedy and His Times*, p. 514 - but at the time the President included them in his charge of bad faith.

looking for any weakness in the West that they could exploit. Khrushchev two years ago had talked about competing with capitalism and beating it in industrial production and in aid to other countries. Why not? There was plenty to be done there, Kennedy said. It was a challenge that the Americans would like to meet. The previous day he had entertained the President of Honduras, 60 per cent of whose people were illiterate. The day before that he had talked to the Ambassador of Brazil, whose country was nearly bankrupt, and three days earlier to another Latin American ambassador, half of whose people were undernourished or near starvation. How much more profitable it would be to compete with the Russians in trying to raise standards in these countries.

He believed that there was no need for a European nuclear force – and it could not be made effective, because of its cost and because of the difficulty of political control. 'The bomb is great until you've got it,' he said. But the US could not be negative in its response; hence the proposal for a multilateral force, in submarines, with crews drawn from different nations. When the Europeans faced the true cost, he didn't believe they would go on; nor were they capable of solving the problem of political control. There must be one man who took the decisions. De Gaulle would never accept anyone but himself. 'You can't run a nuclear force,' Kennedy concluded, 'with a committee.'

We went on to talk about the Common Market, on which he said, 'We've got to shame them [the Europeans] into accepting Britain.' He wanted to talk also about Macmillan's political prospects and about Hugh Gaitskell, of whom he was suspicious. (Max said afterwards that he had been scathing about Gaitskell's use of the word 'alleged' of the Cuban missile sites.) He talked also about the press and about its never admitting to any mistakes – though he mentioned Altrincham as a rare exception, with the grace to say he'd been wrong.[13] The Southern press were building up a completely new version of history, in which the federal marshals were responsible for the fighting on the university campus at Oxford, Mississippi.[14] He spoke also of the 'synthetic hard line' of some

13 Lord Altrincham, now better known as John Grigg. From 1960 to 1969 he was one of the *Guardian*'s regular columnists, and a great asset because of the range and originality of his writing. On the Thursday morning of the crisis week his column had criticised Kennedy for getting worked up about a side-issue, important only in relation to US domestic politics, instead of concentrating on the more serious matter of China's attack on India in the Himalayas. The following week he said it was now clear that he had misjudged the situation and seriously underestimated President Kennedy, for which he apologised unreservedly. The President remarked to me that in making that apology Altrincham had surely broken the press's unwritten code. (For John Grigg's contribution to Irish coverage, see Chapter 12, pp. 296 and 299.)

14 Federal marshals were sent to the campus to protect a Negro, an Air Force veteran who wished to register as a student at the State University. No Negro had ever done so before. For the whole story, see among others Arthur Schlesinger's *A Thousand Days*, pp. 940–49.

American newspapers – no backing down, no negotiations, no give and take in our dealings with the Russians. That, he said, meant nothing but nuclear war. It was one of the real dangers in the American situation.

To me, no other political leader – European, Asian, or American – has ever sparked such an instant response as Kennedy did. He was friendly, relaxed, and cheerful though his questioning was tough. He had an excellent knowledge of British politics and policies, as well as the British press, and of the intricacies of European affairs. During our talk, he was as unhurried as if he had nothing else in the world to worry about.

Before meeting him I had heard a series of tributes – from Johnson, Rusk, Rostow, Max Freedman and others – to his calm and self-control during the Cuban crisis. During that week, he was master of himself and his team. In the end he alone had to decide and direct the American action. The strain upon him must have been beyond anything that most men can bear. He nevertheless kept an orderly routine, eating whenever possible with his family and sleeping normal hours. When he spoke of the burden of nuclear responsibility, he knew better than anyone else in the West what that meant.

A year later he was dead, and the Presidency passed to LBJ. Five years later Johnson gave up, broken by failure in Vietnam. When nuclear decisions put the world's survival at stake, it is proper to ask whether a lesser figure in the White House would have handled the Cuban crisis as well as Kennedy did. Under pressure from Congressional diehards, the Pentagon, and hard-line elements in the press, his response might have been less exactly judged. And with Khrushchev taking risks which nobody has taken since, the result could have been catastrophic. With this in mind, I never grudged the many hours and the many columns that the *Guardian* gave to nuclear policy, to covering the Cuban crisis, and to discussion afterwards of its implications. Nor did we ever cease to give thanks for the presence of Jack Kennedy in the White House in October 1962.

4 Parties, leaders, and politics

General elections, viewed from a newspaper office, seem rather like the fourth movement of Beethoven's Choral Symphony, with lots of noise and a triumphant crescendo. Just because these are the one occasion in four or five years when every citizen can cast his vote, they are also the occasion for newspapers to stretch themselves in covering the campaign and in trying to influence the outcome. Elections often bring out the worst in newspapers as in politicians – but luckily the electorate are resilient and not easily fooled.

The 1959 general election

On September 8 Harold Macmillan announced the dissolution, having astutely stage-managed a curtain-raiser to the campaign, with a visit from President Eisenhower just beforehand. Ike was seen visiting Balmoral, looking in at Oxford, and then taking part in an after-dinner fireside chat with Macmillan televised from Downing Street. It gave a world states-man's tone to 'Super Mac's' campaign. Polling was to be on October 8.

Lines of the *Guardian*'s election coverage had been sketched out months before – with constituency surveys, special articles on the major issues, and reporters on tour with the party leaders. Wadsworth had run previous elections by instinct night by night, and that was how we worked in 1959. The constituencies for survey were mostly chosen by Francis Boyd,* our political correspondent – a Yorkshireman who had been working for the *Guardian* since 1934, apart from five or six years in the Army. Tony Howard,* a young reporter who had joined us early in 1959, contributed forcefully to our thinking and tactics by nudges and pinpricks to editor, news editor, and London editor. He also wrote a private guide for other reporters on how they should approach constituency surveys, having been scandalised by the random guesswork that went into some of the early ones, and his memo became an office classic reissued in later elections.

In the leader writers' 'corridor' I was assisted by Paddy Monkhouse, whose instincts were cautious and whose political home was on the right of the Labour party; and by Harold Griffiths, who handled the economic issues. John Cole and Leonard Beaton were also important – John with an Ulsterman's aggression in argument but also a charming warmth, and with roots on the left; and Leonard with cool Canadian detachment and loyalties on the right, having been a founder-member of the Bow Group.

Traditionally the paper was Liberal, but on the reforming side of the Liberal party. C. P. Scott, while editor, stood as a Liberal in North-east Manchester in 1886 and 1892 and sat for Leigh from 1895 to 1905 – much to the dissatisfaction of some of his staff, who disliked having an absentee editor, but to the betterment of the Liberals in Parliament. C.P., however, had a friendly feeling for Labour and recognised why the Labour party was bound to grow. With the decline of the Liberals, in 1945 Wadsworth in his first election as editor had to steer the paper towards support for Labour but if possible without alienating loyal Liberal readers. Labour's great victory, which had been foreseen by few, gave him retrospective justification. In 1950 he maintained his Lib-Lab line; but in 1951, on the Monday before polling, with much unhappiness he wrote that after Labour's recent 'impotence and stumbling' it was time for a change. In 1955, while advising voters to get rid of extremists on both sides, he again concluded that Labour was not yet ready to be returned to office.

In 1959 I had no hesitation in reviving Wadsworth's 1945 approach. With the amiable exception of Leonard Beaton, there was no dispute among the senior staff about our general policy. Paddy Monkhouse, as my deputy, saw every leader that I wrote and apart from recommending an occasionally more gentle phrase he never dissented. In my room were the leather-bound volumes of leaders written by C. P. Scott and his son Ted, who was editor from 1929 until most unhappily drowned in Windermere in 1932, as were the bound volumes of Wadsworth's leaders. (Crozier's, for the period 1932 to 1944, had been taken away by his family.) I consulted these volumes quite often, to see how my predecessors had turned awkward corners. If C.P.'s ghost ever looked over my shoulder, as some thought it might, elections were the time. But it was an encouraging ghost.

Both C. P. Scott and A. P. Wadsworth had taken account of the personal qualities of party leaders, and I continued that. Especially with the example of Eden's highly personal and highly damaging conduct of the Suez crisis in front of us, it was not to be neglected. In the last few days before polling I asked Francis Boyd to write, in two signed articles, his personal assessments of Macmillan and Gaitskell as the rivals for Prime Minister and of their potential Cabinet colleagues. He noted that, after Eden's troubled era, Macmillan had set out to renew the confidence of the Conservatives in themselves. Hence his nurturing of the 'unflappable' image, and his cool acceptance of the resignation of three Treasury Ministers. Yet the Prime Minister, Boyd believed, was still rather remote from most of his party. Gaitskell he likened to the 'clever young science master' intent on soon becoming head. As leader it had taken him time to learn not to rise to every Tory bait and not to attempt self-justification too often. He had been criticised in the parliamentary party for too obviously preferring the company of bright young economists and 'intellectuals' but had now made himself more accessible to all sections of the party. No one on Labour's front bench could equal Gaitskell in general performance, Boyd said. But he reached no conclusion on how either candidate would respond to another acute international crisis.

I left the final election leader until the eve of poll, two days later than had been Wadsworth's habit. It was a mistake which I never repeated, for it brought a vehemently hostile reaction from a number of readers. Perhaps their reaction would have been almost as strong if the leader had appeared two days earlier, for it made explicit what had previously been less specific, but I felt that leaving it until the day before polling had aggravated the offence needlessly. The leader contained in a single sentence the essence of what we had previously argued: 'We should like to see Labour in office and the Liberals strengthened.' It was on this sentence above all that the critics picked. Yet the case was put carefully, in a leader of about one thousand words. The country needed a change, we said, 'but it will also benefit if the two big parties are jerked out of the ruts in which they are running'. In times of crisis, Conservative instincts had proved unsound. Who could have believed on polling day in 1955 that Britain would go to war aggressively in 1956? Or that the Cabinet could be so unconcerned when civilians in Cyprus, Nyasaland, and Kenya were killed and ill-treated in Britain's name? Those tragedies were the greater because in Mr Lennox-Boyd we had an outstanding Colonial Secretary and in Mr Butler a most humane Home Secretary. Even on the economic front the Conservatives had not done as well as was to be expected.

Of Labour we said that the doctrine of nationalisation had been its worst liability for years, but under Gaitskell future commitments were being quietly liquidated. Labour had become wholeheartedly expansionist, and the ghosts of 'austerity' had been exorcised. In foreign affairs, however, the Labour party had been slower to respond than the Liberals, who had been the first to propose suspending nuclear tests, sharing deterrents, and seeking ways to stop the spread of nuclear weapons. And we concluded by saying that the quality of individual candidates ought always to be taken into account: 'It would be as hard to vote against Mr Butler in Saffron Walden as to vote for the more extreme members of Victory for Socialism.'

Happily Mr Butler held Saffron Walden easily, while Mr Ian Mikardo lost his seat at Reading. The Conservatives were returned with an overall majority of one hundred – their biggest since the war – about which we were not so happy. Fortunately we had made no public forecast, although privately I had supposed that Labour stood a fighting chance of at least a small majority. In a leader written at about 2 am on the Friday, when the trend of the results was plain, I said that for Mr Macmillan the verdict was 'a clear declaration by the country of its approval for Conservative economic policy.'

In Gaitskell's own eyes he lost, above all, because of a misjudged promise not to increase income tax – a promise he made because he believed that the Conservatives in the last ten days of the election were about to start a scare on the costs of Labour's programme. That error was compounded by a Transport House statement promising a reduction of purchase tax. The way was wide open for the Conservatives to imply that the electorate was being bribed. But on the voting figures it seems highly probable that even without the tax issue Labour would have lost. It failed to hold the new middle class. As the *Guardian* said on the morning after the declaration, people voted for the money in their purses, rather than for the bonus they might get if Labour achieved its promised expansion. Winning the new middle class was a theme to which we were to return frequently over the next four years.

At the end of the campaign, privately a little bruised both by the result and by the flow of critical letters, I was comforted by Paddy Monkhouse, who said that the readers' reaction in 1951 had been far worse. Then, he said, after A.P.W. had recommended voting Conservative where there was no good Liberal some older readers wrote 'as if their bishop had suddenly authorized a mortal sin'.

Laurence Scott, as chairman and managing director, looked in to my room on the Friday afternoon to ask how I was feeling. At that point, having had only a few hours' sleep and with a long leader still to write, I replied, 'Numb.' On Sunday, after twelve hours' sleep, I sent him a note to say that I was feeling fine though somewhat sad about hostile reactions to the concluding leader. In coverage of the election I believed that there had been only one lapse, in an unbalanced late-edition report of Macmillan's Manchester meeting. Some readers in the South had complained that we did not cover the Prime Minister's concluding television address – but that was because it was too late for the Southern editions (at that time with printing in Manchester only), just as Gaitskell's had been.

As to the plain speech of our final leader, I reminded Laurence that his grandfather had never been indirect at elections. I had again looked up C.P.'s leaders in the 1920, 1922, 1923, and 1924 elections 'and they were battering rams – magnificent and utterly uncompromising'. He had spared neither his own party nor its opponents. There was a leader in 1920 about his former friend Lloyd George that began 'What does Mr George care for the Liberal party or the Liberal party for Mr George?' And after the rout of the Liberals in 1924 there was no question of wishing the winners well. C.P. had whacked them hard next day, while lamenting the confusion of his own party. But of course I didn't believe that Macmillan's Government would be as bad as Baldwin's after 1924.

Laurence made no comment. He believed that, in the family tradition, the management must say nothing either favourable or unfavourable about editorial matters. But at Christmas he wrote to me, unusually, saying that he thought I was making 'a terrific success of the job', which pleased me greatly.

Grimond's third force

About midday on the Sunday after polling, Jo Grimond phoned from

Orkney. The 1959 election was his first as leader of the Liberals, just as it was my first as editor. The Liberal vote had more than doubled, to 1,640,000, but the party still held only six seats. The Sunday papers were not yet in Kirkwall, and Jo was a bit bothered about an interview he had given to the *Observer*. I confirmed that the paper was leading with the story – 'Grimond urges union of Radicals' – and it reported him as proclaiming that on certain vital issues the opposition parties 'can and must combine'.[1] Jo said that the emphasis in the *Observer* might not be helpful, since he did not want to appear too eager to work with Labour, or to exaggerate his own strength. Any alliance would have to be very loose. I said that I thought policy questions would have to be settled first – perhaps with a review of nationalisation on Labour's side and a review of attitudes to the social services by the Liberals.

The *Observer* had also reported Jo as being greatly encouraged by the election results. With his usual charming candour, Jo admitted to having said that to them but added that he was really very disappointed. He had hoped to increase the number of Liberals in the House as well as doubling their vote.

Monday's *Guardian*, almost inevitably, led with Labour's suspicious reactions to Grimond's overtures – with the headline 'Shotgun marriage feared'. We had our own interview with Jo and a leader saying that cohesion between the two parties of the left was perfectly practicable and honourable, as indeed C. P. Scott had written thirty years earlier, but that it must spring from cohesion on the major issues of policy.

For some time the *Guardian* had been trying to bring the Labour and Liberal parties closer together. Our aim was to move the Liberals to the left and to persuade Labour to drop 'Socialist' measures when there was no pragmatic case. In the spring of 1958 the Liberals had done well in the Rochdale by-election, pushing the Conservatives, who had previously held the seat, into a poor third place. Then at Torrington in Devon they had won the seat in another by-election, overturning a Conservative majority of nine thousand. Roger Fulford, then writing his royal histories in rural North Lancashire, reminded us that a small party could still have great influence in Parliament. In 1906, he said, when 'a great sea' of Liberals ruled the Commons, the tiny Labour party had succeeded in altering 'the curl of the waves'. So we urged Jo Grimond onwards in his endeavour to make the Liberals a more radical group.

Jo came to stay with me in Manchester one weekend in May 1958. I put it to him that the parliamentary Liberals ought to be expounding two policies – one the ideal, of what they would do if in office with a majority; the other the immediate, of what they would do if a minority but holding the balance in the House. The slightest mention of coalitions or cohesive

---

1 The *Observer* interview was by Mark Arnold-Forster, who had flown to Kirkwall for it.

arrangements was anathema to older Liberals, because of Lloyd George
– as it was to Labour people because of Ramsay MacDonald. Yet while
it was self-delusion for any Liberal to talk as if the party might soon
return to power, there was a real possibility that it might hold the balance
in the Commons. In the office we had identified some thirty constituencies
where the Liberals, with a good candidate and energetic workers, could
repeat what they had done at Torrington. Though we knew that what
could be done in a by-election might prove unattainable in a general
election, it was worth a try. It seemed to me the only way forward for the
Liberals and potentially a healthy course for Parliament. A brake was
needed on both the big parties and a new force not tied to exhausted
doctrines.

All this was close to Jo's own thinking, and we put the argument in a
long leader in the *Guardian* a few days later. We said that as part of their
immediate policy the Liberals ought to determine on which issues – a few
only – they must inevitably vote against the Government. Obvious ones
were steel nationalisation by Labour (at any rate of the full-blooded kind)
and any repetition of Suez-like adventures by the Conservatives. Bomb
tests and anything which added heavily to taxation were in the same class.
But on lesser issues – comprehensive schooling, for example, important
though that was – the Liberals must be prepared to abstain. These were
not issues on which to bring the Government down. We recognised that
this was a politically difficult line to take, the more because of the old
bogey that a third force made decisive government difficult. But we
thought it would have a strong appeal to people who were unhappy with
both the major parties.

I heard later that the Liberal Party Executive had discussed the leader
and its line. Clement Davies, who had preceded Jo as party leader, was
horrified by the proposal, as were others of the old guard. Within his own
ranks, Jo had to proceed with caution. The Liberal Assembly at Torquay
in the autumn was a sad fiasco, with incompetent chairmanship, hours
spent on secondary debates, and no sense of direction. Jo took no part
until the final day, when he made a ringing speech about the 'blimps of
1958' and about the patronage and privilege with which Socialists and
Tories equally manipulated party power. Somewhat optimistically, he
claimed the younger generation for the Liberals. But after the appalling
mismanagement of the Torquay conference he took a more direct part in
future assemblies from the beginning, while reserving his main speech as
a climax for the end. (Later Ted Heath made a similar change in Conservative conferences.)

In the *Guardian* in the winter of '58 and spring of '59 we returned to
the theme from time to time, particularly when the Young Liberals held
a weekend conference in Manchester. But Jo Grimond himself never
openly took up the cause of Lib-Lab cohesion until the *Observer* interview after the general election. From then onwards he spoke about it

frequently. Within the office my line was not universally approved. Paddy
Monkhouse, while recognising that the paper must take some account of
its historic Liberal roots, would have preferred at times a more explicit
approval of Labour policies. Tony Howard told me that I was getting too
involved with a 'sideshow'. Harold Griffiths said much the same. But
there was useful reinforcement for my policy when we commissioned a
psephologist, Dick Leonard (afterwards Labour MP for Romford), to
study the likely effects of Liberal intervention in marginal constituencies.
He found that, given the continuation of the swing to Labour of about 2
per cent showing on the polls in March–April '59, the effect would be a
slight increase in a small Labour majority in the next Parliament. He did
another study in November, based on the actual voting, which showed
that Liberal intervention had on the whole been advantageous to Labour.

The 'sideshow', however, was not our only, or main, activity. I saw
Hugh Gaitskell privately as often as I saw Jo Grimond. I also talked from
time to time with Reginald Maudling and with Lennox-Boyd on the
Conservative side, and about once a year lunched with Harold Macmillan
at Downing Street, though that tended to be more social than political.
With Gaitskell the issues of nationalisation were a regular topic of discussion, and of course nuclear disarmament. Nyasaland was another
frequent topic, for we had been dismayed by the inept and brutal way the
colonial authorities had handled the political disturbances there – as
indeed Lord Devlin's commission of inquiry found. The *Guardian*'s
reporting and comment had helped to secure appointment of the Devlin
commission and a change of policy in Nyasaland. Our major achievement
with Labour and with Hugh Gaitskell was in bringing the party round to
support of the non-nuclear club, which the Liberals had endorsed many
months earlier.

When Jo returned to the mainland after the election he admitted that
the *Observer* interview had been perhaps too sudden and abrupt. He had
felt that he must speak first, both to gain attention and before anyone on
the Labour side suggested it. Also he had so much liked Mark Arnold-
Forster, whom he had never met before, that Mark had easily drawn it
out of him. He didn't regret it though he knew there were going to be
difficulties with his party council. He said a little despairingly that the
Liberals could be kept going only by 'a continuous performing seal act',
but with diplomacy the party council would come round to his view. A
month later it did so, in spite of opposition from the *News Chronicle*
(traditionally Liberal, but now dying).

By contrast Hugh Gaitskell, when I saw him the day after talking to
Jo, said that he had decided to make no statement on policy at present.
Immediately after the results it was a question for him of whether to say
something forceful or wait. He preferred to wait and let the party itself
study the campaign, the defeat, and its future policy. Among his reasons,
he believed that during the campaign the party had been in very good

heart and wholly behind its policy – more so than at any time since 1945 – and it would have been hurtful to his own people if he had come out with an immediate reappraisal. Of Jo's statement he said he was sympathetic to Grimond's ideas and indeed liked Jo well personally, but it was impossible for him to do anything at present. It would conflict with his role of standing above the reappraisal. He also questioned whether, on a hard analysis, an alliance would help or hinder the left in votes actually cast.

On all accounts, he intended to stay silent until the party's two-day conference at Blackpool in late November. I wondered whether that might not prove to be a mistake. In retrospect, it was.

Gaitskell and Labour's death-wish

The Blackpool conference was destructive, ill-tempered, and distasteful. Others had stronger premonitions of disaster than I had, though I wrote a leader beforehand saying that the party was giving an impression of complacency and living in the past – and that it would stay in the wilderness unless it strengthened its appeal to young voters, to the increasingly comfortable wage-earners, and to uncommitted liberals. Hugh Gaitskell himself had done nothing publicly to prepare the ground, though privately it was known that he intended to seek reform of the party's constitution. He wanted the old 'Clause 4' – on the common ownership of the means of production, distribution, and exchange – rewritten in broader terms. He also wanted a revision in the structure and authority of the National Executive.

Soon after the election Douglas Jay wrote an article in a Labour weekly saying that the party should drop nationalisation from its programme, and he was savaged by the left. Worse, although it was known that other Shadow Ministers agreed with him, none spoke up. There were rumblings from the trade union leaders, too, against any suggestion of reform of the block voting system at party conferences or of their automatic right to places on the party executive. John Cole, as the *Guardian*'s labour correspondent, wrote two articles on the party's future – suggesting that the unions should work more through the constituency parties and that union leaders should have to fight for places on the National Executive on their own merits. John argued also that prominent politicians ought to be more active in talking and debating in the constituencies at all kinds of occasions, great and small, and using these to educate their supporters. He wanted a vetting committee from the National Executive, including two or three MPs, to prevent the dull and inadequate place-seekers from becoming parliamentary candidates. While these were signed articles expressing John's personal view, they were written after discussion within the office – and I was convinced, as were most of John's colleagues, that with these reforms Labour would become a healthier and more democratic party. (Some years later, with the structure still unreformed, militants on the left set about using a decaying constituency system for their own ends.)

Even Hugh Gaitskell told me privately that John's proposals were unsound. Not only would the union leaders never accept them, but their effect would be to make senior trade union leaders lose interest in the Labour party. He did not believe that enough trade unionists would join the constituency parties, and transfer of power to the constituencies would lead to some very eccentric behaviour. Finance was a further difficulty, for the party was very hard up and if trade union funds were paid through local organisations it would be hard to get money for central purposes. In passing, Hugh said that we were mistaken in writing of the party's 'complacency'. He himself was dismayed by the signs of its 'conservatism'.

Jo Grimond, meanwhile, had persuaded the Liberals' national council to back his search for cohesion among progressives. He spoke of Labour as 'rather like a man trussed up in a strait-jacket of their organisation and tossed into the sea of modern political problems with nationalisation tied round their neck in the form of a lump of lead'. But he believed that there was much in common between those fundamentally concerned with the cause of an individual in a good society; and that, instead of a dogmatic approach to industry, its problems ought to be examined case by case. He also believed that defence and foreign policy contained greater problems in which there were common interests, and he hoped that Labour supporters might be ready to borrow 'some of our clothes' – not the cast-offs, we said in the *Guardian* next day, but their Sunday best. And we thought it a generous offer from a spurned suitor. For Patrick Gordon-Walker had already said, 'Have no truck with the Liberals.'

At Blackpool the first day was bad but not disastrous. Barbara Castle as party chairman spoke in the morning, blasting the 'commercialised society' and proclaiming public ownership as indispensable to Labour. Hugh Gaitskell spoke in the afternoon, saying that he was not speaking for the Executive but asking for a modernisation of policy and a revision of the party constitution. The boundary between the public and private sectors, he said, could not be permanent and public ownership ought not to be seen as an end in itself but as a means. Of Clause 4 he said that it made no reference to colonial freedom, race relations, disarmament, full employment, or planning, and he believed therefore that it should be rewritten. His speech went down badly, with many interruptions while he was speaking and poor applause at the end.

Michael Foot spoke soon after him, condemning Gaitskell with all his invective and receiving a warm ovation. Others maintained the counter-attack on the lines that common ownership must be kept as the party's guiding light. On the second morning Denis Healey and Shirley Williams bravely called for changes consistent with the party's chief objectives. Healey said that if comrades preferred to remain in Opposition, as Socialists pure in heart, it was not they who would suffer but those whom they were supposed to be trying to help. But the major speech of Sunday afternoon came from Nye Bevan, a speech that I found dishonest and shameful. He attacked Denis Healey in order to attack Gaitskell without naming him. He went in for a tortuous reference to the commanding heights of the economy, saying he agreed with Barbara Castle because he was a Socialist and believed in public owership, but he agreed with Hugh Gaitskell because he did not believe that public ownership should reach down to every piece of economic activity. It was flamboyant oratory, empty of true substance, and it received a great ovation.

After Bevan's speech I left the Winter Gardens, found a quiet shelter on the promenade facing the sea, and settled down to write my long leader (to be telephoned to Manchester). It supported the Gaitskell line and refrained from saying anything directly about Nye Bevan. It began and ended in this way:

The charge against the Labour party is that it lives in a bygone age. On the evidence presented by the party itself at Blackpool this weekend it can neither be acquitted nor found guilty....

... these elementary truths [from Denis Healey and Shirley Williams] were not acceptable to all at Blackpool. Perhaps we, the outsiders, should not have expected too much. Perhaps 1959 is too soon for Labour to revise the views it expressed in 1918. Perhaps we are unreasonable in expecting the party to have digested the experience of its years in and out of office. But a reforming party should itself be capable of change.

Francis Boyd and John Cole, in their front-page reports next morning, reflected a similar sense of dismay. At the end of the 1959 election Gaitskell had stood at a peak of public esteem, in spite of his defeat, inside the party and outside it. At the end of the Blackpool conference his position was openly challenged by a vocal group within the party and was seriously damaged outside the party. It was indeed the beginning of a long struggle, leading to the 'fight and fight and fight again' speech against the unilateral disarmers and the opponents of his leadership at the 1960 Scarborough conference, and onwards to his total victory at the Blackpool conference in 1961. We followed his fortunes closely in the *Guardian*, and I kept in touch with him, seeing him once or twice a month. We gave him as much support as we could, though at times disagreeing with him – for example over the withdrawal of the whip from five MPs in March 1961, after a vote on the Service estimates.

Before the 1960 Scarborough conference we wrote a succession of leaders arguing that unilateral nuclear disarmament was untenable for a country that wanted security in Europe – for it would either drive the US back into a 'fortress America', armed with long-range missiles, or, worse, raise Western Germany to second place in the alliance, with more nuclear weapons in the forward area and greater risks of nuclear war. We said also that on the left the unilateralist issue was being exploited to try to get rid of Gaitskell – a point that he himself made, stingingly, in his Scarborough speech. In the end the Scarborough conference agreed to bury the hatchet on Clause 4; but the fight on unilateralism dominated the party for the next twelve months.

Before the 1961 Blackpool conference the *Guardian* gave emphasis to the findings of Dr Mark Abrams, chairman of Research Services, that Labour must establish itself as more than a one-class party. For victory, Abrams said, it must win back affluent manual workers who now regarded themselves as middle class and were turning towards the Conservatives; it must also produce solid evidence of being a united team. But the nuclear issue preoccupied the conference, leading to Gaitskell's overwhelming victory, which we welcomed in a leader headed 'Golden half-mile'. The other half-mile lay ahead, and we hoped that he would now be able to attend constructively to Labour's future policies without looking over his shoulder at opponents in his own ranks. We were sorry that the non-nuclear club, once embraced by Labour, was now nearly forgotten – especially when President Kennedy was coming round to it; but in Britain the first need was for Labour to prove its unity.

After the 1962 Brighton conference we wrote that Gaitskell had put Labour well on the road to winning the next election. I believed that, as did others in the office. But, reading some of those leaders again twenty years later, I notice an ambivalence. For example, the long leader just before the 1960 conference consisted of a series of eight quotations – starting with one on the need for a progressive Government of the left to take Britain through the sixties, and continuing by way of nuclear disarmament and public ownership to the issues of urban decay and inner-city renewal – each with a commentary on its relevance to the Labour conference. At the end the quotations were identified as all coming from Jo Grimond or Mark Bonham Carter at the Liberal Assembly, and there was a clear hint that, ideally, a Lib-Lab alignment was the way to unite the progressive left. Yet I well knew that any attempt to press that point must further divide the Labour party, and that the trade unions were adamantly against even the reforms of Labour's structure that John Cole had proposed. It was understandable that Tony Howard and others thought alignment with the Liberals a dangerous 'sideshow'. But if Labour was not willing to reform itself and was all the time having to cover up its own divisions, could it govern effectively? As the 1964 election neared, I suppressed my doubts – but they grew again in later years.

The leadership after Gaitskell

Hugh Gaitskell died after a short illness, aged fifty-six, in January 1963. It was a personal, political, and national tragedy. Harold Macmillan moved the adjournment of the House – the only time it has been done for a leader of the Opposition who has not been Prime Minister. As the *Guardian* said next day, because his talents were creative he would have been a better Prime Minister than leader of the Opposition. He had shown this already as Minister of Fuel and briefly as Chancellor of the Exchequer in Attlee's Government, and in his courage in handling the Bevanite and bomb controversies. He had never waged the kind of personal warfare against colleagues that some of his colleagues had waged against him; but in office his construction of his Cabinet would have been uninhibited, for while he saw little purpose in axing 'shadows' he was determined that his party must give the country the strongest Government it could.

Who was to succeed him? Gaitskell had warned me more than once that Wilson was distrusted by others. When Hugh had been about to leave for a holiday in the Caribbean at Christmas in 1959 I had said that he should be fairly safe from sudden recall since Harold Macmillan would be out of the country. 'Yes,' Gaitskell replied, 'and Harold Wilson will be out of it too.' Wilson had been much upset by the proposal to replace him as shadow Chancellor by Roy Jenkins, because he feared that it would jeopardise his chances of succeeding to the leadership 'say fifteen years hence'. Wilson was clever, quick, and an excellent parliamentary performer, Gaitskell said, but not a deep thinker and of doubtful quality as a leader.

He went on to speak of others who might lead the party, perhaps about 1975. Brown and Robens were tough, but not up to it. The man he picked was Denis Healey – also tough, and with plenty of political courage. Healey was a lonely figure but in time would gain support. He would never commit the party to anything – for example on defence or foreign policy – through cowardice. That was a rare quality.

Hugh Gaitskell had died on a Friday evening, and on the Monday I phoned Jim Callaghan. I had been seeing him quite often in the past five years and had come to respect and like him. He said he'd spent the weekend thinking very hard about his position. The more he thought about it the more he realised his inadequacies. He didn't want to run but was ready to do so if others thought he should, and already he'd had a visit from three members of the Shadow Cabinet who had said that he must stand. They believed that George Brown was not a satisfactory candidate and that there would be strong trade union opposition to Harold Wilson. Jim said that he would do no canvassing and take part in no pacts or manoeuvres. He would work loyally with whoever became party leader.

On the phone I told Jim the way we were thinking at the *Guardian*. If George Brown were to be elected leader that would be a grave handicap to the party – we regarded him as excitable, erratic, and of unreliable judgement – and we should have great difficulty in supporting a party with him at its head. On the other hand, I was ready to see Harold Wilson in the post, for I thought his worst defects would disappear once his ambition was realised and he became leader. But, still more, I would prefer to see Jim in that place and I thought he ought to run if there appeared any reasonable prospect of his coming above George Brown. He said it was a comfort to know that, but he was still conscious of his own deficiencies. I said that that wasn't quite the point: he had also to consider the qualifications and possible policies of the other candidates.

Next day, Tuesday, I went to London. At that time I was renting the top-floor flat in Dick Crossman's house in Vincent Square. I had been doing so from just before the start of the *Guardian*'s printing in London in September 1961 and continued there until we moved the editorial headquarters to London in February–March 1964. Most weeks I spent one or two nights in London, and sometimes more, and in the year 1963 I spent a horrifying sixty-eight nights on the sleeper train between Manchester and London. In fact it was while on a short autumn holiday in the Lake District with my wife that year – our third child was then six months old – that I finally decided to move the editorial headquarters to London, in hope of a more settled home life.

In the train going south I drafted a very short leader about Labour's choice, and in the London office showed it to one or two others, John Cole and Harold Griffiths in particular. We knew we had to be careful, for the parliamentary party might be resentful of outside advice. But since the parliamentary party was choosing not just its leader but a potential Prime Minister who might soon have to govern, we felt justified in offering advice, discreetly phrased.

While we were discussing the leader Dick Crossman telephoned. Was I to be at Vincent Square that evening and if so what time would I be coming home? I replied that if he was to be there and wanted to talk I would come about 10 pm or soon after. He said nothing about anyone else being there, but I knew what he wanted to talk about.

John Cole and Harold Griffiths thought that the leader was pitched about rightly, so it was duly put into type. Since the party had announced that afternoon that it was to proceed to an election of leader at once, instead of after the usual month's delay, the comment was timely. Apart from its opening, it said only this:

It would be a mistake to choose a man because he can most obviously hold the party together, unless he can also win an election. It would be a worse mistake to choose one who has the popular appeal to win an election, unless he can also govern. Steady judgment, a reasonable consistency of policy, the courage to take unpopular decisions, administrative ability, and robust health are the requirements. Mr George Brown, in spite of his great service and long devotion to the Labour party, hardly measures up to all these requirements. There are other candidates who come nearer to doing so.

That was all. We made no direct mention of Wilson or Callaghan, and indeed we did not know whether there might be other nominations.

When I left for Vincent Square, I took a proof of the leader with me, intending to let Dick see what he would read in next morning's paper. On reaching the house, I found Harold Wilson with Dick in the sitting room. So I thought it best to show them the proof at once; the first edition was being printed by then anyway. I said that at that stage I didn't think the *Guardian* could do any good by going further than expressing its doubts about George Brown. Personally I would be content to see either Wilson or Callaghan as leader, but to say that plainly might be unhelpful. If George were to be leader we should have great difficulty in supporting the party at an election, and I thought it essential to say so now rather than leave it until the election came. Wilson agreed with this.

Rather to my surprise, he seemed delighted with the leading article when he had read it. He thought the *Guardian* the only paper that could have a positive influence on parliamentary party members, who might be encouraged to think in a larger context. He believed he stood a good chance of winning. In a straight fight with George, he said, he would probably win. The implication of his satisfaction was not completely clear: but if he regarded Callaghan as a more dangerous rival than George Brown, then at least we had not backed Callaghan at that stage. And if it came to a straight fight between him and George, the *Guardian* might have marginally reduced George's chances.

Harold said that he had agreed with George that neither would say anything in public about the contest or about the other, and that they would do no canvassing. Wilson said he had not undertaken to serve under Brown if Brown was elected; in that event he thought he would channel his energies elsewhere. I asked how he would feel if Callaghan was elected. He said he thought Callaghan had changed his mind too often and was not strong enough for the job, but he did not reply directly to the question. I kept quiet about my previous day's conversation with Callaghan.

He went on to talk enthusiastically about Labour's great task in releasing the untapped energies of its own people and of the country as a whole. In a comment no doubt designed to appeal to me he said that if the millions of pounds now going into the independent deterrent could be spent on medical research, agricultural research, electronics, and other new things it could yield immense results. He mentioned the quite small amounts that, under his guidance at the Board of Trade, had gone into the National Research and Development Corporation – from which had come computers and the Hovercraft. The Tories were trying to frighten people in Stevenage and other new towns by asking what would happen if Labour cancelled defence contracts, but he would go round saying that there were great new research tasks to be undertaken and he knew that numbers of scientists were only waiting for such a chance.

Harold puffed happily on his pipe in Dick's sitting room for more than an hour. Next day and later in the week I discussed the choice further with others in the office, but we wrote about it in the leader columns only once more. That was eight days later, when the ballot papers went out to Labour MPs, who then had five days in which to return them. This time we made our choice more explicit:

Of the three candidates all are capable of holding high ministerial posts. But the choice now is potentially for the highest post in Britain. Mr George Brown has courage, tenacity, and force ... Even so, it is hard to see Mr Brown as an effective Prime Minister. His judgment is sometimes too hurried, his knowledge too limited, his words too offensive, and his tactical course erratic....

That narrows the choice to Mr Callaghan and Mr Wilson. Either seems likely to make an effective Prime Minister, though there may be preferences between the two. For leading the country out of an economic wilderness Mr Wilson has better qualifications.... He also has the advantage of previous Cabinet service.... Justly or unjustly he came out of the 1960 party conflict with an equivocal reputation [after Scarborough he stood against Gaitskell for the leadership] but he can plead that his course was governed by the interests of party unity. As an administrator, as a national leader, and as an international negotiator his standing is good.

Nevertheless a number of people, inside and outside the Labour party, will prefer Mr Callaghan. He has a deserved reputation for directness and fair dealing. He is a man of great ability, though he has had fewer opportunities for showing it than his immediate rivals.... In 1960 he took no hand in party intrigues. For that reason, among others, he is acceptable to sections of the Labour party that will not tolerate Mr Wilson.... To some extent he is untested; but his reliability and good judgment commend him.... Either Mr Wilson or Mr Callaghan would be welcome as Labour's leader and as a potential Prime Minister. Of the two, we should prefer to see Mr Callaghan elected.

On the first ballot the voting was Wilson 115, Brown 88, Callaghan 41. To our disappointment Jim Callaghan then dropped out, and on the second ballot a week later the voting was Wilson 144, Brown 103. George Brown remained as deputy leader and Wilson recast the Shadow Cabinet, moving Denis Healey to defence and bringing in Dick Crossman to science. We welcomed him to the saddle, hoping he could pull the party out of its fratricidal battles. We welcomed his statement that Britain stood fairly and squarely behind the Atlantic alliance. We hoped also that he could indeed find ways to release Britain's untapped energies and revitalise the economy.

Eight months later the Conservatives, too, had a new leader and the country a new Prime Minister. The process of choice was almost entirely private, though the veil was lifted a little more than in the past. Harold Macmillan's illness was announced on the eve of the party conference at Blackpool in October, to the consternation even of his Cabinet, for he had assumed that his ailment would not keep him out of action long. From his hospital bed he took a leading part in the consultations on who should succeed him, and, with the rest of the press, the *Guardian* was able to follow the comings and goings. Eight days after the first announcement of his illness the Prime Minister's letter of resignation was taken to the Palace, and an hour later the Queen drove to the hospital to discuss the situation with him. Twenty minutes after her return to the Palace Lord Home arrived, to be invited to form a Government – which he did only next day, after persuading some hesitant colleagues. He resigned his six peerages and fought a by-election in West Perthshire, which was conveniently vacant. Thus the former fourteenth earl came to face, across the despatch boxes, the Opposition leader to whom he referred, in a jocular retort, as the fourteenth Mr Wilson.

'A new Britain'

That autumn of 1963 at the *Guardian* we thought it was time to try to focus attention on where Britain was going. Nearly twenty years earlier there had been the great achievements and the disappointments of the post-war Attlee Government: the revival of peacetime industry, creation of the National Health Service, a start with rebuilding the cities, and more opportunities in education – but with a long period of austerity and extensive Government controls as part of the price. Then twelve years of Conservative Government had brought greater prosperity, more freedom, and improvements of housing and slum clearance – but still with disappointingly slow progress and too many people unable to move out of uncivilised living conditions. Three years earlier we had run a series of articles on the theme 'North v. South', showing statistically and descriptively the disadvantages in health, education, and prospective earnings to which anyone born in a Northern city was unavoidably condemned. We thought it was time to return to the theme and see where each of the political parties intended to take Britain.

In all the series ran to twenty-two articles, published between mid-September and the end of October. All but one of the articles were by *Guardian* staff writers, and they were reprinted as a fat little pamphlet which sold well.

The opening shot was from Drum Street, Openshaw – 'locked in by industry alongside the main road to Sheffield out of Manchester' – and was accompanied by an aerial photograph of row after row of tiny Victorian houses, each with its back court and back lane and interspersed with factories and chapels, but utterly devoid of trees or green space. It described the life of the young Bennett family (not their real name, but it served): better off than they were ten years ago, now with hot running water in the house but with no bathroom and only an outside lavatory. Their son went to a well-built modern school, though with large classes and teachers who tended not to stay. They longed to live 'in a place which is cleaner, where the shops are not strung out along a main trunk road, where you do not see a factory wall the moment you get out of bed, and where the social divisions are less marked'. (The Bennetts lived on the wrong side of the canal: an uncle who lived 'over the bridge', in Higher Openshaw, had never been to visit them in eleven years though he received them affably enough when they ventured to his side.)

From Drum Street the series moved to the bricks and mortar of housing, slum clearance, and urban renewal – and to the related questions of jobs, restrictive practices, transport, and regional planning. It noted that in Britain nearly fifteen million people were still living in houses without baths, and it discussed the achievements of Sir Keith Joseph's Conservative housing programme as against the claims made for Labour's proposed Land Commission (in the end a failure), and Labour's policy of accelerated slum clearance and faster modernisation, together with repeal of the Rent Act and provision of special interest rates for owner-occupiers. It took a look also at the Liberals' six-point plan. That section of the study concluded that against the sheer physical mass of the housing problem it was impossible to plump for a 'best buy' among the party policies. 'As well as ceaseless and bold Government action from the top,' it said, 'the housing problem needs a vast, articulate, and ceaselessly demanding push from below.'

The transport study showed the switch away from rail and to private road travel. 'Traffic jams and crawl, Mr Marples and his parking meters, Dr Beeching and his axe' – these were the well-known results. The Liberals wanted to charge for the use of road space in cities, by a technically feasible system of metering. To the Conservatives this was alien State intervention (though why, then, our study asked, was it not alien to tax each drinker for his use of a glass of beer?); instead they were thinking of new urban motorway grids, in spite of their enormous cost, and Mr Marples had admitted that the whole concept of life in cities was being challenged. Labour was looking towards ways of restricting the use of cars in cities, through the provision of peripheral parking and efficient public transport in city centres. Labour at last accepted the need for integrated planning of transport, land use, industrial location, and regional development.

The failings of the Restrictive Trade Practices Act and of the Monopolies Commission were another topic. 'Breakfast cartels' as they were called on the Continent – informal arrangements to manage prices – were one flaw, though Tony Crosland in a caustic aside had doubted whether much British business was done at breakfast time. 'The vice of certain large British enterprises,' Peter Jenkins wrote, 'is not that they are engaged in squeezing the public but that they are coasting along comfortably with a nice secure home market and a large public relations department.'

One of the most telling contributions was John Cole's on manpower. 'Perhaps the only part of Britain which really needs to be modernised', he began, 'is the national mind and will.' The problems which flowed from the under-use of men, resources, and space in one half of the country and the stifling congestion in the other half overlapped all other problems considered in the series. It had taken all the post-war years for the need to disperse industry and to develop a better regional balance to be accepted. As long as the shortage of labour and of skill reappeared in the

South and Midlands each time economic expansion got under way, 'so long will we face inevitable wage inflation and a continuation of "stop-go" economic policies'. These in turn must worsen the economic and social difficulties of the North, Scotland, Merseyside, and Ulster and so drive more and more people south. As to remedies, John Cole wrote that industry would believe that the Government meant what it said about the development areas only when the inducements to move north were clearly stated, guaranteed for a period, and not subject to the appalling delays of the past – and when the policy of refusing industrial development certificates in congested areas became firm and consistent.

In a final comment on the series we concluded that good management in government mattered as much as an imaginative policy, and that whatever choice was made at the election, we must not let the Drum Street legacy pass to another generation.

Almost a generation later, the Drum Street legacy is less common, but not extinguished. Nor has Britain come anywhere near to an economic miracle, as in 1963 and 1964 we hoped it might. We have not even achieved a steady rate of growth. The national will has never been mobilised. But the 'New Britain' articles were worth writing and publishing, and indeed the phrase became a cliché by the end of the 1964 election.

The 1964 general election

Two issues dominated the 1964 election – the economy and nuclear weapons. The 'New Britain' ran a good third. After the 1959 election Harold Macmillan had looked towards entering Europe as the way to economic salvation, but after long negotiations de Gaulle had slammed the door in his face. Alec Douglas-Home promised continuing prosperity through the modernisation of industry, regional incentives, and an incomes policy (unspecified) to curb inflation. Harold Wilson called for a more active central direction of industry, with tax incentives to stimulate exports, better credit terms, and a more rapid application of scientific discovery. It was a choice between slightly tired Conservatives and the Wilson 'tomorrow's men'.

The nuclear debate was livelier than in 1959, for the Prime Minister was more at home in the fields of foreign policy and defence than with economics. Maintenance of the British independent deterrent and the right to decide for ourselves were his frequent theme. Early in the campaign he declared that the Conservatives would 'never hand over the right to decide our future to another country', nor would we ever 'hand over Britain's defences'. That provoked us, in a leader, into asking four questions.

First, did Sir Alec mean that Britain's forces must be strong enough to defend us in all circumstances, without relying on the alliance? We believed he could hardly want to go as far as that, for apart from the enormous cost of such a policy our small and compact island was bound to remain vulnerable in a nuclear era. As in the past, greater security was offered through the Atlantic alliance. Second, did Sir Alec mean that Britain must retain a veto over all alliance decisions? We had no such veto now and were unlikely ever to be granted it. The right course was to work for closer consultation within the alliance, on which Mr Wilson seemed to have thought out his course more fully than Sir Alec.

Third, in the absence of a veto did Sir Alec mean that Britain must retain the right to stand aside from allied decisions or allied action? In practice every nation had that right; but it would be more difficult for Britain to stand aside than, say, for Norway just because we were one of the key elements in the alliance. And even if we tried to stand aside we might find ourselves dragged in by events. Geography and historic associations reinforced the case for seeking more effective consultation within NATO and in Washington. Fourth, did Sir Alec really mean that Britain must retain the right in the last resort to act alone? The precedents were unfortunate – the most recent having been Suez in 1956. In the last resort any Government, Conservative or Labour, could withdraw the British V-bombers from NATO. In essence, we said, Sir Alec overrated the importance of independent action and underrated the need to strengthen the alliance.

Mr Wilson's approach was to seek interdependence rather than independence in nuclear defence. Along with the *Guardian* – and partly because of its advocacy – he regarded the separate deterrent as a costly waste. With the Americans already providing nineteen-twentieths of NATO's nuclear protection, there was no value in further duplication. The occasions when Britain might want to act alone were now remotely hypothetical. The Republicans' choice of Senator Goldwater as their Presidential candidate – their elections were due one month after ours – had caused us some concern. But even Goldwater did not want to dismantle the alliance; and even thinking 'two Presidents ahead', as one must, the case against separate deterrent seemed strong. Sir Alec continued to speak of nuclear weapons as giving Britain a 'ticket' to the top conference tables, but in a leader the *Guardian* quoted the old comment that when Oliver Franks (now Lord Franks) was ambassador in Washington he was worth the whole of Bomber Command, because his advice was known to be shrewd and was trusted. No less, a solvent and prosperous Britain was likely to carry as much weight in the world as a nuclear Britain.

Over the previous eighteen months I had had a number of private discussions with Harold Wilson on this topic, as with Hugh Gaitskell earlier, and I was confident that Wilson had planned the way he would negotiate within the alliance. Especially after the experience of the Cuban missile crisis two years earlier, it was essential to find means of access to the decision-making process in Washington, day by day. The President was bound to insist on handling a crisis from his own headquarters. And the McNamara doctrine of a 'flexible response' – keeping open a choice of action – made crisis decisions still more important. Hence the need for a more subtle approach than Sir Alec's to the way the British involved themselves in alliance decisions through Washington.

In August Leonard Beaton (by then at the Institute for Strategic Studies, but still writing occasionally for the *Guardian*, and always very welcome when he came to call) had written a pair of articles for us on what he called 'An Alliance War Cabinet'. His proposal was for a small secretariat in Washington, parallel with the staff of the National Security Council, and for frequent meetings of NATO Prime Ministers or senior Ministers within that framework. In June Leonard had spent some time in Washington and Ottawa, and while the ideas were his own he had discussed them with members of the policy planning staff in the State Department and others in the White House. I thought he was on the right track. Harold Wilson, in a discussion at the beginning of September, also favoured Leonard's concept but was wary of putting anything so precise forward during the election campaign. Afterwards, as will be seen in the next chapter, he was readier to embrace the idea.

In his election speeches, Wilson preferred to concentrate his attack on the state of the national economy and on the Prime Minister's performance. But he devoted one major speech to the nuclear issue and was questioned from time to time at his press conferences. He spoke of the need for nuclear sharing within the alliance, for more effective consultation in Washington, and for the creation of stand-by forces for the United Nations. He also spoke of the need to renegotiate the 1962 Nassau agreement, and that caused some confusion – not least because the Nassau agreement itself was long and at one or two vital points ambiguous.[2]

During the election Wilson declined to be drawn too far on what he meant by renegotiation. He did, however, make clear that the Polaris programme would be reviewed and if cancellation or conversion were too

2 The Nassau meeting in 1962 had been held in a strained atmosphere just before Christmas chiefly because of the British Government's anger and embarrassment when Skybolt failed – for Skybolt, carried by the V-bombers, was to have constituted the British independent deterrent. At Nassau, somewhat reluctantly, Kennedy had agreed to let Macmillan have Polaris (less warheads) instead. He made the concession because in 1960 Macmillan had let the Americans have their base for Polaris submarines at the Holy Loch, on the Clyde, in return for the promise of Skybolt. But until Nassau the Americans had set themselves against providing any further nuclear weapons (or launchers) to any individual country, though they were willing to provide them for a multilateral NATO force with multinational manning and control (the so-called 'MLF'). Nassau damaged Kennedy's policies both for fostering West European unity and for stopping further independent forces. And, though Macmillan did not foresee it, Nassau finally torpedoed the Common Market negotiations at that time – for de Gaulle saw it as proof that the British cared more for their 'special relationship' with the United States than for Europe. For two versions of Nassau, see Macmillan *At the End of the Day*, pp. 355-62 and 553-55 (text of agreement); and Schlesinger's *A Thousand Days*, pp. 860-66.

costly the submarines would be completed and 'irrevocably' assigned to NATO. This would mean revision of Clause 8 of the agreement, which gave Macmillan and Sir Alec their right to withdraw the British submarines from NATO when 'supreme national interests' were at stake.

Through an irony that was not lost on me, Alec Douglas-Home made one of his major speeches on the bomb at Belle Vue, Manchester, not far from the *Guardian*'s offices. Harold Macmillan had done the same in 1959. But whereas Macmillan had spoken of the non-nuclear club as 'completely unrealistic', Sir Alec appeared to approve of it. Not only that, but he spoke of the Irish resolutions at the United Nations Assemblies (1959, 1960, and 1961) as the possible basis of a treaty to stop the spread. The difference, of course, was that he now took the British independent deterrent as an accomplished fact and outside the negotiations. While we welcomed his partial conversion, in the *Guardian* we preferred Harold Wilson's approach. We also reminded Sir Alec that without greater prosperity and a better economic performance Britain's status at the 'top tables' was bound to be in jeopardy.

The economy in the end occupied more newspaper columns and more platform wordage than the nuclear issues. Could Britain's industries be mobilised more effectively and exports be stimulated? Were Labour's plans for import-saving likely to work, and which party could generate a higher rate of growth without fuelling inflation?

The *Guardian*'s disenchantment with Conservative economic policy was expressed in a leader right at the beginning of the election. The sight of the Prime Minister grappling with the thorny problems of the British economy, it said, 'suggests nothing so much as a rather puzzled housemaster trying to put down smoking among his prefects'. The smallest extra effort from each individual, he had announced in his constituency, would increase national earnings to a point which ensured that prosperity continued. His proposition had a classic simplicity but left a great deal out of account. From 1951 to 1962, when the Conservatives belatedly decided to set up the National Economic Development Council to plan for growth, the Government had believed as an article of faith that the way to run the economy was by the law of the market, with the minimum of interference. In 1951, the leader recalled, the Conservatives were the party which would 'set the people free', and in 1955 and 1959 they were the party whose 'freedom worked'. They had dismantled the rudimentary structure of planning developed under Attlee; and, more important, they had deliberately turned their backs on the ethic of 'fair shares'. Those who had benefited most under the Conservatives were by no means the ones whose 'efforts' were of most value to the community. The rich had become notably richer, especially those with the sharpest eye to the main chance; and while the poor had not become poorer, 'they did not become less poor at anything like the same speed.' We believed that a new direction was needed to evoke the effort of which Sir Alec spoke.

From the beginning, in this election, the *Guardian*'s position was made plain. We wanted a Labour victory, because we believed it would bring better economic management and a fairer society, and we also wanted a 'solid block' of Liberals in the House of Commons. As before, we tried to see that editorial views did not colour the reporting.

The paper was bright and lively throughout the election (or so I thought, and still think having looked back at the files). There was first-class cover from the reporters out with the party leaders and in the constituency surveys. Tony Howard's guide for constituency students was reissued, slightly revised, as it was again in 1966 and 1970. One light-hearted bonus we enjoyed in this election – a Horner daily strip cartoon, Horner having come over to us from the *News Cronicle*. He poked fun at the Conservative party and Laboratory party candidates in equal measure, and at one point had a witch thinking of turning both lots into pigs but deciding that they would get the party votes just the same. The Stock Exchange provided less cheerful headlines towards polling day, as shares lost value on the expectation of a Labour victory.

The Nuffield book on the election – with David Butler and Anthony King as its main authors and Alan Beith on the press – says this of the *Guardian*'s coverage:

> Although occasional comment seeped into the news columns, it was usually confined to the editorial. Such criticism as can be made of the *Guardian*'s objectivity in campaign reporting would be prompted only by occasional imbalances in the selection and presentation of news. The *Guardian*'s high-minded policy of giving prominence only to those issues which it wished to be considered important, and its emphasis on the economic crisis probably worked more to Mr Wilson's benefit than exhaustive reporting of his campaign would have done. On a more partisan note, Papas contributed numerous cartoons of a horned, tailed, Satanic Sir Alec; the *Guardian* also produced an envied scoop on October 2 when it published extracts from a 'suppressed' report by Mr John Corbett containing criticisms of the Government's dealings with BOAC.

The voting was close, giving Labour 317 seats, the Conservatives 304, and the Liberals 9. The Liberals' popular vote had almost doubled, to more than three million, but they gained only three new seats. At least, though, they were bound to be of some account while the Government had an overall majority of only five.

On polling day and the day after, nuclear shadows again hung over the world. On Friday, October 16, the *Guardian*'s front-page headline, with the election results still not final, said 'Khrushchev out: Wilson in?' And indeed the sudden removal from office of Nikita Khrushchev was the lead story, while the British election hung in the balance. The Central Committee in Moscow was exacting its price for Khrushchev's misjudgements over the Cuban missiles and over the ideological conflict with China. Next day, along with the final count in Britain, the *Guardian* reported that China had exploded her first atomic bomb in the Sinkiang desert. A few days later our front page carried a map prepared by the American Atomic Energy Commission, showing radioactive fallout from the Sinkiang desert stretching two-thirds of the way round the northern hemisphere and covering most of Canada. At the same time, though on a different plane, the paper's Rome correspondent reported the Pope's ecumenical conference under the headline 'Hell still the great deterrent'. But man could create his own hell, and we wanted to avert it.

5 Tickets to Washington and Bonn

To be told personally by the President of the United States that he did not know what to do next in Vietnam was extraordinary. To be told that he wanted 'the British flag' alongside the American flag on the battlefields of Vietnam, when previously there had been no public hint of this whatever, was worrying. And to be told that the British Government had made serious mistakes of economic management in the past six weeks, with adverse effects on the United States, was more worrying still. That was, however, my experience soon after the 1964 British general election – which was followed by the American Presidential election in which Lyndon Johnson won a landslide victory. The talk with Johnson in the White House came chiefly because of the *Guardian*'s interest in nuclear policy and the Atlantic alliance, and it immediately preceded Wilson's first visit to Washington as Prime Minister. How it happened and what followed are the substance of this chapter.

Sterling crisis and Chequers meeting

The afternoon that Wilson arrived at Downing Street, even before he began the formal appointment of Cabinet Ministers, he was presented with the Treasury's forward estimate of the British balance of payments deficit. It was more than twice as bad as the worst of Labour's expectations during the election campaign – a deficit not of £400 millions for the current year but of £800 millions. With total sterling reserves at no more than £1,000 millions, it created an acutely difficult situation. Neither press nor public knew of this until ten days later, when the Government issued its first economic statement. This was in fairly neutral terms but still came as a considerable shock. Because the new Parliament was not yet in session, the statement was published simply as a White Paper, and the new Chancellor of the Exchequer, James Callaghan, held a press conference to explain it.

The statement said that, having taken stock of the situation, the Government were satisfied that with the resources available 'the strength of sterling can and will be maintained'. This was an immediate and direct reply to those who expected Labour to devalue the pound. But the statement went on to announce a temporary 15 per cent surcharge on all imports except food, tobacco, and basic raw materials, together with a tax rebate scheme to assist exporters. It also announced the start of consultations with industry on an incomes policy and the imminent creation of a price review body. The previous Chancellor, Reginald Maudling, issued his own statement saying that while there was 'an element of exaggeration' in the balance of payments estimates (in fact prepared by the Treasury before they knew who had won the election), he was not opposed in principle to the Government's measures. In the *Guardian* we accepted them as necessary.

The reaction abroad, however, was highly adverse. Next day the Secretary-General of EFTA said that the measures were a contravention of the 1961 Stockholm treaty and 'illegal'. He was followed by the European Commission, which said that the British action was 'not appropriate' and ought to have been preceded by consultation, and the European Coal and Steel Authority also said that the measures were a serious obstacle to trade. Hostile statements from a number of otherwise friendly Governments came in the next few days, including one from the Irish Prime Minister describing the surcharge as 'a body blow'.

A fortnight later the Chancellor introduced a form of autumn Budget. This increased pensions and social benefits, as promised, and improved the tax allowances in relation to dependants. It also put up the petrol tax by sixpence a gallon at once and proposed a sixpenny increase in the basic rate of income tax from April. It announced that the new Capital Gains Tax would apply from April and that Corporation Tax would replace other forms of company taxation. Again, in the *Guardian* we accepted these as reasonable measures in keeping with the Government's declared intentions. But immediately after the Chancellor's statement the flight from sterling became deadly.

So much so that it upset the Prime Minister's preparations for a study weekend at Chequers on defence policy, in readiness for his Washington visit. I saw him both on the Thursday before the Chequers gathering and on the Thursday after, and on the intervening days the sterling crisis dominated the headlines. On the first Thursday, although he admitted that the weakness of sterling had been his biggest worry in the past week, he remained reasonably optimistic. He had made his own Guildhall speech at the Lord Mayor's banquet at the beginning of the week, deliberately making its main theme the Government's determination to 'keep sterling strong and see it riding high', and he believed that that had stopped the run. But I had been warned by the *Guardian*'s financial editor, Richard Fry, that the position was again deteriorating – and Harold said that some of the European bankers, who after the Guildhall speech had expected that the British bank rate would go up that day, were now selling sterling because it hadn't. It was something that the authorities would have to watch.

Watch it they did, all day Friday and until 3 am on Saturday, as he told me a week later. By then they were at Chequers, and he had agreed with the Chancellor and George Brown that they must raise bank rate first thing on Monday. They had to get American acceptance for it; and the Treasury Minister in Washington, Sir Eric Roll, was just about to leave to return to London as George Brown's permanent secretary in the new Department of Economic Affairs, which was being carved out of the

Treasury. Eric Roll was already on the plane, and according to Harold they'd had to get BOAC to divert it late on Friday night so that he could return to Washington. (In fact it was not quite so dramatic, for he was intercepted while changing planes in New York and spoke to Wilson at Chequers from there, though on an open line so that they had to talk in parables which fortunately Roll understood.) The reasons for the British action were put to the American authorities on the Saturday morning, Wilson said, and they'd readily given their approval to an increase in British bank rate from five to seven per cent. He remarked that they had been very good about it, which did not entirely accord with what Lyndon Johnson told me a fortnight later.

But the Monday change of bank rate did not succeed. The attack on sterling continued to develop. 'We were in the dark about the enemy,' Wilson said. He believed that some Tory ex-Ministers were 'in it up to the neck', for they'd been asked for advice by big international companies and had said Labour's policies would not work.[1] He drew a bitter contrast between this behaviour and the way the Labour party had helped to defend sterling after Suez. He went on to tell me – with great relish – about a meeting on Tuesday night with Lord Cromer, the Governor of the Bank of England. He was sure that no Governor in this century had been talked to like that. As soon as the Governor was in the Cabinet room Wilson had asked why the Bank was not operating in the forward market. Lord Cromer had given his reasons, which to the Prime Minister had seemed poor. He had said that the crisis was being caused by lack of confidence in the Prime Minister and Labour Government. Asked what steps were wanted, Cromer had said that to restore confidence there must be extreme deflationary measures – more severe than Selwyn Lloyd's in 1961. It was the only way.

Wilson had said 'no'. It was the wrong policy and he would not accept it, for it amounted to saying that a democratic election in this country counted for nothing. The country could elect whomever it liked so long as it was a Conservative Government. Was the Governor saying that the country had to be ruled by the international bankers? He had told the Governor, he said, that he would go to the country on this issue; economic expansion had been a main issue in the election only six weeks ago and the country's verdict ought not to be repudiated. He would come back with a huge majority. The Governor, he said, was horrified. The Prime Minister had added that during the election sterling would be on 'floating' rates, which Lord Cromer said would wreck not only sterling but the whole European system. Wilson had replied that it was the City's choice, not his.

On Wednesday – the day before – the attack on sterling had gone on. In the evening he had called a small meeting of Ministers, expecting to

---

1 This is, of course, Harold Wilson's version; but I know of no reason to doubt its accuracy.

have to take bitter decisions. Just as they had assembled the message had come through that the central banks were making available a massive credit. Obviously the Governor, having slept on the matter, had been telephoning to the other bankers and this was the result. Probably he had told the others that he had 'a raving lunatic' to deal with as Prime Minister but had also told them that Wilson meant what he said. The tough line had paid off better than he expected. There was no ground for euphoria, he said – though he seemed in an unusually cheerful state – for we had only won an opportunity and must use it.

We went on to talk that second Thursday about the Chequers meeting and defence, but as soon as I got back to the office I set about making sure that the measures of international support for the pound were properly covered. I need not have worried. Richard Fry and his City Office team, who had in fact reported the central bankers' action that morning were ready with extensive reports for the Friday paper. Richard had gleaned a great deal from the Bank of England and other financial sources, as well as from friends in Zurich. Alistair Cooke, too, came in with a long report from Wall Street on 'how the pound was saved'. And to top it all, looking ahead, John Cole had prepared a leader-page article on our industrial performance and exports, indicating what must be done internally to give Britain a good reputation abroad. The background provided by the PM was nevertheless invaluable; and wary though one must be in contact with Ministers, who are looking for favourable publicity, the safeguards lie in one's own judgement and their realisation that to give unsound information is short-sighted.

On the defence front, I had myself written two long articles in the previous week (before seeing the Prime Minister), on the coming Chequers meeting and the choices before Britain. I said that the renegotiation of Nassau was probably not now of the first importance, since the Polaris programme was likely to be already beyond the point of no return.[2] While assigning the Polaris submarines and the V-force to NATO, the Prime Minister ought to concentrate on the questions of political control and crisis management. He should endeavour to seek a British seat on the National Security Council or the President's executive committee – or better still four seats, giving one each for Britain, France, West Germany, and the fourth for a representative of the remaining NATO nations. Much must depend on personal relationships, but since any major crisis was bound to be run by the President, backed by a group of advisers, it was better to be there beside him.

When we discussed the matter before the Chequers meeting, Wilson

2 Just after the election, one of the out-going Conservative Defence Ministers had told Mark Arnold-Forster that Wilson would find there was no cash saving in cancelling any of the first three Polaris submarines, and the operational advantages of having a fourth were so great as to be almost irresistible.

seemed to me to be drifting somewhat towards the Douglas-Home position. He declared himself still in favour of some form of 'Alliance War Cabinet', but said that he must first establish his working relations with Johnson. He had already been talking on his own direct line to the White House, and he must begin by making this a close relationship. Asked whether he saw this as an exclusively British matter, he said it was: it was something he must work up for himself as an individual and for Britain as an individual country. And although publicly he intended to hold to the 'irrevocable' assignment of all our nuclear weapons to NATO – partly in order to prevent the coming of the MLF – he nevertheless knew that none of the channels of communication with the submarines would remain wholly British and by that means we could retain control over them.[3] The 'double key' system meant that the missiles could not be fired without NATO's consent and our consent, but the British channel of communication meant that, in his phrase, the submarines could be told 'The Queen wants you' and would then return home.

After Chequers he was further along his 'personal' line. The President had sent Richard Neustadt, one of Kennedy's men, across to prepare the ground for the Washington meeting, and Wilson saw this as an indication of the way he should move. He must get to know the President and his senior advisers closely, so that in emergencies he could hop on a plane and take part in White House discussions – perhaps in the National Security Council or the executive committee. He intended also to have an ambassador of ministerial level in Washington – someone, he said, who could be a kind of 'War Cabinet Minister'. This seemed to me to differ little from the way Oliver Franks and Ormsby Gore (Harlech) had already been used. He said he was not going to try to negotiate anything formal, because that would diminish his chances of individual success.

As to the MLF, he was still against British participation and hoped to persuade Johnson that our assignment of our nuclear forces to NATO diminished the need for the MLF. He acknowledged that the Under-Secretary of State, George Ball, was still pressing hard for an MLF that could lead to a separate European deterrent. But, Wilson said, if there was any sign of the Americans lifting their veto over the use of the MLF – giving the decision to the Europeans on some weighted voting system, electronically controlled, for example – then Britain would withdraw its nuclear forces. Irrevocable, clearly, was not going to be irrevocable. On his main-point, however, I judged that the Prime Minister was being too optimistic in expecting to pare down the MLF. Having sat next to the American Ambassador, David Bruce, at a dinner earlier in the week – and he had had to take a telephone call from George Ball in the middle

3 The MLF was to be NATO's multilateral, mixed-manned nuclear force (see Chapter 4, footnote on page 99); the ANF, or Atlantic nuclear force, was Wilson's alternative. The ANF was to consist of American and British units only, under a multinational command but without mixed manning.

of dinner – I believed the MLF to have strong supporters in Washington. In the end, the Prime Minister proved even more successful than he himself foresaw.

Finally, since I was due to leave for New York and Washington at the weekend, with a provisional appointment to see the President on Wednesday, he wished me luck. He asked me to come to see him as soon as I got back to London. That would be about forty-eight hours before his own departure for Washington, and he wanted to discuss my findings first.

Pentagon, State, and Capitol Hill

My first calls were at the United Nations headquarters in New York, to discuss UN peacekeeping operations with U Thant, General Rikkye, and Brian Urquhart. These talks were important in the later shaping of *Guardian* policy but are not relevant here. (Rikkye's analysis of the real needs of a multinational UN force was fascinating.) Plainly, the proper establishment of UN peacekeeping forces was far away.

In Washington next day I received the first indication that Vietnam was to be on the agenda for the Prime Minister's visit, though he did not know it. The Defence Secretary, Robert McNamara, was forthright. People who wanted a share in crisis decisions, he said, must take a share in the action. The United States could not continue to carry the whole load in South-east Asia, for 'our people' would not stand for it. It was politically unsound for the Americans to be acting alone in that area without the willing support of others. The British ought to be taking a share instead of talking of reducing commitments east of Suez. I countered by saying that in Malaysia we felt we had been left to carry the whole burden. McNamara replied that we could have had more help there if we, in turn, had shared in Vietnam.

Richard Scott was with me, having lately taken over as Washington correspondent preparatory to Max Freedman's departure to become a freelance – and later an adviser to the Canadian Prime Minister, Lester Pearson. Richard asked the Defence Secretary whether he wanted military or economic help in Vietnam. McNamara replied that 'British squadrons' were wanted there, though it was not clear whether he meant fighters, bombers, or naval units – or simply a visible British military presence. He said that the American casualties in that area since the Second World war amounted to 175,000 (presumably including Korea), which was more than even the French had suffered in ending their hold on Indo-China.

While Richard and I were separately digesting this bolt, I brought the conversation back to crisis decisions in the North Atlantic context. McNamara said that you could not participate in crisis management 'unless you participate in the tools and the assets'. So I asked whether assignment to NATO's nuclear forces of our V-bombers and Polaris submarines was not enough, to which he said he would want to look at the terms and conditions of the assignment. He then made a scathing comment on Wilson's speech in the Commons defence debate a week ago, in which the Prime Minister expressed outright opposition to the MLF. The Foreign Secretary, Gordon Walker, had said in Washington that the British forces could join with the MLF in an Atlantic nuclear command. But here was Wilson saying the opposite.

To this I replied that Wilson was stonewalling in reply to an Opposition motion. In the Commons debate he had said nothing that he had not said publicly during the election campaign, and he was taking care not to pre-empt his own discussions in Washington. (George Ball's call to Ambassador Bruce had been on the same point, and since I had been in the House that afternoon and had written a leader immediately afterwards, before going to the dinner, I had made the same comment to Bruce who did not know exactly what had been said.) McNamara replied that that was not good enough. Wilson was now Prime Minister, and he and the Foreign Secretary could not say different things to the United States.

The Defence Secretary said that it would be good for the Germans to share in the MLF. It would give them a sense of involvement, and it embodied American integration with Europe. He did not believe that the MLF could or should develop into a separate European nuclear force. On the contrary, he said, the Germans were anxious to tie the Americans in to Europe so that it was impossible for them to withdraw. At this point I could not help wondering whether it was all right for McNamara and George Ball to say different things, but of course I had heard only Wilson's account of George Ball's view.

Having been escorted out through the strict security checks that guarded the inner core of the Pentagon, Richard and I walked back across the Potomac in the brisk December sun. We went on to a long series of meetings in the State Department, where I got the impression that the *Guardian*'s brains were being well washed to try to favour the MLF, and then to a more sociable meeting with Senator Fulbright on Capitol Hill.

The State Department men were all very friendly, and there were no hard words about Harold Wilson. (We did not see either Dean Rusk or George Ball.) Ambassador Gerard Smith, who was in charge of MLF affairs, took me through all the British objections to the scheme. Was it a superfluous addition to American deterrents? No, because it would let the United States cut back on its Minuteman programme.[4] Did it amount to nuclear proliferation? No, because the safeguards built into the system with mixed manning and international control meant that no one nation had access to the weapons by itself. There was no question of the United States giving up its veto over firing. Might the US not withdraw later, leaving the force as a European deterrent? That was not intended and the Germans were wholly against it. What about cost? The US was ready to

4 Minuteman, a land-based intercontinental ballistic missile. Range 6,000 to 7,000 miles. About 1,000 still deployed in US, 1981.

help with Britain's Polaris costs if we would contribute some naval personnel to the mixed-manned force, where their skills would be valuable. Would not the MLF's ships – they were to be surface ships, not submarines – be vulnerable? No, because they were to be exceptionally fast and could use inshore waters and straits to shake off pursuit.

Ambassador Smith's exposition of the control system was also technically fascinating. In brief, it amounted to a computerised system with a whole series of safeguards, but with separate national channels from each head of government to the master computer and a weighted authorisation system under which there had to be, say, a 75 or 80 per cent 'affirmative' including the US affirmative before the firing mechanisms could operate. It reminded me also that Robert McNamara had said that the system must be capable of reaching decisions in not more than half an hour.

Henry Owen, deputy chairman of the Policy Planning Staff, was with Ambassador Smith most of the time. He had read my articles on an 'Alliance War Cabinet' and crisis management, but he said that I had modelled them too much on the experience of the 1962 Cuban crisis. Each President, he said, worked in a different way; and although the Executive Committee of the National Security Council had been the significant body then, his impression was that President Johnson would now work with a smaller group, preferring more intimate consultation.

That was echoed when we went to call on Senator Fulbright, chairman of the Foreign Relations Committee, at his office on Capitol Hill – the kind of office that in Britain only a Minister would enjoy, though senior Senators after all are as influential as most British Ministers, if not more so. He said that Johnson tended to lean on a small number of close advisers such as Acheson and McGeorge Bundy. Richard was quick to take up Acheson's name, for although an outstanding Secretary of State he had been out of harness for twelve years and now had a rather conservative and hard-line reputation. Fulbright seemed both amused and slightly embarrassed at this, but did not retract it at all. He clearly had a good regard for Mac Bundy, too.

Fulbright said – presciently, as it turned out – that he did not think Johnson himself was enthusiastic about the MLF. The drive was coming from others. For his own part Fulbright did not feel strongly about it; if the Europeans wanted it, he said, then let it go ahead. But he felt that it should not have been pressed so hard. Towards the new British Government he seemed well disposed, asking a number of questions about it. But, as I had found years before, with his Oxford background and interest in British affairs Fulbright was always congenial to talk to.

One other chance encounter was with a very senior British officer whom I had also known some time before. He was attending a NATO session on nuclear matters at the Pentagon. The trouble was, he said, that only the Americans and British understood the tactical aspects at all. The others of the thirteen just made set speeches which were a bore. Even the

French still seemed to think that if a couple of Bulgarian battalions crossed the Thracian border you had to hit Moscow with a nuclear attack. It might be good for NATO's tactical thinking if it had to forget about the strategic weapons.

Next day – Wednesday, December 2 – I was due to see the President at the White House in the afternoon. Richard Scott and Max Freedman were coming with me. I had dictated notes into a little recorder late the previous night, and to clear our heads Richard and I had a good walk in the morning. So far as I can remember we went along by the Potomac again from his house in Georgetown and down by the Lincoln monument. It was cold but invigorating.

After lunch, having been checked through an unusually tight security cordon at the White House, we had a short session first with McGeorge Bundy. He had remained at the White House after Kennedy's death, continuing as the President's special adviser on international affairs. He told us at once that 'upstairs' we would be hearing about Vietnam. He confirmed that the Administration wanted Britain in and that this was not just McNamara's own thought. He was sceptical about Wilson's ideas on an Atlantic nuclear force, saying 'You're giving us nothing new'. America's commitment on its Polaris submarines was just as 'irrevocable' as ours.

One other aside from Mac Bundy, during a few words on crisis management. He suggested that whatever Wilson might feel de Gaulle would rather be 'vapourised' than take part in any National Security Council or Executive Committee proceedings in Washington. And with that it was time to go upstairs.

Lyndon Johnson

LBJ was not in the sunny mood of two years ago. He seemed tired and grumpy. He received us not in the oval office, as with Kennedy, but in a tiny room next door. It was rather dark, and he seemed to be just waking up from an after-lunch nap. Beside him were three small television screens, with the picture from each of the three main channels running all the time, and he could punch up the sound of any of them when he wanted it. He hardly ever looked at Richard or me – only at Max or the floor or the TV monitors. He seemed to be having trouble with his throat and complained of asthma. He telephoned for hot coffee ('Sanka') twice at the start and was quite ratty because it did not come at once.

At midday he had been at the Arlington cemetery, at an earth-moving ceremony to start the Kennedy memorial, and the cold seemed to have got into him. Max warmly congratulated him on his speech but chided him for standing in the open without his overcoat. The President said he was wearing a heavy English suit especially for the occasion, and he showed us the Savile Row label inside, though it was mostly concealed by the eight or nine pens he was carrying in his pocket. He bantered with

Max, saying that he didn't come down to stay at the ranch in Texas as he used to, because Max daren't bring his beautiful new wife.[5] It took him a little time to get round to anything of real substance. His style was rather like a Welsh non-conformist sermon, going round in seemingly great discursive circles but gradually homing in on the message. But the message was there all right.

He complained at first of continuous misrepresentation in the press, especially during the election campaign, citing examples from the *New York Times*, *Newsweek*, and others. Why did they do it? The press should look on the leaders of the nations – embracing, it seemed, Wilson, Erhard, and de Gaulle as well as himself – as men of goodwill confronted by very great tasks and should write about them with better understanding. He mentioned Wilson specifically for the first time, saying he knew him and hoped to get on well with him.

He then talked about his personal security. Even at the White House he was not supposed to stand or sit by the windows. During the campaign he often stopped to meet people in the crowds and there was little risk in that, for unplanned and unscheduled stops were not dangerous. Nobody was going to knife him or shoot him then. If people in their thousands came to see him, he felt he must stop to talk to some of them. In any event, the Secret Service surrounded him as soon as he got out of the car. The danger, he said, was on occasions like today – when he was standing still, up on a platform, with only 150 or 180 people around him. He could be shot at from the highways. He seemed much preoccupied by the risks. Perhaps that was not too surprising, since it was the Kennedy memorial occasion.

He spoke of his work in the past two days and its range. Yesterday he'd begun with Asia, mainly Vietnam, and ended with commerce; today he'd started on Africa and ended on money, with most of the day taken by economic troubles. He'd had a meeting with his economic advisers before going to Arlington. Of the British Government, he said that they were good men but had made a bad beginning. They had put Britain into a bad situation, which was affecting the United States. Wilson had put up British interest rates, so the United States had had to do it too. It did not mean a recession, he said, but there was a serious risk of still higher interest rates, lower capital investment, lower production, higher prices – and so onwards to a slump. He would have to discuss this with the Prime Minister. He sounded excessively gloomy about the outlook. His morning session with his economic advisers had not been cheerful.

He moved obliquely onwards. There were difficult problems to be discussed with the Prime Minister, he said, but he believed they could meet each other's needs and resolve their mutual difficulties. Neither

5 Max had married the widow of Herb Elliston, editorial page editor of the *Washington Post*.

should take a hard and final stand; both should speak freely but be ready to accommodate each other. Had we seen the reports of his press conference at the weekend? We had. He drew attention to his statement that he was taking up no adamant attitudes; on which reporters had asked him about Mr Wilson's advance bid to block the MLF. Neither of them should be taking up fixed positions beforehand. I started to try once again to explain that the Prime Minister was stonewalling in reply to an Opposition motion in the Commons, but Johnson waved that aside. He appeared much irritated about it.

With Alec Douglas-Home he had had some good visits, he said. But last time Douglas-Home had gone out from the President's office and told the press that he had said 'no' to Johnson on not selling buses to Cuba. If the Prime Minister had said that Britain had to live by trade and that sort of thing to explain his position, then it would have been acceptable. Crowing and boasting were not acceptable.[6] After the coming visit as President he could say 'Ah screwed Wilson', or Wilson could say 'Ah screwed him'. But it would do neither of them one bit of good.[7]

Coming round in another of his full circles he referred to untrue press reports about Maxwell Taylor's visit. Maxwell Taylor was then US Ambassador in Saigon, having previously been Chairman of the Joint Chiefs of Staff. Taylor had flown back to Washington for consultations at the end of the previous week, because of the deteriorating situation in Vietnam. (The Americans at that time only had 'advisers' in Vietnam, though their aircraft and gunship helicopters were in regular action against the Vietcong and North Vietnamese.) According to Johnson, some of the press had said that Maxwell Taylor was coming back to thump the table and demand tougher American action, and to resign if the President did not agree. The Ambassador had been much upset by these reports, which he had seen while his plane was refuelling at Hawaii, and had phoned the President to say so. There was no 'Taylor plan'. They'd been talking much of yesterday morning, and Taylor had had 'no more goddam idea what to do than I have'.[7]

That was chilling enough. What came next was no better. Since the Buddhists, Roman Catholics, student groups, and armed forces in South Vietnam were frequently in conflict, they'd discussed this yesterday. He had told Dean Rusk 'to find the best Buddhists' to help with the Buddhists in Vietnam, 'to find the best Popes' to help with the Roman Catholics, and 'to find the best student groups' to help with the students. In Vietnam

6 Lord Home, in a letter to me in January 1981, says he told the President that we could not stop selling buses to Cuba. 'But what words I used I cannot remember; an unembroidered "no" is very unlikely.'

7 For Maxwell Taylor's view, as revealed through the *Pentagon Papers*, see pp. 326–38 and 370–73.

they could not go on waking up in the morning and starting the day with rioting and killing among themselves.

And what about the British? He said that the United States did not want to be there alone, 'in a colonialist position'. They wanted us there, too. Why had Britain only eight men in Vietnam, he asked. 'I sent for the roll,' he said, and Britain had eight, Canada only one, and Australia eleven. We ought to have two hundred or four hundred men there. Richard, remembering McNamara, asked whether he wanted 'a squadron or two'. Yes, said Johnson: 'We want your flag.' Britain should be in there, wherever freedom was being fought for, in the front line. They wanted the British and others to stand alongside them, to show that it was not an American colonialist action, and they wanted to draw on our experience in guerrilla warfare.

He had asked why Canada had only one man there. Yesterday he'd been given the reason – that the man was a member of the International Control Commission, in contact with the Russians. He accepted that and withdrew his criticism. But what about Australia? They had only eleven men there; but they were a great people. And here he set off on another of his long digressions, telling of his experiences in the war when he landed in Australia after his bomber group was shot up. He had landed on a sheep farm and he had been cared for by a Lady Brooke. Years later he had described her, without naming her, to Prime Minister Menzies. He had identified her at once. 'Ah like that Prime Minister Menzies,' he said. 'He's a good Prime Minister: he knows his constituents.' The Australians were a great people, and they should be with the Americans in Vietnam. He wanted their flag.

To find a way back from all this to NATO was not too easy, and my next question was perhaps too general. Did he see a link between Southeast Asia and Europe? Afterwards I could not recall the precise words, but the sense was plain. 'If you want us to be there in your front line when you are in trouble,' he said, 'you'd better be with us.'

Other topics were touched on. China – he objected to the British line, saying we were ready to let the Chinese 'shoot their way in' to the United Nations; but he was also totally against Joe Alsop's line in his syndicated column, which was (he said) that we should take care of Vietnam by bombing China. The Congo – another case where the United States was not backed as it should have been, for there were no British planes, no Canadian planes, no German planes, and only the Belgian paras. And de Gaulle – 'we must be patient'.

We had had almost an hour, and he seemed much more cheerful by the time we were leaving. He said that, unlike Joe Alsop, he did not believe that the end of the world was at hand. Joe believed that the alliance was about to break down, that we were going to lose in Vietnam, that the Germans would go nationalist, that a slump was coming in America, and all that. He didn't. These problems could be solved; and he was hoping for a good meeting with Prime Minister Wilson next week. He shook each of us by the hand and thanked us for coming to call on him – almost as if there was an election and each of us had a vote. But Max got a special farewell, and an injunction to come to see him again soon, before going off to Ottawa.

Reporting back

Outside, standing in Lafayette Square, we consulted Max. How much did he think the President intended for use in the *Guardian*, and how much only for relaying to Harold Wilson? Max had no hesitation. Everything was intended for 'unattributed' use, subject to some care with phrasing and discretion with detail. We must not say in the *Guardian* that we had been to see the President, because this had not been a formal interview, but he had no doubt that the President wanted the substance of his message relayed in the paper.

By then it was after 4 pm in Washington, so the *Guardian*'s first editions would soon be going to press in London and Manchester. We therefore decided to send nothing that night. Instead Richard and I set to work writing – in his case preparing a long front-page report, and in mine first making notes before dictating to my recorder and then writing a leader-page article to go with Richard's report. Since I was to fly out from Washington with the earliest flight to New York next morning, and then go straight on to London, we had little time to spare. All the copy, mine and Richard's, was to be left with him for transmission across the Atlantic next day. I could not risk taking any of it with me because my aircraft would not be landing in London next evening until just before that night's paper was going to press – and I was determined that the first results of our work must be published before I went to Downing Street on Friday morning.

On the transatlantic telephone from Washington I also had a short talk with Frank Edmead, the *Guardian*'s specialist on South-east Asia. He was less surprised than I had been by the request for British troops for Vietnam, but he was even more strongly against conceding anything to the President than I was. We agreed on the lines of a brief leader, to go in Friday's paper.

Richard's report duly appeared as the front-page lead on Friday morning, by which time I had had a short night's sleep back home in Blackheath. Under the headline 'British troops wanted for South Vietnam', it began:

Washington, Thursday

Mr Wilson will almost certainly be asked during his discussion with President Johnson here next week what he is prepared to do to help the United States to sustain South Vietnam against the Vietcong guerrillas and their Communist supporters, and in particular whether Britain will supply token units of troops and aircraft.

The Administration feels very strongly that the United States has for too long been left virtually alone in its defence of freedom in South-east Asia. In the case of Vietnam, the United States is definitely thinking in terms of military as well as moral and economic aid. . . .

The report went on to refer to the President's wish for 'more flags' alongside the American flag in Vietnam – not only the British flag, but if possible the Australian flag and others too.

The leader, picking up that theme, was headed 'No more flags for Vietnam'. It said that the answer 'can only be "no"'. The President's request was not prompted by belligerence: on the contrary, it testified to his agonised anxiety not to let the war get out of hand. He had constantly resisted pressure from his advisers to carry the war to North Vietnam. But additional flags would not solve the Administration's problems: they would merely involve other Governments in the collapse now threatened. Most Vietnamese, the leader said, were now utterly weary of the war. The only solution lay in negotiation among the Vietnamese themselves.

The neighbouring article, signed with my name and datelined from Washington, said that the Prime Minister would receive a friendly and attentive hearing, though he would be faced with the request for the Union Jack to fly beside the Stars and Stripes in Saigon. But it went on to deal with the NATO aspects of the meeting – with the hard bargaining to be expected over Wilson's proposal of an Atlantic Nuclear Force (American and British units only, assigned to a NATO multinational command). In spite of torpedoes launched recently by de Gaulle, Wilson himself, and Gromyko, I wrote, 'the MLF is still afloat'. The project – for twenty-five fast vessels armed with Polaris missiles and manned by multinational crews – still held an important place in American thinking. While the Prime Minister's broader proposal of an Atlantic force could be accepted, the MLF was still seen as a constituent part of it. And, I said, Wilson's speech in the Commons ten days earlier had gone down very badly in Washington where its parliamentary context was not understood.

The article went on to summarise the American position as it had been put to me by Robert McNamara, Ambassador Smith, Henry Owen, and others, though without naming any of them. It went through Gerald Smith's five main points in reply to British objections to the MLF, and outlined the safeguards that were to be built into the system. A second article, to deal with NATO's control of its nuclear forces and Britain's voice in Washington, was promised for next day.

On the flight home from New York I drafted the second article. Oliver Franks, former British Ambassador in Washington, was another passenger. He was far from happy about the way the arrangement with the European central bankers might work out. They had us 'by the short hairs', for the £1,000 million credit was renewable every three months. We had created hostility and resentment among the European Governments – not so much by imposing the 15 per cent surcharge as by failing to send Ministers (not just ambassadors or Notes) round the European capitals forty-eight hours beforehand to explain what we were doing. The Europeans did not believe that Wilson's measures would work. On the plane Franks wrote a letter to the Prime Minister and asked me to deliver it at Downing Street next day, which I did.

Next morning I went to Downing Street and was received, as usual, by Wilson alone in the Cabinet room. He had read his *Guardian* well, both the front-page report from Washington and the leader-page material. He said that there seemed to be 'a flap on' about Vietnam, and he wanted to know who had said what. When he had heard about McNamara, Mac Bundy, and the President, he asked whether that was the main message we had taken away from the White House. So I described Johnson's circuitous Texan equivalent of a Welsh sermon and said I thought its main message was on the need for both to speak freely and try to resolve their mutual difficulties. 'Yes,' said Wilson wryly, 'on his terms.'

On Vietnam I suggested that the Prime Minister might find himself with a delicate dilemma. The commitment, say, of two RAF squadrons was not large and we could surely spare them, buying immense goodwill from the Americans in doing so. But Vietnam seemed a hopeless case, where no amount of American intervention could succeed; and any association there would do great harm to Britain's standing with many nations in Africa and Asia. I thought we should keep out, but if Wilson felt that we ought to go in I was willing to turn the paper's line round over the next week or two. (It was an exceptional offer, made because of my sense that a sound start to Wilson's relations with Washington was vital.) To this Wilson said, referring to that morning's leader, 'You've given him the answer already, haven't you?' The *Guardian*'s answer that morning was the one the Government would have to give, he said, and there were other areas of the alliance where we could help the Americans.

He asked whether there had been any mention of bombing North Vietnam, and I said none. Contrary to some reports, Maxwell Taylor had apparently not brought back hard proposals. If they were to bomb the North, the PM said, the British position would be more difficult.[8]

On the MLF and the ANF, he said that he had had a clumsy visit from George Ball on Monday when I was in New York. Had the President said much about the MLF? I said not much: only indirectly and obliquely. George Ball, the PM said, had come here to discount the whole of our

8 Thanks to the *New York Times*'s publication of the *Pentagon Papers* in 1971, we now know that bombing of the North had been discussed at the White House meeting on December 1, 1964, because the generals in the Pentagon wanted it; Maxwell Taylor considered it a possibility but limited his support to proposals for bombing the supply routes from the North, and Lyndon Johnson was against it.

negotiating position in advance. He had told Wilson that the ANF was worthless, that the assignment of our Polaris submarines was nothing new, that the revocation of Clause 8 meant little, and that emphatically we must join the MLF. I told him that that was what we'd been hearing from McNamara and Bundy, and they were angry about his Commons speech. Wilson said he had had to talk straight to Ball, who was hard-headed and could take it. He was not going to negotiate until he reached Washington. If they told him that the ANF wa. 'worthless' then all bets were off. If they took that line then we would go back to the beginning, for we were not yet committed to completing the submarines. As to the Commons speech, the trouble was that Gordon Walker had gone too far in Washington and revealed the second stage of our negotiating position.

The PM said that he had been giving a lot of thought to how he would get on the right terms with the President. He hoped that the two could have the whole of Monday morning together by themselves, while their advisers met separately. (He was taking Denis Healey, Gordon Walker and Lord Mountbatten with him.) He wished to explain to Lyndon Johnson that, while they had both recently won elections, in Britain he would have to fight again soon. In the October election the Conservatives had chosen to fight on Nassau and Clause 8, with their independent deterrent, but Wilson had held the line for the alliance and for friendship with America. Johnson as a deft politician would understand. From the Washington meeting it must be clear that we had our seat at the top table and that the Administration did not share the Conservatives' Gaullist interpretation of Nassau. It must be clear also that we would be consulted next time there was a crisis of the Cuban kind.

When I doubted whether this could be achieved, since it was not something that could be put into a formal public commitment, Wilson disagreed. Wasn't it what I had been arguing for in the *Guardian*? They could set up machinery like my Alliance War Cabinet, though that was the wrong name for it. At any rate, Johnson must provide him with the answer to the Conservatives for the next election.

On the ANF/MLF controversy, he said that we were making a big concession to the Americans in completing the submarines and that should be acknowledged. They would be assigned to NATO on the same terms as the American submarines. If he had to, he would be prepared to put our 'eleven men' into the MLF at the same time (rather implying that it would be the third or fourth XI). But he still hoped to achieve what he had thought of in his bath during the election, which was to use the ANF to eliminate the MLF.

Finally, on monetary matters, I mentioned Johnson's concern with the risk of a recession and his comment that the British Government were 'good men' who had made 'a bad start'. Wilson said it was not true that we had caused them to raise their interest rates. We had deliberately refrained from raising bank rate during the American election because he knew that Johnson was a 'cheap money man', brought up in the Roosevelt tradition. And we had cleared the 15 per cent surcharge with them before imposing it. Then in the week of the Lord Mayor's banquet, when pressure on the pound had continued, we had again not raised bank rate because we had not secured American concurrence. It had had to wait until the Monday. (But in that case, I wondered, why all the flurry about getting Eric Roll off his plane at New York: he could have been asked to discuss it before leaving Washington if we were already thinking of it.) The PM appeared more put out about this part of Johnson's message than about others. He was nevertheless in a resilient mood in readiness for his departure on Sunday morning.

George Brown, with whom I had dinner a few days later, said that he had spent 'anguished hours' with Harold that Friday discussing Vietnam. In his view we ought to accede to the American request. We ought to 'go to the Yalu' with them, by which he meant that we should stand beside the Americans on the border between North and South Vietnam. I said (echoing Frank Edmead) that we should be involving ourselves in a civil war which the civil population did not want. George said that in principle we must back the Americans; but Harold was against it and party opinion was strongly against it. Considering George's own heavy tasks in establishing his Department of Economic Affairs, securing tripartite agreement on an incomes policy (its ratification must have been his main business with Harold), and starting work on his 'national plan' I judged that the 'hours' on Vietnam must be an exaggeration. But his conviction was real.

Saturday's *Guardian* carried a further leader, written by Frank Edmead, arguing that however much we might wish to support the Americans we must not become involved in Vietnam. It also carried my second signed article about decision-making in Washington. To cover the Prime Minister's visit jointly with Richard Scott, one of our two political correspondents, Ian Aitken, was on his way to Washington. He had previously worked there for the *Daily Express* and knew his way around. I was satisfied that the *Guardian* had given its readers greater insight into the issues than any other paper had done – as well as making its own contribution to governmental thinking on both sides of the Atlantic – and was well placed to cover a vital White House meeting effectively. So it proved.

Wilson gets most of his way

The Ian Aitken–Richard Scott joint report on Tuesday's front page was headed 'Off to a good start in Washington', and Wednesday's 'Now Mr Wilson must convince West Germany' – for already it was clear that the Prime Minister's Atlantic Nuclear Force was several lengths ahead of the MLF. Although the full story did not emerge until the Commons debate a fortnight later – by which time Ian Aitken had already done a remarkably good job in piecing most of it together – we knew that the MLF had lost its prime place in American policy. In fact, Harold Wilson's handling of his Washington and Bonn negotiations led to its burial. On that point he achieved even greater success than he foresaw in his September bath.

The agreement reached at the White House provided for an Atlantic Nuclear Force with four components: the British V-bombers, except for some reserved for use outside NATO; the British Polaris submarines; US Polaris submarines of at least equal number; and some form of mixed-manned or jointly owned element. The force was to be controlled by 'a single authority' in which all the contributing countries were to take part.

Of the mixed-manned element, the Prime Minister told the Commons that the Americans had not dropped their proposals for a surface fleet, but the British had entirely reserved their position and made no commitment. This aspect was to be the subject of further consultation, and the British view was that land-based weapons were preferable to sea-based. On this, therefore, Wilson in Washington had secured three-quarters of what he wanted and would now have the initiative in talking further to the European Governments – the Germans particularly.

On South-east Asia the White House communiqué was diplomatic: it recognised the importance of the military efforts which both countries were making 'in support of legitimate Governments in South-east Asia, particularly in Malaysia and South Vietnam'. And at his Washington press conference the Prime Minister replied entirely in terms of Malaysia, turning aside questions about Vietnam. In the Commons he indicated that Britain was to provide additional civil aid for South Vietnam. Plainly he had said 'no' to the President on combatants but was covering the issue up as discreetly as possible.

I saw him again at Downing Street the day after the Commons debate and he was in a jubilant mood. The start of his meetings with Lyndon Johnson had been harsh, he said. In the first minute when they were alone together, Johnson had brought up the business of Alec Home and the Cuban buses, and had said that he doubted whether he could ever trust a British Prime Minister again. For a time Wilson had doubted whether they were going to get anywhere. He had had to spend almost the whole of Monday trying to establish trust, instead of discussing specific proposals. But when they came to the ANF/MLF complex it turned out that the President did not want to discuss detail. Wilson had been filled with foreboding that Johnson might start by taking the George Ball line, saying that it was no use talking unless the British conceded first that the MLF was to be incorporated in the ANF and that they would take part in the mixed-manning. Johnson had not been like that at all, and therefore the British working paper on the ANF had been presented to the full meeting with their advisers later on. Nor was the President tough about Vietnam. He had put his request for British combatants and that, too, had been brought up at the full meeting in the afternoon. But by then Wilson was feeling safe enough to offer only civilian aid and to say that we could not 'hoist our flag there'.

Wilson told me that we would probably extend Brigadier Thompson's mission in Vietnam. He was the man who had devised the 'strategic hamlets' which had worked well in the defence of Malaya, and he had been seconded as an adviser to Vietnam. We might also increase our police mission. But that was as far as we had gone, and there were no recriminations.

His greatest jubilation was over the second day's events. There was to be a full meeting at 11 in the morning, and the British were sitting there waiting. About 11.30 Johnson himself came in and said they were sorry but they were not ready, because they were still discussing among themselves the British paper on the ANF. At about noon Healey had said to the PM that this must be 'Ball's last stand', and so it had proved to be. There was no proper discussion before lunch, and after lunch, when the American working paper was presented, the British found that the ANF had been accepted. Though there had been much discussion with Rusk, McNamara, and Bundy in the afternoon the President had said little. Wilson now believed that the President was prepared to abandon the MLF if the next stage of discussion with Europe went well. Harold said that he had been astounded.

He said there was much still to be discussed about political control over the nuclear forces. Something like the 'war cabinet' might well emerge, for such possibilities had been mentioned in the White House sessions. The immediate proposal for a 'single authority', parallel with the North Atlantic Council, was simply a device to bypass de Gaulle's veto.

Of the monetary discussions he said little, for they appeared to have been overshadowed. Of the continuing crisis he said it was a battle and we must not show fear. It was our Waterloo, but he had told Jim that 'Blücher is here already'; the £1,000 million credit was our Blücher. He had told Jim also that the money must be used, for there would be a flow back to sterling as soon as confidence was restored. All this was said with his feet comfortably up against the Cabinet table in a relaxed way. While I admired his performance in Washington, I was less sure about economic management.

One lesson he had taken – the criticism over his post-Chequers Commons speech. He said that his opening speech for this week's debate, or those parts that related to the Washington meeting, had been sent to Bundy in good time and a copy had also gone to Paris with Gordon Walker for handing to Rusk at the NATO meeting there. Rusk and Bundy had both responded favourably.

The next stage was to talk to the Federal Government in Bonn. Healey was talking to von Hassel in Paris this week, and Gordon Walker to Schröder. De Gaulle wanted him to go to Paris before going to Bonn, but he had refused this. He wanted to succeed with the Federal Government first, and he thought there was a fair chance of doing this.

It was in my mind to go to Bonn in early January anyway, so I mentioned this. Wilson replied that my report on Washington had been most helpful, and he would welcome it if I could make a similar sortie to Bonn shortly before his own visit. I reckoned that, apart from any value to the Prime Minister, it was likely to provide valuable information for the paper. As Richard had found in Washington, extra doors were opened for the resident correspondent when his editor turned up – though the *Guardian* staff almost everywhere were accorded ready access to Ministers and their advisers. So I phoned our Bonn correspondent, Norman Crossland, and bought a ticket for the second week of January.

On the banks of the Rhine

Two deaths and another sterling spasm took some of the value out of my Bonn visit, though it was still well worthwhile. My father died suddenly in London on my second day in Bonn; and then Winston Churchill's terminal illness, followed by his death on January 24, forced a postponement of the Prime Minister's visit to Federal Germany. By the end of January the MLF itself had died of asphyxia, and Harold Wilson did not make his journey to the Rhine and Berlin until mid-March.

Bonn as usual had the air of being a capital by mistake – as if the paraphernalia of Chancelleries, Parliament, civil service, and embassies were to be imposed on Maidenhead or Henley. The January weather was surprisingly mild; and the hotel in which I stayed, in the old town, was one of the most quiet and comfortable I had encountered for years. The preliminaries included meetings with the American and British ambassadors and with German officials. The US Ambassador, George McGhee, argued with both charm and ferocity that the British were trying for too much and might lose everything. He remained an MLF man, saying that Wilson's ANF would never satisfy the German wish to share in nuclear matters without having a national force of their own. Dr Diehle, from the Federal Press Office, said that British moralising was insufferable. Wilson's repeated use of 'no German finger on the trigger' implied that the Germans were vicious, untrustworthy, and uncouth.

State Secretary Carstens, in the Foreign Ministry, was more emollient. Although the Federal Government had reservations about the British proposals, the discussions with the Prime Minister could be fruitful and constructive. He raised one particularly strong point. The Germans wanted to continue with one Supreme Commander for Europe and were against having a separate nuclear command. (The Supreme Commander's post was the one first held by Eisenhower in 1949, and then by Gruenther, Ridgway, Norstad, and now by General Lemnitzer.) The reason was political: SACEUR in the past had been an invaluable channel for representing European views to the President, for he was in close touch with the European Governments. To split the post would be a mistake.

The climax was the conversation with the Federal Chancellor, Ludwig Erhard, at the Palais Schaumberg. Dr Erhard had been Chancellor for only just over a year, and in the past few months had had a rough ride, with his predecessor Konrad Adenauer being something of a thorn. A former professor of economics, Erhard had been in charge of the currency reform in 1948 and then Minister of Economics for fourteen years.

The conversation with him was awkward, for at first he seemed determined to say as little as possible. He sat with three officials, a stenographer, and an interpreter; he was a bulky man with big feet and leather boots that stretched out in front of him, and much of the time he chewed an unlit cigar. While I was talking the interpreter whispered in his ear, but when he spoke he made a complete statement before the translation began – and since I understood about 40 per cent of the German I often felt I was being given an incomplete version of his words. Norman Crossland sat with me.

Knowing that the Chancellor was due to spend Monday with de Gaulle at Rambouillet and then meet Harold Wilson in Bonn on Friday, I said that he had two very important meetings next week. We hoped for a happy outcome to both, but especially of course to the second. Unsmiling, Erhard replied that he hoped for a happy outcome to both. Turning to the Atlantic Nuclear Force, I hoped that the British proposals were satisfactory and helpful (ill-chosen words, perhaps) to Federal Germany. Erhard replied that he did not wish to expose his views on the British plan. He would discuss them with the Prime Minister.

I said that the British proposals were aimed at giving Germany a greater share in decision-making and at extending consultation within the alliance to areas outside Europe. He seemed to have slightly misconstrued this and replied with emphasis that European security was of the first importance. A fault of the British proposals was that they did not strengthen the defence of Europe. We must match any weapons that might be used against us with weapons of our own, and there must be absolute parity of nuclear forces. I agreed, suggesting that Wilson's proposals fully provided for this. We went on to disarmament, East-West relations, and the Common Market.

When we came to the state of Britain's economy, Dr Erhard at last became quite genial. He said he thought that we had come to ask him, as a professor of economics, how to get the British economy going again. He thought his answers might not be acceptable to us or to the British Government – but was not the *Manchester Guardian* a Liberal paper? I said that some of the Wilson Government's measures were less than fully understood abroad, its incomes policy for example. The Chancellor laughed openly at that, so I said we took it seriously; he retorted mockingly that it was our patriotic duty to do so.

Thus the discussion went on, not very fruitfully. He concluded with rather heavy irony that he must ask whether the socialist method was the right one for Britain. I replied that I wished I could be present next week to hear two such distinguished economists argue that point. And with that we ended the interview on apparently friendly terms.

I went back again that evening to see the British Ambassador, Sir Frank Roberts, to tell him what had been said. He had been trying to see the Chancellor for a week but had been unable to get an appointment. He took the view that Dr Erhard had not yet made up his mind between the Franco-German alliance and the Atlantic alliance, and the coming week would be important. That gave me the cue for the main message of the article I wrote after returning to London, with emphasis that the Prime Minister had put himself yards back from the starting line with the Germans by his repetition of 'no German finger on the trigger'.

I had intended to return to London next day anyway, but a message came about 6.30 in the morning, through the *Guardian* office in London, to say that my father had collapsed after flying to London from Edinburgh the previous afternoon and was seriously ill in Westminster Hospital. He was coming up to seventy-seven years old and had had two previous heart attacks, the second some years earlier, but remained vigorous in every way. I returned by the first flight from Bonn, but was met with a further message at Heathrow to say that he had died in the early morning. He had had a rough flight on an old Vanguard from Edinburgh, and had carried quite a heavy bag, as usual, from the West London terminal to the tube and from the tube to the Athenaeum. There he had had a talk with John Fulton, Vice-Chancellor of Sussex University, but had said that he was feeling unwell; later, when he was clearly in some distress, another of his former colleagues had insisted on summoning an ambulance. He had become unconscious soon after reaching Westminster Hospital.

That evening I was to have seen the Prime Minister, but I called off the appointment, which was reinstated five days later. By then I had been to the family funeral in Edinburgh – a memorial service was to follow in Glasgow later – and my long article on German attitudes to disarmament, East–West relations, and NATO had been published. But by then Churchill's illness had led to the cancellation of Wilson's visit to Bonn and Berlin.

The Prime Minister's interest in Bonn seemed much diminished. He was glad of the postponement and he believed the Germans, too, were glad that there was a dignified reason to put the visit off. The atmosphere was uncongenial there and Sir Frank Roberts was not sorry about the delay. In any event the MLF was virtually dead, he said. He reminded me of a report from Richard Scott in Washington, tucked at the foot of the *Guardian*'s front page about ten days earlier, under the headline 'Death knell sounded in Washington for the MLF?' Its occasion was the resignation of Ambassador Gerard Smith from his post as special assistant in the State Department; and although Richard reported the Department as denying that the MLF proposal was dead, Ambassador Smith's departure was a sign that 'its future is very dim'. The PM said that on his information Richard's interpretation was correct.

He listened, nevertheless, to a fairly full report of what Erhard, Carstens, and others had said to me in Bonn; and we went on to talk of the aircraft industry, prices and incomes policy, Rhodesia, and other topics obviously of greater urgency to him. He could not refrain, though, from saying with great satisfaction how amazing it was, when you looked back just over a month, that the MLF was dead.

Amazing, indeed, but that success had been bought at a price. The Federal German Government remained cool towards the British for some time and stayed closer to the French – with no great improvement until after Erhard's resignation two years later and the replacement of the Free Democrats by Willy Brandt's Social Democrats in the coalition. French reserve also remained strong, though that would have been likely anyway; and any chance of a changed relationship with the Common Market was set back. But the biggest part of the price was Wilson's commitment to continue with the British Polaris submarines. Effectively, he had gone four-fifths of the way towards adopting the Conservatives' policy of an independent deterrent, interpolating his own concept of being able to tell the submarines when necessary that 'the Queen needs you'.

A domestic footnote: just a week after my father's death my own fourth child, Mary, was born at home in Blackheath. One loss, one gain.

6 A permissive society?

The common thread to this chapter is the changing British society of the sixties. Twenty years after the Chatterley trial, those not then alive and at work find it hard to believe that book publishers could be prosecuted for obscenity and for corrupting readers, that the Lord Chamberlain could censor plays, that abortions were few and mostly illegal, that divorce generally took five years or longer and the ex-wife could come out of it impoverished, and that except in factories employers rarely allowed women to go to work in trousers.

After the Chatterley trial

Until October 1960, I had not read *Lady Chatterley's Lover*. After the Obscene Publications Act of 1959, which was meant to liberalise the law, Penguin Books decided to publish it unexpurgated.[1] As editor of the *Guardian* I was asked in late September whether I would be a witness for the defence. I replied that I must read the book before deciding, and Penguin then sent me a copy. Both Miranda and I read it in the next few days; and I consulted John Rosselli, a careful critic in literary matters and one who had read a foreign edition of the book some time before. I had no hesitation in saying 'yes'. Some passages in the book might be shocking, but they were not corrupting, at least to any normal person. In due course I was called as a witness, along with some thirty others; and on November 2 the jury brought in a unanimous verdict of acquittal.

Our leading article next day said that the jury had done what the judge had told them to. They had kept their feet on the ground. Their verdict was a triumph of common sense, the more pleasing because it was unexpected. The *Times* took a contrary view. Their leader, headed 'A decent reticence', said that in spite of the impressive parade of witnesses for the defence, they could have been matched bishop for bishop and don for don, with a similar parade taking exactly the opposite view.

Throughout the trial our reporting refrained from any repetition of the four-letter words. Nor did we use dashes or asterisks, except in the evidence of Richard Hoggart where direct quotation was unavoidable. This restriction created some difficulties – not least, ironically, in conveying the force of Mr Mervyn Griffith-Jones's opening speech for the prosecution. But it seemed the most expedient course.

The morning after the judgement there were no real difficulties, but one cropped up that afternoon. Wayland Young – now more generally known as Lord Kennet – at the time was one of our regular columnists.

1 See C. H. Rolph's *The Trial of Lady Chatterley*.

The columnists were free to write on any topic of their own choice, regardless of conflict with the paper's view, provided they refrained from libel or obscenity, kept within the specified length, and delivered their copy on time. Wayland had sat in the gallery throughout the trial and wanted to write about it. And at one point in his column he felt that direct quotation, unaltered, was essential.

Most of the column was given to an examination of what he called the 'morbid psychology' of the prosecution. For, he wrote, the book spoke of joy, kindness, and trust. But the difficult passage was this:

The defence, conducted by Gerald Gardiner at his sanest and most agreeable, gave an admirable picture of how ordinary people do feel and think. A procession of clergymen held that since human and divine love are not in conflict, the book had a religious significance; a procession of writers said that this or that particular word cannot be evil; schoolteachers said children know them anyhow; a very young woman said, in effect, that she had not been corrupted; and so on.

The hero among the witnesses was Richard Hoggart. I think he made history. In his own evidence, using the word in its correct and proper sense, he said the point Lawrence made was: 'Simply, this is what one does - one fucks.' If ever the English language comes to be at peace with itself again, thereby giving people freedom to be at peace with themselves, the credit will be Lawrence's first but Hoggart's soon after. He also gave a model account of the history of puritanism, dealing most intelligently and profoundly with our moral and literary heritage; the prosecution asked if he was serious, and the judge looked amazed. The jury, on the other hand, heard him.

Wayland went on to write about E. M. Forster's evidence and his influence on our literature and language. He finished with a flourish that personally I would not have risked, saying that 'on November 2, 1960, a giant who had lain in chains, the English imagination, was at last unshackled'.

Wayland's text, teleprinted from London, arrived on my desk in Manchester in mid-afternoon. Having read it I asked our London editor, Gerard Fay,[2] to take a copy or send it round to our London legal advisers. Lovell, White, and King were then, as now, the *Guardian*'s principal legal prop - and extremely good, too, combining knowledge of the law with earthy common sense. John Notcutt was their partner who usually dealt with our affairs; and at 7 in the evening I received a further telex from Fay saying this:

Urgent, Fay to Hetherington.
Notcutt says he would rather have had several hours to consider this matter but his opinion 'off the cuff' is -
1. There is *some* danger of being proceeded against under the same Act as Lady Chatterley was, the Obscene Publications Act. This danger he calculates as about 50-50.

2 The post of London editor lapsed when the editorial headquarters moved south in 1964, and Gerard Fay then became an assistant editor.

2. If we were proceeded against under this Act he thinks the chances of our being found guilty would be about 6 to 4 against.

3. Very roughly the odds on these two points are about 75 per cent in our favour.

4. There is another Act under which we might be in some danger – the Law of Libel Amendment Act – which is normally used to tone down the reporting of evidence in divorce cases, but which could be used in any report which deals with what is known as 'obscene evidence'.

5. It is wrong to think that the Chatterley finding 'takes the brake off' and that anybody can in future get away with anything. The finding in this case applies only to this particular edition of this particular work.

6. Speaking as a reader rather than as a legal adviser Notcutt said that he would think it questionable whether anything could be gained by using this passage. He believes that as the *Guardian* we could 'get away with it' whereas the *Mirror* or the *Sketch* could not. Is it worth making an issue on this particular article and this particular word, he wonders.

7. So do I.   END.

The article had already been put into type, and the page was due off stone in about ninety minutes' time. The last of the leaders had still to be sub-edited and the front page to be discussed with John Putz. Clearly from a legal point of view we were fairly safe, though not entirely so. Equally clearly John Notcutt and Gerard Fay, whose opinions were worth heeding, felt on general grounds that we ought to remove part of the article.

But against this there were three objections. First, our commitment to the columnists not to tamper with their writing. It was an important part of their freedom. In principle what he or she wrote must not be altered without consultation first. There had been one or two slip-ups, but not many. We had had difficulties with Dick Crossman, one of the earliest of our regular columnists, but these were mostly when I suspected that he was writing too hurriedly and without enough thought. Above all, I was concerned to maintain so far as possible the freedom of the columnists to write as they wished.

Second, even if Wayland were to agree to an alteration, the removal of that passage about Richard Hoggart would tear a gap in his train of thought. Readers would see that something had gone wrong. At least for the first edition there was too little time now for any major revision after a telephone talk with Wayland. The third point was that, in all probability, we would fail to reach agreement with Wayland in time and would have to omit his column entirely. That would be remarked on, and the reasons inevitably would become known. Would we not look silly, in the aftermath of the trial, if we funked using one word in its proper context and in what seemed to me a reasonable way?

While I had no intention of letting such words become commonplace in the paper, this seemed to me the occasion to allow a single usage. I knew well enough, nevertheless, that there was likely to be a fuss. So in order to try to anticipate it I quickly wrote a very short leader, just in time to be fitted into the first edition. Headed 'Vulgar or not?' it began by asking whether a word that for years had been regarded as vulgar became any less vulgar because of a court decision. 'The short answer is "no": words are vulgar because their users deliberately intend them to be so, or because they are commonly used by crude or foul-minded people.' The Chatterley court decision could not by itself redeem those words, which civilised people would still prefer not to use. The short answer, however, was not the whole answer. D. H. Lawrence was at least partly trying to restore to some of the four-letter words a decent meaning; and, as Mr Wayland Young was seeking to show, the use of a four-letter alternative need not necessarily be vulgar. 'Whether or not depends on the user, the context, and the manner of its use.'

No sooner was it written and on its way to the composing room when a further teleprint came in from Gerard Fay, saying he felt strongly that this was an issue on which we should not stick our necks out. He had shown the Notcutt message to John Rosselli and Richard Scott, and they agreed. Would it not be better to wait for some occasion when use of the word 'might really do some good'? We should, Fay said, 'hold our horses for a while'. But it was now after 8 and the leader page was due off stone in about twenty minutes, to be followed soon after by the back page with Wayland's column. Anyway, my mind was made up. I doubted whether the 'better occasion' would come; and I regarded Wayland's use as a responsible one.

Two days later Kenneth Tynan in the *Observer* made a point similar to Wayland's and was allowed to use the word. He said that that part of Hoggart's evidence was the crucial incident in the trial, 'the exchange wherein the case was psychologically won'. Hoggart had uttered a word formerly heard only from the lips of Mr Griffith-Jones. 'There was no reaction anywhere in the court, so calmly was the word pronounced and so literally employed.' The same day in *Reynolds News*, Tom Driberg, MP, wrote approvingly of Wayland's article and noted that a Conservative MP had tabled a question asking the Attorney-General to draw the DPP's attention to it – a question which itself was a breach of Parliamentary procedure, Driberg said, since Wayland Young was a member of the House of Lords as the Conservative MP (also a journalist) ought to have known. We heard no more of that.

Nor, surprisingly, was there any strong reaction from readers. In the following week we printed many letters about the Chatterley case, but there was not a single complaint from our own readers about Wayland's passage. His concluding words about the unshackling of imagination brought at least one ribald comment asking whether he had never passed the rows and rows of seamy paperbacks on bookstalls. More substantially, there were letters about Sir Clifford Chatterley's position, about biblical teaching, about risks to the sanctity of marriage from the judgement – and many letters welcoming the verdict. When the Archbishop of Canterbury some days later rebuked the Bishop of Woolwich – saying that his evidence could become 'a stumbling block and a cause of offence to many ordinary Christians' - that set off a further round of letters on each side. There were also suggestions from other clergy as to alternative reading about marriage and Christian conduct.

The Press Council's verdict

Three months later, we learned from a Press Association news bulletin that the Press Council had censured the *Guardian*, *Observer*, and *Spectator* for publishing certain four-letter words used at the trial. The Council's statement was doubly surprising. To begin with, it was a standing rule that the Press Council would not consider a complaint unless the complainant had first taken up the issue with the editor involved. Nobody had written to the *Guardian* to complain about Wayland, still less to suggest that the matter might be taken to the Press Council. Second, we had had no communication of any kind from the Council and therefore no opportunity to put our own view before its members.

We nevertheless printed the Press Council's statement in full next morning, at the foot of the front page.[3] We printed also a short leader saying that while we disagreed with the Council's judgement that our printing of one word had been 'both objectionable and unnecessary', we heeded its rebuke. We added that the matter was one chiefly of taste and consequently no judgement could be final, and that the Council had not had the courtesy to tell us that it intended to consider the question.

That morning I had a telephone call from Frank Singleton, editor of the *Bolton Evening News*, a member of the Press Council, and an old friend. He had written one of the best books about Lancashire and another outstanding one about the Lake District, and he had an exceptional sense of prose and poetry as well as running a prosperous daily newspaper. He said that he had not known that this judgement was coming, and he, too, disagreed with it. He had not been present at the last meeting and had not known that the matter was coming up, for it had not been notified in the papers for that meeting. Privately - the whole conversation was for my private knowledge - he said that he had become very concerned with the way the Council was being run. He thought the time had probably come to resign, but he would discuss it with others first. I was glad to hear his comment but sorry to hear that the Press Council might lose him.

A few days later the *Observer* rejected the Council's finding in stronger terms than we had done. It also reported that only about six of the twenty or so members present at the last meeting had voted for the censure, although it had been published as an apparently unanimous opinion of the Council. The *Guardian* then asked the Council's chairman and its secretary whether this was true: each declined to comment. Instead, the chairman two days later wrote a letter which we published, drawing a parallel with the collective responsibility of a Cabinet or of a company's

3 The *Guardian*, February 16, 1961.

directors. We again wrote a short leader, saying that a closer parallel was with a jury. When divided, a jury could not condemn.

Chairmanship of the Press Council had been taken over about eighteen months earlier by George Murray, chief editorial writer of the *Daily Mail*. His predecessor, the first chairman of the Council, had been the editor of the *Yorkshire Post*, Sir Linton Andrews – a bluff old Tory, but with a broad outlook and an engaging humour. I had the impression that George Murray's horizons were narrower. He still did not answer the point we had put as to why the three journals had not been told beforehand that the matter was to be discussed, saying only that 'no specific complaint' had been made to the Council. I wanted to know whether the members had had before them the whole text of Wayland's article. I suspected that they had not. Had they, in fact, given any consideration to the writer, the context, or the manner in which the one word was used?

Frank Singleton then resigned, being unwilling to accept George Murray's version of collective responsibility, and that left the Press Council even weaker than it already was. I wrote a further short leader regretting his departure and saying that the Council really needed to look again at its procedures. I still wanted to know whether the Council members at their meeting had had the opportunity to consider the *Guardian* article as a whole. (In fact I knew by now that they had not – an odd failing when the Obscene Publications Act itself now required consideration of a work as a whole, not of isolated passages.) In the leader I wrote that the Council had an important job in helping to raise the standards of the British press but could not carry weight if it appeared to be reaching its decisions blindly. I added, perhaps a touch too acidly, that the *Guardian* had never been asked to take part in the Council's work but would not do so while the Council's constitution and procedure remained unchanged.

At the time I was a member of the Royal Commission on the Police, which was then holding fortnightly all-day sessions. At the next meeting one of the more staid members, a distinguished lawyer, said he was glad to see that we were taking a stand against arbitrary decisions reached behind closed doors. Readers' reaction, though not extensive, was also on our side. We had letters from such diverse sources as the general secretary of one of the printing unions, NATSOPA, and a Balliol college don. Not surprisingly, Bernard Levin as deputy editor of the *Spectator* weighed in, calling the Press Council 'a hollow turnip'. But a reader in Aberdeen thanked the Council for delivering 'a well aimed and well deserved cut across the backside'.

There was, however, one adverse comment that stung me more deeply than it can have been intended to. Laurence Scott, our company chairman and managing director, had been out of the country in mid-February – on a skiing holiday in Switzerland, I think. But he had been seeing the paper there, and when he returned home he wrote me a short note. As mentioned earlier, in keeping with the Scott family custom he scrupulously refrained as manager from any intervention in the editing of the paper. He was such a model proprietor, from the editor's point of view, that this one comment jolted me. He wrote simply that we ought to have printed the Press Council's original rebuke and replied very briefly if we wished; but we should then have accepted the situation and said no more.

I didn't reply in writing but instead waited a few days until there was the chance of a friendly conversation. He then said he quite agreed with our criticism of the Press Council's statement, but there were occasions when it was better not to answer back. He mentioned also that my last leader had committed him as well as me to refuse membership of the Press Council. He had no particular wish to be a member – he had more than enough to do already – but he would not have wanted to turn it down summarily. He accepted, of course, that since he had been away he could not have been consulted.

Two years later, following the report of the Royal Commission on the Press under Lord Shawcross, the working of the Press Council was overhauled and Lord Devlin became its chairman. Later still, Laurence's successor as our chairman and managing director, Peter Gibbings, served for four years on the Council – with Lord Pearce as chairman by that time. It was by then a stronger body, though still imperfect.

Vassall, Profumo, and the press

If Lady Chatterley was fiction, Christine Keeler and Mandy Rice-Davies were real. They were high-class prostitutes with some high-class customers. It transpired that Christine for a time had been making herself available both to the Secretary of State for War, John Profumo, and to the Soviet naval attaché, Captain Eugene Ivanov. That came into the open only a few months after a great deal of press speculation and innuendo about an improper relationship between a homosexual Admiralty clerk, W. J. C. Vassall, and another Minister. The clerk was convicted of spying for the Russians; the Minister was wholly exonerated.

The Vassall and Profumo affairs in 1962 and 1963 clouded Macmillan's last years as Prime Minister, caused dog to eat dog in Fleet Street, and were taken by some people as signs of moral degeneration in British society. The *Guardian* from the start was sceptical of the more lurid allegations on Vassall–Galbraith – and was proved right. We were no less sceptical when the Profumo rumours grew some months later – and were proved wrong. When the Radcliffe Tribunal reported on Vassall, it confirmed our belief that a number of Fleet Street newspapers had behaved scandalously, and we said so. Predictably that led to counter-attacks, at times vicious, in which Wayland's post-Chatterley article was raked up. But, personally, I never believed either that the Profumo affair involved great security risks or that it marked any general deterioration in British moral standards – and these judgements, at least, were vindicated.

Of course the Profumo affair had to be investigated, a task which let

Lord Denning enjoy himself as a sleuth. His inquiry put the security hazards in perspective and included again a harsh condemnation of those Fleet Street newspapers which were 'trafficking in scandal'. But in terms of social morality, Lord Denning found no substance in most of the rumours. In retrospect the affair appeared an unhappy aberration but not unlike others among the wealthy in Victorian, Edwardian, and more recent times.

Vassall was condemned in October 1962, on charges of espionage while serving in the Moscow embassy in 1955, and in London in 1956, 1957, and 1962. He had been lured by the Russians into homosexual activity in Moscow, where he had been photographed and blackmailed, though he was paid well for his spying. Between 1957 and 1959, but not at the time any of the offences took place, Vassall worked in the office of Mr Tam Galbraith, MP, then Civil Lord of the Admiralty and afterwards Under-Secretary in the Scottish Office. Immediately after the trial, the Prime Minister appointed a committee of three senior civil servants to go into the security implications, and a fortnight later they furnished him with an interim report. Then, because of insistent pressure from the Opposition in Parliament, Macmillan published the civil servants' report and at the same time ordered a further independent inquiry under Lord Radcliffe. Galbraith resigned pending the outcome of the inquiry; it found no impropriety on his part.

Ironically, in the light of the subsequent anger in Fleet Street when the popular newspapers found themselves in the dock, the *Guardian* at the start took the line that there was no need for the Radcliffe Tribunal. If security was the issue, we said, the committee under Sir Charles Cunningham ought to be adequate. But there were vehement demands from Fleet Street, even more than from the Parliamentary Opposition, that there must be a bigger inquiry; and two of those most vehement in making these demands, the *Express* and the *Mirror*, were among those who eventually found themselves under severely critical examination by Lord Radcliffe. The biters themselves were in the end savagely bitten. Another irony was that the two reporters who went to prison for refusing to reply about sources were from papers rather on the fringe of the affair, the *Mail* and the *Sketch*, in that most of the time they were trying to catch up with the *Mirror* and *Express*.

The main relevance of Vassall and Profumo here is that, coming together, the two affairs created a period of exceptional ill feeling between politicians and much of the press; and that, wrongly in my view, the scent of scandal created for a time the belief that there was degeneration in public life. Radcliffe and Denning helped to clear the air, and looking back I do not regret the *Guardian*'s directness in saying what it thought about the conduct of some other newspapers.

In November 1962, after publication of the Cunningham report, we commented that George Brown and those newspapers which had forecast that the Vassall case was going to 'blow up' in the Government's face were looking 'a little foolish'. The terrible letters from Galbraith to Vassall had turned out to be trivial and unimportant; they contained nothing sinister, and their use for imputations against Mr Galbraith was absurd.

When next day the *Express*, *Mail* and *Mirror* sought to use the letters to justify their attitudes, I wrote again in harder terms. The leader quoted what each of them had said and concluded:

> The personal attack on Mr Galbraith launched by the *Express* newspaper, and followed by others, was vicious and unwarranted. The *Sunday Pictorial* was muck-raking when it flaunted its possession of the letters. The letters in themselves show no particular involvement on Mr Galbraith's part. Much remains to be said about the defectiveness of Admiralty security; but the press has nothing to crow about in this case.

Hugh Gaitskell incidentally had told me that the *Express* appeared to be getting its information from sources in Scotland Yard, who must have known of the continuous watch being kept on Vassall. As a member of the Royal Commission on the Police I had heard some months earlier the Metropolitan Commissioner's evidence on the inducements – free cars, free holidays, and other perks – being offered by Fleet Street newspapers to some CID officers and of his difficulty in controlling this. Gaitskell also mentioned that George Brown, who was retained by the *Mirror* group as an industrial adviser, had been allowed to read the letters in the *Sunday Pictorial*'s possession.

The Cunningham Committee had been able to reach an interim report in two weeks – and its speed of operation had been part of the Prime Minister's justification for preferring it to a tribunal – but now the further aspects of Admiralty security and Moscow embassy security were out of its hands. Lord Radcliffe's tribunal took five months to deal with these and with the further allegations in the press. By the time Radcliffe reported the first rumours about Profumo were circulated, and indeed John Profumo had already made his first (untrue) personal statement to the House. By then relations between Fleet Street and Westminster were poisonous.

Radcliffe at the end of April found nothing improper in the relationship between Galbraith and Vassall, nothing remiss in Galbraith's failure to suspect Vassall, and 'no truth' in the allegation that Lord Carrington had known for eighteen months that there was a spy in the Admiralty. It found failures in the 'positive vetting' procedure and in the handling of secret documents, and it criticised the policy of saving money by sending single men to Moscow instead of married men.

As to the press, it had this to say about a number of specific allegations. Of the *Daily Mail*'s charge that Vassall had spent weekends at Galbraith's home in Ayrshire, mixing with other guests and learning more of Admiralty procedure: 'It is in all essentials a piece of fiction.' As to the report

in the *Daily Sketch* that Galbraith and Vassall had spent holidays together:
'There has never been any evidence whatsoever that Mr Galbraith and
Vassall had ever spent any holidays abroad in each other's company.' Of
the reports in the *Daily Mirror* and *Daily Herald* that Vassall had worked
with the Portland spy ring: 'We have thoroughly investigated the allegation and the nature of the information on which it is based, and have
no doubt that it is completely false.' As to another report in the same
papers: 'These stories ... were also fiction and were not based on any
evidence that could support the story.' Of the *Daily Express* report that
Lord Carrington and other Admiralty officials knew that there was another spy in the Admiralty: 'There is nothing to give ground for the
allegation.' And of that paper's report that Lord Carrington had been
called to explain to the Prime Minister why he had not reported the
presence of this spy: 'This also is without foundation.' Of the *Sunday
Telegraph* report that Scotland Yard had closed its file on the Lonsdale
(Portland) case: 'On examination we found the report ... was in most of
its particulars, though posing as fact, essentially speculation and not
founded on any actual knowledge.'

The list goes on, but no more need be reported here. It was a devas-
tating critique of the methods of the popular press, driven onwards by
competitive pressures, and after its publication there were few signs of
any sense of guilt. The *Daily Express* commented:

The outcome justifies the press campaign for an inquiry into security. The press
is shown to have done its job, to have performed its function to society in its own
way.

And the *Daily Mirror*:

Now the truth is known. The press is not half as bad as the politicians thought.
The Administration is not half as bad as some of the newspapers alleged.

The *Sunday Express* and the *Sunday Mirror* (the *Pictorial*, now renamed)
remained silent, though they had been in the forefront of the attack the
previous autumn.

Over Profumo, as over Vassall-Galbraith, the newspapers lacked hard
evidence but were hearing a great deal of gossip. Over Profumo, however,
a proportion of the gossip in the end turned out to be true. Again the
running was made mostly by the *Mirror* and the *Express*. The *Sunday
Mirror*, though it did not mention it until after Profumo's resignation,
possessed the only tangible piece of evidence - a short letter from John
Profumo to Christine Keeler, written two years earlier. But that was proof
of nothing except that he had written a warmly friendly letter cancelling
an engagement to meet her. The *Express* in mid-March - a month before
publication of the Radcliffe report on Vassall, but after public examination
of *Express* and other witnesses from which they had not emerged too well
- openly showed its doubts about the War Minister. He told the *Express*

that there was no truth in reports that he had offered his resignation to the Prime Minister and that there were no reasons whatever why he should do so. The *Express* suggested that he had been asked by the Prime Minister to stay in his post. The *Mirror* at that time was enjoying itself with pictures of Christine Keeler on its front page and reports, quite correct, that she had failed to turn up as a witness in a criminal case at the Old Bailey, that shots were alleged to have been fired into the door of her flat, and that she was believed to be abroad. All this was unconnected with Profumo.

The following week the War Minister made a personal statement to the House of Commons saying that it was wholly untrue that he had any connection with Miss Keeler's absence from the Old Bailey, that he had met her only about six times, the last in 1961, and that he and his wife had only twice met the Russian military attaché, Captain Ivanov, who had lately been recalled. In the *Guardian* we asked whether, even though Miss Keeler might have an interesting story to tell, newspapers should be trying to buy it from her.

From then onwards, newspapers were circumspect in what they said even though the rumours circulated and grew. Three Ministers apart from John Profumo were being mentioned as having had an involvement either with Christine Keeler or with the so-called 'Wimpole Mews' circle, but, while wary, I was still inclined to discount all these rumours. Gerard Fay in our Fleet Street office remained my principal channel of information, and he too was inclined to discount most of what he heard. But Dr Stephen Ward, who had a flat in Wimpole Mews and had been admitted by Profumo to be an acquaintance, was apparently telling a number of tales. He might be more reliable than Christine Keeler, but I thought not much more so. Her story had been or was being bought by the *News of the World* (for £23,000 we heard later).

In the last week of April Harold Wilson told me privately that he had had a letter from Dr Ward which he had at once passed on to the Prime Minister. He was concerned that Harold Macmillan appeared to be treating it somewhat frivolously, for if nothing else Ward seemed to Wilson to be a security risk. In the third week of May Wilson mentioned, again privately, that he had had another letter from Ward and had again passed it on to the Prime Minister. Ward had said more about the untruth of Profumo's personal statement to the House, and Wilson wanted the new Security Commission to inquire into it. What the Prime Minister in fact did was to arrange for his principal private secretary to see Dr Ward, and then for a senior officer from Scotland Yard to pursue inquiries further. On May 30, just before the Whit recess, he asked the Lord Chancellor to carry the next stage of the inquiry; that would have meant again interviewing the War Minister, who was continuing to insist on his innocence. Four days later, while Macmillan was on holiday in Scotland, Profumo admitted to the Conservative Chief Whip that he had lied to the

House and offered his resignation. Macmillan accepted it with a brief letter from Scotland. Until that day he had believed in Profumo's innocence.

At the time I was in Stockholm, speaking at a conference of the International Press Institute (on the press, security, and D-Notices, as it happened); others in Manchester and London had been briefed in strict confidence on what Harold Wilson had told me, but the resignation still came as a surprise. The leader that appeared next day was too emollient, saying that the sooner the Profumo affair sank into oblivion the better; I rather regretted having been out of the country that night. Wilson's information was still extremely useful in piecing the news report together.

Through George Wigg, Harold Wilson in truth knew a great deal more than he had indicated to me. The *Daily Telegraph* also published an extensive interview with Stephen Ward next day, and it provided a few more clues, not all reliable. Something of the bitterness towards the press – especially among senior Conservatives – is indicated in Macmillan's own diary:

Every part of the Profumo story, now only a ramification of the 'Ward case', was used by an exultant press, getting its own back for Vassall. The *Times* was awful – what has since been called a 'Holier than thou' attitude, which was really nauseating. The 'popular' press has been one mass of life stories of spies and prostitutes, written no doubt in the office. Day after day the attacks developed, chiefly on me – old, incompetent, worn out.[4]

On June 17 in the House Wilson moved what amounted to a vote of censure on the Prime Minister for his handling of the case. Macmillan records his own part in the debate as 'the most difficult and wearing task', for he had to tell the whole story from February 1 onwards as it had now emerged, defending himself, the police, the Security Service, and the civil service. The Conservative ranks, he says, were undergoing an attack of hysteria. After a tense debate, twenty-seven Conservatives abstained from voting – 'not only the usual malcontents but a lot of worthy people, who had been swept away by the wave of emotion and indignation'.

Wilson privately took the view that Macmillan would have to go, and he thought Home the likeliest successor since the Peerage Bill was on its way through Parliament.

On June 21 Lord Denning was appointed to conduct a judicial inquiry, and he spent an extremely busy summer doing so. He reported in late September. As secretary he was given Tom Critchley from the Home Office, whom I knew well because he had recently been secretary to the Royal Commission on the Police. Harold Wilson objected on the ground that civil servants would be chary of giving candid evidence in front of a Home Office man, and the Home Office would have backstairs influence. Knowing Tom, I suggested to Wilson that his objections were misplaced

4 Harold Macmillan, *At the End of the Day*, p. 442.

and he dropped the issue. The Critchleys came on holiday to Langdale in the Lake District at the end of August while we were in our old farmhouse nearby, and we had a fine day out on Scafell and Scafell Pike, via Lord's Rake; nothing of substance about the Denning inquiry escaped Tom's lips. When we got home there were urgent messages for him to ring someone at Scotland Yard, but we never heard why.[5] The Critchleys also looked after our newest (Lucy, aged three months) for part of one night while Miranda and I went to see the sunrise from the top of Bowfell.

Stephen Ward had been arrested and charged with living wholly or partly on the immoral earnings of Christine Keeler, Mandy Rice-Davies, and others. At the end of July he was found guilty but committed suicide before sentence.

The *Mirror* meanwhile was keeping up its counter-offensive on the *Guardian*, directly and indirectly. It summed us up after Radcliffe as 'led by the soft answer, blindman's buff, and a bucket of whitewash'. We retaliated by asking what freedoms the *Mirror* thought it was protecting by giving excessive prominence to a handful of Fascists (Colin Jordan's group), putting money into their pockets for 'exclusive' pictures and interviews (Gerard Fay had supplied me with the evidence), and paying large sums for the memoirs of a convicted spy (one of the Portland ring). The *Mirror* damned our 'faint-hearted' about-turn on entry into Europe: we replied that unlike the *Mirror* we had taken the trouble to follow the negotiations in 1962 and report them in detail, and it was the adverse terms that had altered our view. It made more sense to study the facts than blithely to turn a blind eye.

In August Cassandra, the *Mirror* columnist William Connor, had a go at the 'querulous' *Guardian*, 'dwindling into a less than mediocre paper'. He got round to Lady Chatterley again, saying that the *Guardian*'s present editor 'gave the green light for the scribes of the graffiti to scribble F to their hearts' content on a quarter of a million pages'. Cassandra was always good fun to read. At the back of it all, I suspected, was Cecil King's anger over the *Guardian*'s leaders in 1961 saying that it would be better if the *Mirror* Group did not acquire the *Daily Herald* – a take-over which led to the appointment of the Shawcross Royal Commission with a brief to look particularly at the concentration of control in the press. Cecil King did not soon forgive opponents. (Though in fairness it should be said that after the Royal Commission reported Cecil King, as chairman of the Newspaper Publishers' Association, worked hard both to rebuild the Press Council and to secure agreement with the printing unions on improved working practices.)

Lord Denning's report at the end of September was in its way a masterpiece of journalism.[6] It was lucid, well written, and convincing. It

5 Tom Critchley apparently kept a diary, which will be of some historic interest.
6 Cmnd. 2152. *Lord Denning's Report.*

began with a survey of the character and activities of Ward, Ivanov, Christine Keeler, John Profumo, and Lord Astor, at whose house they had met. It went on to an examination of the security services and a criticism of the way Ministers, including the Prime Minister, had exercised their responsibilities. It dealt critically also with the press, and it contained a final section on 'rumours affecting the honour and integrity of public life'. As our leader said in its opening sentence 'the report blows away a cloud of vile suspicion'.

Ward emerged as an accomplished but utterly immoral man, in sympathy with the Soviet regime. Ivanov was quoted as telling people when he met them that every word would go back to Moscow; but he was an intelligence officer nevertheless. He had a sexual relationship with Christine but apparently not sexual intercourse. Christine, not yet twenty-one, was an attractive girl but had been 'enmeshed in a net of evil' since she was sixteen. Denning said that she should not be judged too harshly. He quoted Ward – for once believing him – as saying: 'Quite honestly, nobody in their right senses would have asked somebody like Christine Keeler to obtain any information of that sort [about nuclear weapons] from Mr Profumo – he would have jumped out of his skin.' Of Profumo, Denning said that his record gave no reason why his colleagues or the Security Services should have suspected him. And 'one of the most redeeming features' of the affair was the way Mrs Profumo (actress Valerie Hobson) stood by her husband after he confessed.

Denning's main criticism of Ministers was that in interviewing Profumo they had not asked the right questions. He also disclosed that through lack of coordination no one Minister was in possession of all the information, most of it circumstantial rather than conclusive, then held by the Security Services and separately by Scotland Yard. The head of the Security Services had decided in any event that since Ivanov had gone home the matter was now primarily political and not one that his people should pursue. Denning also asked why the *Mirror* or *Pictorial* did not disclose to the Prime Minister or Home Secretary or Scotland Yard the information they held (the letters to Christine Keeler). They had a 'secondary responsibility' though if they judged that there was no security risk they could keep their information to themselves. Chequebook journalism, however, came in for sterner treatment. Lord Denning said that 'scandalous information' about well-known people, whether true or false, had become a 'marketable commodity'. He condemned those newspapers, few in number, who dealt in it; he said that something must be done 'to stop this trafficking in scandal for reward'. This was a task, he suggested, for the new Press Council.

The *Observer* at an early stage had commented that the efficiency of Rhine Army and the condition of the Brigade of Guards were more important matters than the War Minister's relationship with Miss Christine Keeler. After Denning, we said that Britain ought now to concentrate on real issues – on economic growth, efficient planning, how to build more houses, defence and the Atlantic alliance, and on the quality of political leadership. A fortnight later Harold Macmillan announced his intention to resign. It was genuinely because of illness and not because of recent events, painful though those must have been to him. His own humanity had led him into judging a colleague too generously.

Denning provided a great relief by clearing the air. All kinds of scurrilous stories had been in circulation; and it took calm judgement to discount them, especially after Profumo's resignation. After Denning they evaporated. London was not Sodom or Gomorrah; still less were Nottingham or Manchester.

The women's movement

Did moral standards nevertheless decline in the sixties? And did the *Guardian*, as some critics alleged, contribute to the decline? Personally, I do not believe that morality suffered; and there was a great gain in the sixties through the dissolving of Victorian hypocrisies, the reform of laws on obscenity, censorship, divorce, abortion, and homosexuality, and the growth of artistic freedom. One of the greatest gains was in a woman's right to make critical choices for herself – not least because the contraceptive pill gave women the means to choose when they would and when they would not have children. If the *Guardian* provided some stimulus towards social change, so much the better.

The women's pages were the main forum. Mary Stott,* women's editor from 1957 to 1971, gradually extended their scope – encouraged by our features editors. Mary made a point of giving individuals the opportunity to write about their own experiences – the mother whose daughter had had an illegitimate baby, the woman who ran a farm for herself, the father who had left his wife and children, the paralysis victim struggling to live a fuller life, the girl who had had an abortion, and many more. Mary developed this vein before it became common in other newspapers, and underlying it was a deep concern with personal relationships, social welfare, and family wellbeing. She was both an early campaigner in the women's movement and an upholder of orthodox family life. Meeting her, you might have thought that she was an ascetic spinster, but you would have been wrong. She was married to another journalist and has two grandchildren; and, at seventy or thereabouts, is still writing and campaigning.

Of unquestionable benefit were some of the organisations and associations that grew out of articles and correspondence in the women's pages. The National Association for the Welfare of Children in Hospital was one of the first, one towards which Miranda and I were especially well disposed after a conflict with hospital authorities over visiting Tom when he had a septic boil at eighteen months. That association did much to change the attitude of doctors to the presence of mothers in hospital with

sick children. The Pre-School Playgroups Association was another valuable influence, helping to change Lady Plowden's mind after her report
on primary education, and it had its origins in a letter to the women's
pages. The Disablement Incomes Group came about because of something that Mary herself wrote, together with Ann Armstrong's articles
about life as a polio victim, and it led to legislation on help for the severely
handicapped. In these ways gaps in the social services were filled, by
voluntary and state-financed effort.

The acquisition of Jill Tweedie as a columnist brought another dimension to the discussion of social change. It did not matter that as editor I
often disagreed with the views she was putting as others did, for she was
a stimulating writer with a lucid ability to describe the relationships of
men, women, and children with each other.

In 1967, outside the women's pages but as a sequel to them, the
Guardian published a series called 'The Permissive Society', aimed at
assessing the gains and losses from the new freedoms. Although the series
caused a stir at the time, it contained little that would upset anyone now.
Mary Quant opened the series with a contribution which ranged far
beyond the field of fashion, arguing that the young were less materialistic
and more intelligent than older generations – 'and they've got sex in
perspective; they're not hung up on it any more; it's not difficult, they
take it or leave it'. She sought to justify her style of clothes, too, saying
that although 'sexy to look at' they were really 'more puritan than they've
ever been'; an interesting judgement, whatever you might think of mini-
skirts (and personally I found them attractive on girls with slender legs),
but one that John Knox would not recognise. Her key point, however,
was that because of the pill 'women are the sex in charge' – no longer
trading sex for material gain or marriage, but with an ability never known
before to determine their own way of life.

Altogether fifteen authors and six staff writers took part in the series,
which brought a host of letters and was reprinted as a paperback.[7]
Margaret Drabble followed Mary Quant, dealing directly with the question of morality. She welcomed the fact that women were no longer
haunted by the fear of pregnancy, pain, and possible death through
motherhood, as in all previous generations, and that education, freedom
to work, and personal equality were less likely to be negated by the arrival
of one small unintended baby; but she acknowledged that the problems
of careers and parenthood were far from resolved. She argued that men
were sometimes resentful of the new freedom of women to take up or
drop their careers if they became bored, and felt threatened in other ways.
Children still needed the same protection and attention that they had
always required, and the strains on an exclusive domestic partnership
were increasing.

7 *The Permissive Society*, published by Panther in 1969.

Both Quant and Drabble came in for criticism and praise in about equal measure. A churchman in Kent no doubt spoke for many in saying that love ought still to be the basis of a secure relationship, with chastity both before and after marriage. A woman writer in West London said that monogamous marriage was still the most satisfying relationship. A man in Glamorgan wrote that permissiveness seemed to him another word for spinelessness; 'a little more self-discipline, if you please, sir'.

The 'underground' poet Adrian Mitchell gave only 'three rousing psychedelic ho-hums' for the permissive society, believing it had not arrived, and he cited a long list of continuing forms of censorship. To which a correspondent in Hindhead, Surrey, replied that while he admired the clear sight of the younger generation they should not forget that some of his generation had died in concentration camps in the cause of political liberty and that the use of technology to overcome poverty required intricate organisation. The series continued with contributions from France, California, and Saudi Arabia, from the bishops of Durham and Woolwich, and from *Private Eye*.

Maybe the series broke no new ground, but nothing like it had appeared anywhere else at the time. Judging from readers' letters, it must have caused one generation to think about themselves, their children, and their marriages and a younger generation to think about themselves, their aspirations, and their friends. Though I disliked some of the contributions, it was right to let the *Guardian* open its columns to a wide range of views. And, over all, the inquiry left a healthy taste. Lady Chatterley and the pill had not brought the roof down.

Because we were restyling the section headings throughout the paper, about 1969 'Mainly for Women', as it had been called for most of Mary Stott's time, became 'Women's Guardian' – in line with Arts Guardian, Financial Guardian, Sports Guardian, and so on. That was a mistake, for almost as many men must have been among the readers of those pages. It aggravated also the feeling among women staff and women writers that these pages were a kind of ghetto; it seemed out of key with the freedom from sex discrimination that they were seeking. After Linda Christmas* became women's editor in 1973, she persuaded me to change the title to one that had deep roots in the past, 'Guardian Miscellany'. The pages then became a little less feminine and rather more general, though they retained their strong concern with the women's movement. They also continued to cover consumer affairs, fashion, cookery, and other household topics. The change of title was disliked by the advertisement department, who found it harder to sell space on general feature pages, and by the circulation department; but it had been the objective of a strong campaign inside the office led not only by Linda but by Jean Stead and some of the women reporters. That was a lobby hard to resist.

During Linda's reign the frank discussion of sex and social relationships was carried even further than before. Jill Tweedie remained at the forefront of contributors, going so far as to attend and write analytically about a wife-swopping party ('I put on a pair of my tattiest knickers so that, no matter what temptation assailed me, I would resist: I am a member of the NUJ, after all'). One of the many men who wrote for the pages described, movingly, the tensions and anxieties of a childless couple – who, having begun married life in their early twenties, employed orthodox contraception, but as the desire for children grew within them found that they could not achieve what they wished; and, even with the help of clinics and artificial insemination, had to wait more than five further years before success and happiness were attained. Another candidly introspective article, memorable to anyone who read it, was Bel Mooney's about her experience with a stillborn baby.

As in Mary Stott's time, so in Linda's and afterwards: these were pages with a deep humanity and social concern.[8] They made a powerful contribution to the paper. They were the inspiration of many campaigns; they were good to read, for men as for women; and they were pioneers among the women's pages of national newspapers. They were an influence towards a more liberal, tolerant, and equal society.

8 Peter Preston eventually restored to the pages a variation of the older title, and it now stands as 'Guardian Women'.

7 To London, crisis, and success

The London printing of the *Guardian* was almost a disaster, but in the end proved a success. Laurence Scott knew that the paper must print in London to achieve a national distribution, without which it could not win the display advertising essential to its survival. Neither he nor I foresaw all the difficulties. Our worst mistake was to take the paper to London with too small an editorial staff and too few printing resources to compete properly in Fleet Street. Then, just when we were beginning to get sales going in 1965-66, our revenue was hit by Wilson's retrenchment measures. At that point, as already mentioned, Laurence wanted to merge with the *Times* and opened talks with its proprietors; but eventually the Scott Trust and the company's Board decided against the course, and the *Guardian* fought on alone. The paper and its staff went through another round of belt-tightened austerity, but emerged healthier; and from 1967 onwards began to rebuild its strength. In spite of the millions that Roy Thomson had poured into the *Times*, we overtook it in 1971 - our 150th birthday year.

Printing in London

Loyal Northerners often told the *Guardian* that C. P. Scott would never have taken the paper to London. They were wrong. In spite of his devotion to Lancashire and the North of England, as early as 1890 he talked of printing in London. At that time the company owned a small general printing business in London, and C.P. wanted this to provide the *MG* with a London outlet; he wanted his paper to have as many readers and as great an influence as possible, provided it kept its character. But to the London proposal his senior partner said, 'No: that must be for younger, bolder and stronger men than I am.'[1] In 1914, with Scott himself by now the principal proprietor, there was serious negotiation. Some wealthy Liberals in London wanted to back the proposal but the talks came to nothing because C.P. insisted on absolute control.[2] With the coming of the war, that was just as well. There was more talk of it again in 1924, when C.P. thought the company's prosperity might cover it, but caution intervened.

Laurence, even before becoming managing director in 1947, was convinced that the London project was an absolute necessity. But he did not achieve it until 1961. He knew that once newsprint ceased to be rationed, as it had been since 1939, display advertising would be harder

1 Ayerst, *Guardian*, p. 230.
2 Ayerst, *Guardian*, pp. 354-55.

to get for a provincial paper such as the *Guardian*. Internationally it might have a great reputation, but that carried no weight with advertising agencies. They looked only at the number of readers and at their social group or income group, and at the 'cost per thousand' of reaching them. The *MG* was at a double disadvantage. As a provincial it could charge only a fifth of the *Telegraph*'s rate or a third of the *Times*'s rate; but for the advertiser the 'cost per thousand' was the highest of the three. The *MG* therefore, Laurence argued, must double its sale and prove that it was in every way a national newspaper.

The company's post-war technical director, Charles Markwick, was a man of great ingenuity. Working with Sir Robert Watson Watt and Partners and the electrical engineers Muirhead and Co., Markwick produced a prototype machine for 'facsimile transmission'. This could send the image of a complete page over some hundreds of miles in a matter of eighteen or twenty minutes, and the page could then be printed at the second centre. In 1951 trials were carried out between Manchester and Copenhagen – it was thought more discreet not to use a second centre in Britain, and engineers at the offices of the *Berlingske Tidende* were interested in the Markwick–Muirhead process – and complete success was achieved. The cost of production by this method would be well below that of using full conventional methods at a second centre, as many of the nationals were already doing in order to print in Manchester and Scotland in addition to London.[3]

Laurence approached the printing unions, but was not too surprised by the guardedly negative nature of their replies. If facsimile transmission of whole pages were to be generally adopted, the *Telegraph* and the popular papers would need fewer printers; most of the typesetting at one or other of their centres could go, as well as most of the wire-room (telex, teleprinter, and photoprinting). While some of the Manchester officials were sympathetic, national headquarters were not and he was told by at least one that they could not answer for the attitude of their members in London. He never achieved a meeting with the London Society of Compositors, who at that time controlled linotype operations – typesetting, that is – in Fleet Street.

He had meanwhile negotiated the purchase of a site in Southwark, close to the South Bank, with planning consent for a small industrial building – and indeed took me to see it soon after I became editor in 1956. But by then he had already decided that the facsimile process was almost certainly not feasible, because the response from one of the unions was that they must have a precise proposal, with starting dates, before they could put it to their members. He judged that the risks were too high. The company could incur all the capital costs of its South Bank plant and then be held to ransom at the last minute. He had therefore

3 The *Daily Mail* started printing in Manchester in 1900, the *Daily Express* in 1927, the *Daily Herald* in 1930, the *Daily Telegraph* in 1940, and the *Daily Mirror* in 1955.

decided to try a different approach. The Southwark site was sold soon afterwards.

One day at a Labour party conference in Blackpool I had a chat with one of the printing union leaders, who confidently told me that 'fax' for whole pages would never be used in Britain because it could not cope with demands of large circulations. There was a certain irony in that, for in 1957 the Markwick–Muirhead prototype was bought by Asahi Newspapers, in Tokyo. They then placed a production order with Muirheads, and from June 1, 1959, they used it between Tokyo and the northern city of Sapporo. They were printing six million copies a day of a joint morning and evening paper, and the print at Sapporo alone was well above anything the *Guardian* was likely to require. Later the *Wall Street Journal* and then the *New York Times* bought facsimile machines to extend their operations in the Middle West and California. The *Guardian* eventually brought the process into use in 1976, when it moved from Gray's Inn Road to Farringdon Road in London – but that was after fifteen years of printing in London by more conventional methods.

Not entirely conventional, however, for what Laurence and Charles Markwick eventually did was to adapt for the *Guardian* a system both cheaper and quicker than full conventional printing. It was called 'duplicated teletype setting', and was already in use on a small scale by the *Cumberland Evening News* between Carlisle and Workington and by the *Lancashire Evening Post* between Preston and Wigan. Each of those papers sent copy both ways, to and from each centre, for editions of their papers. In essence, a man working at a linotype keyboard punched out a perforated tape; it was then fed first into a specially adapted linotype to provide metal for printing at the first centre, and then the tape was fed by wire for reproduction at the second centre where it served a second linotype and produced a second set of metal lines. One-way teletype was already quite extensively used by the *Scotsman* from London and Glasgow to Edinburgh, by the *Glasgow Herald* from London to Glasgow, by the *Times* from the House of Commons to Printing House Square; and the unions had become used to it. Never before, however, had it been used on the scale that the *Guardian* planned.

The *Manchester Guardian*'s name was changed to the *Guardian* on August 24, 1959, as one of the first moves towards printing in London. Oddly enough, readership research carried out both in the North of England and in the South – an expensive affair into which we did not often venture – had told us that by changing the name we would in fact increase the paper's popularity in Manchester. So it proved, for sales in and around Manchester increased after the change. The explanation was simply that younger people in the North, and in Manchester especially, did not want a local paper; and until then Greater Manchester had been the only part of Britain where sales were not increasing. There was some nostalgia in the office about the old title, nevertheless, and that morning's leading article said that we hoped Mancunians would take the change as a compliment to the *Guardian*'s success rather than implying any disrespect to our home. We also said that eventually, but not imminently, the paper was to be printed in London as well.

That autumn, after the birth of our first child (Thomas), Miranda and I bought an old farmhouse in the Lake District – and sitting in its orchard next spring, shirtless in the sunshine and with Tom rolling on a rug alongside, I hammered out for Laurence on my old typewriter the first draft of an editorial plan for London printing. It was geared to working with the duplicated teletype. It transferred to London the sub-editing and control of political, parliamentary, financial, and some home news: all that would be typeset from London. It kept in Manchester the foreign, sports, feature, and leader page operations. It failed to foresee the extent to which the paper's centre of gravity would inevitably move south; but, mechanically, it did what was required in providing an even distribution of printing between the two centres – and it worked.

Momentarily I incurred Laurence's displeasure by discussing our London project and its union problems privately with Jim Callaghan. Jim was anxious to help and offered to do a little lobbying on our behalf among the union leaders. Laurence summarily dismissed the offer, saying that we must owe nothing to any politician. I thought we had done enough for Labour in the 1959 election to deserve a little help, without any expectation of future rewards, and I was sure that Jim knew the *Guardian*'s independence too well to expect anything in return. Anyway, I let the matter drop.

The key to the London arrangements in fact came in a deal Laurence did with Roy Thomson in July 1960. Roy had been in Britain only six years, having acquired the *Scotsman* in 1954, the franchise for Scottish Television in 1956, and the *Sunday Times* together with the whole Kemsley provincial empire in 1959. In a light-hearted article when his take-over of Kemsley's was announced, I had suggested that although still a commoner he was now bound to rank among the press peers and ought to have the title 'Thomson of North Bridge', since the *Scotsman*'s headquarters on the North Bridge in Edinburgh had been his first base for UK operations. In fact that was one of the titles he considered when he attained his peerage in 1964, but in the end he chose the metropolitan 'Thomson of Fleet'. He had acquired the *Scotsman*, its evening paper, and their plant and offices effectively for nothing, for he shrewdly noticed that it owned other property around North Bridge which was heavily undervalued; and within a year he had sold off that property and repaid the Royal Bank of Canada what he had borrowed to buy the *Scotsman*. He secured the television franchise because nobody else of substance in Scotland was bold enough to compete for it, and he thereby obtained his famous 'licence to print money'.

But the Kemsley deal was the boldest of the lot, for he obtained a newspaper chain said to be worth £75 millions for no more than about £5 millions in cash (borrowed this time from a Scottish bank), using among other devices a reverse take-over of Scottish Television to complete the transaction. It gave him a controlling interest not only in the *Sunday Times* and the *Empire News* but also in sixteen other papers, including the *Press and Journal* in Aberdeen, the *Western Mail* in Cardiff, and the *Journal* in Newcastle. Even the *Sunday Times* was then nothing like as prosperous as he soon made it; but a serious loss-maker in the Kemsley system was the operation at Withy Grove, Manchester.

Characteristically, Roy cured that within a year – and his deal with Laurence Scott was an important part of it. The two Manchester evening newspapers were our own *Manchester Evening News*, always dominant and with sales 30 or 40 per cent above its rival, and the weaker *Evening Chronicle* published from Withy Grove. The *MEN*'s main strength was in Greater Manchester while the *Evening Chronicle* did better in some outlying areas. In 1959-60 each was spending large sums on extra editions, promotion campaigns, and other costly competition. Laurence was determined if possible to resolve the contest before launching into the *Guardian*'s London operation. He wanted to avoid fighting a war on two fronts.

The arrangement he reached with Roy – and each was as enthusiastic as the other – brought both evening papers under common ownership and common management at the top. A new company was formed, North News Ltd, to own and operate the two. The shareholding was 80 per cent *MG&EN* and 20 per cent Thomson. North News arranged printing contracts for the *MEN* with our company and for the *Chronicle* with Thomson's. Extra editions and the more costly forms of competition were eliminated. The *MEN*'s profits were improved and the *Chronicle*'s losses curtailed. (Ownership of the *Guardian*, of course, remained entirely with *MG&EN* and the Scott Trust.) Thomson had turned round the worst of the Withy Grove loss, gaining a marginal profit instead; and Laurence had averted the war on two fronts – or so we thought at the time.

But there was another part of the arrangement, even more significant for the *Guardian*. Although Kemsley had had a large printing plant at Gray's Inn Road in London, most of the machine room was in mothballs and the *Sunday Times* was printed under contract by the *Daily Telegraph*. Thomson wanted to expand the *Sunday Times* to forty-eight pages or more, and the *Telegraph* could not cope, so Roy ordered new presses for Gray's Inn Road.[4] But those expensive new presses were

4 There was an extraordinary piece of in-fighting over the Thomson-*Telegraph* negotiations, retailed to me at the time by James Coltart, who was Roy's managing director. When Roy found that the *Telegraph* could not print forty-eight pages, he offered to buy the *Telegraph*. Michael Berry (latterly Lord Hartwell) was furious; and the *Telegraph*'s management then decided to start the *Sunday Telegraph*. A letter was sent to Thomson giving six months' notice to end the contract to print the *Sunday Times*; and six months was

going to stand idle throughout the week. What better than to print the *Guardian* there? Laurence was already looking at alternative possibilities in the summer of 1960, but the thought must have occurred to him and to Roy almost at the same moment. The details had still to be worked out, but in principle they agreed. Roy was extending the building at Gray's Inn Road anyway, so there was room for the *Guardian*'s London editorial and commercial offices and for a new composing room. It was a good match of business interests.

The Gray's Inn Road offices, when our embryo London editorial staff moved in, were ghastly. Building work was going on all around; there was universal dust, noise, and disorder. For the existing London reporters and specialists, moving up from their comfortable old Victorian offices in Fleet Street, it was a wretched transformation. It was amazing to me that they put up with it, making so few complaints – though they did complain. For the sub-editing staff moving down from Manchester, including a dozen or more new recruits, it was as dismal. The subs had to share accommodation with the *Sunday Times* sub-editors at first, and they had an extremely noisy wire-room right alongside. Nobody was happy. The greatest strain fell on John Putz,[5] who not only had to make his new London team into a coherent and efficient group but had to deal with all the teething troubles of the new teletype system and with a composing room staff almost all of whom were new to the *Guardian*.

London printing was scheduled to start on Sunday night, September 10, 1961, to produce the Monday morning paper. John Putz had been promised ten days of trials, so that the full system of sub-editing, teletype setting, page make-up, correcting, and onwards to the machine and publishing rooms could be thoroughly tested and run in. In the end, because of protracted union negotiations, there were no trials. Even the manning and payments for certain of the keyboard operations were not finally agreed until the Friday evening before the start. So on the Sunday it had to work; and fortunately it did. Late on the Friday night two senior composing-room men, on temporary loan from Manchester to supervise the new London staff, were in a car crash on their way home for the weekend. Though the car was written off they were back at Gray's Inn Road on the Sunday afternoon. And, luckily for us, on that Sunday in the Arctic the Russians carried out the world's biggest nuclear test – so we had a good story to lead the front page. Altogether, it was a good paper. But the next three years brought many nightmares.

---

nothing like sufficient for Roy to get his new presses working. But Roy's staff realised that the *Telegraph* had slipped, for by the current contract they had to give twelve months' notice; so they in turn held off for a while before pointing this out to the *Telegraph*, thereby winning Roy extra time to install his presses.

5 Night editor, introduced on p. 32.

Towards the crisis

Plotting *Guardian* sales on a graph, there was a steady rise from 1945 to 1961, though with a dip when the price went up in 1951. With the start of London printing, we expected the graph to climb faster. It did, but only for about six weeks; then it stuck, and for more than two years it hardly moved at all. Though careful never to state any targets, we had hoped for something more meteoric. It did not come until 1969, but then came in a most gratifying way.

The figures: from selling about 80,000 daily at the end of the war, the *MG* had grown to around 165,000 by the time I took over. It passed the 200,000 mark in 1960 and stood at 215,000 just before London printing began. The day we opened up at Gray's Inn Road we passed the *Times*, then at 245,000, and by mid-October were at 265,000. But that was where we stuck, indeed with a small dip in 1963. When Roy Thomson took over the *Times* in 1967 it pulled ahead again. But we started climbing again in 1968, passed the 300,000 early in 1970, passed the *Times* again in 1971 and kept ahead, with a figure just short of 350,000.

Why did the London operation at first fail to give the *Guardian* its take-off? First, because the printing restrictions at Gray's Inn Road meant that we were actually producing a less good paper. Laurence had argued, quite soundly, that if the Manchester paper was selling so well even when it could not reach most of the South at breakfast, then with a London outlet we must do better. Even with the special train from Manchester – an engine and two or three vans, which became the front of a Holyhead boat train at Crewe – we were previously reaching only London and a small part of the Home Counties, together with special deliveries to Oxford and Cambridge. But at Gray's Inn Road, with a new and rather raw staff in the composing room and problems also in the machine room, we were limited to twelve 'live' pages. In other words, everything else – feature pages, classified advertisement pages, and even some so-called 'news' pages – had to be prepared the day beforehand in Manchester.[6]

Twelve 'live' pages were just not enough, and the timelessness of the feature pages was too obvious. From a very early stage in the London experience, I had to start pressing Laurence to finance extra printing staff so that we could go to fourteen, then sixteen, and eventually twenty live pages in London. But then, not long after the London launch, we were hit by the very thing Laurence had wanted to avoid – something akin to a war on two fronts. The endeavour to rationalise the relationship between the *Manchester Evening News* and the *Evening Chronicle* was not a success;

6 For those interested in the technicalities: the pages prepared in Manchester in advance were 'matted' to London. That is to say, the page was made up conventionally and a papier-mâché impression (or 'matt') was made. The matts then went to London by train, being collected by a van at the station.

and Beaverbrook's were threatening to start an evening of their own in the city. By the spring of 1963, after two years of unexpectedly heavy expenditure on the evenings, our management decided that the *Chronicle* must be merged with the *MEN*. That was done in July, and it was no consolation that the second evening newspaper closed that year in six other cities – Birmingham, Bristol, Leeds, Leicester, Nottingham, and Edinburgh. Even then, Roy Thomson had to be compensated for the unexpired nine years of his printing contract for the *Chronicle* at Withy Grove and the loss of his share of North News profits. (His holding in North News was bought out, to leave us again in full control.) Our company had a painful year, financially, in 1963-64; and it was not until the spring of 1964 that Laurence could provide the cash for better printing facilities and some extra editorial staff at Gray's Inn Road. That autumn, helped by the general election, *Guardian* sales began to climb again.

There was a third factor for which we had not allowed. Readers in the South had been willing to forgive the *Guardian* quite a lot when they knew the paper was coming from Manchester. Once they knew it was coming from London, they were less forgiving. They expected theatre notices and concert criticisms the morning after the first performance, not thirty-six hours later, and they expected fuller coverage of metropolitan and southern events. They expected more from the City and sports pages, too. They were right to expect all these things, but with only twelve live pages and only two or three extra reporters we simply could not provide them.

What we did provide was generally very good indeed – especially in the news columns – but all this was not enough to give the *Guardian* the take-off it needed. We were working with a staff and resources far below that of any other national newspaper.

The strain was telling, too. Muriel Putz complained that John, having come home as usual about 2 am, threw off the top sheet one morning at six and said in his sleep, 'That's another page gone to press at last.' In fact on many nights John was having to scrap or telescope editions because the composing room was unable to cope even with the minimum output that we had planned. There were some nights in 1961 and 1962 when he had to come down to eleven or ten live pages, though by 1963 he was beginning occasionally to push up to fourteen pages. Physically, the subs' room was still a shabby and uncomfortable place though not as squalid as in the early days. On the news desk John Cole was now in charge and urging his reporters along in fine form. Harford Thomas had taken over from Paddy Monkhouse as deputy editor.

Laurence came to call on me at home in Didsbury on December 30, 1963, and it was an unhappy discussion. We both knew that the *Guardian*'s position was difficult, with losses higher than we had expected, and that the company was having to find £1,720,000 to compensate Thomson, to be paid in stages over the next seven years. We were both disappointed

by the sagging of *Guardian* sales. In addition, he said that he had to tell
me that he had been hearing of discontent among some of the senior
editorial staff because I was showing signs of fatigue, not talking to them
as much as I used to, and becoming 'snappy' in dealing with them. That
was true, and I had already taken the decision to move the editorial
headquarters to London. Most of the leader writers had already moved
themselves to London, because they found it more convenient, and
specialists such as the science and education correspondents had gone
south. I was tired of spending so many nights on the sleeper train (the
Manchester line was not yet electrified, and the day trains took four or
five hours). Moving to London would give me a more settled life.

I asked Laurence whether he would prefer to have a new editor. He
replied emphatically no. So I went in to the office and wrote one of my
regular staff circulars, to be distributed to everyone on January 1. It
acknowledged our difficulties and the paper's stagnation, noting that even
with the 'matted' pages we had an average six to nine pages fewer than
the *Times* and *Telegraph*. I reported, however, that with the evening
newspaper difficulties in Manchester now cured there was hope of
Guardian editorial expansion in 1964; and I looked forward, optimistically, to 1964 bringing a lively newspaper and 'more buoyant sales'.

A year later I was able to tell the staff what most of them already knew
– that 1964 had indeed been a good year for the *Guardian*. Sales during
the election period had briefly touched 300,000 and we had been producing an excellent paper. The half year's average for July to December,
including the summer dip and the election, looked like being about
275,000 – an increase of 14,000 daily. During 1965 the upward trend
continued, in spite of a price increase at the end of 1964. But on November
3, 1965, Laurence dropped a small bomb on my head.

The Haley-Hetherington talks

Out of the blue Laurence telephoned to ask if he could come to see me
at home at Blackheath. There was no indication of the reason, but the
paper was running well and I was almost always glad to see him. My
mind was occupied with Rhodesia – UDI then being imminent – and
with whether or not to try to keep Lib-Lab ideas alive, since Wilson's
working majority was down to one. I met Laurence at the station and we
walked home across the heath. He said that he had been to dine two
nights ago with Gavin Astor, chairman of the *Times* Publishing Company.[7] Sir William Haley had been there as well. Laurence had intended
to bring up an idea about which he had been thinking for some time – a
merger of the *Times* and the *Guardian* – but at the dinner he had found
it difficult to do so. Afterwards, however, he had hinted at it to Haley

7 Since 1971, Lord Astor of Hever, in succession to his father. A cousin of Lord Astor,
mentioned in Chapter 6; and of David Astor, editor-proprietor of the *Observer*.

alone. They had therefore had a long meeting the previous day, and Haley was enthusiastic about the idea.

Laurence had worked out his plan in some detail. Both papers, he said, were in difficulty. Before London printing, the *Guardian* had just about broken even in each of four or five years (from 1956-57 onwards); but in the four years of the London operation the losses on the *Guardian* had grown, from £200,000 in each of the first two years to £350,000 in the third and now to about £440,000. Neither sales nor advertising had grown as we hoped, and he could see no early likelihood of an improvement. His friends in the City - through whom he wished to raise money for a new building in Manchester - were incredulous that he could think of continuing to lose up to half a million a year on the *Guardian*, even though the *Manchester Evening News* was making a profit of over £1 million. He had already quoted Mark Norman, managing director of Lazards, to me on this.

The *Times*, however, had no asset such as the *MEN* and was only just paying its way. Gavin Astor was not prepared to put any more money into it, nor was his brother Hugh.[8] Haley had confirmed this to Laurence. The *Times* was not doing well on advertising, with a rate per column inch per thousand readers double that of the *Guardian* and four times the *Telegraph*'s. Haley had recently been appointed chief executive, and, while continuing as editor, had been charged with finding a way forward.

Laurence said that the idea of a merger greatly appealed to Haley, both because he had come up through the *Manchester Evening News* and indeed had been a member of the Scott Trust until he joined the *Times*, and, Laurence suspected, because he saw it as a tremendous culmination of his career. Both of them could see the *Times-Guardian* as one of the world's greatest newspapers. Haley would edit it for about five years and then, Laurence suggested, I would take over. Gavin Astor would be president of the company and Laurence chairman. Shareholdings would be according to the assets put in, which he believed meant that the *MG&EN* or the Scott Trust would have at least 52 per cent and therefore ultimate control.

Confronted with this proposal, I said that the two papers had much in common - endeavouring to work to the highest standards of journalism, trying to provide a first-class news service, and catering for intelligent readers. But there were differences, of political and general character. By tradition we were left of centre and took a clear political line, whereas the *Times* tended to be right of centre and for long periods took no clear political line. I then put the point which was to become one of the major obstacles in negotiation - that Conservative readers would always have

---

8 Hugh Astor for a short time in 1946-47 had served alongside me at the *Glasgow Herald*, before joining the *Times*'s foreign staff; a director of the *Times* from 1956 and a substantial shareholder; much more approachable than his somewhat patrician elder brother.

the alternative of the *Telegraph* or *Financial Times*, whereas those to the left would have no such alternative; so the paper would always be under pressure not to offend too many of its Conservative readers. All the same, I said, although I had great difficulty in conceiving that his scheme could work it must be given serious study.

We went on to discuss details, and it was plain that Laurence had thought out his ideas carefully. But he was uncomfortably inclined to dismiss my political point. He wanted to move fast, for he believed that if we did not come to an arrangement with the Astors they would go to the *Financial Times* or the *Telegraph*, and the *Guardian* would then be left in a weak and exposed position. Haley was talking to Gavin Astor that morning, and a meeting of both sides could be expected next week.

The next day I could not leave London, but that night I travelled to Manchester by the sleeper and went to breakfast at Laurence's home, at Alderley Edge. We then spent about two hours going over the whole scheme again. He readily agreed that the *Times-Guardian* must be able to take a strong stand on occasions such as another Suez crisis; I no less readily agreed that especially in its early days it must move carefully so as not to lose established *Times* readers. I questioned whether his thoughts on shareholdings would be acceptable to the Astors, the more because Haley had told him that only a 50–50 arrangement would be acceptable to the Board of Trade and the Monopolies Commission. He hoped for a board of five former *Guardian* people and three former *Times* people, and thought that the Scott Trust would probably wind itself up. I suggested that the succession to Haley as editor four or five years hence could not and ought not to be settled in advance, and Laurence, on second thoughts, was inclined to agree. He said incidentally that if I was not there he would want John Cole, which I took as a healthy sign because I had the highest respect for John's toughness and strength of character, and he was most certainly not of a Conservative political outlook.

Next Wednesday the summit took place. It was a strange meeting. It was held at Gavin Astor's house in Belgravia, starting with a polite cup of tea in his drawing room and then moving to business in his dining room. Present on their side were Gavin Astor, Hugh Astor, Haley, Pope (general manager), and Kenneth Keith (merchant banker and financial adviser to Gavin); on ours, only Laurence, myself, and Kenneth Searle (deputy managing director). Gavin asked Laurence to outline his proposal, and then put three questions.

First, did we propose to put in all our assets, including the *Manchester Evening News* and our holding in Anglia Television? Laurence replied that he assumed both companies would put in all their assets, without reservations. There was an almost audible sigh of relief from their side. Second, would it not be possible to continue publication of both papers under single ownership? Laurence said he could see no advantage in this, since neither paper would be gathering a greater revenue than it now enjoyed. He was supported by Haley and Pope. Third, would it not be possible to print the combined paper in the south of England only, saving the costs of production in the north? I intervened on this, saying it would be impossible in terms of our tradition. We must print in Manchester and give Manchester a special service; and as a growing, expanding national newspaper we ought not to print in London only. Haley backed me on this.

The discussion went on to the Monopolies Commission, transitional problems, and finance; and then to the character of the paper, which I said must be given very careful consideration. Since Gavin and Laurence were about to depart for five weeks to the Caribbean, to attend a Commonwealth Press Union conference, Haley and I were asked to meet meanwhile and report on the character of the *Times-Guardian*. At the same time Pope and Searle were to prepare a working paper on the economics of the project, also to be ready by mid-December.

When the *Guardian*'s three emerged on to the Belgravia pavement in the dusk, I had an agonised feeling that events were moving much too fast. Yes, the project was exciting, and I would not mind swapping the squalor of Gray's Inn Road for the comfort of Printing House Square. But was it not going to mean the end of the *Guardian* as we knew it and treasured it? Wouldn't the *Guardian*'s character simply be submerged in the *Times*? How many of our staff would still have the freedom to write in the way they wished? Would anything be left of the *Guardian*'s occasionally cheerful irreverence? And, above all, was there really any need for this drastic course? Laurence could see that I was not happy, and he said that in the talks with Haley I should not accept anything with which I was not satisfied.

Next morning Ian Smith made his unilateral declaration of independence on behalf of Southern Rhodesia, and in the afternoon Harold Wilson declared Smith to be a rebel. In the evening he invited Fleet Street editors to meet him at Downing Street – only the second such meeting since Anthony Eden had called one after the visit to London of Bulganin and Khrushchev in 1956. In fact, although he spoke of sanctions against Rhodesia, he said little that he had not already said either in the Commons or to the Lobby correspondents. But as we filed out of the Cabinet room I overheard the editor of one mass-circulation Sunday newspaper say to another: 'I say, old boy, what was that all about? It sounds rather serious.' In that respect at least, Haley and I were roughly on the same wavelength.

Our wavelengths were tested the following Monday, when we held our first session together. We both lived in Blackheath, and we met alternately at each other's houses. There were three meetings, on November 15, November 25, and December 7. In many ways I liked Haley, but these were eerie meetings; at their best they had the intellectual stimulus of an Oxford tutorial, but at their worst they were like negotiating with a cobra.

I mean no disrespect by that, but I feared that Haley might now have it in his power to kill the *Guardian*.

He opened the first talk by speaking of the difficulties we must expect with the Monopolies Commission, but he then went on to state his conviction that the combined newspaper would be a great undertaking. 'The most mature newspaper in the world,' he called it, and we must think of printing it eventually in more than one country – an American edition being quite feasible. He thought we should discuss policy and content first, then staffing and presentation. That suited me.

Though I wrote a fairly full record of the conversation immediately afterwards, only a little of it can be reproduced here. We went into some detail on issues such as Rhodesia, economic planning and free enterprise, regional imbalance, housing, the Common Market, and Anglo-American relations. Haley agreed that the newspaper could not be neutral and must have a clear point of view. I suggested that it must take great care to provide a forum for opposing points of view, and that in its own writing it must hold a successful dialogue with former *Times* readers and with former *Guardian* readers.

Haley remarked that C. P. Scott regarded the Conservatives as having more than their share of original sin. For himself, he thought that original sin and humbug existed in both parties in about equal measure. I was ready to agree to that. He wanted an assurance that when the time came, which was not just yet, I would be ready to say, 'Wilson must go.' I was willing to do that, though I thought the time was quite a long way off, but in turn I was uneasy about the extent of his support for Heath. He said outright that he had a good impression of Heath and was ready to trust him.

Towards public enterprise and the welfare state he was hostile. State enterprises encouraged the belief that there was limitless money to be tapped: he instanced the BBC, where as Director-General he had left £6 millions in reserve, but then because the Corporation wanted to force more money from the Government it had gone £14 millions into the red. That was wholly wrong, but typical of a public concern. As for the welfare state, it had 'thrown a bucket of water over everything, making it wet and slippery'. It was wasteful and inefficient and had gone too far. While ready to agree that there was waste and inefficiency, I believed that there were areas where it still needed development, particularly in pensions and benefits.

Towards the end of the two hours, I suspected that Haley felt I was pressing him too hard on particular items of policy. But I believed that if we were to understand each other we must explore ideas as thoroughly as possible before, not after, the new paper came into existence. Haley said that there should be no written document on policy, and I entirely agreed. The man in charge must be free to decide in the light of events.

That night I was on the sleeper again to Manchester, for a talk with

Laurence just before he left for the United States. Over the weekend his optimism had partly evaporated, and he was no longer so expectant of early success. He had been reconsidering the purposes of the Scott Trust and the *Times* trust, and he now regarded the appointment of the first editor as a matter of crucial importance. I had always seen it that way; but I now suggested that it might be best if both Haley and I stepped aside. Why not look for someone such as Jo Grimond? Having stayed with Jo and Laura in Orkney at the end of August, I knew that Jo was thinking of soon relinquishing the Liberal leadership and wanted some kind of executive role. Laurence replied that experience in editing a daily newspaper was essential. I thought that, underpinned by an experienced deputy, Jo could do the job. It would be better than having Haley as the first editor.

Laurence was going to the Caribbean via Washington, where he intended to brief Richard Scott, as chairman of the Trust. I decided that I had better visit Richard, too, as soon as the talks with Haley were over.

At the next Blackheath meeting, Haley made an obvious effort to meet some of what he assumed were my anxieties. He expressed rather more reservation about Heath but said that we must talk in terms of principles, not particular policies or people. He defined our objective as amalgamating the *Times* news service with the *Guardian*'s 'articles'. Correspondents such as Alistair Cooke we could keep, but he was inclined to rule out the kind of colourful reporting or parliamentary sketch-writing (Shrapnel, Zorza, Keatley) that the *Guardian* enjoyed. The *Times* sub-editors, he said, believed themselves to be the custodians of the *Times* traditions, and it was 'a newspaper of record'.

We went on to a study of how the paper would be laid out – starting with news on the front page, which the *Times* still did not have – and of the feature content. He was particularly anxious to inherit the *Guardian*'s science coverage. Later I asked whether we might return to the policy issues, emphasising that I was not trying to tie him down but only to understand his mind. He was again conciliatory, accepting that there should be further provision for widows, single-parent families, and retarded children. We also had an interesting but inconclusive exchange on nuclear weapons, with Haley remarking on the importance of Alun Gwynne-Jones, as an individual journalist, in shaping *Times* policy. Haley seemed well pleased with our morning's work, and I sent off a twenty-five-page report to Jamaica, with a carbon to Richard in Washington.

Next time we turned to staffing. The two papers together had editorial staffs of just over 400, not counting secretarial, and of these he thought that one hundred must go. We discussed and agreed in principle the way to proceed. For the senior appointments, we got down to names – for night editor his McHardy v. my John Putz, for news editor my John Cole v. his John Grant (ex-*Guardian*), for financial editor his Bill Clarke (also ex-*Guardian*) or his Egerton v. my Bill Davis. That was a difficult debate, and we decided only on two of the three posts. On more general matters, Haley said that we must be prepared to shed all the old *Times* 'stick-in-the-mud' readers and all the *Guardian*'s radical extremists but try to keep the rest. I was still concerned that, to hold Conservatively inclined readers, we would be under pressure to stay politically right of centre. Haley said that we must 'take a national view'. He again seemed well pleased with the meeting. This time I sent only a short report to Laurence.

The following day I flew to Washington, and, somewhat confused after a rough air journey, had a disjointed discussion with Richard. He mentioned that Laurence had first broached the project in October, when Richard was staying with him at Alderley for a Scott Trust meeting. (I was not then a member of the Trust.) He had gained from Laurence the impression that much more of the *Guardian* would be retained in the merged paper than now seemed to be envisaged. He implied, indeed, that I had already conceded too much to Haley. I replied that that was not the way the talks had been set up. From Laurence's standpoint, I thought that I had probably been too tough with Haley. Richard seemed stunned that events had moved so fast.

Over the next two days – at intervals between meeting Rusk, McNamara, and others, but not the President this time – we went over all the ground again. Richard accepted Laurence's economic analysis, of which I was sceptical, but expressed distaste for the whole project. He believed that the merged paper could meet the intentions of C. P. Scott, but he had extreme doubts about Haley as the first editor. Laurence had not told him of my Grimond proposal; Richard thought that, by an almost unique accident, that might be acceptable all round. The *Times*, after all, had come out for the Liberals at the last election.

A week later, back in Britain, I was astonished to hear from Laurence that during their time together in the Caribbean he and Gavin Astor had never discussed the project. There had never been a convenient opportunity, he said. The managers Pope and Searle had completed their report, though parts of it needed further examination. Laurence was expecting a telephone call from Gavin any day now. As to the first editor, he had now concluded that Haley was acceptable. Caribbean distance had evidently lent enchantment to that view. He still ruled out the Grimond or other third-party solution.

That telephone call never came. A week later, on December 22, Laurence said that we should perhaps break off the negotiations in the friendliest way, so that they could be resumed later if the need arose. That was fine from my point of view, since it postponed the evil. Laurence asked for formal confirmation of my recommendation to the Trust. Was it that Haley should not be accepted as the first editor? I confirmed that it was. I liked Haley, but that was not the point; as first editor he would mould the paper, and I did not believe that there would be much of the *Guardian* left in it.

For months Laurence said nothing more about a merger. When the Trust met in the spring, he asked me to mention nothing of the negotiations while making my annual report. I would have preferred to hear the Trust's views and to be sure that it was all a closed chapter. Of the trustees, only Laurence and Richard knew of the *Times* talks, and of the directors only Kenneth Searle and I. In November I had been unhappy at being unable to consult Harford or John Cole; Miranda was then my only adviser, though an astute one. But I was not too worried. I hoped that the *Times-Guardian* had disappeared over the horizon. It hadn't.

The crisis, November 1966

There were three portents whose significance at first I missed. One was that during the spring of 1966, for the first and only time apart from the Chatterley case, Laurence sent me a number of notes about editorial matters. They were no more than half a dozen in all, and none was of great moment. Their common thread was that the paper contained too much politics and was becoming a bore. Twice he drew unfavourable comparisons with the *Telegraph*'s front page. That was fair comment, though I did not believe that any general complaint was justified. We had a standing rule, well respected by John Putz and others, there there must be something non-political and non-economic on the front page every day. But perhaps our ration of humanity and fun had been a bit thin.

He also sent me, no less unusually, a note midway through the March election campaign to congratulate me on the tone and content of the election leaders. But then in August he sent me a draft paper, intended for the Trust and Board, in which he said that the *Guardian* could not succeed while so many of its writers 'belittle the ethics and outlook' of people in commerce and industry; and that the *Guardian* was unattractive to advertisers. When I indicated that the kind of remedies he implied would have made his grandfather's hair stand on end – the suggestion that commercial necessity should bring a modification of the paper's radical politics, for example – he withdrew it. But it was a sign of his anxiety.

The second and most significant portent lay in the Wilson retrenchment measures, announced on July 20. The Prime Minister's long statement was fully covered and commented on in the paper – with its imposition of a twelve-month 'freeze' on prices, wages, and dividends, its surcharges on purchase tax and surtax, its higher charges for petrol, postal services, and telephones, its restrictions on new building, and so on.[9] It was the end of George Brown's 'national plan', and it proved much too severe. What we failed to foresee was its effect on advertising.

9 The 'freeze' is more fully discussed in Chapter 9, pp. 204-09.

The display and classified categories both suffered. In August the *Guardian*'s display revenue dropped 28 per cent compared with the previous year, and classified by 9 per cent; September was not quite so bad, at 3 per cent down and 14 per cent down; October and November were catastrophic, with display down 37 and 25 per cent, and classified 17 per cent in each month. These were grievous figures, on top of the London printing costs, and at that time over 70 per cent of the *Guardian*'s revenue came from advertisements.

The *Times* suffered only a small drop, being about 6 per cent down in revenue. The *Telegraph* was harder hit, with a monthly fall of 14 to 15 per cent. Our one consolation was a continuing rise in sales, with figures in the autumn months of around 285,000 to 290,000. The *Times*, too, was pushing ahead – with news now on its front page and other benefits from Haley's expansion plans, including one or two ideas he had borrowed from our talks, I thought wryly. Its sales were close on our heels; but, unknown to us, its modest profit of 1965 now looked like being turned into a loss of £300,000 in 1966.[10] The Astors had had enough.

The third portent I had missed was a Rolls-Royce sitting in the middle of Blackheath as I went for a walk at 8 on a fine September morning. I knew it was Haley's and wondered why it was waiting for him so early in the day. That afternoon Roy Thomson's take-over of the *Times* was announced; and some days later Haley told me that he had been driven to Oxford first thing that morning to tell the Warden of All Souls, one of the *Times* trustees, what was afoot.

The Thomson Organisation's acquisition of 85 per cent of the *Times*'s shares came as a complete surprise. There had been rumours of contact between Gavin Astor and the *Financial Times* (Lords Cowdray and Drogheda, and Pat Gibson), but none about Roy Thomson.[11] Laurence was disinclined to believe that anything was happening, or so I understood. In April he had written to Haley – not Gavin Astor, oddly – to say that he assumed talks were in abeyance because of the likely difficulties with the Monopolies Commission, and had had a friendly acknowledgement.

The *Times*-Thomson announcement came at 6 pm. Miranda and I were due to dine at the Polish Ambassador's house at 7.30; she got there

10 The final figures from the Audit Bureau of Circulations in fact put the *Times* just ahead of us in the last quarter, exactly when the Astors were preparing to hand over to Roy Thomson.

11 The negotiations with the *Financial Times* are described in Lord Drogheda's *Double Harness*, pp. 189–93. Drogheda speaks of their failure as the major disappointment during his thirty years as managing director or chief executive of the *FT*. The Pearson-Longman directors were prepared to offer Gavin Astor only 8¼ per cent of the shares in the combined *Times-FT* group, which Drogheda thought too little. Because the directors were divided, the offer could not be improved. It was turned down by Gavin Astor a few weeks before his deal with Roy Thomson.

on time, but I was forty minutes late. I had meanwhile tried to assess the situation and had written a leader – saying that Roy Thomson might find the *Times* as awkward a morsel to swallow as Lord Northcliffe had done, but that his methods would be different. He was not likely to interfere with editorial policy, so long as the *Times* made money, and papers such as the *Scotsman* and the *Sunday Times* had greatly benefited from his ownership. We noted that he had to have consent from the Monopolies Commission but thought he was likely to receive it. We noted also that he would now be printing his national newspapers' chief rivals – the *Guardian* at Gray's Inn Road and the *Observer* at Printing House Square. We looked forward to long and friendly rivalry with Lord Thomson's *Times*.

What followed in the next eight weeks is a story better not told in detail before 1991 or 2001 or whenever Laurence and I are both well settled in whatever Valhalla or Gehenna is reserved for newspaper people. But, briefly, a series of proposals were discussed and the *Times-Guardian* merger featured in two of them. Chronologically they were as follows:

1. Move to Printing House Square. Roy Thomson told Laurence that he wanted to move the *Times* to Gray's Inn Road. Did we object? (At the beginning of the meeting he ribbed Laurence, saying, 'You could have had the *Times* if you'd been ready to pay the price.') Laurence decided to ask the Monopolies Commission to attach a condition to its consent to the Thomson-*Times* deal – that the *Guardian* should be allowed to buy PHS at an arbitrated price. Roy was furious. He told us that it was 'preposterous'. He told the Monopolies Commission that if it attached any conditions he would let the *Times* 'go down the drain'. He had a big and difficult job with the *Times* and if conditions were attached he would say 'no'. It was in Laurence's mind that the *Guardian* would cease printing in Manchester. In that event, I told him, Roy would own the *Guardian* as well within five years. From David Astor, the editor and main authority at the *Observer*, Laurence sought an assurance that they would stay as our tenants at PHS. They were cautious, because they wanted facilities to print up to $1\frac{1}{4}$ million copies, which did not then exist at PHS. Later David Astor put a counter-proposal that the *Guardian* and *Observer* should form a joint company to buy PHS. But the whole project died because of discreet indications from the Monopolies Commission that anything of the kind would be beyond their statutory authority. They could say 'yes' to Thomson unconditionally, or they could say 'No, unless...' They could not say 'yes, provided...' which was what we were asking them to do. That was in late October.

2. The 'Times-Guardian' at once. Laurence then decided to propose to Roy an immediate merger of the *Times* and *Guardian* 'within the next ten days'. I intercepted him at Euston when he was on his way to see Roy, by himself, and mercifully talked him out of it. It was a non-runner for a number of reasons – most obviously because Roy did not yet own the *Times*, and neither he nor Gavin Astor was likely to upset their arrangement while it was under examination by the Monopolies Commission. That was on November 2–3.

3. The consortium. This was the biggest and longest running proposal, conceived on November 6 and killed on November 22. The consortium was to consist of the *Guardian*, the *Observer*, Gavin Astor, four or five merchant banks, and a man called Claud Morris. It was to publish the *Times-Guardian* and the *Observer*, as well as the *MEN* in Manchester. After tense debate on our side, involving the *Guardian* & *MEN* board and the Scott Trust, we rejected it on November 22. That day, also, Lord Goodman effectively turned it down on behalf of the *Observer*. A little more of its short life and death is recounted below.

4. An 'Observer-Guardian'. This was an offshoot from the consortium. David Astor suggested that the *Guardian* should take over the *Observer* and, if necessary, close the *Guardian* in order to use the resources of the *MEN* to sustain the *Observer*. It was not as Machiavellian as it sounds, for David perceived that Laurence had lost confidence in the *Guardian*'s ability to survive; David was looking both for a means to inject new money into the *Observer* and to let the *Guardian* keep something of itself alive. He was willing to sacrifice his own editorial and managerial control. But that project, too, was set aside a few days later. By then we had decided to keep the *Guardian* going as an independent paper and all our resources were required for that.

The Monopolies Commission gave its consent to the Thomson-*Times* deal shortly before Christmas, with no conditions attached. That was immediately endorsed by the President of the Board of Trade, Douglas Jay, a former *Times* man; and on January 1, 1967, Roy Thomson took over.

The consortium really began from Claud Morris, though something of the kind was already running through Laurence's thoughts. Morris was a former *Mirror* journalist who at the age of thirty-two had bought a small newspaper in South Wales, from which he went on to run a successful chain of magazines.[12] About the end of October he approached the Monopolies Commission, suggesting that a rival group might bid for the

---

12 Claud Morris, while a *Mirror* political writer, had also stood as a Labour candidate in the 1950 and 1951 general elections. In 1952 he bought the *South Wales Voice*, published at Ystalfera, north of Swansea; and later he started the *Voice of Welsh Industry*. Later still, in partnership with Roy Thomson, he started other *Voice* magazines, mainly for industry in different regions. Morris and Thomson parted company, however, and in 1966 Claud Morris was strongly antagonistic to Roy Thomson. There was an element of seeking revenge in his attitude; and he argued that under Thomson the *Times* would cease to be a British institution.

Times. He then visited David Astor and Laurence Scott, indicating that
two or more merchant banks were willing to put up money and that
anywhere between £3 millions and £5 millions could readily be raised.
At that point Laurence effectively took over leadership of the consortium.
I became involved in discussions with David, Laurence, Claud Morris
and others, and was extremely uneasy about the proposal. It seemed to
me flawed from the beginning; and, unlike Laurence, I still believed that
the *Guardian* could survive on its own.

Morris spent Sunday, November 13, with Laurence at Alderley Edge.
I offered to join them, but Laurence preferred to talk by himself, especially
as editorial control of the *Times-Guardian* was one of the issues. He said
he was going to be 'tough' with Morris and insist on three conditions.
First, there must be solid City backing, if possible with five merchant
banks each taking 5 per cent of the shares. Second, the *Observer*'s shareholding must not exceed 10 per cent and they must be under our operational control. Third, the *Times-Guardian* must have 'our' editor – specifically, me. I phoned on Sunday night and he said only that the talks
had gone well and that he was asking Richard to return from Washington
some time in the next ten days. As yet, neither the Trust nor the *Guardian*
& *MEN* directors knew what was being discussed.

Next day I had to fly to Israel. In July I had interviewed Nasser on the
tenth anniversary of his nationalisation of the Suez Canal – a strong
interview to which we had given much space – and had wanted to
interview the Israeli Prime Minister, Levi Eshkol, in the same month.
That had been inconvenient to the Israelis, and eventually they had asked
that the Foreign Minister, Abba Eban, should speak for them.[13] The
interview was to take place on Tuesday morning in Jerusalem. I was most
most reluctant to cancel the visit, but on Saturday and again on Sunday
told Laurence that if necessary I would. He said there was no need. No
decisions would be taken while I was away.

My absence from London was for no more than fifty hours, for I was
back at Heathrow at 1.20 on Wednesday afternoon, bringing the Eban
interview with me. But on arrival I found that Richard had returned from
Washington on Tuesday and that the Scott Trust was already in session,
at Laurence's flat near Hyde Park. There was a message to say that he
would see me in the evening.

We met at 5.30 at his flat, and that meeting, for a time, was the breaking
point between us. He outlined the proposals on the consortium as they
now stood. Only one merchant bank, a small one, was at present willing
to take shares. But the *Observer* was coming in and would take 15 per
cent. The editorship of the *Times-Guardian* remained to be determined,
but he had concluded that I was politically unacceptable to the consortium. He had given the Trust a full account of the situation. If the

13 For the Nasser and Eban interviews, see Chapter 10, pp. 237-39 and 245-47.

October drain continued, the company could lose as much as £400,000 next year. The loss on the *Guardian* would be running at £900,000 or more, and the profit on the *MEN* had been halved. We could not continue in this way. He had asked the Trust for a free hand and had been given it.

In reply I asked Laurence to cast his mind back to the undertakings he had given me on Saturday and Sunday. All but one had been broken, and even the City backing had dwindled. As to the editorship, I asked him to cast his mind further back – to a year ago, when I had proposed the Grimond or 'third party' solution. I had been ready to stand down then, and would stand down now on one condition. I had to be sure that enough of the *Guardian* would survive in the merged paper. I was not against a more 'popular' *Times-Guardian*, which was what Claud Morris and David Astor wanted; but I distrusted the way decisions about the consortium were being taken, and I was dismayed by the way he had handled matters in the last few days. I would sleep on the matter and talk to him next day.

It was quite a short encounter. Later I dined with Richard. I told him that I thought the Trust had been given a misleading picture. Had anyone asked about the company's financial reserves? Apparently not: yet to my knowledge they stood at about £1½ millions, the bulk of which was readily accessible. The company still looked like breaking even in this financial year (to next March), and trading conditions ought to improve some time in the next financial year. Why was there such a rush to ditch the *Guardian*? There were many other points that I would have wished to put to the Trust, but I had not been given the opportunity.

Before leaving Washington, Richard had talked to Eric Roll who was on a visit (the former Economics Minister in Washington and now permanent secretary in the Department of Economic Affairs). Eric had told him that it would be at least twelve months before the economy turned upwards, and that, followed by Laurence's long recital about company finances, had influenced him. The trustees had also understood that I was in agreement with the consortium proposals. I asked Richard to reconvene the Trust at the earliest possible moment. He agreed but said it could not be held until Monday or Tuesday.

Next morning I wrote a memorandum of five foolscap pages and posted it to each trustee individually. I telephoned to Laurence and told him I was doing so; they would have the weekend in which to consider it. It began with a restatement of my objections to the consortium, above all that too little would be left of the *Guardian*. From the way 'our' editor had been ruled out, it looked as if the *Times-Guardian* must start from a cautious and conformist point of view. Were we really to accept that the new paper must soft-pedal subjects that the *Guardian*, uniquely, had cared for?

Further, my note said, it was evident that the consortium stood only a slender chance of coming into existence.

At least three hurdles lie ahead. First the Monopolies Commission must say 'no' to the Thomson-*Times* merger – and it must back its refusal with reasons strong enough to convince the Board of Trade, Parliament, and the public. Secondly, Gavin Astor must then choose between our consortium, the rival offer from the *Financial Times*, and possibly a third grouping. Thirdly, the new merger must be placed before the Monopolies Commission and accepted by it – which is likely to happen only if the consortium can present its case in a most convincing manner, with Gavin Astor's willing cooperation. Our group will, incidentally, be questioned in detail about how it proposes to appoint its editor, what names it has in mind, and what safeguards he will have. It is also likely to be asked why the Commission should prefer a solution (ours) that reduces the number of newspapers in place of one (Thomson's) that gives all the opportunity to continue.

Were we going to be forced back, I asked (remembering the questions to Roy), on the argument that in the absence of such an arrangement we should let the *Guardian* die? Was the Trust ready to authorise that answer?

The note went on to discuss the company's finances, saying that although the prospects were black they were not so black as they had been painted. The current forecast was a company profit of £200,000 for the financial year; and there were reserves of over £1,250,000, not counting trade investments such as our holding in Anglia. Some must be held for use in the new Manchester building; but even if the worst forecasts were correct, and the *Guardian* had to be killed next summer, the *MEN* could then quickly finance the new building out of its own profits. I concluded with the recommendation that the *Guardian* should be kept going, with severe 'belt-tightening' in every department, including editorial; and with a major overhaul of the advertisement and production departments, both of which were running badly. 'To abandon hope of saving the *Guardian* now would be a shameful decision, for which we should not be forgiven.'

Over the weekend I had two further meetings each with David Astor and Claud Morris, in which they tried to persuade me to withdraw my opposition; also a further long talk with Richard. On Sunday Mark and Val Arnold-Forster provided a buffet lunch at their house in Holland Park, between my other meetings, for about twelve of the *Guardian*'s senior editorial staff from London and Manchester, so that I could brief them. I asked them individually to brief their departmental staffs that evening on a basis of strict confidence; they did so, and there were no leakages whatever. In a building shared with Thomson's, that was first class. I had prepared a short and non-committal press statement, since there had been rumours in some weekend papers, but it was not required. Paddy Monkhouse, former deputy editor and still a trustee, telephoned from Manchester to say he had found my memorandum invaluable and wished he had known all that was in it before the Wednesday meeting.

On Monday morning the Trust met, again at Laurence's flat but this time with me present. Apart from Richard and Laurence, the trustees were Bill Montague, another grandson of C.P. and now, having retired from the Colonial Service, an Oxfordshire county councillor; Francis Boyd, the *Guardian*'s political correspondent; and Bob Ebbage, who had served with the management side for more than forty years and now was company secretary. The meeting was opened by Richard, who read a personal statement he had prepared over the weekend. It was resounding but diplomatic. Here is part of it:

As I understand the position of our potential partners in the consortium, the merged *Times-Guardian* would be tailored to the tastes of *Times* readers. The radical, and perhaps disturbing, voice of the *Guardian* would be largely suppressed. This appears to be regarded as vital by Mr Morris, Mr Berry,[14] both Gavin and David Astor, and the City interests. Our 40 per cent interest in the consortium could hardly prevail against such combined forces. We would find ourselves surrendering the profits of the *Evening News* to subsidise the *Times* and the *Observer* while the *Guardian* died. Indeed, the new edifice which the consortium is now planning seems to me to be assuming more and more the character of a mausoleum in which the relics of the *Guardian* might be preserved with decorum and without loss of face to nourish and sustain a more thriving *Times*.

He went on to say that if we proceeded with the consortium we must state our minimum requirements and stick to them. This statement must include an agreement on the character of the paper and how that character was to be preserved. He concluded

The maintenance of the character of the *Guardian* is virtually the sole function of the Trust. We are not required to express our views on the economic fight to be or the day-to-day arrangements for publishing our papers. These are questions for the Board. But ours is the chief responsibility for ensuring that actions are not taken which might jeopardise the essential character of the *Guardian*. If we fail in this, we are out of business. And we are not back in business again, however successful the consortium with which we are associated, if it fails to speak with the voice of the *Guardian* and to preserve its essential character.

Richard then invited me to speak in support of my memorandum, which I did. Laurence came next. He was conciliatory in tone – indeed he had telephoned on Saturday, saying he was pruning his roses which was a good way to relax and hoping I was doing the same – but in substance he budged hardly at all. He corrected me on the company's financial reserves. While it was true that we had a cash reserve of over £1,250,000, only about £300,000 was in 'free resources'. The remainder was on loan to property companies in which we had interests, and while legally it could be recalled that would be crippling to them while they were suffering like others from the freeze. On my 'belt-tightening' thesis,

14 Anthony Berry, the only merchant banker who had committed himself; younger son of Lord Kemsley, and MP for Southgate, Enfield, from 1964.

he did not believe that the savings I had outlined were practicable. He conceded, however, that if something of the sort were applied it could tide us over the next two years. He maintained his view that the consortium and the *Times-Guardian* were the right course.

Paddy spoke strongly in my support, and Francis Boyd more cautiously so. Bill Montague and Bob Ebbage asked a number of questions but did not put a view. Richard proposed that since the consortium was to meet again in the afternoon we should insist on three conditions – adequate City backing, revision of the *Observer*'s part, and our editor. That was agreed.

The consortium met in the afternoon at the offices of the Arts Council with Lord Goodman in the chair. (He was chairman both of the Arts Council and of the *Observer*'s Trust, which in constitution was rather different from ours, since it could and ultimately did return a substantial part of the shareholding to David Astor.) Goodman began by saying that the financial aspect must be settled first, and he turned to Claud Morris for an answer. Morris gave a long, circuitous, and unconvincing reply. Goodman said that only 'letters of intent' from the City interests would impress the Monopolies Commission. Could we have a precise list by this evening or tomorrow morning? Morris said there was much preliminary work to be done and he didn't think it would be possible; he departed to a telephone. There was some discussion of editorial aspects, but it was inconclusive. Goodman had to depart after one hour.[15]

The Trust met again in the evening – a much longer meeting this time, again with my presence. I argued that we ought not to let it appear that we were pulling out of the consortium just because of inadequate financial backing, if it came to that tomorrow. We ought to show our commitment to the *Guardian* and its character. Laurence suggested that my interpretation of its character was too narrow. The Trust decided against any modification of its three conditions, agreed in the morning.

At 9.30 on Tuesday 22nd the consortium convened again at the Arts Council. Claud Morris had arranged a meeting in the City at 11.30; Laurence and Kenneth Searle (deputy managing director, just back from holiday) were going on our behalf. At the beginning of the 9.30 meeting

15 Harold Wilson, in a private conversation at Downing Street on December 21, told me that Goodman had been keeping him in touch with the situation. Goodman had talked to him by telephone at Chequers on the Sunday afternoon, seeking advice about the consortium; he had told Goodman to 'stay with it', but in the end to 'kill it'. As soon as he had known that Michael Berry's money was in it – which in fact it wasn't, for Wilson was confusing Michael Berry and Anthony Berry – he had been more determined than ever that Roy Thomson must have the *Times*. He had let the Monopolies Commission know that there must be no delay in getting on with its job and that it was not supposed to be 'shopping around' for alternative buyers. I felt that he was not too well in touch with the situation, however, because when I told him about the decline in the *Guardian*'s advertisement revenue since July he expressed great astonishment.

Laurence said that if the consortium failed the *Guardian* would fight on alone. That cheered me up. David Astor put in a plea for a marriage between the *Guardian* and the *Observer* before Lord Thomson's 'cold winds' began to blow.

Richard and I had a walk round St James's Park in the November sun, then returned to Gray's Inn Road for a meeting of the senior editorial staff. Richard attended, which proved to be important. The meeting was relayed to Manchester by the loudspeaker telephone which we used for all editorial conferences, and from there Brian Redhead* and Geoffrey Taylor,* then Northern editor and foreign editor, took part. I outlined the position as it now stood. There was a universal view that the *Times-Guardian* was an unsound concept from which we ought to withdraw, even if financial backing were to be forthcoming.

Laurence and Kenneth returned at 1.30. An *MG&EN* Board meeting was due at 2.30. The consortium was 'off', Laurence said, not because of lack of finance but because agreement on editorial control was unattainable. The leading banker, however, had put forward another proposal – a straight take-over bid for the *Times*, backed by a pledge of all the assets of the *MEN*. Laurence now proposed to put this to the Board and Trust and to go to the Monopolies Commission with it on Friday.

At the Board meeting, which Richard for the first time attended on behalf of the Trust, Laurence put his proposition. I opposed it; but it was plain that if Laurence took a vote he would carry four of the six directors present. After a while, however, Richard intervened. He recalled what he had heard at the midday editorial meeting. The senior editorial

staff were unanimously against the *Times-Guardian*, believing that it would be the *Times* under another name. At that point Laurence, who knew that I had drafted a public statement saying that we were withdrawing from the consortium, asked to see it. And at that moment I knew that the fight was over.

The Trust met at 6 pm, without my presence. By agreement with Richard, I had arranged a meeting of all editorial staff in the building for 6.30, and some of the management staff had asked if they could attend. At 6.25 Richard came out of the Trust meeting to give me the all-clear. In front of the staff, I began by reading the statement which was to be made public three hours later:

> The *Guardian* has been considering whether to make an offer to take over the *Times*, as an alternative to Lord Thomson's bid, and whether to take part in the proposed consortium being formed for this purpose. It has been decided that neither of these proposals is in the interests of the *Guardian* or of the public. The Scott Trust, which owns the *Guardian*, and the directors of the *Manchester Guardian* and *Evening News* Limited are of the view that the *Guardian* ought to continue as a separate and independent newspaper.
>
> This country's newspapers face a fiercely competitive future. But we are convinced that there is – and will continue to be – a place for the *Guardian*'s radical voice and reforming tradition. The Scott Trust and the directors of the *MG&EN* are determined to keep the *Guardian* strong and to give it every opportunity in the months and years ahead.

Though I don't myself have any recollection of it, because I was too intent on what I had to say, I was told afterwards that when I got to

December 1966

'continue as a separate and independent newspaper' there was something of a gasp from the listeners, followed by a mounting cheer. Having finished the text, I said that we had a very tough fight ahead. We must cut operating costs, exist on smaller papers, and make every inch count. But it could be an exciting challenge. I ended by saying that the project to take over the *Times*, under the right conditions, might have been a useful enterprise. But I and others had held – above all Richard as chairman of the Trust – that our first and overriding duty was to fight on with the *Guardian*. 'I am happy that we shall be able to do so.'

Reconstruction and recovery

The decision had been taken, and the *Guardian* was to continue. Inwardly, Laurence seemed unconvinced. He still believed that within two or three years we should be forced either to renew *Times-Guardian* negotiations in some form – and from a far less favourable basis – or to have to close the *Guardian*. All along he had been concerned by the company's declining profits and by the belief that with Wilson's Government we were in for a long recession. Outwardly, however, he put a good face on our position. He took the lead in approaching the printing and journalists' unions, with proposals for economy and efficiency of operation. He presented the *Guardian*'s case well and with assurance, though he was less at ease in radio and television interviews. He wrote an excellent statement for the staff, with copies for everyone, setting out the company's financial position and prospects, and saying that with cooperation all round the *Guardian* could be put on a sound foundation. He acknowledged, also, the *Guardian*'s debt to the *Manchester Evening News*.

The immediate aim was to save between £500,000 and £600,000 of the *Guardian*'s operating costs. My 'belt-tightening' was being taken literally, but I did not complain. We expected to cut 10 per cent from newsprint costs, by a higher advertisement ratio and thinner papers at weekends; 10 per cent from administration costs; and 25 per cent from the printing and editorial departments. That meant the loss of over a hundred staff, of whom thirty-five were to be journalists, by early retirement or redundancy. The terms were generous, but it was painful.

From the outset, however, we said that the savings must be shared equally in all departments. Consequently, although by early January agreement had been reached with everyone except NATSOPA, we were held up for a difficult three weeks waiting for NATSOPA's Richard Briginshaw. For two days at the end of January it looked as if we might after all have to shut the paper down, and if that were done even temporarily would we ever start again? But George Woodcock from the TUC did a bit of private talking in the background, as did Jim Callaghan and Ray Gunter (Minister of Labour), and that helped us over the last hurdle.

By February 2 the arrangements were complete. In the end, I felt that the journalists were taking a heavier cut than anyone else. We lost our thirty-five, coming down to 158. But that may later have been to our benefit. Although we lost four or five good men, we shed a number of the older and less effective men and women. We retained a number who could have gone elsewhere for higher salaries – the *Times* and *Sunday Times* were both recruiting aggressively with Roy Thomson's money – but they chose to stay with the *Guardian*. And by the autumn of 1967, since the company's fortunes proved to be less disastrous than forecast, the editorial side were among the first beneficiaries. We ended with an appreciably stronger staff.

Another gain was a major overhaul of the management. For some time there had been discussion of giving the *Guardian* its own management, instead of sharing departments with the *Evening News*, but nothing had happened. In February it was agreed that the *Guardian* and the *MEN* should each have boards of their own, under the parent board, and that the *Guardian* should have its own managing director. The *Guardian*'s advertisement and production departments were to have new heads as well, with a long overdue shake-up.

During the consortium negotiations, Laurence and I had seen quite a lot of the *Observer*'s deputy managing director. Peter Gibbings was then thirty-seven, an ex-barrister who had trained in newspaper management with the *Daily Mail*. He had a quick mind, a clear head, and a congenially cheerful manner. Laurence and I had both been impressed. After soundings in various directions, we put him top of our list. But Laurence said he was not going to 'poach' on David Astor, so I did it. Peter came to lunch at the Athenaeum; we had a long talk, and a few days later he accepted. He was a huge asset from the day he arrived.

He in turn recruited the new advertisement manager, someone with no previous newspaper experience but extensive knowledge from the other side – among the advertising agencies. Gerry Taylor was a little older than Peter but a friend of his and a man of concentrated vigour. He put new life into the 'ad.' department and eventually brought us revenue such as the *Guardian* had never seen before. Later, when Peter became group chairman on Laurence's retirement, Gerry moved into his seat as *Guardian* managing director.

The new team – and the new *Guardian* board – was completed with Michael Jack, our circulation manager, who was given greater freedom and encouragement under Peter than he had had before and did well; and Jim Markwick, son of Charles (of the Markwick–Muirhead facsimile machine), who became company secretary and then general manager. Harford Thomas came on the board as a second editorial man, and John Cole also joined later. Peter and I alternated as co-chairmen.

There were changes also at the top, with two new trustees (Jo Grimond and our historian David Ayerst) and two new parent board directors (Jo Grimond again, and a young merchant banker, John Clay, who is still on the board though much in demand as deputy chairman of Hambros Bank and a director of the Bank of England).

It was the beginning of an altogether better era for the *Guardian*, though we could not have foreseen that in the tense days of November 1966. At first, Thomson's *Times* roared ahead of us, with a spurt in circulation but no comparable gain in advertisement revenue. By 1970, with an annual loss said to be between £2 millions and £3 millions, it had to change course and relaunch itself as a more serious paper. By then we were catching up in sales, and we passed it, as already noted, in 1971. Admittedly, since the *Guardian* was deliberately being given the opportunity to build itself up, its loss was just over £1 million; but the *MEN* was making a profit of above £1½ millions, and some of the group's other activities (Anglia, property, and printing) were bringing money in.

An important editorial improvement in the 1968-71 period was the introduction of the so-called 'facing' page, opposite the leader page in the centre of the paper. Peter Preston, as features editor, made it one of the liveliest parts of the *Guardian*, with a blend of political and general topics. We were now also able to talk daily to the senior management, more freely and with fewer inhibitions than ever before, and we gained useful ideas and stimulus from it. The 're-launch' in February 1969 was a joint operation, with a big publicity campaign. Right through the paper there was a feeling of strength and success, with reporters, specialists, sub-editors, photographers, and the management departments working together.

In that period and beyond, the *Guardian* won an unusual series of awards. Having been runner-up in the daily and Sunday newspaper class in the annual Design Awards in 1967, 1968, and 1970, we took the top place in 1971 - a tribute to the handling of type and pictures and the clarity of layout achieved by John Putz and Brian Jones and their staff. Individual journalism prizes in 1967 went to Anthony Tucker as science correspondent, Harry Whewell* as a columnist, and Peter Preston for his Miscellany column. The 1968 National Press Awards brought top place as Journalist of the Year to Victor Zorza, for his accurate forecasting of the course of events in Czechoslovakia, where a month before the Soviet invasion he had said that it was inevitable; and the award as Reporter of the Year to Harry Jackson, for his work in Vietnam, Korea, Israel, and Czechoslovakia, 'as well as an able and sympathetic coverage of events in this country'.

Next year the *Guardian* won top place in the Granada awards, for 'so unexpected and so welcome a come-back', and a special commendation also for its women's pages. The 1970 National Press Awards, announced not long before the *Guardian*'s 150th birthday in May 1971, began with Alastair Hetherington as Journalist of the Year; and in receiving the award I said that the real work was done by my staff, who were 'well chosen and well directed' (so I was not denying responsibility). The citation said that the award was for 'determined and able leadership'. Norman Shrapnel, Peter Jenkins,* and Neville Cardus also won prizes or awards at about that time, adding to the birthday treat.

The next group of National Press Awards, announced in March 1972, had Simon Winchester at the top as Journalist of the Year because of his reporting of events in Northern Ireland, where 'his qualities of courage, persistence, and impartiality have been conspicuous'. There were four more individual awards as well. Notable in 1973, another good year, were Adam Raphael as Journalist of the Year after his reporting on wages and labour conditions among British companies operating in South Africa, and Peter Niesewand as International Reporter for his work in Rhodesia; also in that year two Guardian photographers, Denis Thorpe and Don McPhee, won prizes for their pictorial journalism.

Though these were awards to individuals or to the paper, they were part of the harvest from the combined efforts of the whole staff. There had been a time when I feared that the Guardian was not going to reach its 146th birthday; now it was very far from being eclipsed.

The 150th birthday

The birthday came on May 5, 1971, and was celebrated in un-Guardian fashion with a banquet at the Dorchester Hotel. That morning we were able to announce on the front page that the average daily sale in April had been 330,518 copies.

At the banquet the guests of honour were Willy Brandt, the German Federal Chancellor, and our own Prime Minister, Edward Heath. I had approached Willy Brandt in February – because he was a former journalist, Europe's leading statesman, and a man in tune with the Guardian's character – and had been delighted to hear within a few days that if possible he would come. The day coincided with a European currency crisis, but he came just the same. He made a beautiful speech and presented the Guardian with a superb antique silver goblet, originally presented to a German poet, Ferdinand Freiligrath, on his return from exile after the 1848 revolution. The goblet was nearly two feet high and crowned by a fluttering silver standard. In his speech he paid tribute to the Guardian's ideals and humanity, to C. P. Scott, and to the Scott Trust and Scott family. He took the opportunity to say that Europe needed Britain 'without further delay' – the negotiations were then coming to their climax – and Ted Heath endorsed that, though with a pleasantly barbed comment about the Guardian's leaders.

Laurence presided, and in replying on behalf of the paper I said that Willy Brandt had known what it was to back unpopular causes and be vilified for doing so – an experience shared by the Guardian. He had seen his ambitions near to crumbling, but had had the courage to go on. Politics, he had once said, is not the art of the possible but the realisation of what initially seems impossible. The Prime Minister, too, had shown those qualities of tenacity and courage which had marked Chancellor Brandt's career – and we were glad that the *Guardian*, unlike most of its contemporaries, had not prematurely written Edward Heath off before last year's election.

I concluded with thanks to all those who had written, cabled, and spoken in such friendly terms on this occasion. 'I say this on behalf of all those who create and sell the *Guardian*. Men who put plates on the presses in noisy machine rooms; men who meet trains in the early morning to handle distribution and sales; men and women who sell advertising space to bring us in revenue; telephone copy takers, telegraphists, typesetters – managers and journalists. Everyone who is involved in writing, printing, and selling the paper. On behalf of all of us: thank you.'

Just before leaving for the Dorchester that evening, I had been handed the evidence gathered by two of our reporters proving that Scotland Yard's criminal records, tax office files, and NHS personal records were being tapped by private inquiry agents, illegally, for profit. I had told Jean Stead as news editor that the story must be held for further consultation with our lawyers. Five days later we published it. A month afterwards, sitting in the garden at Downing Street, our second guest of honour at the banquet said that on his information the *Guardian* had breached the Official Secrets Act and had itself commissioned an illegal act. It was a cold warning, of which more follows later.[16] each of us, in his way, was doing his duty.

16 See Chapter 11, pp. 282–84.

8 Slow boat to Europe

When the Messina conference was held in June 1955, laying the foundations of the European Economic Community, the *MG* regretted that Britain was not there. Ours ought not to be 'a dumb presence' on the fringe of Europe. The Common Market came into existence on January 1, 1958; and late, very late, Harold Macmillan applied for British membership in the summer of 1961. The *Guardian* warmly welcomed the decision but had two reservations – did Mr Macmillan really believe in a politically united Europe, and could he negotiate satisfactory terms to protect Commonwealth interests? Thirteen months later we turned against entry, because the terms were wrong, not only for the Commonwealth. The change of course was preceded and followed by acute disagreement within the office, so much so that in October I asked the trustees for the opportunity to explain our position. It was the only time I ever did so; they listened and made no comment one way or the other.

In 1966–67, when Wilson renewed the application to join, there was less disagreement in the office for none of us believed that there was much chance of success. The 'cold bath' theory – jump in and you'll get better – never made much sense; and de Gaulle was against us anyway. In 1971–72 we welcomed Heath's application, and, while uneasy about the terms, we were unhesitatingly in favour of entry when the Bill came before Parliament. Again in 1975, we were wholly on the 'Yes' side during the Referendum. But were we right?

1961–62 – the 'Guardian' changes sides

The switch in 1962 came less because of Hugh Gaitskell – though I had had many talks with him – than because of Leonard Beaton, who was reporting the Brussels negotiations. It was influenced also by the Commonwealth conference in early September, a fortnight before Gaitskell's warning about 'turning our backs on a thousand years of history'. And it came above all because of our analysis of the terms that were emerging from the Brussels negotiations.

When Harold Macmillan announced the Government's decision to apply, on July 31, 1961, he did not really explain why it had changed its mind. Nor did he make that any plainer when he opened a Commons debate two days later. Even his memoirs are obscure about the reasons for the decision.[1] He spoke eloquently in the House about the need for Britain to play her role to the full and use her influence 'for the free development of the life and thought of Europe', but that had applied ever

1 Harold Macmillan, *At the End of the Day*, pp. 1–34.

since 1955. If our right place was 'in the vanguard of the movement', we had been singularly slow in putting ourselves there. And although these ringing phrases were produced at the beginning of the Commons debate, they had been noticeably lacking in the initial announcement two days earlier. The Prime Minister's statement had been so hedged that the *Guardian*'s leader began with the words: 'The plunge is to be taken, but, on yesterday's evidence, by a shivering Government.'

Most of the European leaders in that period were written by Harold Griffiths, with occasional contributions from Harford, John Rosselli, and me. Harold reckoned that he wrote sixty or seventy over about fifteen months. It was he who coined the 'cold bath' phrase, though not until later. From the summer of 1961, it was difficult to escape the suspicion that the Government was beginning to despair of any other way to stimulate the British economy. The Common Market announcement came just a week after Selwyn Lloyd's 'little Budget', in which he had increased bank rate from 5 to 7 per cent (a big jump for those days), called for further special deposits from the clearing banks, put a surcharge on customs and excise duties, postponed or cancelled some £300 millions of public spending, and appealed for a pay and dividends 'pause'. (Someone said five years later, after the Wilson July measures, that the Treasury had just pulled the old file out again.) Macmillan's memoirs say that the Cabinet's decision to apply for full membership of the Common Market was unanimous but give no indication of the economic background.[2]

The *Guardian*'s leader on August 1 said that there was bound to be hard bargaining and painful adjustment. The Community had come into a thriving life and was not going to abandon what it had built. Commonwealth interests, especially New Zealand's, must be protected. But the *Guardian* was clear that, given fair terms, there were great economic and political advantages.

We have far more to gain by partnership in Europe than by standing aside. The European Community is alive and growing. Economically it is moving much faster than Britain. We shall have access to a large market and the stimulus of competition. We shall be going into an area where advanced planning techniques are practised. (Both Mr Gaitskell and Mr Selwyn Lloyd might remember that.) And we shall be better placed to help the Commonwealth find new markets. Politically, we shall gain a voice in determining the policies of a group that can match Russia, China, and the United States. We shall be helping to do away with Europe's old quarrels. We shall still enjoy close relations with America - closer than if we stay on our own. That is why we should embrace the Rome Treaty.

Leonard Beaton put himself forward as a volunteer to cover the Brussels negotiations. They were obviously going to be long, intricate, and extremely difficult to make intelligible to ordinary readers. His thoroughness

---

2 Macmillan's account of the 'little Budget' comes towards the end of the previous volume of his memoirs: see *Pointing the Way*, pp. 373-80.

and his intellectual precision commended him for the task. He was not emotionally committed one way or other: as a Canadian he was more conscious than most people of the Commonwealth dimension, but he was also a supporter of the principle of European union. The neutrality of his reporting could be relied on. He had one other advantage: as an active member of the Bow Group, he was more likely to be more in tune with the somewhat prickly Lord Privy Seal, Edward Heath, who was to be in charge of the negotiations.

Over the next eighteen months Leonard thoroughly justified the choice. No newspaper, I believe, covered the negotiations better than the *Guardian* – though they were well covered, in detail, by the *Times*, *Telegraph*, and *Financial Times*. Leonard mastered the labyrinth of tariffs, preferences, tax systems, agricultural support arrangements, regulations on competition, and so on. Ted Heath invited us both to lunch one day midway through the negotiations, when he was angry because Leonard had been highlighting some weakness, as he saw it, in the British position – and I was soon lost in their technicalities.

The original deadline for completion of the negotiations, in August 1962, was reached and passed. Food price policy remained unresolved, with the anxiety on the British side that the Community still intended to use high price levels to stimulate production within its boundaries. Commonwealth interests were still unresolved – with the Australians still troubled about the loss of markets for wheat, canned fruit, lead, and zinc; the Canadians about their wheat and aluminium exports; the Indians about cotton textiles, and so the list went on. The voting system in the Community and a host of other matters were unresolved. A *Guardian* leader at the beginning of September listed some of the major issues, hoped that they could still be resolved soon, but was headed 'The marriage is not yet arranged'.

Leonard came to the Lake District for one of his periodic weekends. (He was godfather to our eldest, Tom, anyway.) By now he was convinced that the terms were not good enough and were unlikely to become much better, and he aggravated the doubts already in my mind. He wrote two special articles on preferences and the Commonwealth, in readiness for the conference of Commonwealth Prime Ministers due in mid-September, but those articles were factual rather than argumentative.

On Monday, September 10, the paper carried a leader regretting the increasingly anti-Market trend in Mr Gaitskell's statements, but not committing the *Guardian* as to its own immediate view. I saw him later that day and started the conversation by saying that I thought, for once in our friendly conversations, that we might be about to quarrel; he replied that if so I'd better start the quarrel. I said I thought he was wildly unrealistic in expecting the Six to renegotiate points already settled, but he saw no reason why a Labour Government should not renegotiate. He thought that Heath had been weak and the Government in indecent haste.

We had given away the preferences and got absolutely nothing in return. He rejected my view that if we waited two or three years the Common Market countries would have gone so far in their integration as to make our entry much more difficult. He also said that the *Guardian* had been misled about Indian tea, on which we had had a leader, because in practice the tariff reduction meant little since there was an 80 per cent revenue duty on tea in most Common Market countries. The Indians were saying 'thank you for nothing'.[3]

Wednesday's paper carried a front page almost filled with the Commonwealth conference, where strenuous opposition to the Common Market had been the main news of the second day. A bold panel quoted the objections of six Prime Ministers, among them: Menzies (Australia) – 'No Australian Government could sign a blank cheque and survive'; and Holyoake (New Zealand) – 'This is a matter of economic survival.' Patrick Keatley,* writing the main report from Marlborough House, further quoted a Minister from one of the Commonwealth's tropical territories as saying: 'You can't ask someone to commit suicide and then stand up and propose their health at the same time.' A short leader noted the great difficulty for Mr Macmillan in the strength of Commonwealth opposition but did not come down on one side or the other.

Thursday morning brought another Pat Keatley report, topping the front page and opening: 'Is Britain really about to enter a "rich man's club" and leave her old friends behind? That, in its bluntest form, was the question posed by Pakistan and others in the first big day of speech-making at Marlborough House. . . .' A further and longer leader, written by Harold Griffiths after a good deal of discussion in the office, explored the Prime Minister's dilemma. Should he send Mr Heath back to Brussels with instructions to seek substantially better arrangements, in which case the whole British effort to enter Europe was very likely to collapse? Or should he disregard the Commonwealth's objections, try to weather the accusations of bad faith, and take the risk of a revolt within the Conservative party which might bring his Government down?

There was already in draft an exceptionally long leader, trying to assess the gains and losses from going into Europe. Bits of it had been written by Harold, bits by Leonard, and bits by me; I was the coordinator. Harold, with later experience in the civil service, recalls that it went through an almost civil service process. About three drafts went round the senior staff. Two-thirds of it was taken up with the economic reckoning and one-third with the political reckoning. But, even in the first draft, there could be little doubt that the balance was beginning to lean away from entry on the existing terms.

That leader did not appear for another six days. Meanwhile, for the

3 For more on the evolution of Gaitskell's view and on Gaitskell–Hetherington talks, see Philip Williams, *Hugh Gaitskell*, pp. 702–49.

Saturday morning, I wrote one myself on 'the reality of consultation'. It carried further the argument about the Prime Minister's dilemma, saying that the Government could not disregard the massive Commonwealth assault. In Brussels it must seek to reopen one or two of the items already settled, and on some undetermined matters it must insist that there be no further whittling away of its position – the 'nil tariffs' needed to help the Commonwealth and ourselves, the future food price policy, and the arrangements for New Zealand. The *Times* was arguing that Britain must proceed 'with honour and without illusions'. Did that really, we asked, mean 'without regard to past promises'?

On the change of direction in our policy, Paddy Monkhouse as deputy editor was neutral. He was a Gaitskellite and so far as I can remember (in 1981) was tending to sympathise with Gaitskell's own view. Of the three assistant editors, two were strongly against the change. Harford Thomas was an ardent European and took the view that Leonard was making too much of a host of secondary objections. Gerard Fay, not normally much of a politician, thought that we ought to be sticking to the European course. John Anderson, who had lived for a time both in the West Indies and in India, was more sympathetic to the Commonwealth's case. The specialists were about equally divided. Harold Griffiths, whose judgement mattered most along with Leonard's, had been reluctant to see the shift, but, like Leonard, he had studied the existing terms. The debate was not rancorous but the division was deep – deeper than any I had experienced since becoming editor. And it went on for many weeks more.

Meanwhile Harold Macmillan, at Marlborough House, had miraculously succeeded in getting himself out of the corner. He did so partly by arranging for the conference to split up into subject groups for two or three days and then by the device of drafting two communiqués, one very long and listing all sorts of differing views and the other a short one concentrating on four points of principle. The conference agreed to accept the latter, with some modifications, and Macmillan justifiably felt that he had scored a minor triumph.[4]

On Wednesday 19th, the morning of the conference's last day and the opening day of the Liberal Assembly at Llandudno, the *Guardian* published its long leader on gains and losses. It began by saying that Mr Menzies had asked for, but not obtained, a brief from the British Government on gains and losses. We had found ours hard to write because it must contain so many guesses about the future. In Mr Macmillan's eyes it might seem treacherous 'because it might look too closely at details and so miss the glorious prospect on the horizon'; or in Mr Gaitskell's it might look treacherous 'because a distant mirage may blind us to how bad the immediate terms are'.

4 Macmillan, *At the End of the Day*, pp. 131–37.

To reprint the whole leader would be tedious, but a few extracts from the first section, on the economic reckoning, may give the flavour.

British industry: The gain is in being able to sell more cheaply in Europe, because tariffs between Britain and Europe will eventually be abolished. The loss is that preferences in the Commonwealth countries will disappear and that British industry will cease to be protected against imports from Europe. It has been estimated that, working from 1960 figures, the gain in Europe may mean the abolition of duties averaging 10 to 15 per cent on trade worth £519 millions (out of total exports of about £3,600 millions). The loss in the Commonwealth will be of preferences averaging about 10 per cent and covering £800 millions of exports. In addition there will be a loss because of extra imports (at competitive prices) from Europe.

At first sight this is a bad bargain. For two reasons, however, it may be less bad than it looks. One is that the preferences in the Commonwealth countries are declining anyway.... The other is the faster growth of the European market....
British agriculture: Farmers will no longer be subsidised out of taxes but instead will receive higher prices for most of their products.... Most British farmers, being better equipped and generally more efficient than those in Europe, should do well under this system. Dairy farmers and egg producers may have to accept slightly lower prices. The main threat, however, would be to horticulturalists....

A serious loss will be the cheap food that is available to British consumers....
The Old Commonwealth: Exports to Britain consist mainly of raw materials and foodstuffs.... The trade was worth, in 1960, about £300 millions to Canada, about £200 millions to Australia, and about £180 millions to New Zealand. Negotiations on this trade are not complete and will lead to some of the toughest bargaining when the talks are resumed.... For New Zealand and Australia what matters most is whether they can maintain adequate markets for their exports of cereals, dairy produce, and meat....

Britain, while accepting the main principles of these (Community) proposals, is asking for a more precise assurance that future price policy in the Community will not aim at self-sufficiency and will provide reasonable scope for imports from the Commonwealth....
The Asian countries: The main loss to India and Pakistan will come from the progressive application of duties on cotton textiles, jute goods, and other manufactured products which at present enter the United Kingdom free of duty.... On balance, unless the Government is prepared to reopen negotiation on these points, Britain's entry seems likely to harm the Asian Commonwealth.

On the economic reckoning, the leader concluded that it would be wrong to make an unconditional decision until the final terms were known. The political reckoning was also tallied under a series of headings, and one of its points was that Europe with Britain as a member would be less likely to break away from the Atlantic alliance. But unless Europe grew into a political union it would not achieve its own objectives, and unless Britain wanted to enter fully into a political union she could not attain the influence that Mr Macmillan and others sought.

Macmillan in his diary two days later speaks of the *Guardian* as 'still hedging' and of an attitude 'always willing to wound and afraid to strike'.[5] It is surprising, given the temperate nature of our writing then. Two days later we did snipe gently at his broadcast on the Commonwealth communiqué, when he described the terms already obtained for India and Pakistan as 'very good' and the terms for the African countries as 'wonderful'. We thought that their Prime Ministers might 'blink' on hearing him.[6]

The Liberal conference at Llandudno also went overboard on Europe, sweeping aside any serious discussion of the terms or consequences. At least both Jo Grimond and Mark Bonham Carter, from the platform, were explicit in accepting political union within Europe. Jo spoke of it as 'the dream of European statesmen down the ages' that Europe should come together 'freely in unity'. It was not a question of surrendering British sovereignty, he said, but of adding her sovereignty to a greater one.

It was indeed to this point, and to the words of Jo and Mark, that Hugh Gaitskell was addressing himself at Labour's Brighton conference a fortnight later when he spoke of turning our backs on a thousand years of British history.[7] Federalism, he said, 'is a decision which needs a little care and thought'. More generally, his speech expressed Labour's total opposition to entering Europe on the terms at present proposed. It was a powerful speech and rapturously received, except by the pro-Market group led by Roy Jenkins. Denis Healey told the conference that the Government's decision to seek entry was because of 'an inferiority complex', and the culmination of a process started at Suez. The conference rejected, however, a union motion calling for an immediate general election on the European issue.

The *Guardian*'s leader next morning said that a European watching the debate at Brighton might well have asked himself whether any purpose could be served by continuing the negotiations. A Britain which entered at present would be a Britain too deeply divided to be a reliable partner in Europe. Mr Gaitskell had said that the terms he sought did not close the door to British entry, but he had left the door only just ajar. Hardening our own line, the leader said that the terms now on offer were bad – because they abolished the advantages Britain now enjoyed in EFTA and the Commonwealth without any guarantee that Europe would in future pursue a liberal trade policy; because British consumers must pay higher prices for food, while levies on imports went to subsidise expensive and inefficient European farming; and because our pledges

5 Macmillan, *At the End of the Day*, p. 137; also, on King and Beaverbrook, p. 14 and p. 33.

6 For more on the press, see Miriam Camps, *Britain and the European Community, 1955–1963*, especially pp. 287–89.

7 He had used the phrase also on television a few days earlier, replying to Macmillan's broadcast about the Commonwealth conference.

to the Commonwealth were not going to be redeemed. Nor were political benefits now likely, for they could be gained only through a close political union. Neither the Conservatives nor Labour were ready for that. The leader ended by inverting and amending Gaitskell's own conclusion –

To go in on bad trading terms, and unready for political union, would be a disaster. Not to go in would be a pity, but it would not be a catastrophe. To go in on good trading terms, and ready for political union, would be the best solution to this difficult problem.

The sooner that that was realised both in Britain and in Europe, the leader said, the better for both. (It was another of many party conference leaders, written in a hurry on the sea front, where I almost always enjoyed writing; but Brighton in October tended to be warmer than Blackpool.) Harford was glum when I met him next day in Manchester.

At the Conservative conference in Llandudno next week, the burden of putting the pro-Market case was left to Rab Butler and Edward Heath. In accord with Conservative custom, the party leader spoke only at a rally on the final day. Rab and Ted, however, had a runaway victory in spite of some uncertainties beforehand, and an anti-Market amendment was routed.

I had gone to bed fairly early in Llandudno on the night after that debate, in one of the smaller hotels, for the town was bulging. Towards midnight the manager woke me, saying that the Chancellor and Mrs Maudling were downstairs asking to see me, and was it all right to give them a drink? (Licensing laws were strict in Wales, as in most of Scotland.) I had invited Reggie to look in if it suited him but had not expected him so late. However, I was downstairs in five minutes, and we all had whisky. Hugh Fraser, then Secretary of State for Air, had come with them. Reggie launched at once into a vigorous challenging of the *Guardian*'s changed policy. It wasn't so long, he said, since the *Guardian* had been saying that they ought to get in to Europe, while they'd been hanging back. Now it was the other way round: why? He knew Leonard well enough, so I told him of Leonard's revised assessment and of the impact on us of the Commonwealth conference. The issue of Indian tea was mentioned, and Reggie said that the Indian High Commissioner had been leading us and others up the garden path, for in Europe, for the first time, they would now have parity with imported coffee; their earnings would most probably be increased. But about the terms in general, he totally disagreed with us. They were as good terms as could have been obtained, and nothing still to be negotiated or renegotiated (he mentioned that) was of such a character as to keep us out.

On the political aspect, I said I thought it was the Conservatives who were hanging back. Maudling's own negotiations for a free trade association had failed because the British Government was not ready for a full

1 C. P. Scott, 'an encouraging ghost'.

2 Page make-up on the stone, Manchester.

3 The old 'corridor', Cross Street, Manchester, with the editor's room at the end. In discussion – Geoffrey Taylor (left) and Harry Whewell.

4 The *Guardian*'s 150th birthday celebration, 1971. Willy Brandt presents the Freiligrath goblet to Laurence Scott. Alastair Hetherington is on the right.

5 Prizewinners at the National Press Awards, 1973. Left to right: John Cole, Adam Raphael, Caroline Raphael, Alastair Hetherington, Nonie Niesewand, and Harford Thomas.

6 The newsroom in London; Jean Stead at the back on the left.

7 The London end of the 6 p.m. conference between London and
Manchester. The loudspeaker is on the table between Jean Stead and
Alastair Hetherington. From left to right: Harry Jackson (back to camera),
Brian Crooks, Colin Henderson, Peter Large, Peter Preston, John Cole,
Jean Stead, and Alastair Hetherington.

8 The Irish team: Simon Winchester, Harry Jackson, and Simon Hoggart.

9 The sub-editors' room, London. In the background, Brian Jones in discussion with Pat Keatley.

10 & 11 Two award-winning photographs taken by Robert Smithies, staff photographer on the *Guardian*. Street corner assault, Londonderry, and A place for women: Liberal conference, Southport.

12 The author in 1966 with Lucy and Mary.

commitment.[8] Weren't they still unready, and wouldn't we be in for a lot of trouble when the Community moved towards political union? Wouldn't the Community, as an international negotiator, be a fiasco if it did not have a common approach to international questions? Reggie said that it would take time to create a political union, and that there could be no question of any British commitment to any form of federalism. It was an interesting half hour, after which I went back to bed.

Ten days later came the Cuban missile crisis, and that swept almost everything else out of the way for nearly a week. But at the beginning of October, because of the continuing disagreement within the office, I had asked Richard Scott whether I might talk to the trustees about our European policy. There was no need to do so, but I thought it might be prudent when the senior editorial staff were so much divided. The trustees, after all, were the ultimate keepers of the *Guardian*'s conscience; and they might have something useful to say. The date had been fixed for October 29, when my talk could be tacked on to the trustees' normal half-yearly meeting. Trust meetings at that time tended to be very short anyway, or so I understood. I had never been to one.

That afternoon I turned up at the small boardroom at Cross Street, Manchester, well prepared. I was invited to speak, and did so for a little over half an hour. Present were Richard and Laurence, Paddy Monkhouse and Francis Boyd, and Bob Ebbage. Bill Montague had not been able to come. My half hour started from Messina and finished with the Labour and Conservative conferences (and I still have the rough notes from which I spoke). At the end, I think it was Francis who asked a single, fairly simple question. There was then a silence, after which Richard thanked me for coming and asked whether I would like to join the trustees for tea in about half an hour. That was all; it was something of an anti-climax. Its only by-product was that thereafter the editors of the *Guardian* and the *Manchester Evening News* were invited once a year to talk informally to the Trust about progress, problems, and prospects. From 1967 onwards, of course, in the aftermath of the *Guardian*'s 1966 crisis the Trust expected from the management a more thorough twice-yearly briefing on the financial and commercial prospects than it had previously been given. The editorial briefings remained short and with no comment on policy from the trustees' side; I never again spoke for as long as half an hour.

1966–67 – The 'cold bath' theory
After the Nassau meeting, in January 1963 de Gaulle vetoed the British application.[9] He believed that the British Government still gave higher priority to the Anglo-American relationship than to Europe. For more

---

8 The abortive negotiations for an industrial free trade area in 1956–57.
9 For the Kennedy–Macmillan meeting at Nassau, see Chapter 4, p. 99n.

than three years the issue lay dormant. Then, in the autumn of 1966 Harold Wilson took it up again. As with Macmillan and his memoirs, so with Wilson and his: neither in his public statements at the time nor in his reflections afterwards did either Prime Minister make at all clear his reasons for the decision. With Wilson, one might almost have supposed that it was done to keep George Brown busy after his 'national plan' had been torpedoed; but there must have been reasons less frivolous than that.[10]

The economic setting was unpropitious. The July measures in 1966 were brutal evidence of the Government's failure to resolve the weakness of sterling or reinvigorate the economy. The only tangible gain was the improvement in the balance of payments, now moving towards a surplus. After the July measures George Brown had been transferred to the Foreign Office, and on November 10, after a well-leaked 'Chequers weekend' to determine European policy, the Prime Minister announced that he and the Foreign Secretary were to tour European capitals in January to discover whether conditions existed 'for fruitful negotiations'. He said that Britain would enter Europe only when she had secured 'a strong economy, a strong balance of payments, and a strong pound'. It sounded very like whistling in a fog.

On November 10 I was almost totally preoccupied by meetings with Laurence Scott, Claud Morris, and others concerned with the *Times-Guardian* consortium. Harford was about to leave for ten days in India, so the burden was left to Harold Griffiths and John Cole. Harold had little belief that we could even begin to negotiate successfully until the British economy could be seen to be much stronger, but he let Wilson off quite gently. 'Vive Wilson!' the leader began. It wished the mission success, hoping that the Common Market's doors might be opened not only to Britain but to other countries as well, and its only immediate misgiving was that Wilson continued to take too narrow a view of Europe's political future.

This time there was virtually no dissension in the office. Mark Arnold-Forster alone opposed entry, mainly because of the Common Agricultural Policy, but being alone he did not press his point too hard. Harold Griffiths held that the British economy had to be in better shape before entry: we could neither negotiate successfully while weak nor cope with the competitive strains after entry. The 'cold bath' was more likely to cripple than cure. But his leaders were more often concerned with how sterling's role as an international currency could be wound down than with Europe itself.

Three days before the Prime Minister and Foreign Secretary set out on their exploration, I saw Wilson at Downing Street. He said that the visit to Paris, after Rome and Strasbourg, was what mattered. He had

10 See Harold Wilson, *The Labour Government 1964-1970*, pp. 299-300 and pp. 327-44.

October 1965

positive things to say to de Gaulle, among them proposals for strengthening the European computer industry. He knew that the greatest difficulty would be de Gaulle's instinctive dislike of having a rival in leading the Community – he recalled the axiom of 'five hens and one cock, good; five hens and two cocks, bad' – but said he intended to play on the fact that the British and French Governments were the only two secure ones in Western Europe.

Hella Pick travelled with the Wilson–Brown mission, and Francis Boyd also went to Paris. After the opening talks with de Gaulle, Francis said that because of the coming French elections there would be no early answer, but the President had listened to the Prime Minister 'with courtesy, care, and respect'. On the second day he reported Wilson and Brown as 'calm and relaxed' after their Paris meetings; but Hella added that there were major difficulties over the role of sterling as a reserve currency and over the Common Agricultural Policy.

In the middle of February – the weekend after a joint meeting of the *MG&EN* board and the Scott Trust, which had finally set the *Guardian* on its new managerial course after the November crisis – the Prime Minister invited a small *Guardian* group to dine with him at Chequers and stay the night. John Cole, Francis Boyd, Ian Aitken, Mark Arnold-Forster, and Peter Jenkins went with me. A great deal of the discussion at and after dinner was taken up with Europe, though Vietnam, Rhodesia, and economic strategy also were well aired. He remained optimistic. He believed that the problems of agriculture, finance, capital movements, and Commonwealth trade could all be resolved. He acknowledged, however, that de Gaulle was like a grandfather who really did not want intruders coming into his house. From de Gaulle's point of view, Harold said, they were people with new habits and new languages 'who would have runny noses and wet pants and would have to be trained'. But he still believed that he could prevail upon de Gaulle.

He did not succeed. He went to see de Gaulle again in June, but only after an emergency visit to Washington because of the Arab–Israeli war. There was an evident lack of Anglo-French coordination at that moment – but the shadow of 1956 hung over everyone, and French aircraft were again alleged (untruly this time) to have been flying for the Israelis. Once more I had a talk with the Prime Minister just before he left for France, and this time he was less hopeful. He said that if he had been invited to de Gaulle's home at Colombey les deux Eglises it would have meant 'yes'. If he had been invited to Rambouillet, where the President had met Macmillan shortly before Nassau, it would have meant 'no'. He had in fact been invited to stay at the Petit Trianon, near Versailles, which probably meant that de Gaulle wanted to be very nice to him and entertain him in great style but in substance to say 'no'. That proved to be about right.

Wilson kept up the effort nevertheless. The President's public statements at the time of the June visit remained friendly and neither negative nor positive towards British entry. The Prime Minister, on return from France, said he had told de Gaulle that 'we do not intend to take "no" for an answer'. The *Guardian* supported his endeavour, though with no great expectation of success. But November brought another sterling crisis and the devaluation of the pound. Just one week after devaluation, de Gaulle told his autumn press conference that France could not risk breaking up the Community for the sake of British entry.

The President's statement was highly polished and in parts sardonic and entertaining. Reporting from Paris, Nesta Roberts quoted his denial that he had ever wanted to see Britain enter Europe 'stripped naked'. 'For a beautiful creature,' he said, 'nakedness is natural enough. For those around her, it is satisfying enough. But I have never said that of England.' He drew attention to the somersaults executed by Harold Macmillan and then by Harold Wilson in their attitudes to the Common Market. Macmillan, whom the President referred to as his friend, had once compared the Market to a Napoleonic blockade but had then sought to join. Britain, he said, would have to 'transform' herself before she could be ready.

Harold Griffiths that summer departed to become a civil servant in the Treasury. His advice was much missed, the more by me because he had come through the *Glasgow Herald* as I had done, and we had worked together (with a gap between 1950 and 1955) for almost twenty years. He had been writing nearly all our economic leaders and most of those on Europe. Thereafter within the office the only flutter of disagreement, which was not serious, came over the 'mid-Atlantic' question. One or two of the senior staff thought that I was inclined to over-emphasise close consultation with Washington and that that was inconsistent with Europeanism. The question of how the Atlantic alliance would handle another nuclear crisis remained important in my mind, and, apart from that, I would have preferred a form of Atlantic union to European union if there had been any practical possibility of it. Since there was no such possibility, I believed that European union should be used as a means of strengthening transatlantic ties - not as a Gaullist or Marxist device for getting the Americans out of Europe. My thinking was in keeping with Kennedy's; but Vietnam, among other things, caused some anti-alliance feeling among *Guardian* writers.

1971-72 - Heath succeeds at last

British entry was Heath's greatest success as Prime Minister, or so historians may argue. The application was in fact revived by Harold Wilson in December 1969, six months before the general election, and the Heath Government opened negotiations immediately after taking office. The negotiator was Geoffrey Rippon; but it is to Edward Heath himself, above all, that credit must go. He had held all along that Britain ought to be in Europe, and it was he who achieved entry.

Mark Arnold-Forster had secured a considerable 'scoop' in the summer of 1969 by obtaining and publishing the official Treasury and Ministry of Agriculture estimates of the cost to Britain of the Common Agricultural Policy - then put at between £500 millions and £600 millions a year.[11] He secured another 'scoop' as well, when he found out that to reduce the butter mountain the EEC had decided to feed some of the surplus butter back to the cows. But Mark's greatest feat in this context was that, through assaults and asides in leaders and in the Miscellany column, he shamed the Government into publishing a White Paper giving its own assessment of the gains and losses through entering Europe. After Mark's summer scoop, Heath had taken up the demand for publication of the official estimates, much to Wilson's annoyance. The White Paper, published on February 10, 1970, contained about as many guesses as the

---

11 The *Guardian*, July 14, 1969.

Guardian's long leader of October 19, 1962. Its meaning, however, was that the big 'minus' on food prices – with their inevitable effect on wages and so on export costs – was more than offset by a big 'plus' in industrial markets.

The British prospects for entry were much better in 1970 than in 1961 or 1966. In April 1969 de Gaulle had resigned from the Presidency, through which, as Christopher Soames remarked, 'France lost a general and Britain an alibi.'[12] If Britain truly wanted to join, there could be no excuse for not taking the initiative again. The application, indeed, had never been withdrawn after de Gaulle's squelching of negotiations two years earlier. No less important, the British economy was healthier. Production and productivity were up, even if not to Franco-German levels; the incomes policy, while controversial, was working; the balance of payments was in surplus, and three-quarters of the IMF and other loans had been repaid. And the transitional problems for the Commonwealth were bound to be fewer, for in the past ten years the Commonwealth countries had been making adjustments of their own.

So when Mr Rippon set off for Brussels after the June election in 1970, he carried with him the good wishes of nearly all the British press, including the *Guardian*'s. The *Express* was still against entry, though Beaverbrook had died in 1964. For the *Guardian* the reporting of the negotiations fell primarily on Hella Pick, who had been appointed European Economics correspondent. Being fluent in German and French, and graduate of the London School of Economics, and having served the *Guardian* in West Africa, Geneva, and at the United Nations, she was well qualified; and she did not object to immersing herself in the detail of deficiency payments, fishery quotas, and common budgets. She managed to make the negotiations intelligible, even when all-night sessions and 'clock stopping' tactics wore down everyone in Brussels.

As in the previous phases, along with the economic haggling went a major constitutional uncertainty. What political institutions and what political direction was Europe to have? In this field, the Community itself was in trouble. Its constitutional and political development had failed to keep up with its material progress, and there was a partial paralysis of decision-making. So much so that after the first few months of negotiation serious misgivings were evident in the British press – and in the *Guardian* especially because of our belief that Europe could not succeed except as a political reality. A leading article at the end of December 1970 had this to say:

Without political direction, Europe is nothing. The Common Market itself will wither and die. At present it lacks adequate means of taking political decisions. The proof is to be seen in events in Brussels just before Christmas. For the third consecutive year, the Council of Ministers deferred reform of the Common

12 Christopher Soames was then British Ambassador in Paris.

Agricultural Policy, although there seems some hope that this will be tackled within the next few months. The Council also failed to agree on the Werner Plan for monetary and economic union, which was to have been inaugurated on January 1. And it was unable to determine its approach to Britain's share of the common budget.

This is, in truth, the most critical of all issues facing Europe itself. At present the Community can move only on its predetermined course, with little deviation or adjustment. The Commission (the Community's civil service) is frustrated because it cannot secure decisions from Ministers. The Ministers themselves, each with heavy national responsibilities, cannot give too much time to Brussels and must always look over the shoulders at national political pressures. Yet the issues calling for strong central decisions grow each year....

To talk of central decisions, direct elections, and a European Parliament with genuine authority is usually regarded as idealistic, unrealistic, or folly. The truth is, though, that unless Western Europe moves on to such a system it will be unable to cope with the Community's own problems.

A fortnight later another leader returned to the same issue, saying that the pragmatists in Britain said that there was no hurry to settle these matters. In one sense they were right, for the process of giving up some degree of autonomy, sovereignty, and individual tradition must take time. In another sense they were wrong, because too few central decisions were being taken in the Community and on that account it was unable to cope with its own problems and was becoming 'unfit to join'. The Community must avoid the risks of remoteness: 'sensitivity to local democracy matters as much in the Ardèche, West Flanders, and Apulia as it does in the West Riding, Ulster, and Stornoway'. But Europe must learn fast, the leader said. A group of six or ten nations, pulling in opposite directions, 'will not survive – nor will it be outward looking'.

There was extraordinary ambiguity, too, in the attitudes of both the Prime Minister and the Leader of the Opposition when it came to political union. At times in the past Heath had argued for political evolution and democratic control of the Community – most eloquently in his Godkin lectures at Harvard, where he had said that we must feel ourselves and think of ourselves as 'European'.[13] But when it came to negotiation he appeared to adhere to a Gaullist concept of a 'Europe des patries'. He had to remember the patriotic sensitivities of Conservative supporters, but his retreat from a political Europe was disappointing.

Wilson was no better. He had never been specific about the European political dimension, and after the 1970 election he began to feel a cold draught at his back from the ranks of the trade unions. In September the Transport and General Workers, with the biggest of block votes, came out against entry. Clive Jenkins's ASSET was already strongly against; and the Boilermakers now also went over to that side. The hibernation

13 The Godkin lectures were reprinted in 1970, with a fresh introduction, under the title *Old World, New Horizons*.

after 1962 was ending. Harold Wilson in 1969, oddly, had used Gaitskell's 'thousand years of history' in a reverse sense – looking forward to the day when European nations would abandon their antagonisms of a thousand years. But as the anti-Market forces gathered after the election, he began to take cover. At the party conference in late September he held to entry into Europe if the terms were right, and thereby helped to win a narrow victory for the pro-entry forces. But by July 1971, he rejected the terms then negotiated.

Of those terms, the *Guardian* said on July 8 that though not ideal they were adequate – and that 'they are, broadly speaking, as good as Labour could have hoped to achieve'. They held out the prospect of greater prosperity for industry and commerce, provided we worked for it. The disappointment, again, was on the political side. The Government statement, we said, assured everyone that everything from the monarchy to the Royal and Ancient Golf Club would be left intact; it said nothing of the new Europe which Mr Heath, not long before, had said would grow in stature to be the equal of the United States or the Soviet Union. Nevertheless, the verdict was 'Europe, yes'.

Mr Wilson's verdict, broadcast the next night, was that on these terms the answer was 'no'. At the Labour party's one-day conference a fortnight later, he enlarged on his objections and promised 'renegotiations'. Mr George Thomson at the conference and Mr Roy Jenkins outside it both said that the terms were ones which a Labour Government would have accepted. Of the positive side to Europe, Mr Wilson said nothing. The *Guardian*'s comment next morning described his speech as 'disreputable'.

During July the paper published a series of articles analysing the terms in detail, and in August these were republished as a pamphlet. It sold remarkably well; at least among *Guardian* readers there was an appetite for more information. The opinion polls published in the *Mail*, *Express*, and *Telegraph* appeared to show the public as almost equally divided between 'yes' and 'no'.

At times I wondered whether we had been too insistent on the political dimension, though it seemed clear that if the Community was to thrive and become an influence in the world it must have more effective political direction. At one of our occasional editorial gatherings with outside guests, a comment on that was made to me by Heath's foreign affairs adviser at Downing Street, Douglas Hurd, who went into Parliament in 1974 and later became a Foreign Office Minister. He propounded the theory of 'progress by mistakes' – namely, that the Community and its electorates would learn as they went along. The Werner Plan, he said, had stemmed from the mistakes made over French devaluation and German revaluation.[14] The gradual approach was probably the quickest to political

14 For the Franco-German currency chaos of November 1968, see Chapter 9, pp. 211–12.

integration, and it was 'saleable' to voters from Shetland to Sicily. It might be unheroic, but it was practical. The key, he said, was to get into the Community and make it work. That made a lot of sense.

On October 28 Parliament voted on the principle of entry. The Commons majority in favour was 112 and the Lords 393. The Commons debate was the longest since the war, six days. With a free vote on their side, thirty-nine Conservatives went against entry; defying a three-line whip on the other side, sixty-nine Labour members voted for. Five Liberals voted for and one against (Emlyn Hooson, because of agriculture). From the Commons Norman Shrapnel reported the biggest crush of MPs and spectators that anyone could remember; and from the Lords our report spoke of peers crowding past the gilded throne 'like commuters making for the underground' - and of a Labour complaint that in the stampede of backwoodsmen some did not know where to vote.

Thus the decision was taken in principle. The European Communities Act, after a long passage through the two Houses, received the Royal Assent a year later. Britain joined the Community on January 1, 1973; but the debate was not over, nor is it over eight years later.

The 1975 Referendum - 'Yes', again

Wilson let the anti-Market tide rip in the Labour party for about two years, then began to reassert control. But he had committed himself to 'renegotiate', and in April 1972 he further committed himself to a consultative referendum, thereby losing Roy Jenkins, George Thomson, and Harold Lever from the Shadow Cabinet. There was no getting out of it.

Having won the March election in 1974, the new Government gave notice to the European Council of Ministers that renegotiation must follow. The points of renegotiation, however, were not unlike some that Conservative Ministers had already been trying to secure by less abrasive methods - an improvement of the Common Agricultural Policy, above all. Revision on this and a number of other issues was achieved over the next twelve months; and the referendum was set for June 5, 1975. As a curtain-raiser, another special Labour party conference at the end of April voted two to one for coming out of Europe - after Michael Foot, on one side, had argued that Britain must have 'full mastery' of all the instruments of economic management, which was not possible inside Europe, while James Callaghan on the other side said that we should be cutting ourselves off both from Western Europe and from the United States. As a Labour poster said, 'The people will decide.'

The last three leaders that I wrote for the *Guardian* were all on the referendum, on June 5, June 7, and June 9. The one on polling day said that Britain faced massive difficulties whether in or out of the Community. The fact that inflation had ravaged money values in the past two years was not the fault of the Common Market: oil prices dictated by Arab producers and world prices for food and raw materials were the spurs to inflation. Domestic wage pressure had latterly taken over and would destroy jobs and prosperity if not controlled. The leader recalled Vic Feather's comment that the man on a camel in the desert now had as much say over our future as the man in a South Wales pub or coal mine. All the same, it was strongly probable that 'Britain will be safer and more prosperous within a democratic Western Europe', and that with Britain as a full member 'Western Europe will be more securely democratic and less exposed to outside buffeting in a troubled world'. And the morning after declaration of the results, the leader began:

> Fullhearted, wholehearted, and cheerful hearted: Shetland apart, there is no doubt about the 'yes'. Labour's anti-Marketeers asked for the people's verdict and they have received it.

The 'yes' was indeed more massive than expected and more uniformly spread across the country. At 67 per cent of those who cast their votes it remained a minority of the entire electoral roll. But then hardly a Government in Britain had ever had that kind of overall endorsement, and in terms of the existing electoral system the verdict was unambiguous .

The final leader, on the Monday morning, was written after the Western Isles had added their 'no' to Shetland's – and it said that this should not be seen as some quixotic Norse response but as a distress signal to Brussels, London, and Edinburgh. The decline in fishing, knitwear, and weaving had been less than offset by the coming of oil; the fishermen and boatbuilders were angry because so little had been done to look after their interests, and because even Edinburgh seemed so remote. I did not imagine that it was to be my last leader for the *Guardian*; but the tax problems of the Scott Trust preoccupied me in the next six weeks, and Peter Preston had anyway taken over the daily running of the paper.

In the autumn of 1980, while myself on a rocky splinter of the Hebrides, I read a *Guardian* leader which seemed to be written much in Peter Preston's own style. The Labour party was again agonising about whether to stay in or come out of Europe; and I may or may not have been right about the authorship of the leader.

> No one amongst us [it said], no one who urged membership in the fifties and sixties and welcomed the accomplished fact of the seventies, can pretend that the Europe of today is the Europe of our imaginings. It has not infused British industry with a new dynamism (though it has become a dominant trading partner at a time when selective import controls are a two-edged blade for an exporting nation). It has not moved far enough or fast enough towards the sinking of national aspiration in a wider federation (though there stand Greece and Spain and Portugal, banging on the door for their guarantee of continuing freedom). It is not the vision of the founding fathers, nor yet even a necessary joining of great nations. But it is what exists; what we have; what, through our frailties, we have built; the only show in town.
> Within a couple of years the show will either leave town or change out of

recognition: within a couple of years the entire financial foundation of the Community will have to be constructed afresh, because the old bricks and mortar have crumbled. That will be the real moment of decision. Either the EEC is an agricultural benevolent society and a Franco-German mutual admiration association – or it still has something of the potential we saw so long ago. Only when these renegotiations, for everybody, from scratch, are complete will we know whether the dreams are dust and whether the moment has come for Britain to slink away from its 'European destiny'.

Peter once complained because my deletion of some commas upset the poetry of one of his leaders; and of course he was right. Even more abundantly justified, I believe, is that view expressed in the autumn of 1980. On any issue judgement must be inspired by vision and tempered by events, and on none more than European unity.

9 The price of prosperity

The City pages of a newspaper are an unusual place for an Archbishop's letter. But one day in 1968 the retired Archbishop of Canterbury, Dr Fisher, wrote a letter which appeared in the financial pages of the *Times* (not, alas, the *Guardian*). It was about the role of market forces in the management of the economy, and it questioned conventional City wisdom with these words:

Is it not the normal market mechanism which needs to explain itself, since it need not always be right and since, from time to time, it seems to a layman to show some signs of bullying, cruelty, and inordinate love of gain?

Hear, hear indeed! If Clause 4 of the Labour party's constitution was out of date, and Hugh Gaitskell well justified in having challenged it, the philosophy of unbridled free enterprise was no less inappropriate to a caring and humane society.

In all my years at the *Guardian*, there was never a time when Britain seemed safely on the road to prosperity. Sterling crisis followed sterling crisis, and ceased only when inflation had reached double figures. The 'unacceptable face of capitalism', as Edward Heath termed one great City deal, was more than matched by the philosophy of 'I'm all right, Jack' among trade union members. Newspapers were hypocrites when they preached against inflationary wage claims and wage settlements, knowing all the time that their printing workers and their managements were among the worst offenders; but they preached just the same. Like other newspapers, the *Guardian* had to tell its readers what was happening to industry and exports and the balance of payments – and to give advice.

Never having it so good (*1957–63*)

In the post-war years, the *MG* was a strong supporter of the Attlee-Cripps policy of austerity. In the Churchill years, on the whole it approved the more liberal and expansionist approach initiated by Rab Butler – provided health, housing, and the welfare services received their due share of public funds. So the paper's established path was broad. In Wadsworth's last eighteen months the economic leaders had mostly been written by Harold Griffiths and John Anderson, and that continued for some time – with Richard Fry, financial editor already for nearly twenty years, as a fatherly adviser.

Soon after becoming Prime Minister, Harold Macmillan appointed his 'three wise men' – Lord Cohen, Sir Harold Howitt, and Sir Dennis Robertson, a judge, an accountant, and an economist, to advise on prices, productivity, and incomes. Lord Cohen wrote to me as editor asking whether the *MG* would like to offer any private advice that they might take into account. Harold Griffiths, Richard Fry, and I put our heads together and drafted a short memorandum. It said that there ought to be an annual stocktaking to estimate how much the national economy could stand in the next twelve months, whether in wages or in dividends, and that this should be seen as a fair target within which everyone ought to try to keep. In other words, the Treasury should 'present the arithmetic' in public, as was being attempted in Germany and Holland. Improved productivity and a better export performance were, of course, required to justify any higher incomes.

Perhaps the idea was not too original, but it brought a friendly response from Lord Cohen. Allied to it, in our minds, was an old view of John Anderson's that somehow the TUC and the union leaders must be brought into the process of national planning – and that that must include, in some form, the planning of incomes. It was a view not at all popular among the big unions. Nevertheless the proposal of an annual stocktaking and an endeavour to forecast what the economy could stand was aired in our columns quite frequently.

The Cohen commission made its first report only in February 1958, and it was a disappointing document. It emphasised the high level of demand as an inflationary factor, together with the upward push of wages on prices. To maintain the competitiveness of exports, it said, wages must be allowed to rise much less than in the past few years. In this, it said, trade union leadership had a significant part to play. But it said nothing about any common endeavour to work out how this could be related to other forms of income or be brought about. Hugh Gaitskell scathingly dismissed it as 'a political tract, not a scientific report'. The FBI thought it 'weighty, impartial, and carefully considered', while the TUC said it was 'partisan'.

It contained, nevertheless, the seeds of the first approach to an incomes policy. And Lord Cohen might well have replied to us that he had, after all, made the first serious attempt to assess what the economy could stand. A second report came in August with more detailed calculations and statistics.

Twice while the Cohen commission was at work Richard Fry had had private talks with the Chancellor, Peter Thorneycroft, and both times had brought back foreboding news. In July he was told that the injection in twelve months of an extra £900 millions into the economy through wage settlements where production had not increased was 'an explosive force', and no cuts in defence or welfare or tighter credit squeeze could match it. On the other hand the external current account was in surplus and improving. In November the Chancellor was even gloomier.

There had been a sterling crisis in September, with heavy pressure on the reserves and speculation against the pound. (Labour Ministers seven

November 1958

to ten years later tended to think that it only happened to them; but it had happened before.) Bank rate was raised from 5 to 7 per cent – 'a thing practically without precedent', Macmillan says in his memoirs, but that too was to happen again – and a tighter credit squeeze had been imposed to damp down demand.[1] Macmillan accepted these measures with some reluctance, believing that a slump might follow. But Peter Thorneycroft was convinced that they were right, as were the other Treasury Ministers, Nigel Birch and Enoch Powell.

When Fry saw the Chancellor again in November, he was told that another wage round like the last could be the end of sterling. 'It is doubtful whether sterling could ever recover its position.' The Government must persuade employers to stand firm, and it must persuade arbitration tribunals to understand the national background. He was hoping that Cohen's first report would be strong enough to make an impression on wage negotiations this winter.

But in January Thorneycroft himself resigned, along with Nigel Birch and Enoch Powell – a clean sweep of the Treasury Ministers, on the eve

1 Harold Macmillan, *Riding the Storm*, pp. 355-60.

of Macmillan's departure for a Commonwealth tour and after less than a year of the new Government. The issue was the saving on public spending, the counterpart to the autumn credit squeeze. When the civil estimates came before the Cabinet in December they had not been cut as much as the Chancellor wished, and he also wanted deferment of a forces' pay increase. The Prime Minister argued that since sterling had regained much of the ground lost in the autumn and the savings on public expenditure were substantial, no issue of principle was at stake. Nevertheless on the day before Macmillan was due to leave for India, Pakistan, Australia, and New Zealand all three Ministers resigned. It was the 'little local difficulty' of which Macmillan spoke at the airport next day.

He resolved it promptly, before leaving. Heathcoat Amory became Chancellor, John Hare went to Agriculture, and Soames moved to the War Office; and the Prime Minister issued a resolute statement lest there was renewed speculation against sterling.

Our own comment in the *Guardian*, from Harold Griffiths, was that the loss of Mr Thorneycroft mattered less than the possible loss of confidence in sterling. The resignation of the entire Treasury team was without modern precedent, and it might be taken abroad as implying a retreat from the Government's stern economic policy in defence of sterling. But since the difference between Mr Thorneycroft and others in the Cabinet amounted apparently to no more than £50 millions, it seemed hardly to call for the ex-Chancellor's drastic course. The statements from the Prime Minister and the incoming Chancellor were reassuring; and Mr Macmillan was right to keep to his Commonwealth journey. To have stayed at home would have been taken abroad as a greater sign of weakness.

It was impossible not to admire Macmillan's tactical skill, and his economic judgement proved better than Thorneycroft's. In his memoirs Macmillan puts much of the blame on Birch and Powell, who, while they had great gifts, 'introduced into the study of financial and economic problems a degree of fanaticism which appeared to me inappropriate'.[2] Heathcoat Amory was a steady if unexciting Chancellor, guided by his professional advisers and more responsive to the Prime Minister's anxiety about a slump. He fitted in with Macmillan's concept of economic management through a modest touch on the brake or a light thrust to the accelerator – a concept far preferable to the more drastic methods of later years. Two months after the 'little local difficulty' bank rate came down to 6 per cent, and by the end of the year it was at 4 per cent.

The three main strands of *Guardian* economic policy in the late fifties were that there must be growth to provide the resources for better housing and social welfare; that the neglected areas of Northern England, Central Scotland, and South Wales must be put to better use; and that to prevent

2 Macmillan, *Riding the Storm*, p. 372.

growth leading to inflation there must be some form of incomes restraint, agreed if possible through the TUC. On public ownership the *Guardian*'s view was always pragmatic: let it be judged on the merits of the case, for or against, according to the circumstances of the industry or other activity. We were perhaps too optimistic about the prospects for growth – being influenced in this by Gaitskell's philosophy – and perhaps too critical of the Macmillan Government's performance as the 1959 election drew near. Almost all of us in the office did indeed believe that the Conservatives had more than their share of original sin and were somewhat insensitive to social justice, as shown by their increase in NHS and National Insurance charges. Growth appeared to be top priority in order to build a better Britain.

Because I lived in Manchester and every day saw the depressed and run-down condition of industrial East Lancashire, and because of frequent visits to Glasgow – and much the same applied to John Anderson, Harold Griffiths, and others at Cross Street – it seemed obvious how far the country had to go before anyone could justly say that its people had 'never had it so good'. Whether Harold Macmillan ever used those words in the 1959 election has since been disputed; but they were taken as the hallmark of his philosophy. It was a perfectly good philosophy provided that prosperity was being increased and being fairly shared, and that was what we doubted.

Curiously, not long after the election Macmillan wrote to his Chancellor drawing attention to the 'good sense' of a *Guardian* leader which was against severe disinflationary measures. The economy, it said, was not working at full stretch; many industries still had unused capacity and there were reserves of labour in many parts of the country. Macmillan was opposed to the deflationary measures and fierce Budget that the Governor of the Bank and the Treasury advisers wanted. It would be either 'very foolish or very dishonest' after the previous Budget and the autumn election, Macmillan said. A gentle squeeze might be right; a violent push might work too well. 'What will happen if the motor companies cancel their plans for expansion on Merseyside, etc? What will happen if Pressed Steel decide after all not to set up in the North-east? What will happen if our Scottish plans, on which so much depends, break down?'[3] At Cross Street, of course, we did not know of his letter; but, along with other pressures, the letter led to modification of the disinflationary plans. 'Less harsh than was feared' stood out as one of our front-page headlines after the Budget.

Selwyn Lloyd replaced Heathcoat Amory as Chancellor in July 1960 – with Home moving to the Foreign Office (as Francis Boyd foreshadowed a day or two earlier) and with Thorneycroft back as Minister of Aviation and Powell as Minister of Health. Selwyn took some time to play himself

3 Macmillan, *Pointing the Way*, p. 220.

in, and by the time he was ready to put forward ideas on national economic planning he had another sterling crisis on his hands. So July 1961 brought another 'Stop' in the stop–go cycle, with bank rate up again to 7 per cent, another credit squeeze, more rigorous exchange controls, cuts in defence spending, cuts in local authority housing, and curtailment of proposed increases in teachers' and nurses' pay. It also brought the first public hint of Lloyd's 'pay pause' – his words being that, in relation to salaries and wages, 'there must be a pause until productivity has caught up'; and that in relation to profits and dividends no general increase could be justified in the coming year. A pause, he said, was no lasting solution; 'we must work out methods of securing a sensible long-term relationship between increases in incomes of all sorts and increases in productivity.' That autumn he opened discussions with the TUC and the employers' organisations which led to the creation next year of the National Economic Development Council.

While the freeze was unwelcome, the approach to national economic planning was warmly welcomed in the *Guardian*. Here at last was formulation of something for which we ourselves had been searching in our paper for the Cohen commission four years earlier. In the autumn of 1960 we had carried a number of leaders, Harold Griffiths's again, on the need for planned growth. In November the Government had published its first White Paper on Public Investment, which we saw as an important advance, though we also wanted comparable forecasting for the private sector. While the leader on the July measures said that they were bound to deter investment in the private sector – and that the Chancellor seemed to have no idea how he was going to bring about his pay policy apart from hitting the public services – it applauded his long-term intentions. It said also that the tax concessions to the wealthy in his last Budget were a bad starting point, and that his call for dividend restraint would fool nobody.

The autumn brought some stormy meetings between the Chancellor and the TUC on how the NEDC was to be established, for the unions were suspicious that its only practical effect would be to impede wage increases – and some stormy meetings also among Conservatives, who wanted legal enforcement for the pay pause. The *Guardian*'s leaders argued that the broader functions of 'Neddy' must be made plain, and that its value depended on its being able to prod Government departments and industry into giving higher priority to long-term expansion. Until near Christmas it looked as if the TUC would boycott Neddy, though in mid-December George Woodcock, its general secretary, dropped a hint that it might be more amenable if the Chancellor convinced it that the pay pause among the public services was temporary. In the paper we seized on that, urging the Chancellor to respond. In a Commons debate a week later, he spoke of an 'intermediate phase' to follow the pause, but was not specific about timing. While critical of his handling of the unions, we urged the TUC to join and so be able to exert its influence on future policy. The postmen's 'work to rule' at the beginning of January added to the difficulties: it was, the paper said, the penalty of Mr Lloyd's rigidity, for he had screwed down the safety valves and invited an explosion. The T&GWU and the NUGMW were at the same time suing the Admiralty for withholding from dockyard workers a pay increase awarded by the Industrial Court. Mercifully, at the end of January the postmen ended their 'work to rule', the Chancellor agreed that the pay pause would cease on March 31, and the TUC decided to join Neddy.

The interlocking of wage inflation, industrial investment, and the location of industry was explored by John Cole in a series of special articles in January. He began from the simple question of supply and demand in the labour market, mentioning the example of unskilled car workers at Cowley, whose high pay was attracting skilled men from the electricity industry, the railways, the police – and the local bus company, with whom there had to be an agreement not to poach bus drivers, because otherwise there would be no one to drive the special coaches bringing motor workers from outlying districts. In the Midlands there were 220 unfilled vacancies for every hundred unemployed, whereas the figure in Northumberland was only twenty-six unfilled vacancies; and the national average ninety-two. Men were coming from Aberdeen to Luton and from Newcastle to Oxford in search of work. Since skilled labour was available more cheaply in the North and Scotland and Northern Ireland, ought not companies to take that into account to offset distance from major markets? Beyond doubt, excessive concentration in the Midlands and South-east distorted the British wage pattern and was a leading agent in inflation.

A further special article from John Cole appeared a few days before the inaugural meeting of the NEDC in March, saying that 'growth' must be its guiding light and that that was bound to take it into the whole range of problems from wages and the local imbalance of industry to training, transport, taxation, and decisions on investment.

By the autumn it was known that Neddy was talking of a 4 per cent growth rate – how could it be achieved, and what would be its effect in key industries? But not much more was heard until February 1963, when one Monday morning the *Guardian*'s front-page headlines were 'Neddy shows signs of flagging' and 'Gloomy Sunday'. The Council's long-awaited first report, it appeared, was now unlikely to be published before June because of disagreements among the members. Two days later, Peter Jenkins produced for the *Guardian* an interesting 'scoop', which again led the front page and took up more than half a page inside the paper. It was the draft report, prepared by Neddy's staff under its director-general, Sir Robert Shone, and discussed and disagreed about at the weekend meeting. It said that for Britain a 4 per cent growth rate could be achieved in the years to 1966, given an increase of 3.2 per cent annually in output per man. But, the report said, changes of Government policy were essential – among them, an incomes policy agreed between unions and employers; tax reforms, shifting the emphasis from earned incomes to wealth; a great increase in adult training; and a less rigorous application of Industrial Development certificates, so that industry could grow in the middle regions of neither unduly high nor unduly low unemployment. This was the first time that an incomes policy had been formally proposed, and the means of its achievement was not spelled out. Some guidance was still needed on how a bargain could be struck between Government, employers, and trade unions, and on how it could then be policed acceptably.

The 'scoop' caused quite a stir. Reggie Maudling, now Chancellor after Macmillan's sweeping Cabinet changes of July 1962, was asked whether the Treasury had attempted to prevent publication of the NEDC documents. He replied that they would have 'looked awfully silly' if they had tried. A group of Liberal MPs tabled a motion calling on the Government to endorse Neddy's conclusions. The president of the Federation of British Industries spoke approvingly of the draft report. When the NEDC formally released the document a week later, the *Financial Times* still thought it worth a whole page and the *Times* also gave it extensive cover. The report received a generally good press, not least because of its encouraging belief that a steady rate of growth could be attained.

In April the Council itself published a further report, but this still left in mid-air the shape and instruments of an incomes policy. Over the next few months, Maudling tried hard to persuade the Council to agree at least on a general statement. Four drafts went forward, and all four were rejected by the TUC representatives on the ground that they were being asked to underwrite the principle of wage restraint in return for no positive guarantees about prices and profits. The employers' organisations tried their hand at drafting something, and they too failed. The productivity and growth rates, meanwhile, lagged behind Neddy's targets.

In April also, Maudling brought in a cautiously expansionist Budget, with heavier duties on wine, beer, spirits and tobacco but a big increase in public spending. 'Expansion without inflation', he called it, which was not unfair with the retail price index having risen less than 2 per cent in the past year. But exports were running behind imports, and the balance of payments was already moving in the wrong direction before his expansion thrust up the import bill; and the general election was imminent. If Maudling had remained as Chancellor, it is at least conceivable that recovery would have come much sooner. Looking back nearly two years afterwards, Maudling argued that the sterling crisis in the autumn could have been ridden out by the Conservatives. The deficit, he said, would have peaked in the last quarter of 1964 and then come down again.[4] We

4 Reginald Maudling, writing in *The Director*, summarised in the *Guardian*, June 6, 1966.

shall never know. The election came, and with the full backing of the *Guardian* Harold Wilson defeated Alec Douglas-Home. In no time at all, Britain was back in a sterling cyclone.

White-hot to devaluation (1964-67)

The afternoon Wilson arrived at Downing Street (as noted in Chapter 5), he was confronted with the Treasury's bleak estimate of an £800 millions deficit - twice as bad as Labour's worst forecast. That blew his Government right off its intended course even before it had been formed. Share values on the stock exchange had already tumbled in expectation of a Labour victory. In the City and abroad there was anticipation also that the new Government would devalue the pound almost at once. After ten days in office Callaghan announced his first set of measures, including the 15 per cent levy on imports, tax relief for exporters, and a 'strict review' of Government spending. He did not make public the extent of the deficit - the *Guardian* speculated that it might now be above £500 millions - and the European reaction to the measures was generally hostile. A fortnight later, on November 11, the Chancellor brought in his autumn Budget, with higher rates of income tax, higher duties on petrol, and increased social welfare benefits. Again the foreign reaction was unfavourable, on the basis that the British were awarding themselves social benefits that they could not afford.

At that point the run on sterling became a torrent. Some of it was legitimate anticipation by traders of their future requirements of foreign currency, but some was the work of speculators after quick profits, or so it was believed in the City. Both because of sterling's position as one of the world's major reserve currencies and because of the extent of Britain's dependence on overseas trade, the state of the pound was something that no Government could disregard. But in this situation sterling's international role was a great liability. The week after the autumn Budget, bank rate went up to 7 per cent - following Selwyn Lloyd's course three years earlier. But Wilson and Callaghan refused demands from the Governor of the Bank of England for deflationary measures stiffer than Selwyn's. That was not what they had been elected to bring about. After the Prime Minister's threat if necessary to 'float' sterling, as he told me a few days later, in late November the Governor, the European central banks, and the Americans mounted the great 'rescue' of sterling. The central bankers knew that if the threat to 'float' were carried out it would probably wreck the whole European payments system. (Juicy information of that kind did not often find its way into the paper, at least through me; but it was relevant when one came later to assess the Government's performance and the pressures on it.)

On the positive side, the new Government had immediately set about creating its improved planning system. In principle and in most of its detail, the *Guardian* welcomed this. Harold Wilson had made great play with his intention to exploit the 'white-hot' technological revolution for Britain's benefit, bringing industry into a more scientific era and planning economic development more coherently. To this end he at once carved the Department of Economic Affairs out of the Treasury and created the new Ministry of Technology. The DEA, with George Brown as its Minister and Sir Eric Roll as permanent secretary, took responsibility for framing a national plan, and for supervising industrial expansion, regional expansion, and the allocation of physical resources. It took over much of the work of the NEDC, though that remained the body which brought together Government, employers, and unions. The Treasury retained control of financial and monetary policy, and regulation of the economy. The Ministry of Technology – with Frank Cousins as Minister, on leave from the T&GWU – took over atomic energy, civil electronics, and industrial research and development. All this was set going within days of the election, and there were hints that the civil service also would be somewhat shaken up.

George Brown's first task was to secure agreement to a 'statement of intent' from unions and employers on an incomes policy. That took him eight weeks, but to achieve it even in eight weeks was a feat. Its terms were general, but it agreed to the setting up of machinery to keep watch on prices and on the movement of money incomes of all kinds, and it was endorsed by the TUC, the FBI, the Employers' Confederation, and other bodies. In the paper we gave the statement a friendly reception, though George Brown complained to me that we were not enthusiastic enough. He felt that a great fanfare was called for. The intent was given effect in February with the creation of the Prices and Incomes Board, under the chairmanship of Aubrey Jones, a former Conservative Minister. Its job was to examine cases referred to it by the Government – with rules laid down in advance for permissible price rises (and some for required price reductions), and guidelines for increases of income, including a current 3 to $3\frac{1}{2}$ per cent annual 'norm'. We gave two and a half cheers for this, saying it was probably as good and adaptable as anything that could be devised, though it was likely to prove somewhat leaky.

Another George Brown measure, which won a full three cheers, was the establishment of regional economic councils for six English regions, Wales, and Scotland; and, after some speedy legislation, also the Highlands and Islands Development Board in Scotland. The HIDB was an executive body, with an initial budget of £33 millions. The regional councils were mainly to gather and digest information, feeding it to the DEA, and in some degree were mini-Neddies. In practice the councils were not a great success, though they were a recognition of the regional dimension. The HIDB worked wonders in the Highlands and the distant islands, though its work brought much criticism and it had to overcome Celtic caution.

Thus the foundations for Harold Wilson's 'brave new world' were laid.

By the end of February, in spite of a precarious external payments position, it was possible to look forward with some confidence. The *Guardian*, it is true, carried a cautionary article by Ely Devons - a Mancunian teaching at the LSE - in which he warned Wilson against economists in general (the main effect of appointing economists in the DEA, he said, had been an inflation of demand for economists in other departments) and against 'godsibbologists' in particular (economists who were also sociologists and based their analyses on a mixture of fact, esoteric jargon, half truth, rumour, gossip, and anonymous ministerial statements). Sam Brittan, whose later writing I much enjoyed, was named as 'godsibbologist' No. 1. Professor Kaldor was exempt.

More seriously, the real test of the new measures lay in whether or not the national plan, once prepared, had any practical effect, in whether productive industry received the promised stimulus, in whether under-used regional resources were mobilised, in whether inflation was kept in check, and in whether steady growth was at last achieved. Only with all this could prosperity and greater welfare be guaranteed. Was stop-go-stop at last at an end?

No: it was not. The 1966 election was fought in March, giving Harold Wilson a working majority (ninety-seven overall), and in May came the seamen's strike. It lasted seven weeks, stopping nearly all exports but letting many imports continue as ships came home. Its effects on sterling were disastrous. During the strike sterling was being sold short (advance sales, that is, at lower than the current value), and after the strike publication of the trade figures caused further heavy speculation against the pound. The strike ended on July 1; and on July 14, after warnings in the press that nasty medicine was coming, bank rate went up again to 7 per cent and restrictions were again imposed on bank lending. (Bank rate had been brought down to 6 per cent in June 1965.) Like most newspapers, the *Guardian* reluctantly accepted these and other measures as a necessity - though we noted that growth, already sagging, must now come to a stop and unemployment was bound to rise.

As to the further measures to come, the leader of July 15 spoke directly of devaluation as a possibility. Harold Griffiths in fact wanted to argue the case for it, believing that it was overdue. I was against this, remembering Harold Wilson's private words the previous summer when he said that if the papers talked of it the markets would take over and it would become a self-fulfilling prophecy, without the benefits that theoretically it could bring. The leader therefore did no more than indicate devaluation as a possibility, though one unlikely because of the Prime Minister's unequivocal commitment to defend sterling, which he had renewed that day. (In an interview with the *Guardian* a year earlier, published as the front-page lead, he had gone so far as to say that the 1964 decision against devaluation was 'permanent'.) That being so, we said, a 'zero norm' for wages and salaries seemed the likeliest course. Harold Griffiths nevertheless phrased the July 15 leader so that, between the lines, a perceptive reader could deduce that the *Guardian* was not against devaluation.

Francis Boyd reported the day before the further statement that use of the 'regulator' - the surcharge on purchase tax, alcohol, and petrol - was virtually certain for the first time since Selwyn Lloyd had used it in 1961. So it proved: when the Prime Minister made his further statement on July 20, after three days away in Moscow, the 'nil norm' for six months and use of the regulator were both there. Also there were major cuts in public investment, lesser cuts in defence spending, and restrictions on private building. It was a tough package, but the run on sterling had continued while Wilson was in Moscow. It meant the end of George Brown's 'National Plan', which depended on growth - including a steady growth of incomes. George Brown's on-off decision to resign went through all its phases, edition by edition, as mentioned at the beginning of this book.

Peter Jenkins on the front page reported - correctly, as became clear later - that George Brown would have preferred devaluation to this severe deflationary package.[5] But, Jenkins said, for the Prime Minister devaluation was not a possibility: apart from anything else, he believed it would still involve severe deflation. It was 'the last and most crushing disappointment' to Mr Brown. A year previously the Treasury had advocated a wage freeze, and George Brown had beaten it off. Now there was to be the standstill for six months, followed by 'severe restraint' for a further six months. Peter Jenkins ended his report with an indication that Mr Brown was still interested in British membership of the Common Market; and that, too, proved to be prophetic. In principle I never asked about sources unless there were overriding reasons, and then I asked only with caution; but in this instance it was not hard to guess to whom Peter had been talking.

Next morning's main leader, 'Brakes but no new engine', was abnormally long because of the occasion. Harold Griffiths and I had both been in the Commons gallery to hear the statement - protracted and badly delivered it was, too, for Wilson was tired after his Moscow visit and had not had time to prepare it properly. Harold Griffiths wrote the leader at high speed, after a discussion between the two of us in a taxi on the way back to the office. The leader said that the measures were orthodox and not sufficiently constructive. They ought to bring the nation's spending under control, as must be done, but they would not stimulate the higher production or higher export earnings that were the only way to prosperity. They might please the international bankers, but would anything short of mass misery ever please some of those bankers? For a Government that was supposed to be taking us into an advanced technological age, they had an old-fashioned flavour.

5 Confirmed by Harold Wilson in his memoirs, *The Labour Government 1964-1970*, p. 252.

A more detailed examination of the measures followed, among its points being that the 'shake-out' of labour which was supposed to help export industries was a completely hit-or-miss affair. The cuts in public investment were difficult to judge, since the Prime Minister had given no details. The cuts in defence spending were all too likely to be a series of small economies instead of one big one (east of Suez being the obvious target).

One section dealt with the wage and price freeze. It followed a line that had been hammered out by John Cole some months earlier, and it was written with the knowledge that a fortnight earlier the Government had introduced legislation giving compulsory powers to the Prices and Incomes Board.

The Government (it said) has opted for a voluntary standstill rather than one with the force of law. If it works, this is to be preferred. Statutory control over all prices and wages would involve wholesale regimentation and the growth of a new bureaucracy. At the same time it has to be recognised that a voluntary stop will be open to all kinds of evasions... On prices, where expectations must anyway be allowed to cover increases in the costs of imported materials, the difficulty of enforcing the standstill may be even greater.

The Government is right to rely in the first instance on the force of public opinion to see that the standstill is observed. But if necessary it must be prepared to take tougher action.... There will also need to be some further refinements of policy to ensure that after the initial period of complete standstill wage increases take place 'in accordance with national priorities', as the Prime Minister promised. One such refinement would be to declare a 'nil norm' for incomes increases until further notice except where the Prices and Incomes Board rules that there is a special case – one, particularly, based on effective improvement in productivity.

With hindsight, that leader was too gentle with the Government. Harold Griffiths would still have preferred to argue for devaluation – or at least to have written in a way that indicated the practical alternative to deflation. But I had been reluctant to let him do it before the measures were announced and could see no gain in doing so now; which, with the benefit of a long-range view, was probably a wrong judgement. The prices and incomes section, however, stood up well in the light of the next six years. John Cole had argued that legal enforcement against employees and unions would prove a mare's nest; whereas some others on the staff, Harford especially, were insisting that without enforcement by law only the weak would comply. As experience grew, John's stand was vindicated. He as much as anyone, however, believed that there had to be a prices and incomes policy, and that unearned incomes must be brought into it.

Among many other contributions to the debate in the *Guardian*'s columns in the next few days was one from Mark Arnold-Forster, 'Stop, Go & Son – or Mr Lloyd revisited', recalling some of the things said in the House five years earlier. Leonard Beaton wrote a column on Puritanism and the economy, saying that puritan remedies generally did the economy as much harm as good. He also suggested that 'another decade of Macmillan-type booms will have people seriously questioning whether the British people are yet mature enough for parliamentary democracy'. And on the women's page Mary Stott noted that the World Cup, on crisis night, had enjoyed two hours and ten minutes of television time – much more than the Prime Minister or anything else of the kind. She found the World Cup easier to comprehend than the crisis, though she could readily imagine fishy-eyed bankers in Zurich disapproving of our mini-skirts and pop groups, our gambling clubs and 'swinging city', our morals and our times of getting to work.

A letter writer, someone who had recently been a research assistant in the Cabinet Office, suggested that the way Mr Wilson was going he would soon have no policy left – except by trying to out-trump Mr Heath with a plan to solve the nation's difficulties by taking us into the Common Market. In the Commons debate a week after the announcement, Mr Heath angrily charged that the Government had been gambling with the economy – and, worse, gambling unsuccessfully. As Norman Shrapnel reported from the gallery, Mr Heath rose to a rhetorical peak, demanding fresh and virile leadership.

As if on cue, Mr George Brown walked in. There was a great roar of cheering and laughter. Mr Brown, whom even the Tories love like a brother, particularly when things are going badly for Mr Wilson, blinked like an owl in the sunshine. Nobody suspects the Commons of stage managing things quite as effectively as that, so the moment was sheer good luck for somebody or other. This was not inappropriate, since luck was a strong feature of the debate.

We knew that the measures had to be tough. I thought that they were too tough and too negative, but criticism was muted by the severity of the sterling crisis. Just how the decisions had been reached took a little time to emerge. Two days after the announcement there was an extended report by William Davis,* financial editor since Richard Fry's retirement in 1965. It presented Brown as a less than lovable chap, in a 'frenzy' when deflationary measures were discussed, and having used emotional insistence over the past twenty months to force Cabinet colleagues into accepting decisions they thought wrong. It presented Callaghan as thoroughly fed up, though without ever quoting him, and it followed the past three weeks as seen through the Chancellor's eyes. He had wanted neither deflation nor devaluation (George Brown's alternative, with backing from two other Cabinet Ministers). Until publication of the sterling figures after the seamen's strike, he still believed that Britain could pull through, but after that he accepted deflation.

According to Bill Davis, when the bank rate rise and the special deposits had been agreed as a first stage, the Chancellor had wanted nothing said about the second stage. The Prime Minister had over-ruled him, on the ground that to announce imminent further measures would steady City opinion, and had himself taken over making the Commons statement. He had then gone off to Moscow. Far from steadying opinion, his statement had accelerated the loss of sterling because the City concluded that the situation was far worse than they knew. As to the future, Davis said that according to the Chancellor's close friends there were two possibilities. There must be a Cabinet reshuffle. Either Wilson could make Callaghan Foreign Secretary and Roy Jenkins Chancellor; or he could merge the DEA with the Treasury, admitting the failure of his experiment, and let George Brown shine instead as 'Mr Europe'.

At the beginning of August the Prime Minister and Chancellor invited editors to a general meeting at Downing Street, the first since Rhodesia's UDI. It was intended as a reassurance, with the message that 'Britain *is* being put on its feet again'. But there were some cold cross currents – as in the admission that Maudling's reference in the Commons to the possibility of floating the pound, quite proper in itself, had caused some big companies once again to think that they had better cover themselves. The French dimension was exposed, too, with the Chancellor saying that de Gaulle wanted Paris to displace London as an international banking centre and was 'actively hostile' to sterling, though the dollar was his real target. Asked why they did not talk direct to de Gaulle, Wilson replied that the general dismissed discussion of liquidity and currency questions as 'quartermaster stuff'.

A couple of days later I saw the Prime Minister by myself. He was furious over the Bill Davis article, saying that Jim Callaghan was 'crazy' to have said all that to Bill and crazier to let him publish it. It made one thing certain: that what Jim wanted could not happen. On the other hand he had read with 'deep pleasure' something that Ian Aitken had written that morning – something perhaps connected with 'a word or two in passing' when he had encountered Ian a day or two ago. He blamed Jim for aggravating the crisis by 'moping' for days at the beginning of July, when anyone seeing his face would have sold sterling, and for talking far too freely to the French. Pompidou and Couve had used his words to damage sterling immediately afterwards. On the home front, I asked why he was not doing more about the productivity drive he had long promised – with joint productivity committees in factories and allowing productivity bargains during the pay freeze. He admitted the failure but blamed it on George Brown, saying that George had never got down to it.

More light on the July decisions came much later, in Douglas Jay's memoirs, and some also through Dick Crossman's diaries.[6] Douglas Jay records that since June he had been asking for meetings, as in the summer of 1965, between Wilson, Brown, Callaghan, and himself as President of the Board of Trade. These could have discussed moderate measures of

6 Douglas Jay, *Change and Fortune*, pp. 342–45; *Crossman Diaries*, Volume 1, pp. 572–74.

restraint, because of the consequences of the seamen's strike. But none was held. Four or five times meetings were arranged but each was cancelled an hour beforehand – apparently because George Brown refused to attend. Crossman speaks of that, too. On July 12 and 14, Jay says, the Cabinet had some discussion with the bad but temporary trade figures in front of it. Another meeting of the four Ministers had been fixed for July 13 but was again cancelled for the same reason. 'Ministers thus moved into the final stages of the crisis with no proper discussion, one senior participant lurking in his tent, the Treasury preparing an unnecessarily severe package, and a pro-Marketeer minority clouding the issue by urging devaluation for irrelevant reasons.' (The last were the group who, it was said, believed that devaluation would ease Britain's entry into the Common Market.)

Douglas Jay goes on to say that Wilson returned from Moscow at midday on July 19 for a Cabinet meeting that must take final decisions. The Treasury papers, making precise proposals and offering no alternatives, had been in Ministers' hands for only thirty hours. 'This was a mockery of sensible government,' he says, 'and I had never seen anything like it during the eleven years which by that time I had worked in the government machine.' As a result, in his view, the disinflationary measures overshot the mark substantially, caused unnecessary unemployment, and undermined the Government's reputation.

From July 1966 to October 1967 there was a steady improvement in sterling. Unemployment rose to over half a million – regarded at that time as a very bad figure – and the recession was felt in other ways. For industry credit controls were eased in November; later bank rate came down, investment grants went up, and there were other easements. In his Budget speech in April the Chancellor said that the country was back on course, the ship picking up speed, and the command 'steady as she goes'. The *Guardian* at the time was sceptical; and in July, on the anniversary of the disinflation, carried a leader critical of the Government and of industry saying that the recovery was too slow. Incomes restraint had worked better than price restraint, and the result had been unfair and inflationary. Devaluation, which had been discussed a year ago, was no solution; it was 'escapist, an evasion of the issue'. The real trouble lay in what was now called 'the English disease', and it was a matter of mood and national character. Industry was failing to compete through the introduction of new techniques; restrictive practices were not disappearing. The Government's problem was to convince the public at large, and management and trade union leaders in particular, that a British economic miracle was still attainable.

At the Labour party conference in October, the Prime Minister was optimistic. A number of motions critical of the Government's economic conduct were defeated. 'Mr Wilson,' a *Guardian* leader said, 'could have convinced the Titanic's passengers that hitting an iceberg, though unfortunate and unplanned, would eventually lead to valuable improvements in navigation and ship design.' Neither the Prime Minister nor anyone in the press realised how near the next iceberg was.

It was struck in mid-November, and with very little warning. A dock strike this time, together with more French manoeuvring and rumours at an EEC ministerial meeting, had started another speculative run. Bank rate was raised on November 9, but without too much flurry; the papers on November 16, a Thursday, reported that new loans from the central banks were being negotiated – the previous year's having nearly all been repaid by the summer. In Friday's paper Bill Davis confirmed that a new support operation was being discussed and said that rumours from France had forced Callaghan and the Bank of England on to the defensive.

Saturday morning's paper, twelve hours before the devaluation announcement, told most of the story. Under bold headlines across eight columns of page one, the choice was set out: a 30 per cent devaluation, or 15 per cent and a $1,000 million loan, or massive deflation. Hella Pick wrote the story from Paris – and parallel reports appeared that morning in the *Times* and *Financial Times*. They had a common source, as I learned later from Hella, but each correspondent had obtained the story separately. Hella's had been secured in a discreet conversation at the OECD headquarters, in a former Rothschild château.

The announcement came late on Saturday evening: the devaluation being $14\frac{1}{2}$ per cent, and bringing with it a string of other measures – the 'regulator' again, limits on bank advances, bank rate up for the second time in ten days, another round of cuts in public spending, and higher corporation tax (in itself not a bad thing, since restraint so far had been a bit one-sided). Monday's leader was almost a re-run of the points made in July 1966. What else was there to say? This was the third major deflation in three years. Nothing had been done to build a new international payments system or relieve the strain on sterling, though that was in part because of French objections. Until the IMF created a new reserve currency Britain was bound to be vulnerable. As for the domestic position, the weekend's measures could yet prove a springboard rather than a slide; but the modernisation of British industry had inevitably been set back.

The planned economy was not faring at all well. But there were some plus points. Spending on education, health, welfare, housing, and slum clearance were all up by about 25 per cent in three years, even discounting inflation; there were improvements in production and productivity; the Northern areas were not so neglected as before; and, if imperfectly, a start had been made with a prices and incomes policy aiming both at fairness and at countering inflation. Though there might be no Hallelujah chorus, the record was not all bad.

Strife and hope (1968-70)

'Two years of hard slog' was what Roy Jenkins forecast soon after becoming Chancellor. He took over from James Callaghan ten days after devaluation, for Callaghan insisted on resigning because events had forced him to break his word to foreign, Commonwealth, and British holders of sterling. Two years of hard slog they were; but with one further recessionary spasm. By the winter of 1969-70 the balance of payments was moving safely into surplus and a growth rate of about 3 per cent had been recovered. Unemployment was down to about 550,000, after its post-devaluation peak of 630,000. The industrial production index seasonally adjusted stood at 125 (100 = 1963), compared with about 117 at devaluation. And while the hard slog continued after the two years, Britain was moving once again into a more expansive climate.

The spasm came just a year after devaluation, in November 1968, in circumstances that illustrated again the perilous lunacy of the international payments system. 'Kafkaesque' was the way a *Guardian* front-page report described the proceedings between November 20 and 22 – the latter being the day the Chancellor returned from Bonn in an RAF Comet, drove to the House of Commons with a police escort in thirty minutes from touchdown at Heathrow, spent barely fifteen minutes with the Prime Minister in his room, and then went into the Chamber to announce another deflationary package. 'It was a bucket of cold water in the middle of the afternoon,' our report said.

This sudden stamping on the brakes followed three days in which London's foreign exchange markets had been closed – and it was induced by chaotic Franco-German disagreement about how to adjust the values of the franc and mark. The British devaluation, thanks to swift but secret consultations with other countries, had been achieved without competitive devaluations. In July at Basle – largely because of a British initiative, with Harold Lever leading the negotiations – the central bankers agreed on improvements to prevent sudden currency fluctuations.

Federal Germany, however, with its hard work and high productivity, was running a large surplus. In November, at a meeting of the 'Group of Ten' (or participants in the 'General Arrangements to Borrow'), there was pressure on the Federal Government to revalue the mark upwards. As pieced together by our City team, the effect of rumours and reports produced a flood of currency into Frankfurt and Bonn, in anticipation of the revaluation – the equivalent of £750 millions in the three working days to November 19, according to figures later given by the German State Secretary for Information. On the night of November 19, the exchange markets in London and Paris were closed on Government instructions, though the New York and Swiss markets remained open. Reserve holders had already moved a huge sum of sterling into marks, and the outflow continued.

The Germans, meanwhile, were refusing to revalue. They were not going to 'import recession', and Dr Kiesinger said it would never happen while he was Federal Chancellor. The US Treasury Secretary was in Bonn, along with the managing director of the IMF, and on the afternoon of November 19 other governments were asked to send their Finance Ministers. (Wilson was accused by the Opposition of having sent for the German Ambassador in the middle of the night, but that turned out to be an exaggeration of what happened when the invitation arrived.) Roy Jenkins went to Bonn, at a few hours' notice, on November 20. The Germans offered an adjustment in their import and export taxes, but no revaluation; they also offered the French a large loan, and the French agreed to devalue the franc subject to de Gaulle's consent. Roy Jenkins came home, having sent Harold Lever ahead of him for consultations with the Prime Minister and Cabinet. And so the brakes were applied, with the regulator as usual and a stiff new imports deposit scheme.

De Gaulle was not persuaded and France did not devalue. Instead his Government introduced its own package of deflationary measures, cuts in public spending, and exchange controls. But de Gaulle resigned in the spring, after defeat in a referendum on constitutional reform – ending a remarkable twenty years as the effective leader of France. Kiesinger, too, resigned in September after the break-up of his Coalition and Federal elections. Although sterling remained a major reserve currency, the international payments system produced no more such severe crises – partly because from the later months of 1969 onwards the British overseas trading account remained safely in credit. The 'hard slog' was beginning to pay.

While the *Guardian* was generally sympathetic to Roy Jenkins as Chancellor, a major social and economic reform was being planned on another front. To its purposes the paper was wholly favourable, but not to all its intended practice. Since April 1968 Barbara Castle had been First Secretary in charge of employment and productivity. In January 1969 she published *In Place of Strife*, a White Paper on industrial relations. Harold Wilson wanted Barbara to find ways to reduce the damage done by official and unofficial strikes – for although the number of strikes and the number of days lost were fewer than in Macmillan's time, strikes were a flagrant symptom of the 'English sickness'. Wilson was sensitive because the seamen's strike in the summer of 1966 had forced the Government into harsh deflation and the Liverpool dockers in 1967 had made devaluation inevitable. Barbara on her side saw the opportunity to apply socialist theory to a big sector of British life and she tackled her task energetically.

In Place of Strife proposed both to strengthen the unions by further legal recognition of their rights and to regulate by law the conduct of industrial relations. It was partly based on the findings of the Donovan Royal Commission, but it drew particularly on the minority reservation written into the Donovan report by one member, Andrew Shonfield, a *Financial Times* journalist who had moved over to the Royal Institute of International Affairs. The Castle version gave the Minister power to order a twenty-eight-day 'conciliation pause' before a strike, provided for compulsory strike ballots in some circumstances, removed from 'wildcat' strikers their immunity under the 1906 Trades Disputes Act, and created an Industrial Relations Commission to try to bring about a better trade union structure and thus diminish inter-union disputes. These proposals were much too mild, according to the Conservatives, but they were strongly opposed by some trade union leaders and some of the Parliamentary Labour party.

John Cole, in a special article before the Donovan commission reported, advised against the 'short cut' of legislation while persuasion and voluntary policies, though slower, were likely to have better effects. John applied his view equally to incomes policy and to industrial relations. He said that the conciliation pause and compulsory ballots would introduce rigidities that prevented settlements, and he drew on American experience to prove this. Some others among the senior staff, Harford Thomas most notably, were extremely sceptical about whether voluntary policies would work. They believed that a better order must be backed by legal sanctions. John replied that the first time a trade unionist went to prison, either under the Prices and Incomes Act or under *In Place of Strife*, the issues in dispute would become immensely magnified and harder to settle. It was no safeguard that civil law was involved, not the criminal law, since the militants would disregard penalties and eventually be committed for contempt (which was close to what happened in 1972). Nor, John said, was it any help to insist, however justly, that trade unionists must be subject to the rule of law like anyone else, because the whole object of the legislation was to improve production and industrial harmony. Harford thought this a feeble stance; John replied that it was practical. My view tended to fluctuate, but I generally came down on John Cole's side. The issues became more intense in the Heath and Michael Foot phases, in 1971–74 and 1974–75, but the *Guardian* line was effectively set in 1968–69.

Barbara Castle was not happy about the persistence of *Guardian* criticism of her brainchild and indicated that she would like an invitation to lunch. It was a fiery occasion. She started her attack on John Cole even before she had a drink in her hand, and he replied in kind; so it went on right through the lunch. Walking back to Gray's Inn Road afterwards, John apologised to me for having been so outspoken. By his recollection, I replied that he had been provoked and it was 'about 50–50'. As the verdict over a conflict with a Cabinet Minister, he thought that a fair vote of confidence.

Politically Barbara lost her battle, in the sense that no legislation was laid before Parliament in her time. She won part of it, however, in that by June the TUC undertook to tighten up and amend its rules, particularly so that it could mediate in inter-union disputes. In the words of Peter Jenkins, the carthorse snorted and was seen to move.[7] The opposition from the trade union side was led by Jack Jones of the T&GWU, in the Cabinet by James Callaghan, and in the parliamentary party mainly by Michael Foot – a formidable combination. The first test of the TUC counter-proposals came within two weeks of the TUC's 'solemn and binding' agreement with the Government, through a steel dispute at Margam in South Wales. The TUC tried conciliation and failed, and there was no solution until in August Mrs Castle appointed a court of inquiry. Thereafter the TUC mediated or took successful action a number of times, but did nothing or failed a number of other times. Industrial relations remained a major area of strife, an electoral liability to Labour, and a severe handicap to prosperity and progress.

In Place of Strife caused acute strain within the Cabinet, so much so that in April, when a Bill was about to be put before the Commons, it looked like provoking another run on sterling. There was a 'Jim must go' faction, and there was a 'Harold must go' faction, stronger outside the Cabinet than in it. Peter Jenkins wrote an incisive article saying that unless they soon sank their differences one or other would have to go. He put much of the blame on the Prime Minister, who was governing by clique. 'The Prime Minister', Jenkins wrote, 'has created around himself a Byzantine structure of constituted and ad hoc committees which enable him to include or exclude Ministers regardless of their standing or competence but according to their political disposition and loyalty coefficient.' But he was hard on Callaghan, too, saying that many members 'who like the sound of his hiss on the trade union question recognise him as a political snake in the grass roots'. Each of two Cabinet Ministers whom I encountered soon afterwards remarked on Peter Jenkins's article, one saying how uncomfortably close to the truth it was. Even Dick Crossman complained to me that he had not had a proper talk with the Prime Minister for nearly six months.

Harold Wilson at that point was nearer destroying himself, his Government, and his party than at any time in his career. But in mid-April Roy Jenkins introduced a Budget which kept to a fairly steady course, with reductions in personal income tax but another increase on petrol and liquor. The balance of payments was improving, though it did not go into surplus until August, and the industrial production index was rising slowly but steadily. In May the threatened Bill was withdrawn, and finally abandoned in June. The corner had been turned, but it was nearly a disaster for the Government, for sterling, and for Britain.

An election in 1970 was highly probable anyway, and the usual pre-

7 Peter Jenkins wrote a good book about the whole controversy, *The Battle of Downing Street*, published in 1970. See also Barbara Castle's memoirs, published in 1980.

THE PRICE OF PROSPERITY

election easements came. They were justifiable, however, because of the real improvement in the country's trading position. Less comfortable was the early 1970 increase in wages and prices, with the retail price index in the first quarter running up to an annual rate of almost 9 per cent. Growth was coming, and a better export performance, but again at the cost of inflation. And industrial investment was still lagging.

It was impossible for the *Guardian* to approach the 1970 election with the enthusiasm of 1964 for Labour's economic policy or with the determination of 1966. Nor was it possible to disregard the Conservatives' antipathy for economic planning, their devotion to the free play of market forces, and their low priority for social welfare. The election as such is discussed in a later chapter,[8] but economic management was again a key issue. Sam Brittan had lately published an updated edition of his book on the Treasury's role, with an epilogue concluding that the country's need was 'not for highly original measures but for an application of a consistent combination of those that are already known'.[9] Agreed!

Sir Alexander Cairncross, with long experience both as a professor of applied economics and as a civil servant (latterly as head of the Government's economic service from 1964 to 1969), had spoken of the limits to successful planning. Although economic forecasting was a prerequisite to decision-making, he said, all forecasts ought to be taken with a pinch of salt – and no amount of economic or other theory could tell us how much salt to add. It was a 'political figment' to suppose that there could be precision or scientific detachment in shaping policy; but there had to be policy nevertheless, he said, not economic policy in isolation but an overall policy. Accepting Sir Alexander's unspecified measure of salt, I still believed that to leave too much to the free play of market forces was inefficient, wasteful, and inhuman. Remember the Archbishop. Any Government ought to begin from the target of shared prosperity, and so far as possible ought to avoid drastic change. Britain needed continuity and consistency of management.

How many U-turns? (1970-75)

Edward Heath became Prime Minister on June 19, 1970, with an over-all Commons majority of thirty-one. His era began uncertainly. Iain Macleod as Chancellor wanted quick tax cuts, as a stimulus to incentive, and an easing of the credit squeeze; but the Conservatives had campaigned on Labour's 'roaring inflation', and the Treasury advised caution. Macleod died suddenly after only five weeks in office, and Anthony Barber was appointed in his place. But that meant a further delay while the new Chancellor took stock. The Prime Minister meanwhile was busy preparing for the European negotiations, dealing with Northern Ireland, reshaping

8 For the 1970 general election, see Chapter 13, pp. 330-31.
9 Sam Brittan, *Steering the Economy*, 1969 edition, p. 327.

the structure of Whitehall departments, and creating the 'think tank' under Lord Rothschild. Robert Carr, as Secretary for Employment, went to work at once on a Bill to replace Barbara Castle's lost measure.

The new Government's policies were paraded before the party conference at Blackpool in October, and the *Guardian* on the whole was friendly. Robert Carr's Bill had yet to be seen, but he put 'a cool and reasoned case'. He did not expect his Bill to transform labour relations overnight or scare the life out of wildcat strikers, but he hoped it would subtly alter the climate in which managers and union officials were operating. John Davies, the new Minister of Technology, was one of the idols of the conference, but the *Guardian* was not bowled over – mainly because his 'disengagement' from the nationalised industries could be damaging and disruptive after their recovery of morale and vigour; and also because he promised to cut back on Labour's regional incentives. Our most pressing advice to the Conservatives was not to dismantle the Prices and Incomes Board – which they refrained from doing for nine months, but then did it, making one of their worst mistakes.

In the first months of Heath's Government *Guardian* criticism was directed mainly to excessive 'laissez-faire' – leaving too much, as we saw it, to the free play of market forces. By March 1971 inflation was rising towards 9 per cent; unemployment at 721,000 was the worst for thirty-one years; and, having seen Robert Carr's Industrial Relations Bill, we believed that it would increase the incidence of strikes. Inevitably, the Prime Minister's election promise 'at a stroke'[10] to reduce the rise in prices, increase production, and reduce unemployment was thrown back in his face. A *Guardian* leader just before the March Budget said this:

Like the offensives at Passchendaele and the Somme the Government's economic policy is running according to plan. The casualties, of course, are colossal. Rolls-Royce is bankrupt and so is the Vehicle and General Insurance Company; ICI and Shell are both cutting major investment programmes in Britain; shipbuilding, the motor industry, and engineering are likely to produce both cuts in investment and some painful lame ducks. The retail price index has been rising faster than at any time since Labour's worst days....

A bracing climate and the discipline of market forces: these were foreseen. Raging inflation combined with the conditions for a major recession: these were not.... In spite of Downing Street's stoic calm, we are being led into a downward spiral from which it will be difficult to pull out.

Anthony Barber's first Budget, at the end of March, contained extensive tax cuts and a restructuring of the tax system. We did not complain then, as we and others did later, that the move towards reflation was too violent. On the contrary, we welcomed 'a major reversal of economic policy', and hoped that by setting the economic signals to 'Go' he would succeed in making the traffic move. The economic leaders at that time

10 Made on June 16, 1970, at the Conservatives' morning press conference.

were mostly being written by Anthony Harris, a lively writer who had lately come to us from the *Financial Times*. In July the Chancellor removed a number of credit restrictions, lowered hire-purchase requirements, and cut purchase tax. This further reflation was partly in response to an appeal from the CBI, which offered voluntary policing of price increases – a move which the *Guardian* welcomed, along with most newspapers, and we said that the TUC in its opposition to Carr's Bill should be looking at the CBI's example and preparing to police labour relations.

Another of the Government's U-turns, again welcomed, came with its assistance to the shipbuilding industry. Through this John Davies was able to offer substantial help to the Clyde, Tyne, and other areas, reversing his January promise that there would be no more money for 'lame ducks' such as Upper Clyde Shipbuilders.

We were not so happy about parts of Robert Carr's Bill, though much of it was useful and acceptable. The strengthening of the Commission on Industrial Relations and some other legal provisions were worth having. The objectionable parts were the legal enforcement of collective and procedural agreements, the cooling-off period, and the compulsory strike ballots (which through enforced delay could serve to prevent agreement). The argument inside the office continued as fiercely as before, but John Cole's line again prevailed mainly because of his close and extensive experience in that field. The *Guardian* was virtually alone in Fleet Street in its criticism of the Bill, apart from the Communist *Morning Star*. As early as November 1970, on the eve of the first Commons general debate on the Bill, John suggested in a leader that the Government should take warning from the way employers were beginning to back away from the implications of the Bill and from the way moderates in the TUC were being silenced. The Bill became law in August 1971, with its provisions taking effect during the winter of 1971-72.

In January 1972, when the miners went on their first national strike since 1926, Anthony Harris remarked that the Prime Minister had trodden on a banana skin. The Carr Act still gave the Government no useful leverage. After a month of the strike, with coal stocks running low and the Government refusing to assist the Coal Board with finance for a better offer to the miners, a State of Emergency had to be declared. The use of electricity for space heating in shops, offices, and most public places was prohibited from February 12, and on February 14 most industrial consumers were strictly rationed. Nearly all manufacturing industry was restricted to three days each week, a foretaste of Heath's more extensive 'three-day week' two years later. More than one and a half million workers were laid off almost at once. A court of inquiry led to a settlement which, directly or indirectly, cost the Government more than double the amount needed to settle at the beginning of January.

A leader on the day the settlement was reached said that, not only in the coal industry, the concept of 'partnership' must replace nineteenth-century industrial strife. The change would have to start from the Government's own thinking: it must move away from its free-for-all competitive philosophy back towards the Macmillan–Butler middle ground. It would have to work with the CBI and TUC – and the first requirement was a voluntary approach to a prices and incomes policy. The second requirement was that both sides in Parliament must accept a mixed economy: the Conservatives must not treat the nationalised industries as pariahs nor continue to hive off their prosperous parts. And when the Europeans were creating equivalents to the Industrial Reorganisation Corporation we ought not to be dismantling ours. The third requirement was for sustained growth, which was primarily a matter for the Chancellor; the fourth was that, instead of relying on the Industrial Relations Act, both sides in industry must patiently practise consultation, communication, and if necessary arbitration.

Pious hopes, perhaps, but I wrote that leader myself to try to broaden the area of debate. John Cole was a bit sniffy about it because it was tending to move towards consensus policies and coalition politics, which I intended, but it accepted much of his long-standing advice. Harford was in favour of the political middle ground but still not convinced about a voluntary prices and incomes policy and voluntary codes of industrial practice. Anthony Harris remained a 'growth' economist. I ended the leader by saying that the Conservatives ought by now to have learned that a tough, abrasive approach was not enough. Labour ought by now to realise that sitting back, being negatively critical, was not enough 'for its own leadership is discredited'. Industrialists must have begun to see the limitations of a Conservative free-enterprise philosophy, and strong unions with leapfrogging claims should see that they were digging their own graves, and hurting the pensioners and the less powerful. 'It is time to make our system less destructive, more efficient, and more humane.'

If my hopes seemed pious, they were less futile than the Government's own expectations. The miners' dispute had not gone to the new Industrial Relations Court, fortunately, but six weeks later the dockers' dispute over container terminals went there. Initially a fine of £5,000 was laid upon the T&GWU because of its members' action, and to that a further fine of £50,000 was added for contempt when the union refused to pay. In May, on the advice of the TUC's general council, it paid up but continued its appeal, reaching the law lords in July. Meanwhile picketing of container terminals had continued, and in June the NIRC committed three dockers to prison for contempt in disobeying a court order. In the Commons Mr Wilson accused the Government of acting as 'agents provocateurs' for political purposes and of deliberately causing an unnecessary and dangerous confrontation.

When the three dockers went to prison, an unofficial national dock strike appeared imminent. But by the curious device of getting the Official

Solicitor to appeal on their behalf, without their knowledge, their release was ordered by the Court of Appeal. Again, however, after picketing at another container terminal in the east end of London seven more dockers were committed for contempt. This time an appeal by the Official Solicitor failed, and a national dock strike began on July 22. Sympathetic action followed in other areas, including Fleet Street, where sections of the printing workers brought all newspapers to a stop for five days.[11] To secure a settlement, the Government had to appoint a special committee on the ports industry which made a rapid interim report on the container question and some other aspects of the dispute; and on the basis of this report, plus some tortuous legal reasoning, the Official Solicitor succeeded in getting the seven out of prison. If nothing else, the episode demonstrated how right John Cole had been in saying that the Industrial Relations Act would neither bring harmony nor achieve what the Government expected of it.

In mid-July, just before the dockers went to prison, I held a senior staff gathering at which I posed, head-on, the question 'Who will the *Guardian* support if there is an autumn election?' Even Labour stalwarts such as John Cole, while highly critical of the Heath Government, were notably reserved in their view of the Labour alternative. In September there was a wider-ranging Saturday seminar for any of the staff who wanted to come, staged at the LSE. From the Manchester staff twenty-eight attended (in their own time but with their fares paid); also one each from Scotland and Wales, and forty-six from the London staff. Five members of the management team attended as friendly observers. No simple consensus emerged, for none was sought, but the general lines of the paper's policy were supported – the search for voluntary restraint of prices and incomes, the call to reverse the Government's running down of regional incentives, the call also to reverse the Government's tax favouritism for the rich, and the establishment of social priorities (housing first, better provision against poverty, NHS overhaul) once the economy could afford them, but only then. Some of the radical Mancunians argued for a national minimum and a national maximum wage, and for 100 per cent mortgages by right; the Welsh and Scottish voices were sceptical of how regional incentives had worked so far, even under Labour.

The Government had in fact done another big U-turn, again a welcome one, and had set about seeking a tripartite agreement with the TUC and CBI on wage and price restraint. Unluckily its first formal meeting came only a few days before the seven dockers went to prison, and the second meeting could not be held because the TUC representatives would not come while the dockers were in jail. Further meetings in August and in

11 For the less than complimentary view of the dockers held by some of the *Guardian*'s printing workers, even though they struck reluctantly for five days, see Chapter 14, pp. 354-55.

the autumn made some headway, but failure was acknowledged at the beginning of November. And on November 6 the Government announced a compulsory freeze, to last ninety days, and to be followed by two further stages of compulsorily controlled restraint. The necessary legislation was guillotined through the Commons within three weeks (Enoch Powell voting against the Government on the critical vote but the Liberals with it). The Pay Board and the Price Commission were created. The *Guardian*'s scepticism about compulsion remained.

Before the freeze was imposed, the retail price index was showing an increase of about 9 per cent over the previous year, and the index of wages an increase of about 15½ per cent. Unemployment stood at 750,000 – having come down from a peak of 870,000 after the three-day week. In June the pound had been 'floated', as a gentler alternative to devaluation but with international agreement, and its value had effectively declined by about 6 per cent by the end of the year. Reserves were down, too. The balance of payments on current account was just in surplus, but including capital movements it was in deficit. Now on the horizon, however, was the prospect of substantial revenue from North Sea oil.

On January 1, 1973, Britain entered the Common Market. The first stage of transition inevitably meant an upward push to prices at home – food prices especially. That probably about offset the restraining effects of Heath's 'Stage 2', which ran from mid-January to October. The average retail price increase for the year came out at 12 per cent. World commodity prices were rising, too, pushing up manufacturing costs; and the pound continued to drift down in value. The *Guardian* still wanted greater growth, and suggested a deal with the unions in which the 'failed parts' of the Industrial Relations Act should be sacrificed if the TUC were willing to shoulder more responsibilities. Someone said that we were trying to make the cart-horse into a motor car with five-speed synchro-mesh: but why not? If the unions wanted a responsible share in managing a twentieth-century industrial society, then they must streamline and modernise themselves.

In October came another bolt from the blue – the renewed Arab-Israeli war, with a dramatic effect on world oil prices. For the first time the Arab Governments used their oil weapon effectively, both to put pressure on the Americans to force the Israelis into a cease-fire and to exact penalties from those whom they believed to have helped the Israelis. The war began with concerted Egyptian attacks in Sinai and Syrian attacks in the Golan Heights. After three weeks of violent fighting, the Israelis were well established on the west bank of the Suez Canal, on the road to Cairo, and they had routed the Syrians. The Arabs placed a total embargo on oil exports to the United States and the Netherlands, and a partial embargo on exports to Western Europe and Japan. And having raised prices by 70 per cent in October, they more than doubled them again in January 1974: in all, a trebling of the world price in three months. That affected, of course, not only fuel for transport and industry but feedstocks for the chemical and artificial fibre processes. It gave a thrust to inflation more fierce than any wage push.

On top of that, forcing the threat from oil prices into second place, came the more immediate threat from the British miners. The conflict with the miners was what brought the Heath Government down in February 1974, for the public had no stomach for the fight. Yet this time Heath was really right, since the miners were grossly overplaying their hand. For the *Guardian*, as for any un-Conservative paper, that created a dilemma. Who was running the country and who was ruining it? More is told of the election issues in a later chapter.[12] Most of British industry was back to a three-day week, because of the fuel shortage, and Heath's incomes policy was in tatters – in spite of his offer of exceptional treatment to the miners.

Had it not been for Barber's tax policies – discriminating in favour of the rich instead of maintaining redistribution to the less well-off – the *Guardian* might well have supported Heath in the February election. He and his Government had learned from experience, and having made all its U-turns it was likely to offer competent economic management. Among the *Guardian*'s senior staff there was no great confidence in Wilson. But because of the sources of Conservative party funds and because we believed that social justice was never close to their hearts, their tax policies seemed extremely unlikely to change.

Wilson was elected, but without a working majority. He governed pragmatically, playing for time until he could go to the country again – as he did in the autumn, this time winning a tiny overall majority of three. Being in a minority from March to October prevented Wilson from going too far or too fast in undoing Conservative measures. There was no new nationalisation, though help was rightly given to the public sector over deficits incurred during the three-day weeks. The new Chancellor, Denis Healey, promised partnership with the private sector and said that to Labour there was nothing wrong with 'profit' while it was honestly earned and put to social use. He brought about a major revision of tax burdens – as we wished – and started work on reform of inheritance taxes and some forms of company taxation, though his budget was broadly neutral. An interim Trade Union Act was pushed through by Michael Foot, now in office for the first time, repealing virtually all the Carr Act apart from the provisions on unfair dismissal.

After the October election he introduced a further Trade Union Bill, which had serious implications for newspaper editors because of its closed shop provisions under which they could be subject to directions on policy and content of their papers from the NUJ. Because of preoccupation with that and with the threatened taxation of the Scott Trust, on both of which

12 The 1974 elections, see Chapter 13, pp. 332–36 and 339–45.

more is said in the final chapter, I have only a hazy recollection of economic discussions in the office in the winter of 1974–75. Frances Cairncross, recently acquired from the *Observer*, was writing most of the economics leaders; Peter Jenkins, in addition to his own columnising, occasionally offered some crumbs of lofty advice to his colleagues; John Cole brooded over the whole political and economic scene, undeterred by past failures to persuade the TUC and its component unions to move into the twentieth century.

My own main contribution at that point was on offshore oil. I had become increasingly interested in it, both because of the sheer drama of North Sea exploration and, contrarily, because of the threat to favourite parts of the Scottish coastline. Miranda and I had camped in the summer of 1957 at Loch Kishorn in Wester Ross, and the sea meadow where we had pitched our tent was now part of a gigantic oil platform construction yard. But the big issues were financial. The *Guardian* had long called for a revision of the terms of offshore licensing and for greater public participation. Both were now in prospect, though not with the priority that we thought they needed.

The handling of offshore concessions had been a sorry story from the beginning, with little realisation either by Labour before 1970 or by Heath's Government afterwards of the staggering sums that they were putting into the pockets of the oil companies – admittedly in return for major risks in the then unknown northern North Sea. The Public Accounts Committee in 1973 drew attention to the way that, through manipulation of the British tax and capital allowances system, the nine major international oil companies were likely to pay almost no UK tax on their enormous North Sea profits. (The exact method was described by the PAC, involving artificial pricing between an overseas subsidiary and a parent company to create a huge theoretical tax loss.) The PAC hearings and report spurred us on, strengthening the case for a larger public stake in North Sea operations. There was some angry correspondence, with Shell in particular, for they thought we were being unfair.

No less important was the need to plan effectively for the use of the Government's share in offshore revenues. And that, too, was another sorry story – extending well after the period of this book. It was never properly done, and the opportunity for major industrial investment in Britain was squandered.

By June of 1974 inflation was running at an annual rate of 15 per cent, and by September by 20 per cent and still rising. Wilson eventually abolished the Pay Board but did not recreate his old Prices and Incomes Board. Instead he sought to rely on the voluntary guidelines laid down in the 'social contract' negotiated with the TUC and on the work of Shirley Williams's new Department of Prices and Consumer Protection. By May of 1975 the Prime Minister was calling for tripartite agreement between Government, CBI, and TUC on how much the economy could

bear and how it should be divided between consumption, exports, and
investment – a marvellous echoing back, I thought, to what the *Guardian*'s
memorandum to Macmillan's three wise men had said seventeen years
before. After publication in the early summer of a price index showing 25
per cent inflation at mid-May compared with a year earlier and a wage
index at the end of April 31½ per cent up on a year before, the social
contract seemed to be having deplorably little effect. In July the Government announced a £6 limit on pay increases – and nothing at all for those
earning over £8,500 a year – together with a 10 per cent limit on dividend
increases and other revised guidelines. Again there was to be no legal
enforcement, but the shadow of compulsory measures could be seen in
the background. In fact, at long last, voluntary action appeared to be
beginning to work. The Government's cash limits in the public sector
had an influence, of course, but the guidelines operated too.

Wilson retired from office in the spring of 1976, handing over to James
Callaghan; and over the next three years Callaghan's Government halved
the rate of inflation in spite of frequently adverse external conditions. It
was a steady Government, even with virtually no working majority, and
it achieved a great deal. Since the *Guardian* had backed Callaghan against
Wilson for the leadership in 1963, I found some satisfaction in that.

One of my own last economic leaders in the spring of 1975 said that
Michael Foot was trying to make Harold Wilson into a Cromwell, with
a 'roundhead commission' to redistribute wealth sternly, but he should
remember that after Cromwell the people lost no time in returning to the
Stuarts. Four years later, when the people voted for Mrs Thatcher, they
chose another Cromwell – though Jim Callaghan had not offered them
the merry life of the Restoration. If there was a keynote to *Guardian*
economic policy between 1956 and 1975, it was to avoid the excesses of
Cromwellians or Restorationists.

A mixed economy, heavily dependent on overseas commercial sales,
needs sensitive steering. Free enterprise and a social conscience must be
blended together, just as managements and trade unions must commun-
icate and co-operate. Platitudes, perhaps; but ones that in a social democracy it is perilous to disregard. Britain is fortunate in still having great
resources in its industry, its workers, and its designers; it will be fortunate
also if, some day, it elects a moderate government not committed to
myopic theory or to instantly undoing what its predecessors have done.
Many Continental countries with coalition governments handle their
affairs better than we do; more often than not, Britain has been badly
served by one-party economic management. The Attlee Government of
1945-50 was one of the outstanding exceptions. Beware of anyone who
pins too much faith in Karl Marx, Ho Chi Minh, Milton Friedman or
any other single source of guidance.

10 War and peace

The *Times* could advocate 'getting a foot in the door first' at Suez – in other words, armed invasion of a foreign country – without bringing the wrath of readers and advertisers on its head. When the *Guardian* suggested armed action in Rhodesia – a British territory in rebellion – some readers were incensed, though many wrote in support, and the management was seriously worried by the possible effects on advertising. There were differences, of course, between the bombardment of Port Said as a preliminary to landings and the proposed knocking out of the Rhodesian air force. Even if it was not instantly evident in Epsom and Godalming, in fact Port Said could not be attacked without causing civilian casualties, whereas the Rhodesian air force consisted of only thirty-six combat planes parked on open airfields; but then the Egyptians, unlike the white Rhodesians, were not our 'kith and kin'.

To advocate force at all ran counter to *Guardian* tradition, and the editorial decision was not lightly taken. Over Vietnam and the Arab-Israeli wars of 1967 and 1973 there were comparable dilemmas. The *Guardian* generally regarded the American involvement in Vietnam as a tragic mistake, though for a time in 1967, after I had myself visited South Vietnam, we took a less hostile view of American action there. Within the office that 'wobble' was regarded by some of my staff as a grievous aberration; events vindicated their view, though I still think that the true situation was not quite as they saw it.

Vietnam: the lost cause

On February 5, 1965, Vietcong guerrillas mortared a US air base at Pleiku, in the Central Highlands of Vietnam. They destroyed six helicopters, then being used to support South Vietnamese forces, and damaged fifteen other aircraft. At the same time another group of guerrillas attacked a nearby US billet, which was not well defended. Altogether, eight Americans were killed and 126 wounded. In itself the Vietcong attack was not large nor the target of great importance, and in half an hour it was all over. But it triggered a decision in the White House next day to start air bombing, in reprisal, against targets in North Vietnam. That decision marked the beginning of a deeper American commitment to the war; and it was followed in June 1965 by the use of American ground forces, for the first time, in an offensive north-west of Saigon. By the end of 1965 some 185,000 American military personnel were in South Vietnam.

In December 1964 when LBJ asked Harold Wilson for the 'British flag' to fly alongside the American flag in Saigon – as reported in Chapter 5 – there were no more than about 21,000 US military in Vietnam. Most of these were training South Vietnamese units or providing air support (helicopters to lift SV units or air strikes to counter-attack Vietcong movements), though about one thousand men of the Special Forces were raiding or patrolling in small units in Vietcong areas. At that time, in Congress and the American press as much as in Europe, there was great reluctance to see any more extensive US commitment. While Harold Wilson avoided argument about Vietnam with the President, since he had so much else on which he needed presidential support, critical voices were being raised in the Senate. Richard Russell, chairman of the Armed Services Committee, said that US involvement in Vietnam was 'a terrible mistake'; Senator McGovern, later a presidential candidate, said that the US was backing 'a Government incapable of winning a military struggle or governing its people'. The *New York Times* was against further American involvement, while the *Washington Post*, though behind the President, had reservations. Kennedy had inherited the US commitment to support South Vietnam, in spite of the frailty and corruptness of its Government, and Johnson was continuing that policy.

The *Guardian* at that time regarded with dismay the deepening American involvement. Richard Scott, reporting from Washington on February 7, 1965, said that the targets in North Vietnam were officially described as 'barracks and staging areas'. The key to the decision remained 'the cessation of infiltration from North Vietnam'. A leader in the paper that morning said that the Vietcong attacks were probably intended to provoke an American reaction. President Johnson's known resistance to the pressures of the more bellicose 'suggests that even now he may not fall into what looks like one of those ambushes that the Vietcong are notoriously skilled in laying'. Possibly the provocation was aimed at bringing all the parties to the Geneva conference table once again – 'where they should have been long ago'. Of one thing the leader was sure: bombing the North was not likely to improve the US position in the South. If continued it would prove only 'an acceleration towards disaster'.

This leader was written by Frank Edmead, already mentioned as the *Guardian*'s specialist in Middle Eastern and Asian affairs. It was he who had written in December that Wilson must say 'No' to the President's request for the British flag to fly in Vietnam, for additional flags would only involve other nations in the impending collapse. Most Vietnamese, that leader said, were utterly weary of the war and the only solution lay in negotiation among the Vietnamese themselves.

For Frank Edmead's knowledge and judgement I always had the highest respect, but we differed because of Frank's pacifism. His Quaker principles made him an opponent of all military action. Generally this caused no problems, because he (and the paper) argued on the grounds of practical policy – and we shared common support for the United Nations, respect for international law, and detestation of violence or torture. The divergence came only occasionally, for I believed that the

Western nations must defend themselves, as some had done between 1939 and 1945. Without NATO, Western Europe could be overrun by Soviet forces at any time and must always be open to diplomatic blackmail; and without the Americans NATO would collapse. In the Middle East, too, I believed that the Israelis were justified in using force to destroy guerrilla bases from which their territory was being attacked; Frank differed from me not only because he felt that reprisal raids were wrong in principle but because he believed that they would strengthen the hand of extremists and prevent reconciliation. For seven years, however, Frank had written leaders and special articles on whose practical reasoning we were in harmony.

We were in full agreement on the line to be taken during 1965 and 1966, as the US military operations grew in scale. We continued to believe that the war could not be won and that the Vietnamese themselves must be allowed to find their own solution. I was more worried than Frank lest American generals were allowed to go so far that, as in Korea, they provoked Chinese or Russian intervention – for I had written most of the *Guardian*'s leaders during the Korean war. At the end of March 1965, Wilson told me privately that he had made strong representations to Johnson about the conduct of the war in Vietnam. He had told the President that the 'measured response' in bombing the North was being 'measured in gallons, not pints'. He had objected to the use of free-ranging bombers over the South, looking for targets while in the air, and had said in the plainest terms that the use of napalm was unacceptable. He had also been trying to find the basis for negotiation, but was not optimistic. In its public comment, of course, his Government remained reticent. His private comment confirmed in my own mind that the *Guardian* was working on the right lines.

In early April, when the President offered 'unconditional' negotiations, Frank Edmead wrote a leader welcoming his intention but questioning whether the offer was truly unconditional – for it contained at least three conditions that the other side could not overlook. The most serious was that the US remained unready to let the National Liberation Front, representing the Vietcong, take part in the talks; yet they were one of the main belligerents. (It was a point that Bobby Kennedy took up later, saying that the NLF would have to have some share in governing the South.) And, hardly less of an obstacle, the President had stated as his objective 'the independence of South Vietnam', thereby ruling out re-unification. 'By insisting that South Vietnam is an "independent nation"', Frank wrote, 'you cannot beg one of the main questions and then claim to be imposing no conditions.' The North Vietnamese counter-proposals, a week after the President's offer, put forward the temporary division of Vietnam pending peaceful reunification but required the Americans to withdraw as part of the settlement. There was no conference, and the bombing of North Vietnam continued.

Dean Rusk, in London in May, told four British editors at a private talk that if the Americans by their action could dissuade the North Vietnamese and others from supplying the Vietcong, then the South Vietnamese forces could take care of the situation in the South. But the 'sanctuary' in the North must be eliminated. I was less than happy about this echo of General MacArthur's use of the term 'privileged sanctuary', in relation to Chinese help to the North Koreans fourteen years before. Rusk, however, was far from seeking a conflict with China.

In the South the war was not going well. The terrain was ideal for guerrilla operations, and in spite of all the bombing, military supplies were still coming down from the North. Northern units were fighting, too, and they showed much greater determination than most of the South Vietnamese forces. Nevertheless the generals in the Pentagon – and at headquarters near Saigon – still believed that they could win.[1] They were used to winning and had become more confident. Towards the end of 1965 General Westmoreland asked for a further 450,000 US troops and airmen to be sent during the coming year, and the President eventually agreed. U Thant endeavoured to mediate at the end of 1965 but was rebuffed.

Harold Wilson, having won the March election in 1966, came under even greater pressure within the Labour party to speak openly about Vietnam. When I talked to him about it privately, he indicated that he wished to remain in a position where he too could try to mediate if an opportunity came. In the paper we accepted the unspoken premise of his foreign policy, that Atlantic unity must come first, but we said that the Americans had trapped themselves in one of the most barbarous wars of this century. Therefore the Prime Minister must take the risk of speaking openly, though it was understandable that he might wish to state his view to the President privately first. (He was due to visit Washington in June or July.) In a leader in late May we said:

> The barbarity of the war ought by itself to make the President pause. Fire bombing and explosive bombing of suspected villages in the South, massive raids on targets in the North, the torture and murder of prisoners and civilians, the uprooting of peasants and splitting of families, the burning of crops – these have been characteristic of the war's conduct. Mr McNamara, again with the best of motives, has tried to devise ways of applying America's vast military power to limited political objectives. But, with each frustration, more American troops and more American aircraft have been thrown in. Now the bombing has reached a rate slightly higher than that of all the US bombing in Europe during the last three years of the Second World War....

That was one of my leaders, not Frank's, for he preferred not to write

---

1 Their estimates are available in *The Pentagon Papers*, published by the *New York Times* in 1971, a study secretly commissioned by Robert McNamara.

when the paper's broader acceptance of British foreign policy had to be stated.

In the autumn of 1966 we carried a series of articles by Martha Gellhorn, who in the ten years from 1937 had reported war at the front and in the attacked cities of Spain, Finland, China, England, Italy, Northern Europe, and Indonesia. (She was a former wife of Ernest Hemingway.) She did not dispute that the United States had become involved in Vietnam through a genuine desire to save a small country from Communist oppression; but she brought home, more effectively than anything I had read until then, the horror and the human cost of the war. She began with an account of visiting a hospital at the old provincial capital of Qui Nhon, where a New Zealand doctor had taken her round the grossly overcrowded wards. They had stopped by the cot of a child burned by napalm:

He is seven years old, the size of a four-year-old of ours. His face and back and bottom and one hand were burned. A piece of something like cheesecloth covers his body; it seems that any weight would be intolerable but so is air. His hand is burned, stretched out like a starfish; the napalmed skin on the little body looks like bloody hardened meat in a butcher's shop. ('We always get the napalm cases in batches,' the doctor said. And there's white phosphorus too and it's worse because it goes on gnawing at flesh like rat's teeth, gnawing to the bone.)

An old man, nearly blind with cataract, was tending this burned child, his grandson. The napalm bombs fell a week ago on their hamlet.... In theory the peasants are warned of an air attack on their hamlet, by loudspeaker or leaflets forty-eight hours in advance, but as the military say, this is not always possible. In this child's hamlet the people were warned to leave by loudspeaker from the air in the night; but no one in Vietnam moves readily by night....

The family had gone, nevertheless, but in the dark they had had to leave the buffaloes on which their livelihood depended. In daylight, with the child to guide him, the grandfather had gone back to find the buffaloes. The fighter-bombers had come, burning and killing many people and the buffaloes. The survivors now were penniless refugees. The hospital conditions, Martha Gellhorn said, were suitable to the Crimean war. And any neutral American there would learn, she said, 'that we, unintentionally, are killing and wounding three or four times more people than the Vietcong do, so we are told, on purpose'.

There were six articles in the series, and they were harrowing. From the Qui Nhon hospital Martha Gellhorn went to a rehabilitation centre, where an ex-Vietcong nurse gave her a painful account of village life on each side; then to a Catholic orphanage, a refugee camp, and a suburb of Saigon; and finally to the American and South Vietnamese centres of well-meant misinformation, where some 400 correspondents obtained most of their news.[2] The moral did not need stating.

2 Martha Gellhorn's articles appeared on September 12, 15, 19, 23, 26, and 29, 1966.

Once American ground troops were committed, much of the American press began to take a more friendly and confident view of operations in Vietnam. John Hohenberg, professor of journalism at Columbia University, attributes this partly to the President's success in putting a monumental domestic programme through Congress, headed by civil rights legislation and Medicare, and partly to the President's own missionary efforts with the press.[3] (Hohenberg has a fascinating study also of the way the US information service operated in Vietnam, providing comprehensive information at its briefing centre in Saigon so that only a strong-minded correspondent went into the field, but also making front-line facilities available at once to any who sought them.) Casual readers in the United States probably gained the impression of American troops fighting a fine crusade against the Vietcong. More realistic assessments came, among others, from reporters working for the *New York Times*, *Washington Post*, *Herald-Tribune*, and *Chicago Daily News*; also from Morley Safer of the CBS network, though for a time he was moved to other duties. Martha Gellhorn's articles were among those helping to complete the picture.

Wilson took his first opportunity to try to mediate, in February 1967 when Kosygin visited London. The visit coincided with Tet, the Vietnamese New Year and a time when some form of cease-fire was usual. Noticing the coincidence, the Prime Minister had consulted the President well beforehand and was strongly encouraged to sound Kosygin on negotiations. The Americans stopped their bombing of the North for the Tet period, and President Johnson wrote to Ho Chi Minh – the letter being delivered by three separate routes, by Moscow, by Warsaw, and by a third channel. The letter was sent on February 8, the third day of Kosygin's visit to Britain, and it offered either completely secret talks or conditional talks which would be publicly announced. It was a good offer, and Wilson and Kosygin, as the Prime Minister told me privately a fortnight later, set about trying to refine some aspects of it – like 'two lawyers trying to get an "out of court" settlement between their clients'. Yet the letter, according to Hanoi, did not reach Ho until Friday, February 10.

That evening, as Wilson told me at the time, he was subjected to a 'switch sell' in which the White House altered the terms of the offer. He was incredulous and furious. His memoirs tell the story in more detail.[4] By sending a strongly worded message to the President early on Saturday, he was able to secure an extension of the bombing pause until Monday morning. Kosygin meanwhile was endeavouring to get a positive response from Hanoi. On Sunday evening the Soviet party dined at Chequers, after a short visit to Scotland, but there was too little time to secure any

3 John Hohenberg, *Between Two Worlds*, p. 291.
4 Harold Wilson, *The Labour Government 1964-1970*, pp. 345-66.

further reply from Hanoi. Wilson sought more time, but was granted an extension only until Monday afternoon. On Monday night, soon after Kosygin had left for home, the bombing was resumed.

In the paper we could not report all that the Prime Minister had told me; but on March 22 Hanoi, surprisingly, published the texts of the exchanges with Washington. We were then able to report and comment more fully, ending a leader in this way:

> It remains a tragedy that in February the Americans were not prepared to extend the pause in bombing. If the full text of the President's letter did not reach Hanoi until the Tet truce had fewer than forty-eight hours to run, ... then there was too little time for Hanoi to consider it. There, as in Washington, hawks argue with doves. By refusing to extend the pause, President Johnson undermined his own best effort to secure negotiations.

Three years later the President's special representative, Chester Cooper, published his account.[5] He had been sent twice to brief Harold Wilson, and had been taken aback by the Friday change of White House terms; on the Sunday night he was hidden in an upstairs bedroom at Chequers, with an open line to the White House, while the British and Soviet Prime Ministers dined below. His book substantially confirmed what Wilson had told me. Reviewing it in 1970, I said that it cast a sad and ironic light on the Tet offensive of 1968, just one year after the abortive peace effort. The peace mission had failed; and in the end, because of the 1968 Tet offensive, President Johnson had lost his job.

In the spring of 1967, not long after Kosygin's visit, I was invited by the Asahi newspapers to a meeting of editors at Kyoto, to discuss China and Vietnam. I took the chance to spend a week in South Vietnam, on the way to Japan. The experience of seeing the country caused me to waver in the belief that the Americans were doing no good there, and it caused a distressing breach with Frank Edmead.

Through the US Embassy in London, I said beforehand that I wished to visit a town in the contested part of the Mekong delta and a village in one of the central provinces; also to see General Westmoreland and if possible General Walt, who was commanding the US forces on the North Vietnamese border. All four requests were granted, and it was arranged also that I should visit an Australian fighting unit about forty miles from Saigon. Miranda, who had also been invited to Kyoto, insisted on coming with me on all but one of these sorties; she also spent a half day with a British medical team in Saigon.

At the famous briefing centre I was given a choice of two or three possible towns in the delta, and chose Tam Binh. Early next morning I went there, accompanied by an American civilian interpreter and an American army officer. We went by helicopter, and I wrote this in the first of four articles for the *Guardian*:

5 Chester Cooper, *The Last Crusade*, published in the United States.

Flying low over the delta, one's first impression is of its richness and beauty. The villages and hamlets line the banks of rivers and canals. They are immediately surrounded by vegetable fields and thick coconut groves. Beyond the groves are the open rice paddies. These stretch for perhaps half a mile clear of trees until one comes to the next thick grove and its hamlet settlement. Although the delta is the most thickly populated part of Vietnam, it is not overcrowded. It has none of the congestion and poverty of the Ganges valley or the Chinese deltas. It could readily double its population and, one is told, could quadruple its food production. But for the war, it would be a pleasant place for its people.

Tam Binh had been attacked by a Vietcong battalion early on a Sunday morning a fortnight previously. Nearly all the houses in two streets had been destroyed by mortar fire and some others burned out, but only five civilians had been killed and twenty-three injured. Every family had a 'bunker' - a tiny dugout, made for themselves under the living-room floor and covered by earth - and in these they had sheltered as soon as the attack began. Five other people were said to have been killed in the previous three months by mines laid on roads at night or grenades with trip-wires across footpaths. Luckily for Tam Binh on that Sunday a fortnight previously, an American air patrol - a slow-flying Dakota with flares and heavy machine guns - had been only ten minutes away. It had been called up by an American major living with an 'Arvin' (South Vietnamese) unit beside the town. Because of the air patrol, the attack on the town had not developed, and at first light an Arvin reserve unit had been flown in by helicopters to surround the town and check sampan movements on the main canal. According to the American major, the bodies of 174 Vietcong had been counted by the end of the day.

Village elections were being held on the Sunday of our visit, and there was a milling crowd of cheerful, gossiping people at each of the three polling booths in Tam Binh. They gazed at us with as much curiosity as we gazed at them. With the two American officers keeping a discreet distance, but having to use the civilian interpreter, I tried a few simple conversations. The replies to the first question were uniform and, I am sure, genuine: what everyone wanted was more security, more protection from attacks, more prevention of booby traps. Their second and third priorities varied. The commonest answers were help with fertilisers and 'Make the landlords live in the villages', for they were said to be away in Saigon or Can Tho and coming only at harvest time to collect their rents. They also wanted the big canal reopened in time for the summer's rice crop - and the preparations to reopen it were thought to have been the main cause of the Vietcong attack.

My second article, of the pair written about Tam Binh and the delta, ended in this way:

Vietnam is a beautiful, cruel, and puzzling place. Its people have lived with civil war for twenty years. Would they be better off if left to Vietcong rule? I do not know, but I greatly doubt it. Anyone who advocates it must reckon what it would cost in the killing and uprooting of many thousands of men and women who have worked with the Americans. It could be worse than all the misery and bloodshed that have come already.

Two days later, walking round a hamlet about thirty miles west of Qui Nhon, I was left with the same uncertainties. It had been overrun twice by each side, and its people were more withdrawn than at Tam Binh; also there were no groups like the crowds at the polling booths with whom one could readily talk, only twos and threes coming in from the fields and anxious to get home. But the hamlet had been rebuilt, crops were growing, and there was a surprising air of peace – and again the extraordinary beauty of the country.

General Westmoreland I met at his heavily defended headquarters. He was just back from Washington, and tired. His staff said that I must not stay more than fifteen minutes, but he insisted on prolonging a political discussion, which he had started, to nearly half an hour. He was adamant that there could not be another bombing pause to pave the way for negotiations, for the Tet pause had been used by the North to pile supplies into the South, and he was convinced that if Vietnam were allowed to collapse the whole of South-east Asia down to Singapore would soon be under Communist control. He had two huge Bibles and the *Thoughts of Mao* on his desk.

General Walt, commanding the northern corps, had the fierce direct-ness of a good field commander but also talked freely of the political context. He had a map plotting the incidence of mortar fire, and he said that in the month before the Tet truce 690 mortar bombs had fallen; during four days immediately after the truce 1,200 were fired, and the monthly average was now up to 3,000. In addition Russian 140 mm rockets were now in use and had been fired against the airfield at Da Nang itself at the end of February. He suggested that his task in holding the frontier would be a great deal easier if, instead of running on the artificial line of the 17th Parallel, it was moved to a natural line of hills about twenty miles to the north. In the middle of lunch he was called away to the front line, because of an outbreak of ferocious fighting in the western hills, and we heard afterwards that he had been pinned down at the forward headquarters and unable to return that night. (I had been on the verge of asking whether I could go with him but was relieved that I hadn't; in Normandy there had been enough bombardment to last more than a lifetime.)

At the US Embassy in Saigon the deputy ambassador, Mr Porter, briefed me on civil reconstruction. He was sharply critical of the Viet-namese civil administration, because of its incompetence and corruption – more than 30 per cent of construction materials and fertilizer brought in by the Americans was disappearing – but believed that progress was being made. He admired the dedication of many of the Vietnamese 'cadres' who were being trained for the rural development programme.

Visiting the Australians, we went by road and saw more of the delta's fringe. Within twenty miles of the city was the edge of the dense jungle, perfect cover for guerrillas. The Australians were mostly operating in that jungle; and in the evening we flew by helicopter to see two patrols 'inserted' at dusk in clearings, from which they would move out to watch tracks by night and day. They were cheerful, down-to-earth men who did not doubt the usefulness of their task. This time we saw at close quarters the effects of heavy bombing, which had devastated tracts of the jungle, and of defoliation, which had stripped other tracts of all life. But these terrifying sights were in areas that had never been inhabited by farmers or peasants.

After six exhausting days in Vietnam, we flew out to Hongkong. To reach conclusions about Vietnam was intolerably hard. Nobody at any point had questioned the accuracy of Martha Gellhorn's reporting, which had been mentioned a number of times, and indeed through the British medical team in Saigon we had gained some further knowledge of the appalling problems of the civilian hospitals, refugee camps, and orphanages. That there were over two million refugees by 1967, nearly all near destitution, was I supposed about equally attributable to the Vietcong and the American air attacks. The bombing of the North seemed wrong and probably unproductive: I had been chilled at Da Nang seeing jet after jet taking off and heading northwards to bomb targets in the Red River delta and round Hanoi and Haiphong. It was wrong, too, in spite of the figures produced by Westmoreland and Walt that the Americans were refusing another pause in the bombing to permit an approach to negotiations. Yet I was no longer prepared to condemn American policy in Vietnam as unequivocally as the paper had done in the past. Nor was I so sure that they were bound to fail, even allowing for the corruption and incompetence in the Vietnamese administration. It was an extremely perplexing picture.

At the Kyoto conference I spoke initially along these lines. The participants were the editors of *Le Monde*, the *Times of India*, the *Christian Science Monitor*, the *Guardian*, and the *Asahi Shimbun*, together with the deputy editor of the *Times* and a Vice-President of the *New York Times*. Monroe Green, from the *New York Times*, said that for once politics could not end at the water's edge and that, even though his country was at war, his newspaper was opposed to the escalation of action in Vietnam. There was general agreement among the editors that 'de-escalation' ought to be the immediate objective, and there was talk of trying to set timetables for an American withdrawal. Having just been to Vietnam, and being conscious of the difficulties encountered by the Wilson–Kosygin effort, I argued that we must be realistic; the Washington Administration could not be expected to talk in such terms unless there was a clear response from the other side. So far Hanoi had yielded nothing, nor had the NLF. Wrong though the bombing of the North was, and long though the next pause ought to be in order to give Hanoi time to respond, it would come to nothing if Ho and the NLF believed, as had been suggested, that inevitable forces of history were on their side.

The sessions at Kyoto were open to reporters, though outside Japan only the *New York Times* carried anything extensive. I had cabled to London from Hong Kong, with a summary of what I intended to say on the opening day. During the exchanges on the third day I said that while I believed the *Guardian*'s line had generally been sound there was likely to be at least some modification of policy when I got home. That was picked up by the *New York Times*, repeated by Reuter from New York, and therefore seen in the *Guardian*'s London and Manchester offices. I was unaware of this until I reached Washington on the way home, when Richard Scott told me. Indeed he had messages from Harford, who was acting editor in my absence, and from Frank Edmead; and plainly Frank was very much upset. My four articles from Vietnam had been factual, an account of my impressions there, though the shift of my thinking was evident. Frank, however, had taken the Reuter report as almost a vote of no-confidence – which my words were not meant to be. I had intended to discuss future policy fully on getting back to London.

The stop in Washington was brief, barely thirty-six hours, but it included a session with Robert McNamara at the Pentagon and a combative one with Dean Rusk at the State Department. Both mentioned the possibility of building a kind of 'Hadrian's Wall' between North and South, with a strip cleared of all vegetation and electronically monitored; but that of course would not prevent infiltration and supplies passing through Laos. McNamara rejected my contention that they were going too far in bombing the North, saying that the people there were guerrillas and could live without electricity and industry. He dismissed also the risk that they might draw the Chinese in. As to operations in South Vietnam, he said that for the past two years there had been severe restrictions on the use of napalm – which was allowed only against enemy strong points and where there was no alternative – and on the use of heavy weapons. I asked whether I might see the standing instruction on napalm carried, I had been told in Vietnam, by all pilots; he gave instructions that it should be made available to me, but it never was.

Rusk also rejected any suggestion of removing the pressure on the North. The will of the Hanoi Government must be weakened, he said. As to casualties in the North, the Americans were suffering casualties too. He said caustically that it might improve understanding if he leaked to the *Guardian* the British contingency plans for dealing with a confrontation with Indonesia, which included heavy bombing if the Indonesians made headway in Borneo. 'It depends whose men are being killed,' he remarked.

He was caustic also, uncharacteristically so, about the 'hundred applicants for Nobel peace prizes', among whom he appeared to include Wilson
and Kosygin. We clashed on the February timetable, when I argued that
they had given Hanoi only three days to reach a decision; that ended with
my saying that they themselves did not appear to have treated seriously
Johnson's letter to Ho. He was sharp also on the British press and
'escalation', saying that when the other side mined the Saigon River we
did not report that as escalation, but if the Americans were to lift the
mines and put them back where they came from, round Haiphong, 'you
will call it escalation'.

The day after my return to London the Middle East took over top
attention. Nasser required the United Nations to remove its forces from
Sinai and Gaza, where they had been since 1956, and then closed the
Tiran Strait to shipping bound for the Israeli port of Eilat. Tension
mounted fast. Wilson went to Washington the following weekend but
said little on his return. I used the occasion, however, to write about
Vietnam – making the adjustment in the paper's line that I thought
desirable. The leader began with a general look at American and British
attitudes to South-east Asia:

The British, broadly speaking, see Asia as a place for Asians. White men with
guns ought not to be there unless their presence is strongly wanted by the
indigenous Governments and people. To most British eyes today, a permanent
Western military presence in South-east Asia is likely to cause as much trouble
as it cures. Most Americans, by contrast, still see their country and others as
having a duty to protect smaller and weaker nations. They regard their presence
in Vietnam and Thailand – like their presence in Germany – as a constant check
to Communist aggression, insurgency, and subversion....

The leader went on to say that while the Americans wished the British to
stay in Singapore and Malaysia, the British Government was committed
to bringing its garrisons home unless there was an explicit public demand
in South-east Asia that they should stay. In Vietnam, however, the
President could not so readily prepare to pull out even if he were to wish
to. The human cost of pulling out could be still greater than the cost of
staying.

The situation today, so far as can be judged among conflicting versions, is that
the major military operations are mainly away from populated areas. The B52
raids, the fire raids, the large 'search and destroy' operations, and the pitched
battles near the 17th parallel are chiefly in jungle, swamp, or mountain country.
Yet if the Americans were to desist – if they were to prepare for the withdrawal
that many of their critics here want – the fighting would return to the coastal
valleys and the Mekong delta.... It is a mistake to assume too readily that people
in South Vietnam would prefer Communist rule to an extension of the security
that American operations have brought to many populated areas. The Vietnamese
have been through a terrible experience and their sufferings are not finished. It

does not follow, however, that the shortest route to a peaceful life is by letting the
Vietcong take over.

Frank deeply disagreed with the terms in which the issue was presented.
Whatever they felt about living under Vietcong rule, he believed that the
Vietnamese would be happier after the end of the war. I remained hopeful
that the breach between us could be healed; but it was immediately
aggravated by the Six-Day War in the Middle East. On that subject, too,
although Frank continued to give advice and draft, I took over the main
leader writing myself. As a conscientious Quaker, he felt that he was now
out of place, and in the autumn he resigned to take up an academic
appointment. He never returned to journalism. Not long afterwards
Christopher Driver wrote to thank me for a salary increase, but took the
opportunity to stick a few friendly pins into me. He lamented Frank's
departure, saying he doubted whether my arguments on Vietnam would
outlast a year, let alone a decade. He added, as had been said of another
Guardian man who had gone, 'You can't hire people like that – you have
to grow them.'

We maintained unceasing criticism of the bombing of the North. On
New Year's Day, 1968, under arrangements made by the Asahi Shimbun,
six newspapers simultaneously published editorials of their own and five
others. They were *Izvestia*, *Asahi* itself, *Le Monde*, the *Chritian Science
Monitor*, the *Times of India*, and the *Guardian*. Knowing that mine was
to appear in *Izvestia*, as in the other papers, I wrote it with special care.
It began by quoting President Johnson's comment that he was not so
'pudding headed' as to stop his half of the war in hope that others would
stop theirs, and it went on to ask whether he was not in truth being a
little pudding headed in refusing another bombing pause, longer than in
February. It suggested a number of ways in which the ground for negotiation could be prepared. *Izvestia*'s leader, not surprisingly, demanded
that the bombing should be stopped immediately and unconditionally.
The BBC's monitoring service confirmed that the Moscow paper had
fulfilled its part of the arrangement, publishing all six editorials.

The Tet holiday in 1968 began on January 30, and that day the
Vietcong and North Vietnamese launched their greatest offensive. They
infiltrated Saigon itself, camouflaged as country people coming in for the
holiday. They captured and for three weeks held the old northern capital
of Hué. They attacked the US air base at Da Nang and the naval base at
Camranh Bay. For a month there was the most bitter fighting ever seen,
even in Vietnam. Harry Jackson was there for most of that month, and
towards the end sent a despatch saying that the Americans had really lost
the war. Eventually the American and South Vietnamese forces re-estab-
lished control over most of the country; but Lyndon Johnson's will had
been broken. On March 31 he announced that he would not again stand
for the Presidency.

Richard Nixon won the election in November, having pledged himself to seek peace in Vietnam. But the fighting in parts of the South and the bombing of the North went on for four more years. The gradual withdrawal of US ground forces and the process of 'Vietnamisation' – handing over control to the South Vietnamese – began in the autumn of 1969. Most of the time most of the Mekong delta and the coastal valleys remained fairly peaceful, in spite of frequent Vietcong and North Vietnamese offensives in the northern provinces and the hill areas, but nowhere was ever completely secure and rocket attacks around Saigon were common. During this period the *Guardian* frequently had correspondents in South Vietnam, Ian Wright* being there for nearly two years from the autumn of 1968.

At Tet 1973, there was a cease-fire based on peace agreements reached in Paris and the final American withdrawal began. In spite of the peace agreements, fighting between the NLF's forces and the South Vietnamese was resumed during 1973, and in the summer of 1974 the North Vietnamese and Vietcong launched a further offensive aimed at capturing the coastal areas, Saigon, and the delta. Saigon did not finally fall until April 30, 1975.[6]

More than 56,000 Americans died in Vietnam during the war. The number of Vietnamese dead will never be known.

Sinai: the search for peace

To mark the tenth anniversary of Suez, in July 1966 I interviewed President Nasser. Frank Edmead came with me to Alexandria, where the meeting took place on the veranda of Nasser's seaside bungalow, and Frank's presence had a curious outcome. Most of the interview was taken up with Anglo-Arab relations, still impeded by the legacy of distrust from 1956 and by suspicion over the supply of British aircraft and British aircrew to Saudi Arabia, with whose rulers Nasser was on bad terms. But after the formal interview was over we had nearly an hour of informal talk with Nasser and Mohamed Heikal, editor of *Al Ahram* and a close friend of the President.[7] (Only the four of us were present.) Frank asked Nasser about the Egyptian military operations in the Yemen, implying that they were not going well. The Egyptians were supporting the republican regime against the conservative Imam of the Yemen, who was backed by Saudi Arabia.

6 A remarkable account of the US withdrawal and the last two years of the war, written by a CIA officer then stationed in Saigon, can be found in Frank Snepp's *Decent Interval*, published in the UK in 1980.

7 Mohamed Heikal, editor-in-chief of *Al-Ahram* 1957–74. Closer than anyone else to Nasser throughout the years of his Presidency; less well regarded by Sadat. Autobiography, *The Road to Ramadan*, published in 1975; and a study of Soviet-Egyptian relations, *Sphinx and Commissar*, in 1978.

Nasser said that the stories of setbacks were not true. Frank mentioned a *Daily Telegraph* report that the town of Sada, close to the northern frontier with Saudi Arabia, had been lost. Nasser repeated that this was untrue, and then asked whether I could spare Frank for a few days to visit the Yemen. Why not let him go and see for himself? He could be flown to the capital, Sana, and then travel the 150 miles by road to Sada.

So two days later Frank flew to the Yemen. But there he was told that floods had closed the road northwards. His time was short. Therefore, since the President had said that he was to visit Sada, the only way was to fly him there – but apparently the floods had closed the landing strip. The pilot of his small aircraft had orders, however: to Sada they flew, and then, at low level, circled the town three or four times to make sure that Frank could see the republican flags on all the main buildings. By this time Frank was feeling very sick, but his ordeal was not over. The pilot insisted on visiting other towns near the Saudi border and flying in tight circles round them so that the flags could be seen. Frank was convinced that whoever might control the space between, the towns were in republican hands. His stomach forbade any further scepticism.

Something else that Nasser said in passing caught my interest, bearing as it did on the perennial question of press–government relations. He remarked how helpful Mohamed Heikal was to him. When, for instance, there had been allegations of corruption among officials in Upper Egypt, Heikal at Nasser's private request had sent a couple of reporters to investigate. They had uncovered some disagreeable corruption. And, I asked, did *Al Ahram* then publish their report? No, Nasser replied; that was not what he wanted. But the officials were dealt with. In an open society, most newspapers would be unwilling to use their reporters in this way and most reporters unwilling to be so used. But in a competitive situation the corruption would probably be uncovered and publicised anyway. (It took a long time, though, before it was uncovered in the city councils of Dundee and Glasgow.)

Nasser talked with engaging candour. He was intent on reform throughout the Arab world, and, as in the Yemen, that meant backing rebels. He was no less intent on bringing his own country into the twentieth century, and he advised us to look at the new irrigation, land reclamation, and community education programmes on the edges of the Nile delta. Everywhere in Egypt education and living standards had to be improved. Feudalism and corruption must be ended. But Nasser himself mentioned the danger of losing touch with popular feeling – as Nkrumah had done in Ghana – and said that he was careful about this. His sources of information were the Arab Socialist Union (the political organisation of his movement), the police, and the newspapers.

When asked in the recorded interview about negotiation and recogni-

June 1967

tion of Israel, he was reserved. 'Nobody knows,' he said, 'what the future holds.' The Israelis were refusing to let the Palestine Arabs return, and unless the Palestinians went back there could be no settlement. Israel was expansionist, and that was a danger. Israel had refused safeguards against atomic weapons, and that was another danger. In that context, preventive war was possible; but he did not want war. Nor did Egypt seek any new territory for itself.

The war came less than a year later, and it was Nasser who lit the flame – though in Frank Edmead's view he had fallen into a trap dug for him by the Israelis. On May 16, 1967, Nasser demanded the removal of the UN forces from Sinai and secured it within a few days. On May 19 and 20 he moved armoured units east towards the Negev frontier and put his own forces in place of the UN detachment at the Sharm el-Sheik, dominating the Tiran Straight. On the 16th I was still in Tokyio, and on the 20th in Washington on the way home; Dean Rusk privately damned U Thant for having conceded so quickly to Nasser's demand for removal of the UN forces, saying that the Secretary-General ought to have found excuses to play for time. The Israelis mobilised on May 20-21 – nearly half their forces were reservists anyway – and on May 22 Nasser closed the Tiran Strait to Israeli shipping and to vessels with 'strategic' cargoes for Israel. Israeli counter-action seemed imminent.

Just back from Washington, I discussed the situation with Frank. He was less sympathetic to the Israeli case than I was, but critical of both sides. Neither of us knew, at that time, the extent of division in the Israeli Cabinet.[8] We agreed on the urgency of diplomatic action. Nasser's closing of the Tiran Strait could not be left unchallenged, but the first steps should be through the United Nations and the International Court. The news broke too late on the 22nd for a leader that night, but next day Frank wrote of Nasser's 'rashness' – saying he was risking the retaliation that the Israelis had threatened. This new rashness, the leader said, was all the more alarming for being uncharacteristic of Nasser.

It must be remembered, however, that before the June war Israel did not appear the invincible military genius that she later seemed. Geograph- ically she was vulnerable, especially in the narrow corridor north of Tel Aviv and in the Jerusalem salient, and her forces were numerically inferior. The Egyptians, having been re-equipped by the Russians after the disaster of 1956, now had some 1,200 tanks and assault guns, against Israel's 800 to defend the Sinai frontier, the Syrian frontier, and the exposed Jerusalem. The Egyptians also had a substantial navy, seventy bombers, 200 MiG fighters – and a separate Missile Command, with weapons capable of reaching Haifa and Tel Aviv. While Dayan (now Defence Minister) could deliver a swift blow such as he had delivered in 1956, the element of surprise would be absent.

The main difference between Frank and me was that he regarded an Israeli blitz, if it came, as unjustified. He believed that Nasser had been trying to avoid any exacerbation, at least until two months before, but had been goaded into action by Israeli reprisal raids on Jordanian villages and their air attacks over Syria, and by jeering at his inaction from Arab and Israeli critics alike. I thought the Israelis were morally justified if they attacked in self-defence, after commando raids against their territory and now the closing of the Tiran Strait, but I feared that they might fail to achieve the victory they needed for their own security. Worse, if they looked like losing it would be exceedingly difficult for the Americans to intervene without bringing the Russians in on the other side. And having recently been to Egypt and to Israel, I foresaw a tragic setback to the building of better relations in the Middle East. With that Frank concurred.

In fact on May 24 Miranda and I went off to the island of Arran, having promised our children that we would all have a holiday together after our absence in the Far East. (The boys were willing mountaineers, and Alex had his first short climb on a rope, above Glen Sannox.) But on May 31, returning from a day out on the hills, I heard on the evening

8 See Walter Laquer, *The Road to War 1967*, pp. 109–59.

news that ten Soviet naval vessels were moving through the Bosporus to
the east Mediterranean, and at the same time the US Sixth Fleet, with
two large aircraft carriers, was concentrating off Crete. So I took the first
steamer back to the mainland next morning, flew to London, and was at
Gray's Inn Road by 12.30. I found that, to cover news needs, Harry
Jackson had already been despatched to Tel Aviv and Michael Wall to
Cairo.

The House of Lords was due to debate the crisis that afternoon, so,
having brought myself up to date, I went to listen. Lord Avon (formerly
Sir Anthony Eden) was among the speakers, but he said more about the
thirties than of 1956. If we were to do to Israel today what we had done
to Czechoslovakia then, he said, we should 'deserve all we got'. It was
indicative of the common view then that he was primarily concerned with
Israel's chances of survival. In a leader next morning I noted that his
concern was something that nearly everyone in Britain would share. In
marked contrast with 1956, I wrote, there was unanimity in British
opinion. All parties were advocating much the same approach – go to the
United Nations; urge restraint on both sides meanwhile; try to get the
Tiran Strait opened by diplomatic action; if that failed, then let the
maritime powers consider what they could do collectively to secure its
reopening. But I said that, from the tone of Cairo's comment, Egypt
might be intent on driving Israel into a desperate act. If that was a correct
reading, diplomacy stood little chance of success.

Three days later, in the early morning, the Israelis attacked. Effectively,
they won the war not in six days but in six hours. By midday the Egyptian
air force had been put out of action, even faster and more thoroughly
than the British had neutralised it in 1956; and not one of Egypt's missiles
had been fired against Haifa or Tel Aviv. The first Israeli squadrons
crossed the Egyptian coast west of Alexandria and then flew east to attack
at 0745 local time; a second wave followed later, and then airfields in
Syria, Iraq, and Jordan were attacked as well. In the afternoon Israeli
planes were able to fly over Cairo unopposed. On the ground Gaza was
surrounded and tank columns were thrusting into Sinai.

The *Guardian* was fortunate in the June war in having available a
military analyst, Hugh Hanning, with access to special sources. (Radio
traffic in the battle areas was being monitored by a number of intelligence
systems.) Each day he provided a page one story which, when full knowledge of the campaign became available, proved remarkably accurate.
Consequently the staggering scale of the Israeli success in Sinai and in
knocking out the Egyptian air force was clear from the second day.
Censorship in Israel prevented Harry Jackson from giving an over-all
picture, and he would anyway have been able to visit only one small
sector of the front on any one day; and Michael Wall was able to send
nothing useful from Cairo until the fighting was over.

Harry Jackson went, however, twenty-five miles into Sinai on the second day, on the road to the Jidi Pass, and described the 'awful' desert. 'It may suit tanks,' he wrote, 'but it certainly doesn't suit humans.' On the third day he reported that the Israelis were close to the Suez Canal and that the Old City of Jerusalem had been taken in an attack launched that morning. On that day also a combined naval and parachute force occupied Sharm el-Sheik and the southern tip of Sinai. On the sixth day Harry went to the 'muddy chaos' of the Golan Heights (using a route he had previously found, to dodge military road blocks). Working alone, and restricted by the Israeli authorities, Harry was not able to send as much as he wished. I was worried, too, that because of the economies forced on us by the *Guardian*'s 1966 crisis we had effectively only one man on any of the battlefronts. Harry nevertheless succeeded in giving us almost as much as three or four men from other papers were getting into print, and together with Hugh Hanning's analysis readers were receiving a clear report. There can have been no war, until then, in which the elements were made so plain so quickly.

Michael Wall, after ten days of frustration, took the first civil flight out of Cairo and cabled from Athens. He said that people in Egypt, apart from those able to listen to foreign broadcasts, 'have no conception of the extent of the disaster which has overtaken their country in the past ten days'. He had encountered two men with 'appalling' stories of the casualties in Sinai – 'of wounded being left where they fell, of the hundred mile struggle back in the tense burning sun, of Israeli planes trying to mow down individuals staggering towards the canal.' A bonus came through Bill Papas, our artist-cartoonist, who had got himself (at his own expense) into Israel just after the fighting started. He sent drawings from Kuneitra in the Golan Heights and from Sinai – with gaunt Egyptian soldiers sitting by the roadside or on the dunes, corpses in the sand, and straggling files of men on the road home. He drew more cheerful pictures from Jerusalem, though the Old City was still closed.

The war had no formal ending. The Israelis obeyed a cease-fire call from the United Nations; but for six years they stayed where they were, on the shores of the Suez canal, holding all Sinai, and occupying all Jerusalem, the west bank of the Jordan river, and the Golan Heights. Not long after the cease-fire Frank Edmead resigned – the more unfortunately, from the paper's point of view, because I do not believe that we should have differed seriously again until 1973. But university teaching claimed him as, from personal preference, it had claimed John Rosselli three years earlier. It was a long time before I found anyone of comparable quality to take his place.

In the six years between the third and fourth wars, mediation of many kinds was attempted. In 1970, trying to clarify the attitudes of each side, I again undertook interviews in Cairo and Jerusalem. I set out with no greater intention than to try to discover – and to describe for the benefit of readers – whether there was any common ground on which a settlement

ISRAEL ARAB
PEACE TALKS

Rapas.

AN EYE FOR AN EYE FOR AN EYE FOR AN EYE

January 1970

could be built. Also I wanted to see the Aswan High Dam, now nearing
completion, and to look more closely at some of the Egyptian irrigation
and land improvement schemes. If the agricultural skills being employed
both by the Egyptians and by the Israelis could be applied to desert areas
round Gaza and El Arish (on the coast midway between Gaza and the
canal), might this not help to solve the problem of Palestinian refugees?
In other words, these journeys began as normal journalism; but because,
as editor of the *Guardian*, I had access to people at high levels on each
side I found myself being questioned on my impressions of the prospects
for peace and war almost as frequently as I put questions.

The risk of a new war seemed uncomfortably close that January. While
I was in Cairo the Israelis raided Egypt's Red Sea coast and stole a
complete Russian radar station, lifting it out by helicopter, and their jets
were flying over Cairo from time to time, apparently trying to tempt the
Egyptian air force into battle. But the Egyptians were biding their time,
and because my plane returning from Aswan had been diverted by a
storm I had seen at close quarters two of the new military airfields with
concrete bunkers, angled to the runways for quick take-off, where the
new MiGs could be kept safe from surprise attack. By chance I had also
glimpsed some of the Egyptian troops undergoing tough amphibious
training at the edge of the delta.

George Brown was in Cairo at the same time as I was, and his presence complicated my inquiries. In 1968 he had resigned from the post of Foreign Secretary, but he was now conducting a one-man mediation mission with funds from a private foundation. We were staying in the same hotel and, on his insistence, exchanged impressions once or twice daily for two or three days. (That had its lighter side: he arranged one talk with me in a nightclub around midnight, but the band made coherent conversation hard; I suspected that he really wanted to dance with Miranda, who was with me.) George was maddening to deal with, because he expected me to tell him everything that Ministers and others said to me but he was not prepared to tell me all that Nasser had said to him. Mohamed Heikal, however, willingly filled me in on the gaps.

In January 1970 after visiting Egypt and in March after visiting Israel, I wrote reports each of which took up most of the *Guardian*'s leader page.[9] The headings for a settlement were clear enough in the United Nations resolution of November 22, 1967, or 'Resolution 242', originally sponsored by George Brown: the main ones being the Israeli withdrawal, the ending of 'belligerency', free navigation at Suez and Tiran, a refugee settlement for the Palestinians, and demilitarised zones. But there were great difficulties. First, a timetable of action must be agreed in outline. Second, a method must be found to bring the Arabs and Israelis face to face in negotiation. Third, each side had to reckon with bitter opposition – from Palestinians and others denouncing any Arab settlement with Israel; and from hard-line Israelis who were demanding impossible terms.

On the timetable the Israelis were adamant that they would not start withdrawing from Sinai, nor even pull back from the canal, unless guaranteed free navigation from the day the canal was reopened. In Cairo I was told as adamantly that Resolution 242 put withdrawal first and so it must come first, though there was nothing in 242 to justify that claim. The question of 'face to face' negotiations further indicated the depth of distrust – on the Israeli side because they believed that Nasser wanted a 'mechanically applied' agreement without face to face negotiations, which in the Israeli view was a frail and unreliable approach to peace; while Nasser, on his side, had a rooted dislike of direct negotiations since he did not want to be 'Egypt's Pétain' and feared that they would be seen among the Arabs as capitulation.

Thus there was a gulf wider than Sinai itself. Yet the leaders on both sides, it seemed to me, genuinely wanted a settled peace. Nasser was preparing if necessary for another war – three, five, ten or fifteen years ahead, when the Aswan Dam and Cairo would be completely protected by Russian SAM missiles, and when his own forces were thoroughly retrained and toughened. But he would much prefer peace, releasing Egyptian energy for the tasks of education, land reform, and emancipation

9 The *Guardian*, January 13 and March 24, 1970.

- for the advancement that was already taking place in parts of the Nile delta. Mrs Meir and her Government had at least as great an interest in permanent peace, provided the settlement was one that they could rely on, provided that some boundary changes were accepted – and provided, most difficult, that Israel's claim to the whole of the old and new cities of Jerusalem was accepted.

In the articles in January and March I set out a formula, starting either with 'simultaneous statements' from each side in public outlining their procedure for arriving at agreement, or with a 'simultaneous presence' in which each side came to an agreed location (Cyprus, Rhodes, Geneva, or London) with an agreed chairman (such as Dr Gunnar Jarring) who would contrive by stages to bring them face to face.[10] Jarring himself had already been working along these lines, trying to break the deadlock. If there was truth in all that had been said to me in the Foreign Offices in Cairo and Jerusalem and at other private meetings, one or other of these approaches ought to work. The two *Guardian* correspondents out there – David Hirst on the Arab side and Walter Schwarz in Jerusalem – had provided much advice, too, though both felt that inhibitions on each side and Russian activity were likely to prevent a settlement. So it proved. Peace in Sinai again shimmered as a mirage on the sand; and land that could have blossomed through irrigation, giving a livelihood to many of the refugees, remained barren desert. More SAMs arrived from Russia instead, and they were part cause of the Yom Kippur war in 1973.

While in Israel in March 1970, I had another talk on a balcony – not in isolation, as at Nasser's bungalow, but with farm workers and tourists frequently passing at Ygal Allon's kibbutz, at Ginosar in Upper Galilee. Allon was Deputy Prime Minister in Mrs Meir's coalition; he had been a sergeant in the British Army (the highest rank Jewish Palestinians could reach) and then, while still in his late twenties, one of the commanders of the Jewish Army in the war of independence in 1948. He was a man whose courage and sanity brought an instinctive response, or so I felt. A fortnight before this the *Guardian* had carried an open letter to Allon and to Abba Eban, the Foreign Minister, which I had written as a leader because I knew both were to be in London that day. Allon said that they had read it together at Heathrow – they had met when he was leaving and Eban arriving. Eban had jokingly said to him that being described by the *Guardian* as a 'moderate' would weaken his position in Israel. With the leader's proposals, however, he had much sympathy.

He agreed that Resolution 242 could still be the basis for a settlement, though there were parts of it that Israel disliked. He agreed also negotiations could begin by being indirect, but he said it must be clear from the beginning that eventually they were going to become direct. At the

10 Dr Gunnar Jarring, previously Swedish Ambassador in Moscow and currently UN special representative in the Middle East.

Rhodes meeting in 1949, initially the two sides had been apart and an intermediary had gone between them; then they had come together with the intermediary in the chair, and finally they had met without the intermediary.[11] If Nasser was not strong enough for a face to face meeting, he said, then Nasser was not strong enough to make a lasting peace.

Allon outlined his proposals for security, which, he said, had been lying on the Cabinet table since the summer of 1967. At that time, in Eshkol's Government, some had said that Israel must keep all Sinai, some that Israel must keep half, some one-tenth, and some said keep none. Allon had proposed that they should give back almost all of Sinai and two-thirds of the West Bank. But the West Bank must not be remilitarised by Jordan, and Israel must be permitted to establish 'security belts' under Israeli sovereignty on the heights above the Jordan valley, with 'Nahals' or security settlements in these belts. (His proposal envisaged a small number of settlements, not the great number that have now been established on the West Bank.) Sharm el-Sheik must remain with Israel, and an access corridor to it. For religious reasons a Jewish community must be established in Hebron, south of Jerusalem, for one had existed there throughout the ages until the massacre in 1929. As to the status of Jerusalem itself, that should be treated as a religious rather than a political question, and there must be respect for all the faiths represented there; he believed, too, that Moslem access to their shrines from Jordanian territory could be discreetly provided by bridges and tunnels, so that there was no need to enter Israeli land. The whole proposal was imaginative, and much less damaging to Arab interests than *de facto* annexation of the West Bank. But how much chance was there of persuading Nasser or Hussein to accept it?

Few meetings in my life have left me with as strong an impression as that morning at Ginosar. Only Willy Brandt and Jack Kennedy had as powerful an effect. Ygal Allon had both a natural humanity and a calm authority. He said that a solution must be reached that would last not just for this generation and the next but for two hundred years and beyond. He did not want his children and grandchildren to have to fight. When he himself was fighting in 1948, his son had been an infant. That son had been a corporal in the Six-Day War and was an officer now. Allon did not want his grandson to be in the same situation. Allon's parting words were that I must heed this: everyone must think in terms of history, for a temporary armistice would not do. A living peace settlement must be found.

Back in Jerusalem Abba Eban again cross-questioned me. From my visit to Cairo two months previously, did I truly believe that they were willing to talk? Yes, I did. Eban doubted it: he had seen nothing to

11 The intermediary was Dr Ralph Bunche, a black American who was UN Assistant Secretary-General.

convince him. Did the Israelis then, I asked, discount the messages that George Brown had brought from Cairo? No, Eban replied, they were taking those messages very seriously – though George at times was an infuriating messenger. A 'simultaneous presence' could be achieved, he said, and 'we're ready to go if they will'. But what advice did I believe that Nasser was getting? From Heikal, I said, probably anti-Jewish and anti-negotiating advice; from Mahmoud Riad, the Foreign Minister, cool and reasonable advice and readiness for a settlement. And from what I'd heard, since the Six-Day War Riad's advice had been uppermost in spite of the close friendship between Nasser and Heikal. Finally, from Eban, were they prepared to go back to anything other than the situation on June 4, 1967? To that I said 'yes', for they were ready to accept demilitarised zones, provided they were on both sides of the frontier; they were ready to accept free navigation at Tiran and Suez, though they wanted Suez left late in the timetable of action; they were now more practical about refugees, and, a great change, they were ready to recognise Israel. Nasser had said specifically to George Brown that he would meet the Israelis and sign.

Eban remained sceptical. He told me about the delivery of Soviet SA-3 missiles, about which nothing had yet been published (though unknown to either of us there was a message in that morning's *New York Times*). From Eban's house I was driven to Tel Aviv for my last appointment, which was with the Chief of Staff, General Aharon Yariv. He, too, talked about the new SA-3 missiles – and provided me with a small scoop for next day's *Guardian*, with news of how Israeli aircraft had photographed them on arrival from Russia. They were being deployed round Cairo and Alexandria, with Soviet crews it was presumed, and they differed from the SA-2 missiles in being effective against low-flying aircraft.

By the end of August, those missiles had created another crisis – for further photo-intelligence showed that Nasser, disregarding the cease-fire agreement, had moved some of them up to the Canal Zone. Mrs Meir was already denouncing Nasser in what seemed to me extravagant terms, quoting his reference to 'rivers of blood' as proof that he wanted war, whereas in every speech he had said that he would prefer a peaceful settlement. Now the Israeli anger over the SAMs was extreme, and Dayan threatened to bomb the missile sites. Had he done so, Russian action would have been probable since the Russians had supplied the SA-3s only after Israeli destruction, to the Russians' embarrassment, of many radar and SA-2 sites the previous winter. At the beginning of September, the outlook for peaceful negotiation was bleak; but I did not let the *Guardian* stray from its commitment to trying to persuade both sides to talk, not fight.

Even the tension over the SAMs, however, was overshadowed on September 6 when Palestinian commandos hijacked three airliners – one each from TWA, Pan-Am, and Swiss Air. They failed to take over an

El-Al flight, whose crew killed one of the hijackers and overpowered the other, Leila Khaled; the plane, on a flight from Amsterdam to New York, made an emergency landing at Heathrow and Leila Khaled was taken to Ealing police station. Three days later, because the British Government refused to release her, a BOAC VC-10 was hijacked. The Pan-Am jumbo was blown up at Cairo airport after the passengers and crew had been released. The three other planes were taken to a remote airstrip in the Jordanian desert, 'Dawson's Field' (so called after Air Marshal Dawson who built it in 1948 for the RAF). About a hundred women and children from the Swiss Air and TWA planes had been allowed to leave on the second day, being taken by bus to Amman. Over 400 passengers remained as hostages for a week, including the women and children on the British plane, living in the aircraft in temperatures above 100°F.

The Palestinian Popular Front demanded the release of three terrorists imprisoned in Germany for previous attacks on civil aircraft, three in Switzerland, and Leila Khaled. After four days the British, West German, Swiss, and US Governments agreed to this, provided all the hostages were released, including Israeli citizens. Their attitude was that there could be no distinction between Israelis and others, and in this they were backed almost unanimously by the British press, including the *Guardian*. The International Red Cross were asked to negotiate, and they were greatly assisted by the former *Guardian* correspondent in the Middle East, Michael Adams, who was on private business in Amman. He provided the main contact with the Palestinians and eventually persuaded them that release of the hostages was the right course. All but fifty-four were freed after a week; but the fifty-four were dispersed and hidden in Palestinian camps, after the three aircraft had been blown up, and they were not freed until the last week of September. Civil war had meanwhile broken out in Jordan, with fighting in Amman and other towns.

Early on September 22, a day when representatives of the Palestinians, Syrians, and Hussein were to meet in Cairo under Nasser's chairmanship to try to end the civil war, Edward Heath sent a message to Nasser from Downing Street asking him to intercede with the Palestinians to secure the release of the last thirty-eight hostages (including the Israelis and those with dual citizenship). Nasser replied that he would try, in the context of the Cairo peacemaking. Three days later the remaining thirty-eight were freed. The week was an extremely strenuous one for Nasser, and on September 28 he suffered a severe heart attack from which he died. He was fifty-two, and had been Egypt's leader for sixteen years.

The news reached us in London, without any advance warning, at about 8.30 pm – with an hour and a half to the first edition. Consequently, I found myself writing both the front-page lead and the first leader. It would have been possible for us to use agency copy for the front page – but I felt it was vital to put Nasser's death in its context in Arab affairs and in Arab-Israeli relations. Therefore I wrote a short summary and analysis, to go in bold type at the top of the front-page story. It said that the strain of the past few days must have told on the President, for the Arab world had just gone through its worst crisis since the June war. For Nasser it had been a bitter time. Earlier in the year, against the advice of other Arab leaders, he had accepted the American peace initiative and stated his readiness for a settlement with Israel. Only King Hussein among the Arabs had supported him, and then Hussein had come into conflict with the Palestinians on his own territory just because he had said that he was ready to accept a negotiated settlement. Nasser had worked ceaselessly in the past six days to bring about a cease-fire in Jordan and a reconciliation of the warring factions. Against all expectations, he had succeeded ... but with Nasser's death, the Arabs might soon return to fighting.

To save time, I moved temporarily to a spare desk in the sub-editors' room that evening. Editors do not usually write the front-page lead, but I felt that since the story was at my fingertips it was the quickest way, and John Putz welcomed it. The leader and the main news story had to be written and sent to the composing room page by page. The leader said that Nasser had never been liked in Britain, but he was a far greater man than had been commonly acknowledged. He was personally modest, not seeking his own aggrandisement, and he did not live in the style of a dictator. (I could not imagine anyone having with Hitler, Mussolini, or Peron the kind of easy conversation that Frank and I had had with him on his veranda.) He enjoyed exercising power and was a born politician: 'but his greatness lay in his feeling for Egypt, for the Arab world, and above all for the Arab peasants who had to be brought into the twentieth century.' Without Nasser, I wrote, peace was far away. The effort of trying to turn the Arab world away from fruitless and endless war with Israel had come close to costing him his political power and in the end had cost him his life.

Anwar Sadat succeeded Nasser, promising his people that if the Israelis did not withdraw from Sinai the Egyptian forces would drive them out. Three years later, on October 6, 1973, the Egyptians and Syrians launched the fourth Arab-Israeli war with offensives eastwards across the Suez canal and southwards into the Golan Heights. The war lasted not six days but eighteen: by October 24 the Egyptians had established a small bridgehead east of the canal in its northern sector, but in the southern sector Dayan's forces were west of the canal and had broken through the Egyptian defences. The road to Cairo lay ahead. On the Syrian front the Israelis had shattered their opponents and the road to Damascus, too, was open. Once again the United Nations brought about a cease-fire.

This time the *Guardian* had two reporters on the Israeli side, Eric Silver and Peter Niesewand, and three trying to get copy out from Arab centres - David Fairhall in Amman and David Hirst in Beirut (with

Syrian contacts), both of whom managed to file a number of useful messages, and Anthony McDermott in Cairo, almost as frustrated as Michael Wall had been six years before. Again the preparation of analyses in London was important, though this time we had no source as good as Hugh Hanning had been, through his military contact, in 1967. By the second week the Arabs' preparations to cut off Western Europe's oil supplies had become as big a story as the war itself.

The Yom Kippur War – so called because the attack on Israel's forces was launched on the Day of Atonement – did not immediately lead to full peace negotiations. A disengagement in Sinai was achieved, thanks chiefly to Dr Henry Kissinger, and the Suez canal was reopened; but it was not until 1977 that Anwar Sadat and Menachim Begin met face to face. They then earned their peace prizes. Although a complete settlement still eludes Israel and her neighbours, peace is no longer so remote.

Two concluding questions and a footnote. Why has the Middle East carried such fascination for some British journalists, myself among them? And is it callous or immoral for journalists to enjoy reporting catastrophes such as the Arab-Israeli wars or the death of Nasser? The second is more easily answered than the first. It is not the war or the catastrophe as such that reporters and other journalists enjoy: I have never known a good war correspondent or analyst who was not horrified by the suffering and personally frightened by the experience. (Or rather I have known only one, extraordinarily a woman, and her cold detachment impaired her reporting.) The enjoyment lies in the challenge of finding out what is happening, communicating it, and feeling that, within human limits, you have done as good a job as possible. For some young journalists, it must be admitted also that war, civil war, and crisis have helped them in their careers – because such events are a severe test not only of physical and mental stamina but also of ability to overcome censorship, find telephones or cable facilities, and meet deadlines.

As to occasions such as the night of Nasser's death, the satisfaction lies again in coping quickly with the unexpected and producing a strong paper next morning. Nasser's death at that juncture was a historic tragedy, and I felt that we had conveyed this to readers – less well than an Aeschylus or Shakespeare might have done, but better than most other newspapers did. In ninety minutes that was not too bad.

And the fascination of Egypt and Israel? Ancient civilisations, conflicts of three thousand years, the territory of the Old and New Testaments – these are one reason. Another is seeing the desert bloom, whether through Arab or Israeli skill, and realising what that can mean in a better life for peasants and refugees. A third is the sheer drama of the Jewish success in building or rebuilding a homeland – of seeing 'Tomorrow in Jerusalem' become today's reality – and at the same time wishing to see reconciliation of Zionist ambition with Arab rights. In the long run, even the aggressive Zionists must come to terms with their Arab neighbours or their homeland will not survive. That is the importance of the vision of men such as Ygal Allon.

The footnote is historic – though it illustrates the extraordinary intensity of experience among Israeli Ministers and officials. It is an episode that deserves record, for I have not seen it written in a connected way. By chance I heard different parts of the story while in Israel in 1970. Ezer Weitzman, who had commanded the air force in the 1967 war and by 1970 was in politics as a member of Begin's right-wing Herut party, had been in the RAF. While in his twenties, piloting a Spitfire he had shot down three Messerschmitts; and then, piloting a Messerschmitt in the new Israeli air force in January 1949, he had shot down two RAF Spitfires. Altogether five were shot down by his squadron after they blundered over the Negev, on a recce from Cyprus, during the last stages of the independence war. One of the RAF pilots was killed but four parachuted to safety, and the four were given a big party in the Israeli mess afterwards.

Aharon Remez, Ambassador in London in 1970, had been in charge of building up the air force in 1948-49, having been called back by Ben Gurion from his post with the RAF's 2nd Tactical Air Force in Germany. They had begun by building small Austers and Piper Cubs from spare parts in caves and warehouses, and flew all of them with the same registration number to confuse the British authorities. Then they had been able to buy old Spitfires and Hurricanes, and some new but very badly constructed Messerschmitts from Czechoslovakia. These were the beginnings of the air force that swept to such triumph in 1967.

The Negev incident was embarrassing to the British Government, which was reluctant to recognise Israel. Arthur Lourie, whom I met in Jerusalem, had been left in charge of the Israeli mission at the United Nations while Eban, its leader, went to England. The day the RAF planes were shot down, an otherwise quiet Sunday in New York, the acting head of the British delegation telephoned and then came to call at Lourie's flat. The British diplomat delivered a note, and only after he had left did Arthur Lourie realise that it was not addressed to anyone though its text referred to 'the Jewish authorities in Tel Aviv', which was not acceptable to the Israeli Government. Lourie therefore went to call on Trygve Lie, secretary-general of the UN and a friendly man, to seek advice. Lie had just returned from duck shooting and greeted Lourie with the words: 'You did better than me – I got only eleven out of fifteen and you got five out of five.'

But the incident mattered, because Churchill next day in the Commons delivered a flaming attack on Attlee and Bevin for their failure to recognise Israel. He referred to Bevin as 'retiring under a cloud of inky water and vapour, like a cuttlefish, to some obscure retreat'. It was more than time, Churchill said, to recognise Israel. 'Whether the right honourable gentleman likes it or not, the coming into being of a Jewish State in Palestine is an event in world history to be viewed not in the perspective of a generation or of a century, but in the perspective of a thousand, two thousand, or even three thousand years.'[12] The Government gave in, and two days later it recognised Israel.

Rhodesia: from UDI to guerrilla war

Over Rhodesia in 1968 – two and a half years after UDI – the *Guardian* was accused of being a war-monger because we advocated a limited use of force. We did it when Smith was about to hang 124 condemned guerrillas, although the Queen, on an application from the British Government, had granted a reprieve. Economic sanctions against Rhodesia had failed – and indeed were hurting Zambia as much as Rhodesia itself. The talks between Wilson and Smith on HMS *Tiger* off Gibraltar had also failed, with Ian Smith side-stepping out of a draft agreement as soon as he got home. When the impending executions were announced in March 1968, the *Guardian* proposed a military operation to neutralise the Rhodesian air force and permit British airborne troops to take over Salisbury, Bulawayo, and the Kariba dam. At the time of UDI the carrier *Eagle* had been in the Mozambique Channel, and its Buccaneers alone would have been enough to knock out the small Rhodesian squadrons, leaving the way clear for unopposed airborne operations.[13] British aircraft carriers were frequently off the East African coast from 1965 onwards, while the oil blockade of Beira lasted; and the Rhodesian air base at Old Sarum, outside Salisbury, was only a half-hour's flight for a Buccaneer. Zambia was ready to offer staging facilities for British forces, provided they were on their way to restore British rule.

The opportunity was not taken. Negotiations with Ian Smith dragged on fruitlessly. Pressure from President Kaunda, other black Commonwealth leaders, and the Organisation for African Unity had no effect on Harold Wilson. Guerrilla war came to the neighbouring countries of Mozambique and Angola – with ultimate triumph for Marxist forces in each – and from 1972 Rhodesia was besieged in its own civil war. For Rhodesia the eight years of guerrilla fighting were bloodier and more

---

12 Hansard, January 26, 1949, cols 951–52.

13 *Eagle* was sent to the Mozambique Channel in November 1965, in advance of Cabinet orders, because the Admiralty wanted to demonstrate the versatility of carriers. In addition to its Buccaneer bombers it had Sea Vixen fighters (with the latest Red Top air-to-air missiles), which were capable of providing air cover over Rhodesia. I had been told about this at the time. Powerful RAF radar units from the British strategic reserve were located near Lusaka and Ndola from soon after UDI, to provide air protection for Zambia; and a squadron of Javelin fighters were sent there in early December. Unfortunately a misleading article in the *Daily Telegraph* caused Zambian Ministers to believe that the Javelins were out of date and ineffective, whereas they were armed with Firestreak air-to-air missiles. Rhodesia's air force consisted of one squadron of Hunter daytime fighters, without missiles, one squadron of ancient Vampires, and one squadron of Canberra bombers – with bases at Old Sarum and at Thornhill, near Gwelo.

costly than any British operation would have been. For Zambia, too, there were fifteen years of economic strain and Rhodesian reprisal raids. If Britain had dealt with the Rhodesian rebellion in 1965 or in 1968, as probably it would have done if the rebels had been black, then Southern Africa could have undergone less violent and less extreme change.

Harold Wilson's personal abhorrence at the idea of ordering British troops into action was the main reason why the opportunity was not taken either in 1965 or in 1968. His feelings were not so much because of Eden's example at Suez, which had little validity in relation to Rhodesia, as because of his own nonconformist Christian background. From before UDI, Wilson had ruled out force unless there was a breakdown of law and order in Rhodesia. He had said to me in September 1965 that he could not contemplate the use of force against a Commonwealth country where the issues were over the electoral franchise and constitutional progress. The only circumstance in which it could be considered was some kind of 'breakdown' within Rhodesia or conceivably if the Rhodesians were to cut off Zambia's electricity power supplies from Kariba. But with quiet conviction he said that he was not going to start any fighting that could be avoided. In 1965 his precarious Parliamentary majority was an extra deterrent, while so many Conservatives were pro-Smith or pro-'kith and kin', but in 1968 he still held out against military action. Even Smith's rejection of the Queen's reprieve was not enough of a 'breakdown' to change his mind – and almost at once, because of the reaction in Britain (including ours), the Rhodesian Government halted the executions after the first five hangings. Whether the *Guardian*'s advocacy of force played any part in that decision I do not know, but our view was certainly publicised in Rhodesia through the BBC.

The Rhodesian story is best followed from before UDI. Smith's camouflaged collision course with the British had been well reported in the *Guardian* – through Patrick Keatley as Commonwealth correspondent, Clyde Sanger* as our staff man in East and Central Africa, and John Worrall as our 'stringer' (or part-time correspondent) in Salisbury. John Worrall was eventually deported in 1969, as was his successor, Peter Niesewand, in 1973. Pat Keatley had written a series after the break-up of the Central African Federation and had predicted that ultimately the choice must be between some form of assured progress to majority rule in Rhodesia and civil strife.

Having never been south of the equator, but having written quite often about Southern Africa, I decided in March 1965 to visit Kenya, Tanzania, Malawi, Rhodesia, and Zambia – in that order. Clyde Sanger was my host in Nairobi at the beginning and end of the tour, but for the rest I travelled alone. On return to London I wrote a series on the likelihood of UDI and the alternative of peaceful change in Rhodesia. My first article began by saying that Salisbury was a deceptive city. Arriving there after Nairobi, Dar-es-Salaam, and Blantyre 'you feel suddenly at home'. Schoolgirls in

November 1965

English school uniform cycled slowly in the street, chatting as they went; there were high buildings, traffic, and paved roads; no dust, no barbed wire, no tattered Africans loitering. Nor were there armed men at road-blocks as around Blantyre, or Ilyushin aircraft unloading secret arms as at Dar, or rebels or exiles waiting to meet you and argue their case in quiet corners. You could even pass the Prime Minister, as I did in a Salisbury street my first morning there, walking unaccompanied by any detective or bodyguard. That was one aspect of the city; another was to be found in the columns of the *Rhodesia Herald*, from which I extracted a number of items in that first morning's issue (shortened here).

A Government request to Parliament for power to detain or restrict people for up to five years, instead of twelve months only. Under the revised powers an individual could be detained for five years without charge or trial, and the only appeal was to the Minister who had made the order.

A parallel request for the death penalty to be imposed for throwing grenades at trains. There had been 16 railway sabotage attempts in the past six months, according to the Minister for Law and Order.

At Fort Victoria 21 Africans had been sentenced to terms of six years or five years for 'malicious injury to property'. The charges arose from an incident at a construction site after a European foreman shot an African in the legs. (Though

the newspaper did not say so, I found out that the African had died and the
foreman had not been charged.)

At the Harari township an African was fined £15 or three months' imprisonment for leading a procession on the day the British Colonial Secretary and the
Lord Chancellor had arrived for talks with the Rhodesian Government. (It was
supposed to be a procession of welcome.)

There were other chilling items in the paper, and much more to be
learned in private conversation. The *Sunday Mail* in Salisbury, for example, was under threat of prosecution under the Official Secrets Act
because it had published parts of a report by the Rhodesian Tobacco
Association on the disastrous effects on tobacco sales that could follow
UDI, the charge against the newspaper being based on its refusal to tell
the police where it had obtained a copy of the report. Still more serious
in human terms was the plight of the detainees and their families – the
official total of detainees being about eighteen hundred but the real total
reckoned to be higher, and their families being generally in destitution.
Add to that the beating of detainees under questioning – one had been
beaten to death a month before – and the picture was wretched.

My second article said that while officially the Rhodesian Government
stated that it would not consider a unilateral declaration of independence
so long as negotiations with Britain continued, in practice UDI seemed
highly probable in the autumn. By then the tobacco crop would be sold
and funds flowing in. The question most commonly asked of me in
Rhodesia was whether Britain was bluffing. White people appeared unable
to believe that Britain would ever do anything nasty to them, such as a
prohibition on tobacco and sugar sales. If it did, the tougher among them
wanted to 'clobber Britain through the copper trade'. That meant stopping Zambian exports of copper through Rhodesia and stopping Zambia's
imports of coal and petroleum products through Rhodesia and power from
Kariba. The third article looked at the franchise question and the devices
by which white supremacy was to be maintained; the fourth looked at
whether, in the light of experience in Kenya, Malawi, and Zambia,
peaceful change offered an alternative course. It concluded that if the
Rhodesians could overcome their own fears this offered the most hopeful
way.

In November UDI came nevertheless – no surprise to any *Guardian*
reader. Harold Wilson had been in Salisbury in late October, trying to
reach an accommodation, and had even taken a telephone call from Ian
Smith at six in the morning of UDI day, though Smith had said nothing
of the declaration that was to follow at midday. The Conservatives in
Parliament were taken aback by the Rhodesian action, and Mr Heath
gave general though guarded support to the Government's decision to
declare the Smith regime illegal and to take economic measures against
it. Although the United Nations Trusteeship Council on November 1
had resolved by 79 votes to 8 that Britain ought to employ 'all necessary

measures including military force' to secure release of the political detainees and repeal of discriminatory legislation, the Prime Minister remained against coercion.

The *Guardian*'s main headline the morning after UDI was 'Britain split on question of sanctions', and the report said that Mr Heath had left the 1922 Committee in no doubt that he would oppose the ban on tobacco imports. Hella Pick from the United Nations said that the African States believed that Britain must use force, and three countries – Ghana, Nigeria, and Ethiopia – were ready to send paratroops. Our leader at that stage did not advocate force, though it came close to doing so: it said that 'all practicable means' must be used to end the rebellion, and it questioned whether economic sanctions would prove sufficient.

Approval for the use of force had already come from an unusual quarter, illustrating the complexity of British opinion. The Archbishop of Canterbury, Dr Michael Ramsey, said a fortnight before UDI that in certain circumstances Christians would have to approve the use of force. He was speaking during a debate in the British Council of Churches, meeting in Aberdeen, and 'with a terrible sense of responsibility' he said that if the Government thought it practicable to intervene to protect the rights of Rhodesia's majority then 'as Christians we have to say that it will be right to use force'. The plight of the African political prisoners had again carried weight among peaceful British citizens.

The Prime Minister, however, continued to believe that quick results could be achieved simply through economic pressure. He told Commonwealth Ministers at a meeting in Lagos in early January that the rebellion could be ended 'within a matter of weeks rather than months'. Pat Keatley from Lagos reported that, in the face of strong Commonwealth hostility, Wilson had achieved a considerable success by keeping his temper when others were losing theirs and through diplomatic support from Canada and the Nigerian hosts. Canada's Lester Pearson had put the straight question to the African militants, 'Are you sure that armed sanctions will now prove quicker?' – and they had come round to accepting Wilson's approach.

But Wilson's 'weeks rather than months' proved wildly unrealistic. Apart from anything else, oil sanctions could not be made effective until Zambia had been provided with an alternative source of fuel, and although an airlift from Dar to Lusaka and Ndola was soon organised, with American and Canadian help, the cash cost was enormous. And in practice the oil embargo had little effect in Rhodesia, since secret arrangements were made for supplies from South Africa – with subsidiaries of British Petroleum and Shell taking a leading part in the trade.[14] On February 15, 1966, the paper carried a report from John Worrall on South African

14 The full extent of their involvement did not become plain until the Bingham report was published in 1979.

assistance to Rhodesia, which midway through said that 'large tankers with the owners' names painted out are coming over the South African border almost daily', and it went on to say that although nominally petrol was strictly rationed in Rhodesia the authorities were now granting generous supplementary allowances. The importance of this message was not fully appreciated on the night it came in, and it was not given the prominence it ought to have had.

Two days later that error was remedied, when Worrall reported the *Rand Daily Mail*'s findings based on a careful count of tanker traffic at Beitbridge, on the South African–Rhodesian border. The *Mail* estimated that 35,000 gallons a day were passing through Beitbridge and that similar quantities were believed to be entering Rhodesia from Mozambique. (That the *Rand Daily Mail* had undertaken its investigation of tanker traffic was typical of its courageous disregard of South African Government pressure to keep quiet.) Worrall reported that the authorities in Rhodesia, while not forthcoming with confirmation, 'are bland with smiles'. This time his story became our front-page lead. Two days later the Foreign Office in London said that these reports were 'highly coloured', and then Lobby correspondents at Westminster were fed the Government's view that 'smuggled petrol' was no threat to the British oil embargo. Unfortunately Ministers and officials in London were deluding themselves.

Nor did the ban on tobacco and sugar sales cause the psychological shock in Rhodesia on which Harold Wilson had counted. There was no sudden urge among white voters to find an alternative to Smith's Government, nor was there any indication of readiness to yield in any way on white supremacy. By April it was plain that sanctions were not going to provide any quick solution.[15]

Harold Wilson nevertheless held to the view that sanctions must be given time to bite. In the two years after UDI I had nineteen private conversations with him, Rhodesia coming in to sixteen of them; and from Easter 1966 he argued that it must be a long process of attrition but would succeed. He had great hope that the 1967 tobacco crop would remain unsold and that oil sanctions could somehow be tightened up. As to negotiations, he fluctuated between optimism and exasperation with Smith's slippery evasions and half truths. He discounted the risk, often mentioned in the *Guardian*, that Britain's failure to end the rebellion could damage Kaunda, Nyerere, and Kenyatta, who had tried to remain friendly in spite of the OAU diplomatic boycott. He continued to reject military action – though the Commonwealth conference in September 1966 again called on Britain to use force – leaving himself only the caveat

15 For a stinging account of British official misjudgement over UDI and miscalculation over sanctions, see a book by the American Ambassador to Zambia from 1965 to 1968, Robert C. Good, *UDI*.

of action in the event of a 'breakdown' in Rhodesia or if power from Kariba were cut off from Zambia.

That caveat gave me my cue, in March 1968, after the Salisbury decision to hang the condemned guerrillas. It was announced on the morning of March 6, when the first three executions were carried out. Those three had been convicted and sentenced before UDI, and a Reuter report indicated that the remainder were to be executed in the order of their conviction. The Queen's reprieve, on the advice of the Commonwealth Secretary and the Attorney-General, had been signified to Salisbury three days previously because of a Rhodesian statement that 'normal processes' were to be applied to the condemned men. A further group of Africans were sentenced on March 8; and it was expected that the hangings would continue at intervals of about one week – with the grim possibility that they would extend throughout the next three or four months. Two further executions were in fact carried out on March 11, though nine Rhodesian reprieves were also announced that day.

The executions were condemned by both sides in the Commons, and the Prime Minister spoke of the 'deep lesson' that the regime with which we had tried to negotiate was 'essentially evil'. The UN Special Committee again called on Britain to restore order in Rhodesia; and the Pope appealed to Ian Smith for clemency for the condemned. It seemed to me that the 'breakdown' might be deemed to have arrived and that the Prime Minister might now be willing to agree to military action. For the morning of March 13, therefore, after discussion with some others in the office, I wrote a leader beginning thus:

The Government has long said that it would not use force in Rhodesia unless law and order there broke down. Today it is at least arguable that that situation has come. An illegal regime is intent on carrying out a series of executions, many of men who can be classed as freedom fighters. Perhaps through incompetence rather than callousness, it is failing to tell the relatives of condemned men whether or not they are about to be hanged. Through fear of invasion and fear of economic collapse it has passed so-called laws under which it can execute men for all kinds of offences. These include unauthorised possession of arms and acts 'likely to cause substantial financial loss within Rhodesia'. In other words, not only guerrillas and those who aid them may be hanged. Anyone who abets compliance with United Nations resolutions, for example on the oil embargo, can equally be hanged. Laws are not applied to all citizens in common, and order is maintained not by consent but by force. If this is not a breakdown of law and order, in any meaningful sense, what is?

The leader went on to say that the Government had refrained from physical action first and foremost because of the Prime Minister's own conscientious objection. That, deriving from a humanitarian outlook and from his Northern nonconformist background, was much to his credit. 'But a time comes when such objections ought to be overruled, either by the man himself or by his colleagues.' That time had come; Britain had a continuing responsibility for Rhodesia, and failure to resolve the Rhodesian question 'can lead only to an extended form of civil war covering all Southern Africa'.

Conservative and other objections were acknowledged. The danger of extreme political dissension at home was real, the leader said. But the danger of worse tyranny in Rhodesia and a gradual degeneration into racial war along the Zambesi was no less real. The dilemma for a British Government was harsh and painful; but, having exhausted all other means of bringing Rhodesia round, it ought to acknowledge its duty to take physical control.

The *Times* answered next day, saying that the proposal made no military sense and that it would create 'a bloody African equivalent to Vietnam'. It seemed to me that the *Times* had not stopped to consider the kind of action that we had called for, since elimination of the Rhodesian air force could be achieved with very few casualties on either side. As we had said, only about thirty-six combat aircraft had to be knocked out, preferably on the ground, and the airfields at Old Sarum (Salisbury) and Thornhill (near Gwelo) were in open country; after due warning to civilians to keep away from them, the operation need last only a few hours. It could be carried out either by carrier-based Buccaneers or by V-bombers from the north. Once the Rhodesians had lost their air force, it was doubtful whether there would be any further fighting, though that could not be relied on. The *Times*, unfortunately, was feeding the myth that the Rhodesians had a powerful air force when they did not. Even the Rhodesian ground forces at that time consisted only of two regular battalions and supporting territorials, with a vast territory to cover. That week, to deal only with a small guerrilla action, reservists had had to be called up. Depleted though Britain's forces were, they remained well able to handle the Rhodesian situation quickly and decisively.

But to speak in such terms inevitably could appear callous or cold-blooded. That worried me, in writing. Yet the risk of bloodshed if Britain did not act was far greater. In replying to the *Times* and other critics I said that 'the African counter-attack will develop even if it takes years'. Arms and training were being made available from Russian, Chinese, and other sources. The white Rhodesians depended on Africans by whom they were outnumbered twelve to one. No farm or factory could exist without its Africans. 'For white Rhodesians, the days of peace are numbered anyway.' Their survival could be better assured, I wrote, with an orderly transition initially under British supervision.

The most material argument against the action was that the British people were not ready for it politically. There was plenty of evidence of that, even in the *Guardian*'s own letter columns. 'Do not give the South Africans an excuse for intervention,' one said; and another told us not to 'start a war on behalf of a few African murderers'. A third said that it was 'fantastic' of the *Guardian* 'to advocate the entry of a nigh bankrupt and bitterly divided Britain into a new Boer war'. Over the next few days we carried many letters, on both sides. I took good note of the critics; yet the occasion seemed to me one where a newspaper ought to lead, not follow.

Our management were alarmed, however. It was the first time since joining the *Guardian* that Peter Gibbings and Gerry Taylor had experienced something that was really unpopular with a proportion of readers, and they were concerned at the damage that might be done just when they were trying to rebuild the *Guardian*'s advertisement revenue. They took it well, nevertheless, expressing only the wish that they might have been told the night before the March 13 leader appeared – and it was a mistake on my part not to have done so. Gerry endured barbed comments from his friends in advertisement agencies; but so far as I know there was in the end no evidence of lost custom. Nor was there any appreciable effect on sales, though Michael Jack, too, was worried at first and outspoken about it. In the end many more of the letters from readers were on our side than against us.

The Prime Minister, questioned in the Commons, held to his position. Sanctions must be given time to work, and meanwhile, after the executions, there could be no question of contact with the Rhodesian Government. (Pat Keatley suggested that contact was nevertheless likely by the autumn; in fact it came even sooner, leading to the abortive talks on HMS *Fearless* just one year after the abortive talks on *Tiger*.) Sanctions were tightened up through a further UN resolution, making them mandatory in the main categories; but Harold Wilson managed still to avoid the commitment to 'no independence before majority rule' demanded by the Commonwealth countries, preferring the commitment to assured progress towards majority rule.

There was no opportunity to see the Prime Minister privately in March, and it was the beginning of May before I talked to him again. Mark Arnold-Forster had seen him meanwhile, but neither of us got much satisfaction on Rhodesia. Of the *Guardian*'s proposed operation, he said that apart from other reasons the military advice was against it. He had been told that, to avoid Rhodesian 'sharpshooters', the parachute landings would have to be at some distance from Old Sarum. He had also been told that a lot of Africans lived round the edges of the air bases at Old Sarum and Thornhill. Also the Rhodesians had lorries ready to block the runways, and these would have to be moved physically by the parachute forces before air landings could follow. All that was no doubt true; but it was still not a difficult operation. The objection remained primarily political.

The guerrilla war came as foreseen, lasted longer than we had expected, and was savage. It led in the end to the 1980 settlement, a great achievement for Lord Carrington. African majority rule had come at last, though at the cost of many thousands of casualties – far more than our critics in 1968 foresaw.

The early stages of the guerrilla war were what led to the trial behind closed doors and deportation of Peter Niesewand, a freelance journalist working mainly for the *Guardian* and the BBC. In November 1972 he sent reports to both of us about Rhodesian raids into Mozambique, in pursuit of black nationalists, with the prior approval of the Portuguese Government. His reports were accurate, but when he refused to divulge his sources he was arrested and charged under the Official Secrets Act. After a secret trial he was sentenced to two years' hard labour; but thanks to his wife's activity on his behalf, and to strong representations from Sir Alec Douglas-Home and James Callaghan, he was deported instead of serving his sentence. He has told the story well in his own book, *In Camera*. (He had to pay for his own one-way ticket to exile.) In London he was offered staff jobs both by the BBC and by the *Guardian*, and, much to our delight, chose to come to us. He has been with the *Guardian* ever since.

There was a curious sequel to the hangings in March 1968 and the *Guardian*'s advocacy then of using force against Rhodesia. Just one year later, though the date itself was a coincidence, I was talking again to Harold Wilson in the Cabinet room at Downing Street. Economic policy, gnomes, industrial relations, and the Nigerian civil war were the main topics, but Rhodesia came up again. He put to me a strange proposal. The deadlock with Ian Smith remained, and sanctions were still not bringing their expected effect. It would be convenient, the Prime Minister said, if the Rhodesians were to believe that the British Government was now thinking of setting fire to Rhodesia's tobacco stocks and oil storage tanks. Setting fire how, I asked? By bombing, he said. If we burned their tobacco stocks and oil storage they would be in a parlous state. I replied that it seemed stretching the imagination pretty far to suppose that the Government which had not been ready to use force in 1965, 1966, or 1968 was now prepared to bomb Rhodesia's tobacco stocks. Harold then admitted that he was not planning to do it; but it was nevertheless a possibility, he said, and in some circumstances the Government might contemplate it. He thought it would be very convenient if the Rhodesians believed it might be about to happen, for it could affect their decisions. Would I, he asked, consider whether something might be written about it in the *Guardian* and come to talk to him about it again soon?

I refrained from going to see him for the next nine months, for the more I thought of it the less I liked his proposal. His reasons for not using force in Rhodesia, particularly the element of personal conscience, were ones that I could and did respect. For four years he had been candid with me in talking about the Rhodesian problem. He had a genuine regard for the *Guardian* and its moral principles, or so I believed (and still believe). But here he was inviting me to arrange publication of a story which I knew to be untrue. It was plainly wrong. I kept away from Downing Street until January 1970, when on returning from the

Middle East I thought that there were some points about Arab-Israeli peace negotiations that ought to be put to the Prime Minister. C. P. Scott's words about 'the unclouded face of truth' were still the soundest guide.

11 The law and the investigators

'Investigative' journalism is disliked by many officials and some politicians – yet it is well justified when it brings into the open facts of genuine public concern. Ann Shearer's reporting of the way mentally subnormal children were being treated at Harperbury Hospital in Hertfordshire, largely because of staff shortages, was one of many such cases. She got into the hospital a number of times, posing as the friend of a parent, and that brought us into conflict with the Press Council; but her findings caused Dick Crossman to set up an inquiry and take action to improve conditions.

The *Sunday Times* campaign on thalidomide – the greatest piece of newspaper investigation in recent years – began with information from readers while Harry Evans, its instigator, was still editing the *Northern Echo* in Darlington. It was a wholly justified campaign, covering a period of twelve years. It illustrated the importance of patience and persistence, and of having good lawyers with whom to resist counter-attack.

Here I want to start with two cases of police corruption, to digress into the issue of Official Secrets, and then to describe two major investigations.

Police and public

In 1973 a man was put in touch with the *Guardian*'s news desk through the National Council of Civil Liberties. At first our reporters were highly sceptical about the man's story, for he admitted to having a criminal record and they doubted whether he was 'going straight'. He alleged that he was being 'shaken down' by two detectives, who were demanding £500 to refrain from bringing a case of theft against him – and he did not have £500. Eventually, because of the circumstantial evidence, two of the reporters (Adam Raphael and Malcolm Dean) equipped him with a concealed tape recorder, with which he recorded a conversation with one of the detectives. The reporters then gave him £100 with which to make a preliminary payment, but the camera which was supposed to record the hand-over outside a pub failed to operate, so we had to arrange another payment of £150 and another tape recording.

At that point I wanted to let events take their course, with the ex-criminal telling the detectives truthfully that he had no more money and their fabricated case coming to court. I thought it would be instructive to see what charges were brought and what evidence was put forward. But that was too much for our normally phlegmatic solicitors. They hustled me along to see an eminent QC, taking the tapes with me; and if he had been wearing his wig I am sure it would have jumped some inches in the air. 'A mockery of the courts,' he declared.

'Unthinkable.' So, reluctantly, I arranged for the tapes to be handed over that afternoon to Scotland Yard's A.10 division, recently established by Robert Mark to separate such investigation from normal CID channels.

In another case, which came to us within weeks of the first, we followed a similar course. It was outside the Metropolitan area, but in both instances I thought it strongly probable that the detectives involved were part of a larger ring. To have let the Met. case continue to court would have given us some chance of discovering more. But Counsel said that we were potentially perverting the course of justice, as well as making our-selves accessories. So the case was handed to A.10, and rather more than a year later the two detectives were convicted and sentenced to thirty months each. (By an extraordinary irony, one of the reporters encountered the senior detective while visiting an open prison – and far from being heaped with contumely received a friendly greeting, for while on bail awaiting trial the man had taken a tradesman's course, and one way or another he now had enough money to set himself up in business; he was looking forward to a prosperous and legitimate future when he got out.)

Lecturing at the Police College at Bramshill, perhaps inevitably I came across the belief that the press made much of such instances of 'bent coppers' while giving too little attention to the positive aspects of police achievement. That was not too difficult to rebut. Between 1960 and 1962 I had been a member of the Royal Commission on the Police; it had looked at coverage of police affairs by press, radio, and television and had found that on the whole they gave a friendly rather than unfriendly impression of the police.[1] A Government Social Survey, conducted for the Commission, had also found that relations between the police and public were generally good – much better, indeed, than most policemen seemed to think they were.

Many valuable reforms in the police service had come through the Royal Commission, and through widespread discussion of the Commission's recommendations in the press. That press publicity helped to persuade Parliament and the Government of the need for early action, including a strengthening of the CID, amalgamation of small forces into larger units, faster routes to promotion, and higher police pay. Member-ship of the Commission was incidentally a useful experience for me – through the insight it gave on the workings of the Home Office and the police themselves – and I hope I contributed something of value to the Commission both on relations with the press and on the policing of big cities.

1 For a good summary of the Royal Commission's work, see T. A. Critchley's *A History of the Police*, pp. 267–322.

'Spies for Peace' and other spies

On May 13, 1963, the *Guardian*'s front-page lead was an exclusive story about the security service. Generally we were sceptical about spy stories, regarding most of them as secondary, but this was an exception. 'Telephone calls disrupt Secret Service' was the main headline, and below "Nuclear disarmers" block lines for 8 hours'. The report, by Clare Hollingworth, said that by blocking the lines of Intelligence headquarters a group of activists had endangered its efficiency, albeit temporarily. They had also entered the office building and photographed people entering or leaving the secret compound. The activists had been making calls at regular intervals, proclaiming themselves anxious to ban the bomb, and ridiculing the junior officials who answered. Some forty lines had been blocked for eight hours. In addition, photographs had been taken inside a security building in the countryside. A further report, below Clare's, said that both the CND and the Committee of 100 were denying responsibility.

Three days later the Prime Minister, at his normal Thursday question time, was asked about the matter. As we reported again on the front page, he said that the story was 'much exaggerated' and that steps had been taken to minimise the effectiveness of such action. It was, Mr Macmillan said, not a serious attempt at subversion – there had been eight calls over a period of one and a half hours, anonymous calls which were 'abusive or obscene'. They were a nuisance rather than a danger.

We also carried a short leader saying that if the original report was exaggerated we were sorry. The information, however, had come independently from two official sources and had been given by people who were in a position to know the facts. It had been checked, so far as possible, by our Defence Correspondent, who had spent some time at one of the offices of a security branch which had been harassed. If the duration of the harassment was as the Prime Minister said, then the interference was negligible. There was a similar discrepancy, the leader said, over attempts to intrude to photograph individuals.

Two points bothered me about the discrepancies. One was that our earliest information had come from Sammy Lohan – Colonel Lohan, acting secretary of the Services, Press, and Broadcasting Committee, which administered the D Notice system, and a man therefore in a highly sensitive post whose reliability was of great concern to us. Rear-Admiral George Thompson, who had been secretary of the committee for about ten years, had lately retired and Lohan had taken over. I had asked him to dinner, hardly knowing him, and there he had shown some cheerful Irish aggression towards the *Guardian*, saying that our opposition to the independent deterrent and our sympathy for the CND were damaging to the country. He had gone on to say that the CND were playing the Russians' game by intruding on Intelligence headquarters, blocking telephone lines and impeding vital Intelligence work. I had asked for more detail and he had given it; I then asked whether he had any objection to a *Guardian* reporter making inquiries. He had none, and offered to talk off the record (unattributably, that is) to one of my staff.

The second point was that Clare had not only talked to Sammy Lohan but, because of existing contact, had been able to spend an hour or two in the main offices of MI5 in the West End. Sammy Lohan had indeed been astounded in turn when he discovered what ready access Clare had there; but her knowledge of that field went back many years, to her time in Paris, Algeria, and the Middle East. While it was possible that someone had given Clare a version that was too highly coloured, it seemed improbable – for what could be gained?

Therefore the morning after the Prime Minister's replies I spoke to Lohan, asking whether he had any objection to my taking the matter up. He appeared a bit abashed, expressing surprise that Macmillan had played it down so much, but said it was not for him to criticise the Prime Minister. He had no objection, anyway, so I both wrote and telephoned to Admiralty House (Downing Street being under repair) to ask whether I might see Mr Macmillan. The reply came quickly, with an invitation to lunch two days later.

Before going to the meeting I thought it as well to ask Clare outright whether she was working or had worked for MI5. There had been a bad incident a year or two earlier when a *Guardian* man had almost been trapped in a foreign country while doing so. I had not known of his involvement until afterwards, having sent him to that country in good faith, and had been extremely angry for a number of reasons (the concealment from me, the risk to other reporters abroad, and so on). That was the only instance involving the *Guardian* of which I knew. To my relief Clare replied categorically that she was not working for MI5 and never had worked for it. She gave me a brief account of the circumstances in which she had come to know some of its people.

Harold Macmillan was both affable and concerned. We talked for a short time before going upstairs to lunch with Lady Dorothy. He questioned me about Clare, believing that he had met her in the Middle East during the war, and asking also about my own dealings with Lohan. He expressed mystification, saying that he had answered according to his brief. It was a long brief, and he had thought it best to give short answers, but he believed his answers to have been accurate. I said that the greatest discrepancies were over the duration of the disruption, for at MI5 Clare had been told that their lines were blocked 'for the whole of a working day', and over the extent of the photography. The PM said that he would like to inquire further; we went up to lunch, where the conversation was on other topics. In the afternoon he had to answer more questions in the House but held to his original brief. The exchanges, Norman Shrapnel reported on next day's page one, were sharp. We wrote no further leader then.

A week later he wrote asking for some additional information, but saying that his senior advisers were standing by their previous advice. He remained puzzled, he said. He was about to go to Scotland and Clare was in the United States, so I delayed a reply until mid-June. In the interval Profumo's confession came – irrelevant to this, but distracting. When replying I was able to give more precisely what Clare had been told, and, still more interesting, details of an interview that Christopher Driver had obtained with one of the 'Spies for Peace'. This showed that the telephone operation had lasted many hours, and it described how two or three people on bicycles, armed with a supply of matchsticks and coins, could prop up receivers in callboxes and 'drive MI5 round the bend'. It did not explain how MI5's numbers had been discovered, but it confirmed that members of the Committee of 100 were actively involved. The *Guardian* had already published much of this in a further report.

Towards the end of June Macmillan sent a friendly but non-committal letter. I was by now convinced that his senior security advisers had not told him the true story, but I felt that there was nothing further we could usefully do, so we let the story drop. But at the beginning of July there was further cause to doubt whether Ministers were being told the whole truth. On July 1 Mr Heath, as Lord Privy Seal, told the Commons that H. A. R. ('Kim') Philby was now known to have been the 'third man' who in 1951 warned Guy Burgess and Donald Maclean that they were about to be questioned, thereby enabling them to escape to the Soviet Union. Philby at that time had also been a Foreign Office official but had resigned, and latterly he had been the *Observer*'s correspondent in the Middle East. Heath said that Philby, between his resignation from the Foreign Service in 1951 and his disappearance from Beirut earlier in 1963, had had no access to official information.

Kim Philby had in fact disappeared at the end of January, and it was some weeks before any report appeared in the British press. The July 1 announcement was the first official admission. But on February 15 Clare had sent by air mail from Beirut, with the strictest warnings about the risk of libel, a report of Philby's disappearance. She said that he had gone without luggage, without a proper exit visa, and without telling his wife. Eleanor Philby had, however, received an affectionate telegram from Cairo – but with no address. Nor, Clare said, did the *Observer* know where he was since they had sent messages asking him to cover the revolt in Baghdad. 'His disappearance follows the familiar pattern of Burgess and Maclean – unexpected departure, affectionate telegram, and letters without an address.' Eleanor Philby, Clare wrote, was at present more angry than worried.

The implication of the message was plain – so plain that we could not publish it without some form of verification. If Philby returned innocently to Beirut, the libel damages could have been colossal. When Clare returned to London a week or so later, she was still convinced that he had gone behind the iron curtain, but there remained no way of checking. She added that in Beirut Philby had been in regular contact with people from the British Embassy and at the Middle East Centre for Arabic Studies, at Shemlan, outside the city. George Blake, the double agent sentenced to forty-two years' imprisonment in 1961, had been at Shemlan just before his arrest – and Shemlan was thought to be more than merely an academic institution.[2]

In July, after Ted Heath's announcement in the House, I wrote a rather sceptical leader. It asked whether the Lord Privy Seal's statement that Philby had had no access to any kind of official information was quite the whole truth, and it noted that while in Beirut he had been able to visit Shemlan. Being in a position to keep a close eye on people passing through the centre, and with his inside knowledge of the Foreign Service, Philby seemed well placed to draw conclusions. This might be a case which the Prime Minister's new Security Commission, when created, might examine. Some way ought to be found, the leader said, to satisfy Parliament that adequate checks had been made in Beirut.

A few days later Heath's office asked if I would call on him, which I did. With him was a tall dark-visaged man whom he introduced so quietly that I never knew whether it was Sir Dick White, Sir Roger Hollis, or some other security man. Heath said that the leader had been less than fair. Why had we assumed either that he himself had been misled or that he had misled others? In fact the leader had made no such direct suggestion, having gone no further than asking whether the statement about Philby's lack of access 'is quite the whole truth'. That Heath had not been told the whole truth was nevertheless in my mind as a probability when I was writing. He said that there were questions on security matters that anyone with experience would know we ought not to ask. I replied that the 'no access' part of the statement could not stand up to what was known of Philby's life and activities in Beirut. As the *Observer*'s correspondent and as a former Foreign Office man he seemed likely to have had access to confidential information through the Embassy. Heath said that journalists had no access to confidential information in that way. That seemed to me an extraordinary statement, knowing as I did that our diplomatic correspondent and two or three others, including Clare, nearly always had privileged access if they wanted it when abroad; but perhaps Heath was unaware of that, and since I did not wish to prejudice their position I let the point go.

The discussion went on to why the Foreign Office had found no means of questioning Philby, after its suspicion that he was the 'third man' had been revived and while he was still in Beirut. This had been touched on

2 Blake escaped from Wormwood Scrubs in October 1966 and was not recaptured.

during exchanges in the House, but had not been raised in the *Guardian* leader. Again, however, our conversation was unfruitful. Heath said that there was no way in which he could have been brought back within British jurisdiction. It was clear to me that Heath did not realise how familiar Clare was with the situation in Beirut. He said to me, speaking in the fatherly but slightly contemptuous manner of a public school housemaster talking to an awkward pupil, that I really must accept his word. He had not been misled, nor had he made a misleading statement, and he must not be expected to answer in detail about the Philby affair.

Six months earlier I would probably have accepted that. But at this point I said that the Prime Minister had clearly been misled at least twice over the Profumo affair, and, of more direct concern to the *Guardian*, I suspected that he had not been fully briefed on another security matter. Heath, rather nettled, asked what that was. On hearing that it was over a report on intrusion at a secret headquarters – a report which, after further checking, we believed to be substantially true – Heath said he knew nothing of it. This suggested to me that either Sir Somebody Something hadn't forewarned the Lord Privy Seal of the *Guardian*'s recent involvement or there was a lack of liaison in the security system. The atmosphere was by this time chilly, but Heath rounded off the talk by saying that he hoped to see me that evening at a Lancaster House reception to which he knew we were both going. Since it was to be preceded by a Command Performance at Covent Garden, we both had something to look forward to.

Altogether these security matters were like dealing with a slippery octopus. There was little satisfaction in them, and I still thought that few were worth the space they occupied in the paper – though readers often seemed intrigued by them. They could not be neglected, though, and Ministers took them seriously.

Sometimes they had their lighter side. The most spectacular action of the 'Spies for Peace' had taken place at Easter 1963, when they published a hand-printed list of 'RSGs' – the Regional Seats of Government, or underground headquarters intended for use in a nuclear war. Part of the Aldermaston march had diverted itself to RSG 6, at Warren Row in Berkshire. That had led me into a tiff with Sammy Lohan, who insisted that in line with one of his blessed D Notices we must not publish its location in the paper next day. Since hundreds of demonstrators had crawled all over its exterior and we had good pictures, that seemed to me daft. Even dottier was his prohibition on mentioning the location of the RSG outside Edinburgh, since the police had obligingly lined the route to it, with the result that anyone wishing to march could easily find the way there. I told Sammy Lohan that night that the *Guardian* was going to publish the locations, regardless of his advice, and I asked the news desk to ring the other Fleet Street papers and the principal Scottish papers to warn them that we were doing so, since I did not want accusations of unfair competition. The *Telegraph*, the *Mirror*, and most of the Scottish papers came into line with us; one other, however, criticised us as 'irresponsible'. Sammy next day said in a resigned tone that he had only been doing his duty.

Not all the information published by the 'Spies for Peace' proved accurate. With their list of RSGs they gave a telephone number for each, so I asked one of the reporters to try ringing all the numbers to see what response he received. At Easter weekend there was no reply from any except one. At the Cambridge number we had a reply from someone living in Parson Road, who appeared delighted at receiving the call. 'We must look under the foundations,' she said. 'This is a perfectly ordinary house and I am a perfectly ordinary housewife living with my husband, who is a university lecturer. It is a new detached house, quite near Brooklands Avenue [given as the location of the RSG]. How exciting to be a secret headquarters.'

Sammy still asked us not to say how deep underground the headquarters were, if we happened to find out. Perhaps he had a point there.

D Notices in decline

In the distant days before sputniks and satellites took hourly photographs from the stratosphere all round the world, the D Notice system served a useful purpose. But since 1970, if not earlier, its value has diminished. Giving evidence to a Parliamentary select committee in 1980, my successor as editor said he had mislaid the *Guardian*'s D Notice file in moving to new offices and did not too much mind if it stayed mislaid. His tongue may have been in his cheek, but his meaning was plain.

The system was always advisory. A D Notice was a private and confidential letter asking editors and broadcasters to refrain from publishing certain categories of information. It was a uniquely British system, depending on goodwill and mutual confidence between officials and journalists, and it was increasingly criticised both as creating a 'cosy' relationship and as tending to mask facts that ought to be public.

An example of the difference between American and British practice will show how it worked. In 1960 I spent a week in Nebraska, partly on holiday and partly visiting the US Strategic Air Command. While staying there I read a story in the *Lincoln Journal* headed 'Where missiles will nest', under which was a map showing the sites around Lincoln where Atlas intercontinental ballistic missiles were to be built in underground silos. The report went on to give the exact locations of the nine installations, their depth, and the names of the farmers on whose land they were to be built. All this information had been openly provided by the US Army engineers.

In Britain in 1958 a D Notice had been issued asking us not to disclose details of ballistic missile sites, and in particular not to give numbers of sites or missiles, precise locations, details of site layouts, or information on operational relationships between sites. There was, however, to be a relaxation in connection with a press visit to one site where photographs could be taken. That notice was issued, like every other D Notice, only after consultation between the two sides on the Services, Press, and Broadcasting Committee – on which four men from the Service Ministries sat with up to ten representatives of the national and provincial newspapers, the news agencies, and the broadcasting bodies. The Service chiefs could not issue a D Notice unless they convinced the press people that there was a good case for doing so.

The case for issuing the notice was that it avoided giving the Russians a quick and easy pointer to where to look. The most valuable time for spying on an underground site, it was said, was during construction; and if precise locations were kept secret until work was finished and the site covered, then secrets of real value were being preserved. I was never on the D Notice committee – where for most of my time the Fleet Street men were the editor of the *Daily Mirror* and a senior executive from the *Telegraph* – but the case seemed to me sound. The D Notice was issued on the day the Minister of Defence, Mr Duncan Sandys, told the Commons that American Thor rockets were coming to Britain and that the 'highest priority' was being given to the development of British missiles to replace them. The D Notice therefore did not inhibit debate in Parliament or the press. In the *Guardian* we said what we had said before – that the Thor missiles, already obsolescent, were not suitable for deployment in Britain; that these islands were too small and vulnerable to become a missile base; and that any British weapons ought to be sea-borne, in ships or submarines. The Americans, we said, were not going to build ballistic missile sites within one hundred miles of New York, Boston, or Chicago. That month the paper also launched its policy of promoting the non-nuclear club.

Strictly speaking, a D Notice carried no legal force. Breach of one was not an offence, nor did abiding by its terms confer legal immunity. In practice anyone who stayed within its terms was unlikely to be prosecuted under the Official Secrets Act. Equally, anyone who disregarded it was safe enough provided his information was obtained legally – without theft or bribery, and without unauthorised entry on secret premises. (When considering whether to publish parts of the 'Spies for Peace' document on RSGs, we were warned by our lawyers that we could be prosecuted as accessories if, as was likely, the 'spies' had obtained their information illegally; but, on a common-sense judgement, the lawyers agreed that we should go ahead with publication nevertheless.) The great difficulty lay in the wide terms of the Official Secrets Act – the 'catch all' clauses as they have been called – which made it impossible to know whether or not a prosecution would hold. Consequently, if in doubt, editors tended to keep within the terms of a D Notice.

Occasionally, but infrequently, newspapers chose to disregard D

Notices. The most significant, in my own experience, was eight months before I became editor when as defence correspondent I wrote about the Government's decision to develop a supersonic bomber. That decision had not been announced, and there was a general prohibition on information about new military aircraft until it was officially released. Britain was already committed to developing missiles and a number of other aircraft, and scarce scientific and technical resources were being spread too thinly over too many projects. In February 1956, in a leader on the Defence White Paper, we said that grand pianos could not be bought for the price of a harmonium, and that the Government must choose its priorities instead of attempting too much. As a result of that leader I received the first hint from Reggie Maudling (then Minister of Supply) of the dilemma over the supersonic bomber, for he disagreed with the decision to go ahead with it; Sir Frederick Brundrett confirmed and amplified what Maudling had said about the strain on scientific resources, and from another civil servant I received confirmation that the supersonic bomber had been approved. The *MG* published the story, with a leader saying that the decision was wrong. There was an immediate threat of prosecution, for the Defence Ministry wrongly deduced that someone in the Avro plant in Manchester had provided the information, but nothing came of it. I never knew whether Maudling had indicated to anyone that he was my first source, and if prosecuted I could not have identified him.

In 1961 there was difficulty when a D Notice after George Blake's arrest asked us not to mention his connection with the Foreign Office. That seemed to me, as to some other papers, to be asking too much, but the difficulty was circumvented by omitting details until the trial. Then in 1963, over the RSGs, we decided to ignore the D Notice; though that was not a serious case, the Official Secrets Act was still a threat. Also in 1963, an attempt was made to use a D Notice in the Profumo affair to stop discussion, but that was vetoed by the press representatives on the committee. There was bother in 1964 over a notice asking us to say nothing about the movement of units in the strategic reserve, because of overflying problems in the Middle East, but loose wording in that notice was revised. Each of these incidents tended to undermine confidence in the system.

The biggest blow to the D Notice system, oddly enough, was delivered by Harold Wilson when he became angry over a *Daily Express* story in 1967. Chapman Pincher, well known for his ability to secure embarrassing stories, reported that cables and telegrams going abroad were being constantly scrutinised by a security department, and he said at the beginning of his story that this was 'Big Brother' intrusion into privacy. The Prime Minister, in a statement to the Commons the same day, said that the story was a clear breach of two D Notices and that the newspaper had been warned of this before publication. He also implied that the story was inaccurate. He mentioned neither the name of the newspaper nor of the journalist, but said that he was asking the Services, Press, and Broadcasting Committee to examine the affair. Mr Heath suggested that it might be better for a committee of Privy Councillors to examine the whole working of the D Notice system.

A meeting of the D Notice committee was called by its chairman, the permanent secretary in the Defence Ministry, but one of the Fleet Street members, Lee Howard, editor of the *Daily Mirror*, immediately resigned. He said it would be a 'gross abuse' of the committee's functions to intervene in a political dispute between the *Express* and the Government, and that he knew of no D Notice that had any bearing on Chapman Pincher's story. Some days later the Prime Minister announced that the issue was being referred to a committee of Privy Councillors under Lord Radcliffe.

Like other editors, I was asked by the Radcliffe Committee for my view on the general working of the system. I said I thought it had been a mistake to appoint as Admiral Thompson's successor someone who at that time was a serving officer in the Defence Ministry, and that a retired officer of more independent status would be preferable. I also thought that D Notices were sometimes too loosely worded; but since that must sometimes be inevitable it was essential to have readily available a reliable intermediary – the secretary of the committee – to interpret their meaning for an editor who was in doubt. The system had worked well in Admiral Thompson's time but less well in recent years.

Having been appointed in February, the Radcliffe Committee reported in mid-June. The day before it was due to be published, Harold Wilson asked me to call. After something of a rigmarole he said, in effect, that Radcliffe had found against him. There had been no breach of a D Notice; there was ambiguity about the advice given by Colonel Lohan to Chapman Pincher and the *Express*, and indeed the Foreign Office and the security authorities had tried to use Lohan to give advice outside the D Notice system, aimed at preventing publication of the story; and in general the system needed strengthening. The Prime Minister said that he was issuing a White Paper along with the report. It would accept Radcliffe's general findings but would contest those relating to Pincher and the *Express*. It would challenge the accuracy of Pincher's story, say that the *Express* had ignored advice, say also that there had been a breach of two D Notices, and say that Lohan had failed to keep his superiors fully informed. Lohan, as indeed the *Telegraph* had already reported, was about to resign.

Wilson clearly was looking for my support. I had to say that there was no chance of giving it to him, which he accepted without too much surprise. It was not clear to me that there had been a breach of any D Notice, and I was unhappy about Lohan's role. (I did not immediately grasp from what the Prime Minister had said just how clearly Radcliffe would point to the misuse of Lohan to try to put pressure on the *Express*.) I repeated my belief in the need for an independent arbiter to interpret the D Notices, but with the confidence and trust of both sides. In view of what Wilson had said, however, I wondered whether the time had not come to scrap the whole system. He replied that this was not possible: it must be kept, and he would be calling a meeting of editors the following week to discuss what should be done.

Our leader the morning after publication was indeed headed 'Do we still need "D" notices?' It began: 'The referee, of course, was wrong – that is the meaning of the Government's White Paper.' It underlined the differences between Radcliffe and the White Paper, accepting Radcliffe as the more objective version. We disagreed with Radcliffe only on one point, where he suggested that the committee's secretary, when in doubt, should take instructions from the permanent secretary at the Defence Ministry. That was a mistake, we said: he must never again be the servant of one side. But we concluded by saying that the D Notice system might not last much longer and its ending would be no great loss.

Harold Wilson called his meeting of editors at Downing Street a week later and opened the discussion by asking for views of what should be done. He received little response from the editors, who knew as well as the Prime Minister that there was now little common ground among them. He offered the name of a distinguished Fleet Street figure, recently retired, as a possible successor to Colonel Lohan, but that fell flat. He said that the matter was urgent, asked us to consider it, and said he would call another meeting soon. In practice more than two months passed before the further meeting was called. There had meanwhile been no consultation among the Fleet Street editors, though the NPA (Newspaper Publishers' Association) had offered facilities if we wanted one. The provincial editors, by contrast, had come to a common view – that the system should continue, with a secretary drawn from the ranks of the civil service but standing outside it. The PM mentioned another possible Fleet Street name, or the alternative of a Privy Councillor as chairman in place of the Defence Ministry's permanent secretary. Again the reactions conflicted, and the provincial editors' spokesman was positively against both propositions.

In the end the PM, with what I thought was a malevolently beatific smile on his face, said that obviously there were divided views and that such consensus as existed was in favour of keeping the present system. He would therefore proceed, he said, to put his own proposals to the D Notice committee as to its future chairman and secretary and he hoped that everyone would accept the committee's decisions without dissent. With that he wound up the meeting. From the start I had been sure that he knew what he wanted anyway and was relying on dissension among the editors to give him a free hand. In talking to me he had once referred to the Fleet Street editors as a bunch of anarchists who, like Arabs, were all ready to cut each other's throats until an Israeli turned up. Individualists might have been a more exact description; and indeed the diversity of view among Fleet Street editors was part of their strength and justification.[3] Anyway, Wilson had neatly got his way. The permanent secretary at the Defence Ministry remained chairman of the committee, and a retired admiral became secretary.

With Admiral Sir Norman Denning effectively in charge for the next five years, the system ran fairly smoothly. A younger brother of Lord Denning, he had both the family charm and a shrewd diplomatic sense. After appointment he called on each of the editors in Fleet Street, and no doubt on some outside London, and soon made himself familiar with the way newspapers worked. Without someone of his friendliness and cool precision the system would probably have collapsed. He was succeeded in 1973 by Rear-Admiral K. H. Farnhill, but by that time D Notices were few and far between. I gather that in later years they became even fewer.

The Official Secrets Act remained – and remains – a blunderbuss and a blight. In 1971, after the costly and dangerous fiasco of prosecution of the *Sunday Telegraph* for its disclosures about Government expectations in Nigeria, the Franks Committee was set up to review the Act. In 1972 it recommended repeal of the 'catch all' Section 2 and substitution of an Official Information Act precisely defining categories of information on which restrictions might be imposed, including defence, currency questions, and law enforcement. Though the system of ministerial fiat proposed by Franks was objectionable to newspapers and broadcasters – because it left Ministers free to determine what kind of disclosure was injurious to national interests – in the main his proposals were a marked improvement. The need for reform was illustrated soon after the Franks Report appeared, when the police raided the offices of the *Railway Gazette* because it published details of Transport Ministry plans to economise on branch lines. That episode led to questions on whether the Ministry feared that the Russians might be thinking of taking over the Melton Mowbray and King's Lynn branch. Unluckily I was out of the country when the Franks Committee invited evidence. The chance to speak to it would have been enjoyable. In 1981, the Franks Report is still awaiting Government action.

3 Not long after Roy Thomson's take-over of the *Sunday Times*, Denis Hamilton invited all the other Fleet Street editors to lunch in its plush premises. There was round-table discussion after the lunch, but Sir William Haley intervened. He had greatly enjoyed the lunch and the company, he said, but this was a most improper occasion. The national newspaper editors must never be seen to be in collusion, he said, for their justification lay in their diversity and individuality. So, while thanking Denis Hamilton, he hoped that there would never be such a gathering again. There never was, apart from the rare occasions when we were summoned collectively to Downing Street – never, that is, until Michael Foot's Trade Union Bill appeared in 1974–75 as a threat to all; of which more is told in Chapter 14.

Leakages from Government files

Dressed and ready for the *Guardian*'s 150th birthday banquet, on May 5, 1971, I was handed a slip of paper. Three figures were written on it. They were the final proof that I had demanded, before being willing to publish a report on the way private detective agencies, illegally, could obtain information from confidential personal files in Government offices. The figures were, in fact, taken from my own last tax return – my salary as returned for tax, my other earnings (from BBC and other outside engagements), and my wife's earnings. Since I did not then employ an accountant, the middle figure could have been discovered in only one of two ways: either by someone who had raided my files at home in Blackheath, or from the Inland Revenue tax office.

The story was not published until six days later. Discussion with our lawyers was essential. We had to be ready for the reaction. On May 11 it became the front-page lead: 'Commercial spies tap State records'. By Peter Harvey, an Australian who had been on the staff for about two years, it said that confidential information on individual citizens was being systematically obtained from Government files and from banks for commercial interests. Tax records, bank statements, security files, and more were being secured through exploitation of leakages. Some of the information was being supplied by Government employees, some through retired employees, and some secured by confidence tricks. The same methods were being used to obtain information about companies.

Peter Harvey said that commercial, industrial, and personal information was being obtained in this way, and that some foreign embassies were using private detective agencies to track and inquire about people in Britain in whom they were interested. His report explained that his investigation had begun after John Pardoe, MP, at a press conference called by the National Council for Civil Liberties a fortnight previously, had claimed that private agencies were openly advertising their ability to obtain – at a price and in some cases within twenty-four hours – criminal records, bank statements, hire purchase records, and other personal information. As a result the *Guardian* had been put in touch with two agencies which offered these services, including commercial information from the Department of Trade and Industry and the Ministry of Transport. (In fact Peter Harvey had a list of twelve and had been in touch with five or six, but had tested only two.)

Peter reported that two sets of tests had been undertaken. Initially one company had discovered within ten minutes details of his own rent and rates payments, through a local government office. Then, within forty-eight hours, a detailed dossier had been provided about the *Guardian*'s news editor, after only her name and private address had been given to the agency without any indication that she worked for the *Guardian*. The dossier included items from the Inland Revenue, Social Security, two banks (including statements of current balances), a vehicle licence office, and a rating office. It correctly stated Jean's employment but incorrectly said her husband was a freelance journalist, whereas he was on the staff of the *Financial Times*. There was one other minor error.

In the second and more severe set of tests, Peter reported, the agency had been asked for the earnings and income tax of a senior member of the staff who did not use an accountant (my own case, though that was not stated in the paper). A correct statement had been supplied within four days, including the total of freelance earnings from a number of sources; the earnings of the man's wife had also been reported, but with a £20 error which suggested a telephone mishearing. Finally, the inquiry company had been asked to supply details of a named individual's dealings with a branch of the Home Office; it had successfully supplied confidential details, including some unknown to the *Guardian* which had since been verified.

Peter went on to explain how most of this information was obtained by telephone, using, for example, a former Inland Revenue employee who knew the departmental ropes and could talk in departmental language. A combination of bluff, inside knowledge, and the old pals' act usually worked. With his report the paper carried a short leader, 'Your secrets for sale', saying that among the remedies was a simple routine of always making return telephone calls to answer inquiries, having first verified that the number being called was a properly authorised office.

On the morning of publication there were, as expected, a number of telephone calls. Most of these were from people who wanted to give further information about detective agencies, and they were noted for Peter Harvey and others to follow up later if necessary. A *Guardian* board meeting kept me out of circulation that morning, but at midday I heard that Peter had taken a call from the office of the head of the civil service, Sir William Armstrong, and had gone to the Civil Service Department to meet him. As agreed with our lawyers, we were ready to offer all possible assistance except on a single point: we could not identify the investigating company. We had given that undertaking to the company, who knew from the start that Peter was working for a newspaper and intended to publish the results. They had therefore, while being keen to demonstrate their capability, asked for an assurance of anonymity which had been given. In the published report we had deliberately camouflaged whether one or two agencies had been used, because in the early stages Peter had run a minor test with a second company.

Peter's instructions were to answer all questions except the one on identity, but if there was any sign of anyone getting tough with him he was to stop the conversation and say he must have legal advice. Geoffrey Grimes and David Shenton at Lovell, White, and King were on call. Peter that morning had also taken a message from Scotland Yard saying that they would like to have 'a chat' with him some time and would make arrangements in the afternoon.

Just after 2 pm he telephoned from the Civil Service Department, saying that the Prime Minister wanted to make a statement at the end of questions, at 3.30, and he had been asked whether it could say that the *Guardian* was cooperating in inquiries. I had no objection at all. On return to the office, after listening to Mr Heath's statement in the Commons, Peter said that the Civil Service Department had wanted to know precisely what we had discovered from the Inland Revenue. They had not pressed him about sources and had not asked about the Home Office side. They had long suspected that leakages of this kind were taking place.

The Prime Minister's statement made the front-page lead next morning – and featured prominently in most other newspapers – with his promise of an immediate inquiry. He said that if the internal rules of security were being broken or evaded, the *Guardian* 'will have performed a valuable public service'. The *Guardian* was cooperating in the investigation, he said, and had agreed that he should mention this. He also said that some of the allegations fell within the scope of the Younger Committee, currently inquiring into the privacy of the individual; but, answering a question, he thought it inappropriate to extend the terms of reference of the tribunal inquiring into the collapse of the Vehicle and General Insurance Company. (From the beginning, our lawyers had been concerned lest after Peter Harvey's story I might be called before that tribunal and, if I refused to answer about the agency we had used, might be held to be in contempt.)

At 4.20 pm I had a call from the permanent secretary at the Home Office, Sir Philip Allen, about the 'bombshell' we had planted in Whitehall. Having considered it, he said, he had concluded that there was 'no avoiding some police investigation'. He was therefore asking the Commissioner, Sir John Waldron, to make arrangements. He took the opportunity to say how greatly he had enjoyed the birthday party, and especially Willy Brandt's speech. The Commissioner rang forty minutes later and we agreed that one of his men would come to my office at 11.30 next morning. I asked about the meaning of Sir Philip's phrase 'a police investigation'; Sir John replied rather formally that its purpose was to find out whether there had been any 'trickery' by which people had obtained information that they ought not to have, and that he could say no more. I therefore asked Geoffrey Grimes to attend next morning.

That presaged, to my mind, one of the most bizarre episodes in the whole affair. A call from Scotland Yard next morning told us that Detective Chief Superintendent John Hensley was coming. Somewhat late, he arrived. It turned out that he had returned from holiday only that morning. He said it looked like being a long investigation, and this was only a preliminary visit. He would arrange to question Peter and me separately, some time later. I intervened to say that we were ready to give every possible help, but we had two reservations: we could not name the agency, for reasons we would willingly discuss, and we had given a promise of anonymity to the man involved in the Home Office case. On the latter, we were ready to provide his name and all the details to Scotland Yard privately, but we must have an assurance in return that his name would not be mentioned publicly.

Hensley replied that he knew about journalists not naming sources, and hadn't the two at the Vassall tribunal gone to prison? Then, he said, there was the one who'd been given a nice holiday in Belfast jail. So far as he could see, breaches of the Official Secrets Act were involved in this case. He would be seeing the Attorney-General in the evening, and he could give no undertakings meanwhile. When I mentioned that there had been conversations the previous day with Sir John Waldron, Sir Philip Allen, and Sir William Armstrong, he was incredulous. At first, he clearly did not believe that the Commissioner had spoken to me. He said he assumed that 'the PR boys' were the ones that dealt with us. He also had no idea that the Prime Minister had made a statement in the House.

He said that we must know his reputation (though in truth I had never heard of him before). He had never failed. Because he was being so heavy, I was inclined to break off the conversation, but Geoffrey Grimes thought we ought to try to make some progress. Since I had a lunch appointment that mattered, and since the meeting looked like being long, I asked another member of the staff to take my place as a witness on our side. Hensley had a detective sergeant with him. I heard afterwards that they had spent most of their time trying to find out what the Civil Service Department had been told and trying to get Peter to name his sources, using trick questions until they were stopped. Geoffrey Grimes later said his impression was that we were being treated like suspects under inter-rogation, and he thought the first meeting had been very badly handled from the police side.

When we knew 'Ginger' Hensley better – and our dealings with him lasted more than eighteen months – we got on very well with him. But the initial encounters could hardly have been worse, for he had not been properly briefed and had little idea of what was involved in the case. His approach worried me both because he seemed intent simply on getting someone into court and convicted, relying only on the evidence of the *Guardian* investigation, and because the broader and far more important aspects of the leakage of information looked like being submerged in the conflict he was creating. So I sought advice from Tom Critchley, with whom I had kept in touch ever since the Royal Commission on the Police. From inside the Home Office he knew well what was going on, and he was reassuring on the point that the broader aspects were not being neglected. The Home Office, it turned out, had assumed that the final case mentioned by Peter Harvey related to the Aliens Office. I told him that they were on the wrong track; it was the Criminal Records Office at Scotland Yard, for which the Home Office was responsible.

Tom said that Hensley was now providing a daily report to the Home Secretary, because Maudling wanted to be kept informed, and that a copy was also being sent to Downing Street. They were aware that things were not going well, but it would be constitutionally improper for the Home Office to intervene in the handling of a case by the Metropolitan CID. There was a problem also over what Heath might say when he made his next statement to the House. The Prime Minister was chiefly interested in the Civil Service Department's inquiry, rather than the CID side, but there were indications that he might say that the *Guardian* after all was not cooperating. I said that if he were to do that I would have no hesitation in publishing a full account of the way Hensley had handled the case so far. It would have to mention that, though Hensley & Co. had spent six and a half hours on the third day questioning Peter Harvey and taking a statement from him, by the sixth day they had still not bothered to talk further to me. Also, as a result of Peter's first report, we now had evidence – with photocopies and tape recordings – of an extremely bad instance of misuse of a file from the Criminal Records Office at Scotland Yard. If relations with Hensley had been better I would have given it to him, but so far I had not done so. It was the work of a detective agency with which the *Guardian* had had no dealings.

Two days later Hensley asked me to come to Scotland Yard for a session, and this time he was much more relaxed and friendly. Although Tom Critchley had said that constitutionally the Home Office could not intervene, it seemed not improbable that a quiet word had been spoken to someone. He said that he must put formally the question about identity of the company, but when I said I could not answer it he did not pursue it. He took a chronological account of my part in the *Guardian* inquiry. When we came to the dossier on Jean Stead, I handed over, as agreed with our lawyers, a retyped copy of its contents. (The original, with the company's name on it, was safely locked away at Gray's Inn Road.) Hensley studied the copy and then asked about the shape of the original, which we had not reproduced. I described it as long and thin, like a lawyer's brief. He seemed pleased. Did it have a cover? Yes. He seemed even more pleased. He went away and came back some minutes later, holding up a thin black document cover and saying that he was sure this would interest me greatly. Was it a dossier on me, I asked? No, he replied, but was it like the one on Jean? I said, truthfully, that I could not answer for the colour but the shape was about right. He was delighted.

They were very anxious to have Peter's original notes, but on the lawyers' advice we provided only transcripts with marks where deletions had been made – and making the transcripts from Peter's illegible writing had been hard work for two secretaries. Hensley asked whether he might talk to the man involved in the fourth test, informally and privately, and since he could not offer an assurance that the man's name would never be used publicly he would refrain from asking it. He had grasped that it was a criminal records case relating to something that had happened twenty years ago. I said that that was difficult because Hensley might recognise him. Hensley looked surprised and said surely not, for he had not been high in the police force then; my real concern was that the man appeared quite frequently on television. (He had in fact gone to prison twenty years before as a conscientious objector, which was why I had asked him whether we might use his case to check the leakages from the CRO; the detective agency had not only provided precise detail but provided detail also of an assault charge ten years later, dropped through lack of evidence, which I thought ought no longer to be in the CRO file.)

Finally, Hensley asked whether Peter had been in touch the previous day with the agency man. After some hesitation, and after consulting David Shenton (my lawyer), I said that I believed there had been a telephone call the previous afternoon or evening. 'I knew it,' Hensley said; so I asked whether they were tapping our telephones. Most emphatically not, he replied, for they would have been kicked straight downstairs if they had asked for the Home Secretary's authority. Our case was not big enough. I was less than convinced.

Going home, I was worried that I had said too much. David Shenton thought not, but he said that I must take Peter off any further involvement in our inquiries. It was too obvious that he was being closely watched. Back at the office we checked Jean's dossier, and it had the identical black cover.

Two days later I handed over to Hensley originals or photocopies of all the material in the fifth case, which became known as the Sidcup case, together with the tape recordings. The involvement of the Criminal Records Office at Scotland Yard could not now be in any doubt, even if the information was sometimes being obtained through CID men in local offices. In every other case which Peter had followed up, we had advised the individuals to take it directly to the police. The Sidcup case we wanted to monitor ourselves. One of the major banks was involved, in that a finance house owned by the bank had commissioned a detective agency to find out about a client and had then misused its discovery that the man had a criminal record. (In the late fifties he had been convicted of receiving, and the finance house had indicated to others in the area that they should not deal with him, although he had run a sound business for fifteen years.) We knew that Hensley's team were following that up, because a fortnight later I had a call from the bank's head office, inviting me to lunch and also wishing to make clear immediately that such employment of detective agencies was contrary to the bank's policy.

On May 27 the Prime Minister replied to another question, saying that all Government departments had now been told to follow the standing rules on security of personal information which had previously applied only to three departments – the Inland Revenue, the Department of Trade and Industry, and the Department of Social Security. A further statement was promised. In early June all the *Guardian*'s relevant information was made available to the Younger Committee, and we answered some additional questions from them. We suggested that to bring private inquiry companies under scrutiny there ought to be a system of registration with the Home Office, recording of transactions, and inspection of their working methods.

On June 17 the Prime Minister made his further statement. While police inquiries were still continuing, he said, the Inland Revenue had established that in one case a tax official had given confidential information over the telephone to a person claiming, falsely, to be from another tax office. He had failed to observe departmental instructions and had been formally reprimanded. Rules to combat dishonest telephone inquiries were already in force. Where an inquirer could not be satisfactorily identified, he must be rung back after the number had been checked. Mr Heath said that, having considered whether former civil servants should be forbidden to work for private inquiry firms, he had concluded that it would be impossible to enforce. On the safeguarding of confidential commercial information, arrangements had been tightened up.

In a leader next day, we said that the Government's action seemed to have been prompt and practical. The telephone remained the first hazard, because most people tended automatically to answer telephone inquiries and wanted to be helpful. But inquiry agents who knew the routine of a department could trick well-meaning officials into giving answers. The rules outlined by the Prime Minister were a simple precaution, though sometimes time-consuming.

From Peter Harvey we knew that the system of telephone deception was skilfully handled. Not only were the inquiry agents familiar with the jargon and working methods of the departments with which they dealt, but the agents we employed had an office organised with ex-directory telephone lines and extensions designated to reply as bank branches or tax offices or social security offices. They were also equipped with various 'bugging' devices, and occasionally employed ex-police officers to assist them.

At the end of June I had a private meeting with the Prime Minister at Downing Street. It was a hot afternoon, and we sat under the trees in the garden; Donald Maitland, his press secretary, sat with us. Most of the conversation was about the Common Market and the British economy, but towards the end I took up the leakages story. Until then the atmosphere was friendly, but as soon as leakages were mentioned it became stiffer and more formal. He said that the *Guardian* had not given the authorities all the help that it should have done. On the Inland Revenue side they had been able to deal with one case because an official had owned up, but on the second tax case they could make no headway because nobody had owned up and we had not given them the name of the agency we had used. I replied that we had given Scotland Yard just about everything except the name of the inquiry agency – surely enough for them to make a thorough inquiry – but we could not identify the agency because we had undertaken not to. They would not have done the job without that undertaking; and we had been horrified by the readiness with which they had proved their ability to get information.

The Prime Minister went on to say that on criminal records our allegation had not been substantiated. That was Scotland Yard's finding in relation to the case mentioned on May 11, and on the more recent case (Sidcup) we had given them too little to enable them to follow it up. I said I was astonished. In both cases the evidence of access to Criminal Records was strong. It was incredible if they were now saying that they had not been given enough detail on the second case, in which the CR number had been quoted. Would the Prime Minister like to nominate someone else to look at the material we had supplied? He seemed reluctant to pursue this. He had become extremely chilly. There were difficulties in this both for us and for them, he said. The *Guardian* had commissioned an illegal act and could be prosecuted.

Unfortunately his PPS arrived at that moment to say that they must leave. While walking back into the house he was more friendly and said that Brandt's visit had gone well; many people had talked of the occasion. He then departed. Next morning, perplexed, I rang Donald Maitland at Downing Street – both to thank him for arranging the previous day's meeting and to ask whether I might tell Hensley what the Prime Minister had said. I wanted to have it out with Hensley. Maitland said that he had been talking to the Prime Minister about it and they, too, were puzzled by the conflict. He was sure that the PM would have no objection to my taking it up with Hensley.

The weekend intervened, and Geoffrey Grimes advised that Peter and I should consider carefully what we were going to say if charged under the Criminal Justice Act. With his help we did so. Hensley that week was elusive – so much so that I asked Geoffrey Grimes to put on formal record with Scotland Yard my request for a meeting. The reasons, however, emerged a day or two later. Hensley's team – now enlarged to about sixteen, including three or four detective inspectors – had embarked on a series of raids on the offices of agencies, and within days charged people from a number of them. Among those charged were the two principals at the agency we had used, but we did not know whether the charges related to anything connected with the *Guardian*. Peter Harvey, however, managed to meet one of Hensley's henchmen in a pub and heard that, while things were going well for the team, their evidence might still not be strong enough to stand up in court. Couldn't Peter just come down and tell them quietly who had done the job for us? They knew anyway, the henchman said. Peter had replied that he just couldn't. Our lawyers offered to restrain Hensley's men from pestering Peter, but we said there was really no need. Peter rather enjoyed it.

Eventually I saw Hensley on July 9 and 10. He said that he had not had time yet to go into the Sidcup case, though someone else had been making inquiries for him and there was a procedural problem. As to the other CRO matter, he still wanted to meet my 'friend'. He seemed now to have visions of some great actor or film star. But he said that on the CRO affair he knew there had been leakages; the question was how to prevent them. He also said that he had identified to his own satisfaction the people whom we had employed. I summarised the discussion in a letter to Donald Maitland, with a copy to Hensley.

Later in July we stumbled on the fact that the agency we had employed had also been working for the South African Government. That happened because an English journalist, married to a South African, told us of his experience of being watched and intruded on and having his bank account and other matters investigated. He had photographed a car from which he in turn was being photographed, and Peter recognised the car and number plate. My sympathy with the agency was now much diminished, but I was still unwilling to break my undertaking to them. Hensley, however, having raided the agency's offices and removed a load of documents, found among them a carbon of the account they had submitted to the *Guardian*. Having asked us to verify that that was an account that we had received on the stated date from that agency, he seemed satisfied that he had all he needed. He sent some roses from his garden for Peter's mother, who was in England on a visit from Australia.

Hensley's team had not finished, however, and they remained at work until well into 1973. They went abroad to pursue their inquiries, and one of them told Peter, again in a pub, that they had been warned off getting too involved in the political end of their investigation. Thirteen people from detective agencies were eventually brought to trial, including four from ours (with the *Guardian* case being used in evidence) and one with a Sidcup connection. The four with whom we had been concerned were found guilty of conspiracy to tap the files of Government departments, including the Ministry of Defence; two were sentenced to terms of one year and of nine months respectively, and two to suspended sentences. But a year later the House of Lords quashed the convictions and set aside the sentences, on the ground that there was 'no separate and distinct class of criminal conspiracy called conspiracy to effect a public mischief', and that if Parliament wanted to create such an offence it must legislate.

Peter Harvey, after three years of working in Fleet Street, went back to the warmer climate of Australia. Ginger Hensley presented me with a tie, embossed with a miniature monkey wrench (for stopping up leaks). Adam Raphael within a year had uncovered another bad case of leakages from Scotland Yard's Criminal Records Office.[4] The South African Government no doubt found someone else to do their snooping for them. I regretted that we had not gone further in uncovering that side of the operation. The Younger Committee on privacy adopted our recommendation that there should be a system of licensing and surveillance for private detective agencies, but so far that recommendation has not been put into effect. (The Home Office apparently thought that registration would confer on the agencies a respectability that they did not deserve.)

Our experience over the leakages story reinforced at least four old lessons. One is that this kind of investigation is costly and time-consuming, eating up many hours for editorial executives as well as reporters, but worth while if the subject is genuinely one of public concern. The second is that nobody in authority will take you seriously unless you push the investigation to the point at which the newspaper possesses hard evidence. John Pardoe's allegations received no attention until Peter Harvey proved them to be true. The third is that to arrive at hard evidence a newspaper may have to take risks of prosecution – for commissioning offences, conspiracy, obstructing the course of justice, or breaches of the Official Secrets Act, as we found in this case. Fortunately the heavy hints of the early days came to nothing in the end, but another time the newspaper might not be so fortunate. Fourth, to be successful any such investigation must be a partnership between journalists and lawyers. Our lawyers not only knew the law but brought solid common sense to bear and a sound tactical judgement.

Starvation wages in South Africa

The most effective *Guardian* investigation in my time began almost by accident. Adam Raphael,* during a spell of duty in Washington, met and married a BBC girl whose father had been editor of the *Rand Daily Mail*.

---

4 In November 1973 Robert Mark invited me to spend a morning looking at the work of Scotland Yard's Criminal Records Office. The old manual system was still in use; the records have been computerised since then. Some twenty-five civilian clerks were taking telephone calls on ex-directory lines from police stations in the Metropolitan area and from other parts of the country; there were places for thirty-six clerks to work at any one time, with a sergeant supervising them. The callers were identifying their stations by a letter or figure code, and all calls were being logged. I was astonished to find that there were files on over one hundred individuals with the same name and first initial as my 'friend' (to use Hensley's term), and eight or nine with the same full initials, but none with the same date of birth. It seemed highly probable that the leakage had been through an outlying police station. In reply to telephone inquiries the clerks were allowed to say only 'wanted' or 'not wanted' or 'no trace'; if further information was needed, they had to ring back – or the outlying station could send a written request for a photocopy of the 'descriptive form', which then went by despatch rider in the Metropolitan area or by post to others. While we were watching there was an urgent call from Heathrow, about a man just boarding a plane, but although he had a long record the reply was 'not wanted'.

With long leave due to him, in the winter of 1972–73 he took Caroline to South Africa to visit her mother. But being energetic, he looked for something about which to write. He suggested to me that an inquiry into the wages paid by British companies could be revealing. I thought this highly improbable, for we had tried in London two years previously and failed to get any useful information. But if Adam wanted to try again in South Africa, I was willing.

Adam's intention had been stimulated by a Congressional inquiry into the affairs of the Polaroid company, following which General Motors, Ford, and other big American employers had taken a sudden interest in the way their South African subsidiaries were run. He had also been told in Pretoria – by Eschel Rhoodie – that British companies were worse than South African employers in paying their black workers.[5] That proved to be an exaggeration, for the British record, though atrocious, was no worse than the South African average. But Adam's inquiries soon showed us why we had failed the previous time: few of the London parent companies had any real knowledge of wage levels or conditions among their South African subsidiaries, and few managements in South Africa were willing to give information.

Being on the ground, however, Adam received a great deal of help from academics and students at the universities of Port Elizabeth, Natal, and Cape Town. He received help also from the black trade unions, who were working under extreme difficulties because of harassment and legal prohibitions, and from many South African journalists. He began by drafting and sending out to one hundred British employers in South Africa a one-page questionnaire on wages and conditions. (Unluckily a letter from me suggesting that he amend it to distinguish between basic wages and average wages reached him late, but that confusion was sorted out.) At first the questionnaire brought few replies, but by telephoning to all who had not answered – in itself a big undertaking – and by seeking interviews with a number of them, Adam obtained answers from nearly one-third. Information on a number of others was secured through the university students and the trade unions. He also gathered figures by talking to workers as they came off shift at factory gates, for once they found he was English, and not from the South African special branch, a number produced wage slips as evidence of their poor pay. But Adam soon found that he was being followed by special branch men, and he lost ground for a time when notebooks were stolen from his car.

After his return to London, his report was published as the front-page lead on March 12, 1973. With it were two striking photographs of the families of black workers at a British-owned wattle farm, and on one of the centre pages there was an extended article by Adam, as well as a

5 Eschel Rhoodie, permanent secretary in the Ministry of Information; later found to have made irregular use of some of his Government's copious propaganda funds.

leader. The front-page story began by saying that the majority of British companies in South Africa 'are paying substantial numbers of their workers below officially recognised subsistence levels'. An investigation of one hundred companies had found only three – Shell, ICI, and Unilever – who were paying all employees above the minimum for an African family to avoid malnutrition. Some British companies earning large profits in South Africa were paying between a third and a half of this minimum subsistence standard.

'If your income is below the poverty datum line (£10-£11 a week for a family of five) your health must suffer: in a real sense this is starvation.' This comment from the research officer at Johannesburg's Non-European Affairs Department, Adam said, proved to be no exaggeration. On two wattle farms owned by Slater Walker SA – the ones where the photographs were taken – he had seen children 'suffering from open sores, distended stomachs, and weakened limbs'. A Natal University lecturer accompanying him said that the children were suffering from kwashiorkor, a disease caused by protein and vitamin deficiency. The farm manager at another Slater Walker estate acknowledged that malnutrition was rife.

The report named other British companies whose subsidiaries were paying substantial numbers well below the poverty datum line – Associated Portland Cement, Tate and Lyle, Metal Box, Courtaulds, General Electric, Reed, Rowntree Mackintosh, Chloride Electrical, Associated British Foods, and British Leyland – and cited supporting evidence. It said that British companies were following closely the practice of much of South African industry. It quoted findings of the University of Natal's wages commission that many workers were living at 'a sub-human level'.

Adam's special article set out the methods of determining the 'poverty datum line' and the 'minimum effective level', two different figures. The first was the minimum income, determined by nutritionists and social researchers, needed by an average African family simply to exist. It did not allow for medicines, education, savings, holidays, furniture, blankets, any luxuries, or even the odd bus ride. According to Professor E. L. Batson of the University of Cape Town, it was not a human living standard but a statement of the minimum upon which subsistence and health could theoretically be achieved. Yet the majority of British employers in South Africa were paying large numbers of workers well below this level. The 'minimum effective level' was an expression of the income needed for an African family to lead a decent life. This 'humane' level corresponded roughly to £13-£15 a week, according to locality, and not a single British company employing substantial numbers was paying all its workers at or above this level.

Adam noted that many companies had improved wage levels and reformed employment practices after the strikes of black workers which had paralysed Durban's industries in February. He also quoted the critical comments of some white trade union leaders whose unions, under South

African law, were supposed to determine wage levels for black workers – the blacks themselves being barred from union membership. He said that British companies were lagging behind their American counterparts, with Ford, General Motors, and Chrysler, for instance, paying much higher rates than British Leyland; and he quoted the managing director of the American oil company, Caltex, as saying that the direction for change must come from the boardrooms of parent companies.

The reaction in many British boardrooms on March 12 was instant and angry. During the day my own office and the news desk took a number of calls, at least four of which demanded an immediate retraction and threatened legal action. For Geoffrey Grimes as for me, however, the case was bound to rest entirely on the accuracy of Adam's evidence and his ability to sustain it – in which I had confidence. From before publication I had realised that the naming of company names and the quoting of figures were what would give Adam's story its sting.

The reactions became a front-page story next morning. As reported, they ranged from that of Mr Jim Slater, chairman of Slater Walker Securities, who said he was horrified and pledged an immediate investigation, to Metal Box and Rowntree Mackintosh, who said that they had been unfairly vilified. The report listed all the companies which had made public statements – Metal Box and Rowntree Mackintosh, Associated Portland Cement, Tate and Lyle, British Leyland, and Hoover – and quoted from their statements. But it pointed out that only one of these (Rowntree Mackintosh) had promised to provide detailed figures. Associated Portland said that they wanted to raise wages but were prevented from doing so by the competitive situation; Tate and Lyle said that they were following local practice, and that within the general South African context they were proud of their employment conditions; British Leyland said that their main plant was in a development area where living costs were lower than average; Hoover said they had only just learned that their rates of pay were so low and that they intended to raise wages for South African workers; Metal Box said that all their adult male employees were earning more than the local poverty line, and that Metal Box employed black as well as white executives.

We did not mention that three of the four companies which had initially implied a threat of legal action were as yet unready to make any public statement. In every case we had said that, if they would provide us with figures, we should most willingly publish them. Though the advertisement department was never able to pin down individual cases, it later reported that whereas display volume had been growing steadily over the previous two or three years, it flattened in the months after Adam's story. In spite of that, the management gave us backing and encouragement.

The *Times* gave us generous support in a leader on the second day, and nearly all the other papers took up the story, some without acknowledging its origin in the *Guardian*. On the third day the paper carried a long letter from Sir Donald Barron, chairman of Rowntree Mackintosh, giving details of the wages now being paid by their South African company, of the other benefits provided (such as subsidised meals, subsidised bus fares, and loans for children's school books), and of their trade union relations. I wrote a further leader for that day, restating the need for British companies themselves to organise some form of voluntary and independent scrutiny of wage levels in South Africa and a code of practice. Already it was all too clear that many good and responsible employers in Britain had no precise knowledge of what was being done in their names in South Africa. That leader also said that Rowntree Mackintosh ought to have been included in our first report as among the few British companies paying all their employees above subsistence levels.

Adam came in to my room next morning, extremely displeased by the leader's reference to Rowntree Mackintosh. He said that his report had been based on figures obtained at the company's East London plant and on conversations with union leaders, and had been correct at the time. He had just had a cable from his contact in East London saying that Rowntree Mackintosh were raising their rates by 40 per cent this week, and he said that these were the rates that Sir Donald Barron had quoted in his letter. He was aware that I knew Donald Barron personally, and he thought I had let the company off too leniently. On my side I was ready to accept Donald Barron's word that the decision to make the big increase had been taken before they knew that anything was to appear in the *Guardian*, and was anyway based on the studies of Professor Potgieter of the University of Port Elizabeth, who was one of Adam's own authorities.[6] Adam said afterwards that, to shut him up, I told him he was the most arrogant young man who had ever worked for me; I do not remember it, and if I did so it was tactical. His story was standing up magnificently to all the assaults being made on it, and we could well be lenient to a company whose record was generally so good.

Later that week the Chloride Group announced that they would take a drop in profits in order to raise the wages of their African workers. Lord Kearton, chairman of Courtaulds, said that the earnings of all adult employees of their subsidiaries were now above the poverty datum line and offered to provide the *Guardian* with full figures. Hoover, British Leyland, and Reed International all undertook that in future no employee would be paid below the PDL. The chairman of Tate and Lyle wrote to the *Times*, to reply to what the *Guardian* had said about his company,

---

6 Sir Donald Barron told me later that the company's position had been particularly difficult, because in 1972 one of the Rowntree Trusts had made a grant to the Mozambique independence movement, Frelimo. The company had come under suspicion in South Africa as people whose profits were subsidising black revolution, and relations with the white trade unions had been strained. Therefore they had deferred one six-monthly increase for the black workers in 1972, which was why the increase in March 1973 was so large.

and stated that the PDL was not applicable to workers in a rural setting, that their subsidiary had paid no dividends in four years, and that wage rates were fixed by the South African Sugar Association. Adam replied with a letter to the *Times* pointing out that there were different PDLs for different areas; that migrant workers had families to feed, house, and educate even if those families were forced to live in reserves; that the sugar industry was paying some of the lowest wages in South Africa, far below officially recognised subsistence levels; and that Tate and Lyle's subsidiary had made a profit of more than half a million pounds in 1972. Was it not time, he asked, for a company with a proud record such as Tate and Lyle to set an example to the South African sugar industry?

In the Commons, after more than a hundred Labour MPs had called for a debate, Mr Callaghan sought a Government inquiry or a select committee. The British Council of Churches published a pamphlet suggesting that Christians should put questions at shareholders' meetings. A number of readers wrote to the *Guardian* with similar proposals. We prepared a list of questions and a list of all the companies with substantial interests in South Africa. One question asked whether the company was willing to accept a private audit of wage levels by an independent inquirer; I had taken private soundings among some of the larger companies to discover whether that was likely to be acceptable. Of the six I asked, five agreed at once, including ICI and Courtaulds. Only one refused. Our own management offered to pay the costs of a trial audit, provided we could find someone of sufficient standing to conduct it.

On April 4, however, all that was overtaken by the announcement that the trade and industry sub-committee of the Select Committee on Expenditure would undertake an investigation. Its chairman was William Rodgers, and the Government had accepted the inquiry. From that point onwards, the Rodgers Committee took the lead – and made a very good job of it.

Between mid-May and mid-July it took oral evidence from about thirty companies and received written evidence from another hundred. It cross-examined civil servants as well, at one point inviting a senior group from the Department of Trade to retire, reconsider what they had said, and return when they had something more positive to say. One of the first witnesses was Lord Kearton, and his performance was a *tour de force*. He must have burned much midnight oil to master every detail of the wages, earnings, and conditions among Courtaulds' various subsidiaries, as well as the relevant PDL and MEL figures, and he was able to announce an increase of over 100 per cent for forestry workers, who had apparently been overlooked. That was one up to Adam, who had found out about the forestry workers in March, but Adam was unstinting in his admiration for Kearton's evidence. The storm set off by the *Guardian*'s disclosures, Kearton said, had enabled Courtaulds to proceed still faster along a course they had already chosen.

He was followed a few days later by Lord Stokes, for British Leyland, who had an uncomfortable time. When he said that his company accepted 'custom and practice' in South Africa, he was asked whether, if he had been in the cotton industry in the early nineteenth century, he would have accepted slavery as inevitable. Other company chairmen were put through questioning more barbed than they were used to. One of the last witnesses, Sir Reay Geddes of Dunlop Holdings, told the committee that his board regarded the wages paid in South Africa as a matter for the company's South African managements. It was put to him that the Dunlop factories in South Africa were paying well below the poverty datum line, and he was asked when wage levels would be raised, but he insisted that that was a matter for the local management. He was asked when the main board had become aware of the wage levels being paid by their subsidiaries, and he replied that they had known since the first factory was opened in 1935. From Conservative and Labour members of the committee, astonishment was expressed.

The public proceedings were extensively reported in the 'heavy' papers, not least the *Guardian*, which frequently gave them a half page or more. Since the reporting was nearly always the work of one man alone – David McKie,* newly appointed as our second political correspondent – that, too, was a feat. Adam wrote occasional front-page stories or analytical follow-ups.

The tally of wage increases grew as the year wore on. Among them were Tootal (English Calico) with three increases during the year, representing nearly 150 per cent for the lowest paid; Slater Walker, which raised wages for its forestry and plantation workers 100 per cent; Metal Box, with three increases giving its lower paid workers an extra 50 per cent; the Anglo-American Corporation, with an average increase of 70 per cent over eighteen months for its African workers; and many others. Some said that these increases were coming anyway, others that publicity had persuaded them to act.

The Select Committee reported in March 1974, one week short of the anniversary of Adam Raphael's first report. It recommended that British companies operating in South Africa should pay their African workers not less than the Minimum Effective Level (that is, about 50 per cent above the PDL) and that they should establish a timetable for achieving this. It recommended also that the British Government should take immediate steps to establish a code of practice for companies operating in South Africa, and that these companies should encourage the lawful development of collective bargaining with their African employees. It found that in the April–June period no fewer than sixty-three major British companies had still been paying a proportion of their African workers the local PDL – and it listed these. Unilever, surprisingly, was in the list with 994 employees below the PDL, mainly in the Durban area. Consolidated, Associated British Foods, Cape Asbestos, and Lonrho were there, with over one thousand each (Consolidated Goldfields, in fact, with a total of over 50,000). Dunlop, Tate and Lyle, Trafalgar House, and other notable names featured, though with smaller numbers.

The Government accepted the main recommendations. A new code was devised, and the Government undertook to publish annually a list of those companies still paying below PDL levels. But, as Adam had discovered, it was neither easy nor straightforward to find out what was being paid.

Having received not a single writ from March 1973 until midwinter, we were taken aback when one came out of the blue on December 14. It was on behalf of Lord Kearton and Courtaulds, and the occasion was the last paragraph of a minor story by Adam on an inside news page four days earlier. This included a Courtaulds' subsidiary, South African Fabrics, in a list of companies which the TUCSA (the TUC of South Africa) was said to have sent to the British TUC, naming them as having refused to recognise the union representing African textile workers. Since we believed that we had given Courtaulds very fair treatment, the writ was unexpected, to say the least. It alleged libel and 'malicious falsehood' on our part, and it cited not only the report of December 10 but 'untrue statements' in Adam's original report of March 12 which had been only 'partially retracted' on March 16.

To recite the whole course of the proceedings would be as tedious as the proceedings themselves became, for they lasted nearly eighteen months. But they had some interesting moments. After discussion, our lawyers pleaded justification and fair comment, though they were as mystified as we were about why the action had been brought. One of the points at issue was whether or not Adam, while in South Africa, had had a telephone conversation with a senior man at South African Fabrics; Adam had kept notes of the conversation, and Caroline Raphael remembered hearing Adam's end of it. In March, Kearton had set up a triangular telephone conversation, with himself and Adam in London and the third man in South Africa. On the basis of Kearton's assurances then, Adam had written in the *Guardian* of March 19 that all SA Fabrics' employees had always been earning above the PDL. Yet eighteen months later, in the course of the legal pleadings, Courtaulds admitted that this had been incorrect. The company meanwhile had told its shareholders that *Guardian* statements about SA Fabrics were 'untrue' and that Adam's account of his telephone talk with SA Fabrics was 'an invention'. The web was extremely tangled.

In the end Kearton typically resolved it by inviting Adam to lunch, after Adam had written him a personal letter pointing out the degree of injury that would have been done if I had believed what Kearton said. He then asked me to lunch, and I replied that I would be delighted to go, for I had had friendly dealings with him in the past, but only when the writ had been withdrawn. It still took the lawyers on each side a little time to agree on the formula for ending the action, with each side paying its own costs. If it had come to court it would have been further complicated by the fact that in February 1974 two of our star witnesses – trade union leaders whom we intended to fly over from Durban – were placed under 'banning' orders, which meant that they were virtually under house arrest and could talk to nobody.

In February the Cambridge Union invited Adam to propose a motion that all British investment in South Africa should be withdrawn – a view that had been supported, among others, by the World Council of Churches – and invited Lord Kearton to oppose it. Adam instead seconded Kearton in opposing the motion, since he believed that investment by companies which paid proper wages was a preferable policy. On the vote, they won. Their encounter that evening helped to move the case to its final settlement, and it was wound up in July.

That Adam's investigation effectively changed the course of some British companies and accelerated the action of others cannot now be doubted. He provided hard evidence which mobilised opinion in Britain, brought about the Parliamentary Select Committee, and caused consternation in a number of company boardrooms. The Church of England was among the investors who started to sell their shareholdings in companies with an unsatisfactory record, and its immense financial resources became a weapon to help black Africans. The World Council's more radical case rested on the fact that apartheid forced most Africans to live in reserves too small and too poor to provide for their needs, and that earnings in the white-controlled areas could never compensate for this. At the *Guardian* we respected the World Council's view, but, for the time being, preferred the Kearton–Raphael approach.

The Select Committee's report had consequences in Europe as well, for in 1977 it formed the basis of the EEC's code of practice on African workers' wages. This was adopted by all nine member Governments, but enforcement has been slow. On the latest figures, it appears that a majority of British and European companies are still not obeying all the provisions of the code. Only the spur of constant publicity will produce reform.

In the end the World Council's judgement may well prove to have been justified. But whatever the ultimate choice of policy, as a work of journalism Adam's reporting on the wages paid by British companies remains an outstanding achievement.

12 Orange, green, and red

Glasgow's buses are painted orange and green to prove that they are non-sectarian. No such simple remedy has ever been found in Northern Ireland. Mercifully the Irish troubles have never spilled over to Clydeside, though at times it seemed that they might.

Like most British papers, the *Guardian* largely ignored Ulster until the Derry disturbances in October 1968. From then onwards, Northern Ireland could not be ignored. A succession of reporters - Harry Jackson, Simon Winchester, Simon Hoggart, Derek Brown, Peter Hetherington (no relation), Anne McHardy, and others - did hard and dangerous duty in the province; and however neglectful we had been before the civil rights marches, we made up for it with thorough reporting from then onwards.

Within the office we had a strong-minded Northern Protestant in John Cole, news editor until 1969 and deputy editor thereafter. He was no Orangeman, for he abhorred the narrow conservatism of the Ulster Unionists. But as mentioned earlier in my view he did more than any other British journalist to dispel illusions about short-cuts in Northern Ireland. He reminded us regularly that there was no simple and peaceful way to unite Ireland, and that poverty, as well as sectarian divisions, lay at the root of Irish troubles. He was one of the earliest advocates of disbanding the B Specials (the armed and partisan police reserve) and of power-sharing between Protestants and Catholics.

John's role, nevertheless, was a cause of tension and friction in the office. He was a powerful influence on me, and therefore on *Guardian* policy; and his influence was resented by some others on the staff, though I was perhaps more aware of it than he was. The leader writers felt that they were being excluded from discussion, and they remarked on it. There were others in the office who took a simplistic view that the troubles were all the fault of the Protestants; they seemed to me too ready to overlook or excuse the violence of the IRA. John's advice never carried greater weight than that of our reporters on the ground, who took no such simple view. I knew also that John was often consulted by Ministers with responsibility for Northern Ireland - Callaghan, Maudling, Whitelaw, and Merlyn Rees - because they trusted his knowledge and his judgement.

For a time in 1972 John and I differed, when I thought he was too unyielding over internment. That came to a head shortly before Bloody Sunday, and for some months I took over most of the Irish leader writing myself. We never again achieved harmony over Irish policy. For a long time I was troubled by fear of repeating over Ulster my misjudgement (if it was a misjudgement) over Vietnam – in having said, that is, that an American withdrawal was not necessarily the way to a peaceful and happy life for the South Vietnamese. The fear about a British withdrawal was that it could lead to an appalling civil war, which the militant Protestants were almost certain to win, driving thousands of Catholic refugees to the West of Scotland, Merseyside, and the Midlands, as well as the Republic. Consequently I was attracted to Conor Cruise O'Brien's proposal that, while not withdrawing immediately, the British Government should set a date for the ultimate withdrawal of its troops. But having taken that position after Bloody Sunday, Conor himself later retreated from it; and I never adopted it in the paper. For what if Britain set the date and civil war still seemed imminent: could we go through with it, and would even the Dublin Government want us to? That left only the option of carrying on.

The missing Ulster moderates

For the first time in years, on July 5, 1966, Northern Ireland made the front-page lead. 'Queen's car hit by block of concrete' was the headline, and our staff man Brian MacArthur reported that a twelve-inch slab, hurled from a roof seventy-five feet above, had dented the bonnet of the Queen's car. A secondary story, with the headline 'Thousands march with Mr Paisley', told how within a few hours the Rev. Ian Paisley had organised a march and demonstration, blaming the incident on Roman Catholics. MacArthur's report ended: 'If Mr Paisley has his way there could well – and this is no exaggeration – be a religious war here quite soon.'

Until then, and indeed for two years after that, the paper took little interest in Northern Ireland. As far back as 1956, John Cole had written a series on Ulster as a neglected province. But thereafter it rarely found its way to any prominence in the news or feature pages: while all was fairly quiet between Belfast Lough and the Foyle – or so it seemed – why trouble too much about the long years of Unionist misrule?

The fiftieth anniversary of Dublin's 1916 Easter Rising began the change. The rising was celebrated by Catholics in the North, after years of relentless Orange marches in Belfast and Londonderry, with parades and speeches and flying of the Republican flag. At last the militant Protestants had something against which to react. The Ulster Volunteer Force was formed, stating that it would 'mercilessly and without hesitation' execute known IRA men, and was proscribed by the Northern Ireland Government soon afterwards. And Ian Paisley, after making little political headway for fifteen years, now had a visible Catholic threat to fight.

Then came the Queen's visit, just before the annual Protestant parading to commemorate the Battle of the Boyne (1690), and the parades brought Ulster back on to the front page pictorially, with Orange marchers in the bowlers and sashes. Ten days later Ulster made the foot of the front page again, when five Catholic pubs in Belfast were ransacked and Paisleyites ignored a restriction order on their march.

Through those July weeks the *Guardian* made only one brief editorial comment and carried no background article. That was extraordinary blindness. John Cole cannot be blamed, because he was in the United States; I was in Egypt from July 5 to 15, then absorbed on return by Wilson's retrenchment, and then on holiday. But these are excuses, for the system ought to have coped. We were retrieved only at the beginning of August when John Grigg, instead of his usual column, wrote a longer article on Northern Ireland – savaging the 'crude fundamentalism' of Ian Paisley, while recognising his cunning and his oratorical skill, and damning those Ulster Unionists who said, 'Of course I am not a Paisleyite, but ...' Unless Paisley was checked, Grigg wrote, another Irish bloodbath was coming.

In September John Grigg returned to the Ulster scene with a column on the challenge to Captain O'Neill's leadership of the Ulster Unionists. He argued that the challenge came not so much from Paisley as from Brian Faulkner, the Minister of Commerce, who was ready to benefit from rank-and-file discontent with a courageous leader much as Harold Wilson had done from the unilateralist opposition to Hugh Gaitskell. Grigg saw O'Neill as some way ahead of the average Unionist in his readiness to talk to the Dublin Government and to be more liberal in his approach to the Catholic community in the North. That challenge to O'Neill became a regular theme over the next three years, though Faulkner did not become Prime Minister until 1971.

In October 1968 police in Londonderry made vigorous use of their batons to break up a civil rights march – Gerry Fitt, a Republican Labour MP at Westminster, being apparently singled out for particularly hard treatment – and that brought the Ulster issue boiling on to front pages, leader pages, and feature pages. The causes of civil rights complaints were clear enough: discrimination against Catholics in public and other appointments, discrimination over housing allocations, gerrymandering in the way local government boundaries were drawn, and refusal of 'one man, one vote' in local elections. Though to those acquainted with the Ulster situation these were familiar facts, they came as a shock to most readers elsewhere in the UK.

In the aftermath of the Derry violence, John Cole wrote his first substantial leader on his homeland. He noted O'Neill's success in lowering tension in Ulster, with steps that none of his predecessors would have contemplated, and said that this was consistent not only with trying to give the Catholics a better deal but also with trying to create a better climate for investment from outside the six counties. Ulster, he wrote, 'needs all the development it can get and this should be the goal of any Prime Minister'. But Mr O'Neill, the leader said, had still to demonstrate that he intended to shift the imbalance between Catholic and Protestant.

If he tried to move faster, right-wingers in his Cabinet might try to oust him – leading perhaps to new rounds of violence and counter-violence. But if he did nothing neither Paisley nor the civil rights movement would remain inactive. O'Neill therefore needed help from the British Government – first and essentially by a restatement of Attlee's 1948 guarantee that there would be no tampering with the North-South border, and secondly through a Royal Commission to inquire into civil rights and how to widen equality of opportunity. About the border, John wrote that within the civil rights movement there were Republicans who wanted to end partition, though there were also many Catholics who simply wanted to live in Ulster on an equal footing with other citizens: and there would be no peace in the province unless the Protestant majority felt secure. A Royal Commission would help to determine just how Ulster must progress, having so far moved too slowly – and help O'Neill to persuade his recalcitrant right that the more progress Ulster made on its own the less the Commission need say.

John's reference to Republicans in the civil rights movement was regarded by his critics in the office as below the belt. What if they were Republicans who wanted to unite Ireland? Were they not entitled to proper democratic rights as equal citizens while within Northern Ireland? So the argument ran, and it was fair so far as it went. But it seemed to me that John had made a strong point about the difficulty of persuading Protestants, even moderate Protestants, to move faster if they feared that the real objective of part of the civil rights campaign was a united Ireland ruled from Dublin. The denial of civil rights to Catholics was outrageous, but reform must come if possible by persuasion. The critics of John's reference to the Republicans also chose to overlook his warning that some were supporters of the IRA, trying to turn the civil rights movement to their own violent ends.

Attlee's pledge was renewed when O'Neill, accompanied by Brian Faulkner and his right-wing Home Affairs Minister, William Craig, went to Downing Street on November 4. Harold Wilson publicly reaffirmed that 'no changes should be made in the constitutional status of Northern Ireland without Northern Ireland's free agreement'. At the same time the Prime Minister made plain the British Government's dissatisfaction with slow progress towards reform of the local government franchise, local electoral boundaries, and non-discrimination. He said in the Commons next day that O'Neill's vulnerability to pressure from extremists (an implied swipe at Craig and Faulkner) must not be used for 'blackmail', and that if O'Neill were overthrown 'we would need to consider a fundamental reappraisal of our relations with Northern Ireland'. The invitation to Craig and Faulkner to accompany O'Neill had been deliberate, and Wilson told me afterwards with some relish that he had 'roughed them up'. Right at the beginning of the meeting he had told them that if they ditched O'Neill he would immediately propose to Parliament the ending of the so-called 'imperial contribution' to Northern Ireland's finances. That point found its way into the *Guardian*'s report next day, as it was meant to.

The Royal Commission did not come so quickly. It was appointed in January by the Northern Ireland Government, not the British Government, with a Scottish judge, Lord Cameron, as chairman. Faulkner resigned because of its appointment; William Craig had been dismissed from office by O'Neill in December. Meanwhile there had been further clashes in Londonderry between marchers and the RUC (Royal Ulster Constabulary). When the Cameron Commission reported in September 1969 - by which time O'Neill, too, had gone - it was highly critical of Craig's handling of the marches in Derry the previous October and November, though it also said that Gerry Fitt had been 'reckless' in the way he led the civil rights march on October 5. It found the Roman Catholic grievances over discrimination 'well documented in fact' and said that the minority had strong ground for their resentment, though it also said that the Protestants had 'solid and substantial basis' in the past and present for their fear of attempts to subvert the UK relationship, and it spoke of the 'ambiguous attitude' of the Roman Catholic hierarchy in the North.

Of the Civil Rights Association which had sponsored the October 5 march, the Cameron Commission said that its purpose was 'non-violent protest and agitation within the limits of the law'. It contained many 'moderate and earnest men and women' who wanted it to keep on that course, but it was infiltrated by others whose intentions were far from peaceful, since they wished to provoke disorder as an instrument of policy. These included members of the People's Democracy organisation, whose objective was a Workers' Socialist Republic embracing all Ireland.[1]

Whatever might be said for an all-Irish socialist republic, the use of violence to achieve it was not acceptable to the *Guardian*'s tradition of liberal democracy. And what Cameron said about infiltration reinforced the disquiet I had long felt about one or two members of the staff who were prominent in criticism of John Cole's policy. There was one leader writer - first class in his own field, which did not include Northern Ireland - whose emotional commitment was undoubtedly towards movements such as the People's Democracy. While not an advocate of violence, he seemed to me too ready to excuse it; fortunately his later career with the *Guardian* took him well away from that kind of association. But discussion among the leader writers and senior staff became difficult, and there were complaints that from 1969 onwards I tended to restrict debate about Irish issues to John Cole, myself, and only one or two others. Mark

---

1 The Cameron Commission's report was published on September 12, 1969; John Cole's main leader on the Londonderry disturbances and the way ahead in Ulster had appeared on October 18, 1968.

Arnold-Forster, though in the critical camp, contributed usefully to the inner debate, as did Harford.

At one point there was a round-robin from some of the reporters, but since the signatories did not include Harry Jackson, Simon Winchester, or Simon Hoggart I replied with an open letter saying that I preferred to be guided by the men on the spot. Especially in the early months all the reporters faced exceptional strains, because people in Northern Ireland were not accustomed to impartial reporting. Apart possibly from the *Belfast Telegraph*, newspapers were either Protestant or Catholic. Harry remarked that you had to treat the story as if you were a foreign correspondent – but the paper was arriving on breakfast tables in Belfast every morning, and local contacts were liable to become angry over what they read, whichever way it went. Later the pressure on reporters came from the physical danger and from the Army's belief that UK correspondents ought to reflect the Army's point of view. Harry and the others nevertheless wrote what they believed to be the truth, regardless of sides.[2]

The tensions within the office back in London were small compared with these, but still worried me. The differences were as great as over the Common Market in 1962, and sometimes expressed less cordially.

On December 9, 1968, O'Neill made a powerful broadcast asking his fellow citizens whether they wanted to live 'in a happy and respected province, in good standing with the rest of the United Kingdom', or in a place continually torn apart by riots 'and regarded by the rest of Britain as a political outcast'. The response to that broadcast was reported to be strongly favourable. Two days later O'Neill sacked William Craig, saying he knew Craig was 'attracted by ideas of a UDI nature'. John Grigg took the view that if O'Neill had called an election then instead of two months later, he would have received an overwhelming mandate. But events at the beginning of January poisoned the atmosphere.

From January 1 to 4, civil rights supporters marched from Belfast to Londonderry in the cause of 'one man, one vote'. They were frequently opposed by Protestants, some armed with staves and sharp-tipped flag-poles. On the last day of the march, they were ambushed at Burntollet bridge, stoned and beaten, and many including women and girls had to be taken to hospital. Simon Hoggart quoted a police inspector the night before Burntollet as saying that his men were 'far too tired' to shift the Protestants who were blocking the marchers; but a few hours after

---

2 There were suggestions that at first the extreme strains of reporting from Northern Ireland were aggravated by dual news-desk control (Manchester normally being responsible for everything in its area, which included Ulster) and sometimes by pressure to 'balance' reports of Protestant violence with reports of Catholic violence; but, in Harry Jackson's recollection, experience showed that what he and the others were providing was a reliable service – and what they sent was printed as written, which was what mattered to them. Latterly the control was exercised from London rather than Manchester.

Burntollet there were violent clashes in Derry, and the RUC broke up a civil rights demonstration with batons and water cannon. People in Derry were asking, Simon said, how the RUC could act so swiftly in Derry when they appeared unable to control the Protestants harrying the marchers on the road to there.

In February O'Neill – having sacked Craig and lost Faulkner, and now faced by a revolt within his own party – called a general election, too late. John Cole and I went to Northern Ireland for a few days, both to see the situation at first hand and to talk to Harry Jackson. We had a private meeting with O'Neill at Stormont, and heard how Paisley's 'bully boys' had been systematically shouting outside the houses of MPs or candidates in and around Belfast, to scare them and to weaken them in their constituencies. Paisley himself was standing against O'Neill in Bannside, and so was a People's Democracy candidate. Disquietingly, O'Neill said that even if he won a clear victory in the Stormont Parliament at best 'one man, one vote' could not be introduced in local elections before 1971. In fact the election resulted in a stalemate, with the Unionists split between O'Neill and anti-O'Neill men and with Catholics apparently voting solidly against the Unionists even where it meant conservative farmers voting for a PD candidate. O'Neill resigned in April and was replaced by Major James Chichester-Clark.

In April also, because of sabotage of power and water lines, the British Government decided that troops should be used for guard duties. A *Guardian* leader reluctantly accepted the decision but doubted whether it would stop the sabotage. So far nobody had been killed. In May John wrote a strong leader saying that Chichester-Clark must not delay the introduction of 'one man, one vote', that he ought to disband the B Specials, and that unless he could prove that the IRA were behind the bombing of water and power lines he ought to wind up the Special Powers Act. (Later evidence confirmed that the saboteurs were not IRA but Protestant extremists.[3])

In August there was serious rioting in the Bogside district of Londonderry and the Ardoyne and Falls Road areas of Belfast, during the Apprentice Boys' annual march in Derry and after Protestant burning of Catholic homes in Belfast. The RUC in Belfast used Browning machine guns and CS gas. There were riots also in Dungannon, Newry, and Armagh. On August 14 and 15 British troops were deployed for the first time on anti-riot duties in Londonderry and Belfast, and as GOC General Sir Ian Freeland took over responsibility for security operations, since Harold Wilson was not going to let the Stormont Government control the British units (and indeed the *Guardian* had urged him not to do so). During the disturbances between August 12 and 17 eight civilians were killed, and according to RUC figures 514 civilians, 226 policemen, and

3 See Martin Wallace, *Northern Ireland*, published in 1971.

one soldier were injured. The Hunt Committee was appointed to examine the role of the RUC and the B Specials; and the Scarman Tribunal was established to examine the causes of the disturbances.[4] At a briefing for editors on August 15, attended by Harford because I was away, James Callaghan said that even if it were possible to withdraw the troops from the streets in a few days, which he doubted, that would not be the end. There would be new outbreaks before long. Twelve years later the troops are still there.

It is arguable that at that stage the paper ought to have taken a much tougher line – saying that either there must be direct rule at once, as the price of putting the troops in, or the Irish must be left to fight it out among themselves. John Cole might not have opposed the first, for he had always been willing to see Northern Ireland placed on the same parliamentary footing as Scotland and Wales, with stronger representation at Westminster. But I was against it, fearing that the British troops would soon find themselves fighting Protestants and Catholics in a major civil war, that relations with the Republic would become intolerably strained, and that the Irish question would again dominate British politics as it had done for nearly fifty years before the 1914-18 war. And the second choice seemed an intolerable abdication of British responsibility. Although most people in Britain knew so little about Northern Ireland and perhaps cared even less, the province was part of the United Kingdom; it was not a Vietnam on the other side of the world, and again a British withdrawal must mean a vicious civil war.

The leader of Saturday morning, August 16, written by John the night before going on holiday, neither explicitly approved nor disapproved of the commitment of the five British battalions. Instead it tackled the question of why the situation had deteriorated so fast. 'A total loss of conviction by a substantial section of the Catholic population that they will get a fair deal from Stormont' was the chief cause; and if more innocent people were not to be killed 'ways must be found of giving the Catholics faith that they will get a square deal'. Since the B Specials were now under the GOC, he ought to remove them at once from the troubled areas. As an emergency measure on the political front, the leader said, there ought to be a 'crisis coalition' – say five or six Unionists, dedicated to maintaining the British connection, and three Catholics, equally dedicated to the unity of Ireland. With Westminster backing, this coalition must force the pace of reform – fairer allocation of housing, an end to discrimination in employment, recruitment of more Catholics to the police, disarming and then dissolution of the B Specials, and so on. Could John Hume and Gerry Fitt be persuaded to sit round a policy-making table with Unionists and not be disowned by their fellows?

4 Respectively, Sir John Hunt, later Lord Hunt, of Everest fame; and Sir Leslie Scarman, later Lord Scarman, a High Court judge.

So far as I know, this was the first time that power-sharing in such an explicit form had been put forward. It was a positive and constructive response to the crisis. I had been consulted by telephone on Friday afternoon, at our Lake District cottage, and John and Madge Cole were due there on the Saturday night in transit to holiday in Northern Ireland. I reckoned that John had done a good final night's work.

Letters from readers flowed in during the next few days. A number said it was absurd to suppose that any good could come while the Unionists ruled at Stormont, and their general tenor was that the Westminster Government ought to suspend the Northern Ireland constitution at once since that was within its powers. Inevitably there were some – one from County Kerry was printed – saying that Irish reunion was the only way and that the Northern 'satellite' ought never to have come into existence. There was the equally inevitable reply that the Southern majority were trying to force their wishes on the Northern minority in Ireland, just as they complained that the majority within the North were trying to force their preference on the minority there. There was a letter from Arundel, Sussex, saying it was 'profound nonsense' for the *Guardian* to call for disarming of the B Specials, who were essential to protect the North against an armed illegal rabble. There was also one from Professor Denis Brogan, in Cambridge, saying that American experience had proved that employment of the National Guard, a rough equivalent of the B Specials, 'is always dangerous and sometimes disastrous'. And there was one quoting Mrs Madigan of *Juno and the Paycock*, '... th' polis as polis in this city is null an' void'.

John kept at the power-sharing theme through the autumn and winter. After the Cameron Report was published in mid-September he put the alternatives plainly. The choice for Protestants was whether to turn Northern Ireland into a fair and generous society where a man's religion was his own business or watch their country slide into chaos and earn the contempt of the outside world. The choice for Catholics was whether to take a full part in the political life of Northern Ireland or sit back and hope that partition would eventually end amid the smoke of riot and civil war. For the British there was no choice, he wrote: without British interest and British troops it would be impossible to create a decent society in Ulster. It was going to be a long task.

In practice, as events proved, power-sharing stood no chance of serious discussion in the North until the Unionist hegemony was broken; and that did not happen for another three years. It was going to be an even longer task than we foresaw.

Army, Provos, and press

Standing alone under a spotlight on a vast empty floor, I faced the embanked tiers of colonels, majors, and captains at the Staff College, Camberley. It was December 1971. The Provos' bombing campaign had begun nearly a year before; many more British troops were in action in Ulster, and so far about fifty had been killed. Internment had been introduced in August; the situation seemed to be getting worse, not better. Brian Faulkner had been Prime Minister at Stormont since March, and Ted Heath had been at Downing Street for eighteen months. I had been asked to speak at the Staff College about the reporting of Northern Ireland. Having checked my facts with Simon Winchester, I began with three elementary case studies.

1. The bogus priests. Ten days before, at 12.45 am, Simon received a 'tip off', but off the record, from a friendly police public relations officer. Two escapees from Crumlin Road prison in Belfast had been recaptured, dressed as RC priests, in a car driven by a genuine priest. Nine altogether had escaped from Crumlin Road, where they were on remand on arms and ammunition charges. As in so much reporting, there were time, space, and staff factors: time because the next editions of the _Guardian_ went to press in London and Manchester at 1.30 am; space because Ireland was only one story competing for space on a crowded front page, with limited typesetting capacity at that hour; and staff because Simon was working alone in Belfast, while in each of the London and Manchester offices there were no more than four or five people on duty after 12.30.

Simon had to ask himself: was the story true or false? What chance had he of checking? Being off the record, was its source reliable? Should he take a chance and send it tonight or leave it until tomorrow? It was a question of judgement; and having thought about it for a couple of minutes Simon decided to send the story. He phoned Manchester at 12.50, but the sub-editor in charge there was not excited by the story, not seeing that the involvement of priests was political dynamite. He had a strong front page already, anyway, and didn't want to dislodge anything. So Simon, breaking with the _Guardian_'s usual chain of command, at 1.05 am rang the production editor in London. The production editor damned Manchester, moved fast, and got a short story on to the front page for 1.30. The _Guardian_ was the only paper to carry it next day, a Friday, but almost every Fleet Street paper was leading with a detailed follow-up on Saturday morning after two Cistercian monks had been charged with aiding the escape.

In that instance Simon did right, but he took a big risk. Our reporters were always sceptical about PR (public relations) information and doubly sceptical of anything that was 'off the record'. I had to emphasise this to the Army audience, saying that it was not just Army and police PR of whom we were somewhat distrustful but nearly all PR. The Foreign Office were the trickiest of the lot, and some big industrial companies not far behind. Everything had to be treated with caution and checked so far as possible, and Winchester had taken a risk that night only because he knew that particular police PR man pretty well. In general we preferred to hear from the operational people direct; the Army, in practice, had done itself a great deal of good in Northern Ireland by allowing even sergeants and second lieutenants to speak directly to the press on factual matters within their own responsibility.

It might be asked why we had not waited until next day. But the *Guardian*, like any other newspaper or broadcasting station, was in a competitive business. Its job was to get the news and give it as soon as possible – though always with an overriding requirement to take care of accuracy.

2. *The Butler Street shooting*. This had happened some months earlier, on the night of February 5–6. Simon quite often drove home late, through the troubled areas. That night he arrived on the scene of an incident, in Butler Street off the Crumlin Road, about 12.30. Petrol bombs had been thrown at an armoured car, which had been set on fire. One shot had been fired into the crowd which had thrown the petrol bombs, and a man was dead. Simon happened to know the officer in charge personally and was told what had happened. It was not clear that the soldier who had fired had actually seen the dead man with a bomb, though he was in the crowd from which the bomb had been thrown. Simon therefore referred in his report to a 'rioter' who had been shot.

But an Army press officer had turned up at the scene soon afterwards, had taken aside the officer in charge, and had then told other reporters who arrived that the dead man had been seen carrying a bomb. And that was how the Press Association and all the other papers reported it. A subeditor in Manchester, having seen the PA version, had questioned Simon's phrasing. Simon had insisted that his version was as near the truth as he could get, and that was how the *Guardian* printed it.

Next day a senior PR man at Army headquarters in Lisburn complained to Simon that he had not accepted the official version. Simon gave him an appropriate reply, though I hope quite politely. That, however, was as nothing to the sequel in the House of Commons. There Bernadette Devlin, the fiery young MP for mid-Ulster, under privilege alleged that the *Guardian* in its London office had 'concocted' the story about a 'rioter' in order to 'condone cold-blooded murder'. The irony was that the *Guardian*'s story was both nearer the truth than any other and less favourable to the Army – while aware of all the surrounding circumstances and making clear that there had been a petrol bomb attack. (But then Bernadette's friend Eamon McCann charged the *Guardian* with having deliberately suppressed the story of another midnight shooting, having failed to realise that the incident actually took place after the edition delivered in Belfast had gone to press; the incident was reported, with commendable speed, in later editions.)

3. *Unity Flats*. This was an incident involving the Royal Highland Fusiliers at the end of February. In essence Simon reported that the use of water cannon against a crowd at the Unity Flats in Belfast had set off a riot instead of calming things down. He had been hauled up to Army

headquarters at Lisburn and told off, but he had stuck to his story and had seen the Commander Land Forces, General Farrar-Hockley. The general had gone into the matter and a week later had issued a public apology about the incident at Unity Flats.

To the Staff College audience I said that our reporters could produce more than a dozen other such cases in the past few months, and there were bound to be conflicts. It was important to remember, though, that the general picture emerging in the paper was one of soldiers doing an intolerably difficult job, and doing it with almost superhuman patience and restraint. Our concern with factual accuracy was as important to them as it was to us, for readers were likely to distrust reports unless they saw our ability to stand up to hostile criticism. The public, Parliament, and the Government all needed the most reliable information with which they could be provided, and official sources were not enough.

The IRA, incidentally, complained as often and in a nastier way than the Army. Simon Winchester, like other reporters, had had a number of calls on the line: 'We've got your home address, you bastard – don't think you're safe in your hotel.' (He had his office in a central Belfast hotel.)

At Camberley I went on to wider aspects of a newspaper's responsibility in reporting political and social trends. The questions from the Army officers were sharp. Above all, they could not understand why newspapers felt it necessary to talk to the Provos, Sinn Fein, and others involved with violence. The answer, I said, was quite simple: unless our staff did so, we could not begin to gauge their tactical and strategic objectives and the way they would try to attain them. Army intelligence was trying all the time to find out what was happening on the other side, for that knowledge was vital. It was just as vital to Parliament and the public, who in the end had to determine policy. I knew that, in the Army's eyes, reporters such as Simon ought to reveal at once any contacts they had with the Provos or the UVF, but that was impossible. Direct contact was infrequent anyway, though Simon knew how to make it when he felt he had to. But if he were to reveal when and how he had been in touch, two things were virtually certain: one was that the *Guardian* would never get any information from that quarter again, and the other that Simon would probably be shot dead soon. In the past our reporters had made the same sort of contact in Kenya, Aden, and Cyprus, so why not now in Northern Ireland?

The normal and legal contact, of course, was through the Provos' political wing. Six months after the Camberley talk, while visiting Simon in Belfast, I was taken to a house in Andersonstown to visit Jimmy and Moira Drumm. Moira was a senior executive member of the political wing and had appeared with Simon in a television programme the previous day; Jimmy had been released from Long Kesh, where he was chairman of the internees' committee, just forty-eight hours earlier. He was reckoned by the Army to have been a senior Provo commander, though he himself dismissed that.

In retrospect it was a macabre conversation, both because a British Army sergeant had been shot dead close to their house the day before (actually while Simon was in the house waiting to go with Mrs Drumm to the television studio some miles away) and because, in 1976, Mrs Drumm herself was shot dead. She was in the Mater hospital for an operation, and it was never known which side had shot her.

What Moira and Jimmy Drumm said, though they emphasised that they were speaking as individuals, represented an extremely hard view. They allowed no room for compromise. Their immediate demand was freedom for all internees, an amnesty for all political prisoners (including Protestants and sentenced men), and the Army, apart from manning posts along the Belfast 'peace line', must return completely to barracks. The next stage beyond that, so far as my questioning could elicit anything precise, must be a 'Dail Ulster' representing the old nine counties and not just the present six. They argued that this was a fair approach because there were a lot of Protestants in the three counties, and a nine-county Ulster, including its Protestants, could make a great contribution to the future of Ireland. As to a plebiscite or referendum, they would not contemplate it unless it was an all-Ireland plebiscite. Since Whitelaw had said that he would not talk to murderers, and since the murdering British soldiers were under him, they saw no reason why their people should talk to Whitelaw. But Jimmy Drumm said that having been in Long Kesh he was out of touch with current thinking. MacStiofain had telephoned to congratulate him on his release, but they had had no chance yet to discuss the situation.[5]

The shooting of the sergeant, they said, came about this way. Regularly at about one o'clock, during the school lunch hour, a Saracen armoured car came round. Sometimes it stopped and stones were thrown at it; sometimes the soldiers fired rubber bullets. They thought the patrol pointless, though they said it was supposed to prevent new 'no-go' areas. Yesterday their house had been flying the Republican tricolour, to celebrate Jimmy's return. Even the old RUC hadn't objected to the Republican flag being flown on special occasions. But the sergeant had torn it down.

Moira Drumm said she had not known he was there until she found him up a drainpipe pulling it down. He had not rung the bell and asked them to remove it. When she appeared he had drawn his pistol and made a number of very offensive remarks. One of her young daughters had said to the sergeant: 'That's our flag – and you'll go home wrapped in yours.' They had thought no more about it until they'd heard, fifteen minutes

5 Sean MacStiofain, at that time chief of staff of the Provisional IRA; born in London, and originally John Stevenson (Gaelicised to MacStiofain).

later, that the sergeant had been shot a bit further down the estate. She, of course, had been with Simon during those fifteen minutes since they had been about to go to the studio. (She had been unwilling to venture through Protestant Belfast to the studio without a neutral escort; Simon said that when she heard of the shooting she was unmoved.) She was hard-eyed in telling the story.

In the afternoon when we were there that part of Andersonstown seemed completely peaceful. Apart from the green hills behind and one or two concrete blocks at road ends, the estate looked like any other modern suburban housing development on the edge of an English city. It made the whole experience the more incongruous. It did nothing to encourage my search for ways towards peace, though it left a vivid sense of the human difficulties.

Bloody Sunday, before and after

When internment was introduced in August 1971, John Cole was on holiday in Brittany. Therefore I myself wrote the leader accepting internment. John reminded me a number of times afterwards that it was I, not he, who had taken that decision. The point had relevance in January 1972, when we disagreed about future policy.

Much of the leader on internment in fact derived its thinking from John's own writing. It began by saying that internment without trial 'is hateful, repressive, and undemocratic'. But in Northern Ireland shooting, bombing, and burning were occurring every day. The men responsible generally disappeared, unidentified. 'Through fear or through misplaced loyalty, others will not say what they have seen.' Northern Ireland's economic life, already tottering, was being brought further towards bankruptcy. Tension between Protestant and Catholic communities was being fanned into bitter hatred. The Army, trying to keep the peace, was being placed under intolerable strain. 'To remove the ringleaders, in hope that the atmosphere may calm down, is a step to which there is no obvious alternative.'

Extreme Protestants and extreme Catholics, the leader said, ought to reckon that unless order and calm were soon restored 'there will be fewer jobs and fewer homes in Northern Ireland'. Burned factories, bombed shops, and damaged homes could not soon be replaced. Nor could the damage be confined to the North: 'unjust and hurtful though it may be, the name of all Ireland will stink'. Orangemen and Catholics were equally to blame, and successive British Governments had done too little to bolster Ulster's economy. Tripartite talks with Dublin were essential. Meanwhile the Army would have to go on bearing its appalling burden.

Maudling as Home Secretary, with responsibility for Northern Ireland, had asked me to call on him that afternoon. Clearly he was concerned lest the *Guardian* go against the Government on this issue, for, as he said, if the opinion polls were anything of a guide (of which he was not sure)

British opinion was moving strongly towards 'pulling out'. He expected difficulties with Dublin in the next few days and a bad reaction in parts of Belfast. But already by midday about 350 of the 500 or so on the list had been pulled in. There would be an appeals procedure, he said, and he hoped to get a good man to take charge of it in spite of the probable threat to that man's life. The police evidence, however, could not be shown to the appellant, who would have to make a case for himself. When I asked why they were pulling in so many PD (People's Democracy) and civil rights people – my man with PD friends had been on to me about this at lunch time – he said that they were not. He fetched a sheet from his desk and gave me the figures. So far as I could remember afterwards they were 270 Provo and kindred men, 140 Protestant activists, only seven PD, no civil rights, and one anarchist. I had already sketched out the probable line of the leader before I went down to Whitehall, and it hardly changed apart from a cautionary insertion about the difficulty of dealing with Dublin in the immediate future.

The trouble in the Ardoyne district of Belfast that night was bad, and in the city nine people died. Protestants set fire to their own houses before fleeing, to make sure that no Catholics could take them over. A further leader next day restated the established *Guardian* line – that there must be power-sharing in the North and tripartite talks with the Dublin Government. It was harsh, however, about the 'phoney' condemnation of internment by the Irish Prime Minister and Foreign Minister, reminding them that the IRA and the Provisionals were continuing to use the South as a sanctuary and that the Army was in Ireland mainly to protect the Catholic community. So the argument continued in the next few days – with another tide of letters flowing in, including comparisons with de Valera's use of internment, with British oppression in Nyasaland and Aden, and with South Africa's treatment of its blacks. We were rebuked for calling Northern Ireland 'British soil', and some of our critics were in turn rebuked for trying to force the North into a backward country dominated by an authoritarian Church.

Unfortunately internment did not bring the reduction of burning, bombing, and shooting that had been hoped. Through the autumn months the paper held steadily to its line, and I probably wrote as many leaders at that time as John. Reading them again nine years later, I find them thoughtfully argued and persuasive – but the proof of that pudding was that neither the Unionists nor the SDLP would eat it. Brian Faulkner in office had proved himself a reformer, carrying out his promises on housing, local government, and the police; but to bring Catholics into the Government was too much, even if they had been willing. Gerry Fitt and John Hume were good and courageous men, ready to stand up against Bernadette Devlin and others shouting the odds against them and to take the risk of being shot in the back; but they maintained their boycott of Stormont, and Catholic attitudes were generally as unyielding as Protestant. In the paper we supported their demands for inquiries into instances of brutal treatment of prisoners, mental cruelty in interrogation, and violence during search operations; but the modification of police and Army methods did not remove the bitterness. Internment came up again and again as an insuperable obstacle to political progress, preventing any constructive discussion either with the SDLP in the North or with the Dublin Government.

The casualty rate climbed, civilian and military. November was as destructive a month as any since 1969, and December brought big bomb explosions and fires in central Belfast and Londonderry. The Irish Government decided to take the issue of internment to the European Court of Human Rights. Although Army briefings suggested that the security situation was coming under control, there was no physical evidence of this.

In January I decided that the paper's policy must change. It was no use sticking to a course that was bringing no improvement. So far we had accepted internment, because of the impossibility of getting evidence in open court against the ringleaders, and we had rejected direct rule on the ground that it would bring no lasting benefit. About the 18th or 19th I started to draft a long leader, shifting the paper's approach and trying to find a new way towards a peaceful settlement. I gave a copy to John and discussed it with him; he did not like it at all. He believed that there ought to be no relaxation of pressure on the IRA and no suggestion of any weakening in British resolve. Harford and Mark also saw it.

John and I gave lunch to Willie Whitelaw on the 25th, but Ireland was not extensively discussed. Whitelaw was then Lord President, and most of the talk was of Rhodesia, the Pearce mission, unemployment, and, most important, the European Communities Bill. Whitelaw said, however, that the Government could not contemplate a situation in which, say, by 1974 the level of violence and the involvement of the security forces remained as high as they were today. He thought it would be a serious mark against the Government if by the next election the Irish situation was not visibly better. John took that as meaning that unless the situation improved the Conservatives might begin to think of pulling out; I doubted whether anything so drastic was implied, but I was reinforced in my judgement that the paper's policy must change. Towards the end of the week, I told John that the long leader would appear in Monday's paper; and after making some small amendments for which he asked I had the leader put into type on Friday evening, January 28.

Thus when I went to work on Sunday afternoon, the 30th, there was already in type a long leader for use that night. It said that for the British it was no solution to get out of Ulster and leave the place to bloody civil war. Nor was it a solution to say 'release the internees', for that led back only to more fighting in the streets and more bombing. The problem was not resolved by saying that the Ulster Opposition must talk to the Ulster

Government, because 'they just won't'. Nor could it be resolved by saying that Stormont was the elected Government and Stormont must decide. Any solution, the leader said, must include three elements: security, a timetable for talks and ending internment, and a programme of economic aid.

Security was primarily a matter for the Army – trying to keep the two communities from each other's throats, and trying to prevent intimidation. The leader's main contribution was a timet.. ble, linking the rundown of internment with stages of political agreement and improved security. Its central passage said this:

Why should not the Westminster and Stormont Governments make an explicit offer, tied to the progress of the talks and the ending of violence? They could say that a proportion (say one third) of the internees will be released as a gesture of good faith as soon as the talks begin. They could say that a further third will be released after three months free of violence. That would leave the final batch – the hardest core – to be released only after all-round agreement in the talks.

The leader went on to acknowledge many objections to this course, but to counter them. People would say that internment was immoral and ought to be ended anyway. Internment was hateful, but the IRA excesses had preceded it. The gunners and bomb men could not be brought to trial as they might be in England, 'because every witness, juror, and magistrate knows that he personally may be the target for reprisals'. Objections would come also from Unionists, exasperated to the limit by the daily violence and disruption, on the ground that internment could not safely be scaled down. But some gesture was needed to get the talks going, and the Catholic Opposition, aggravated by years of being denied parity of civil rights, had made the ending of internment a symbol. Also, if the talks failed or the release of internees led to worse violence, then the full rearming of the RUC must be a possibility, and if the Republican Government then left the IRA its safe retreat across the border something might have to be borrowed from Israeli techniques.

The question, I wrote, was how to reach a settlement. The risks and consequences of a further IRA offensive had to be faced. The IRA would not voluntarily accept a settlement short of full Irish unity; the Ulster Unionists and a majority of Northern Ireland's people were totally opposed to full union. A settlement must therefore fall short of full reunion but contain security against further IRA activity.

It will be extremely difficult. It can be done only if the Ulster Opposition is somehow convinced that it is going to have an adequate stake in the future government of Northern Ireland. Thoughts of a 'Protestant Parliament for a Protestant people' must be buried for ever. Stormont, in whatever form it survives, must be seen to represent and be responsive to both communities.

But is . . . reunion ruled out? The answer must surely be an open acknowledgment that reunion can come only when the majority in the North votes for it. At this stage, the Unionists ought to recognise that Irish unity can be accepted as an aspiration and legitimate aim for Irishmen. The Republicans, equally, ought to acknowledge that reunion cannot be brought about by force. To try to coerce Northern Ireland into union is to repeat and magnify the errors and injustices of the past fifty years.

The leader went on to suggest as constitutional possibilities a system of proportional representation, a committee system in government with guaranteed places for each community, and an all-Irish council. It said that Irishmen deserved 'a future that breaks away from the hatreds and miseries of the past'.

That was the leader already written and in type. In the late afternoon reports began to come in from Londonderry of shooting at a demonstration there. Just before the main news conference Simon Winchester telephoned from Derry to say that the Army had fired on some of the demonstrators and some were dead. He had been fired on himself while sheltering in a church doorway. He would be sending a long report in an hour or so, when he had checked on casualties. There was no doubt about the page one lead that night.

The headline next morning was '13 killed as paratroops break riot'. Simon's story, from Londonderry, began:

> The tragic and inevitable Doomsday situation which has been universally forecast for Northern Ireland arrived in Londonderry yesterday afternoon when soldiers, firing into a crowd of civil rights demonstrators, shot and killed 13 civilians.
>
> Fifteen more people, including a woman, were wounded by gunfire and another woman was seriously injured after being knocked down by an armoured car. . . .
>
> After the shooting, which lasted for about 25 minutes in and around the Rossville Flats area of Bogside, the streets had all the appearance of the aftermath of Sharpeville. Where only moments before thousands of men and women had been milling around, drifting slowly towards a protest meeting to be held at Free Derry Corner, there was a handful of bleeding bodies, some lying still, others still moving with pain, on the white concrete of the square.

Simon next quoted the Army's official explanation – that troops had fired in response to snipers who had opened up on them from below the flats. 'But those of us at the meeting', he wrote, 'heard only one shot before the soldiers opened up with their high velocity rifles.' While it was impossible to be sure, his impression, reinforced by dozens of eyewitnesses, was that men of the 1st Parachute Regiment, flown in specially from Belfast, 'may have fired needlessly into the huge crowd'.

The Army statement, issued at 7.30 pm, said that after an hour of heavy stoning the paratroops were moved from behind the units manning barricades. They had been sent to arrest people in the crowd and had chased and caught several men who were running away. While this was taking place, gunmen had opened up from rubble at the base of the flats and their fire had been returned. Simon's report went on to give a more detailed account of the casualties and the arrests.

His message then gave a chronological sequence. After a three-mile march, with the biggest numbers ever seen in Derry, parts of the crowd were passing barricades erected to prevent them reaching the central area. Men of the 2nd Royal Greenjackets endured a full ten minutes of heavy stoning before opening up with CS gas and shots from a heavy water cannon, 'drenching hundreds of marchers and journalists in purple, indelible dye'. There were fierce tussles at the barricades; huge quantities of CS gas and hundreds of rubber bullets were fired, and many rioters injured. At 4.05 a single shot was heard, fired 'presumably by an IRA man', but not much notice was taken. Some people in the crowd began pushing marchers out of the way at an entry to the flats 'in which, it was presumed, another sniper was lurking'.

Just before 4.15 one of the civil rights organisers went through the crowd with a megaphone, saying that the meeting was starting at Free Derry Corner. Then four or five armoured cars appeared and raced into Rossville Street square, and several thousand people began to run away.

The move had been expected and it is a tactic we have all seen before – nothing, not even gas, breaks up a crowd more effectively than several huge armoured cars careering through the streets. But it was then that the situation changed tragically. Paratroops piled out of their vehicles, many ran forward to make arrests, but others rushed to the street corners. It was these men, perhaps 20 in all, who opened fire with their rifles. I saw three men fall to the ground. One was still obviously alive, with blood pumping from his leg. The others, both apparently in their teens, seemed dead.

The meeting at Free Derry Corner broke up in hysteria as thousands of people either ran or dived for the ground. Army snipers could be seen firing continuously towards the central Bogside streets and at one stage a lone army sniper on a street corner fired two shots towards me as I peered around a corner. One shot chipped a large chunk of masonry from a wall behind me.

The report describes gunfire directed at people with their hands above their heads or carrying white handkerchiefs. 'There was certainly some firing from the IRA,' Simon said. He heard one sub-machine gun open up from inside the flats and intermittent small-calibre weapons. 'But the sound which predominated was the heavy, hard banging of British SLRs, and this continued for about ten or fifteen minutes until about 4.30.'

Later, after sheltering in a Roman Catholic church with two other reporters, he went round a corner and met a civilian armed with a 0.22 rifle, who fired at them. 'He may have been a short-sighted IRA man, but whoever he was he was firing from a Protestant part of the city.' Simon saw seven cars being driven away with bleeding bodies on the back seats, inert and lifeless. 'By 5.30 it was all over. A full moon was rising over a shocked and still numbed Londonderry, and heavily armed soldiers were still keeping Bogside and the Creggan cordoned off.'

In neighbouring columns there were reports of reactions in Dublin, at Stormont, and in London. These grew as the night went on. The television news pictures were having a strong effect – especially those of a priest seeking safe conduct for a dying boy and of dead men on the pavements. Having re-read Simon's despatch after the television bulletins, however, I felt that he gave a clearer and more comprehensive account. To the long leader I gave a new beginning and added a new end, retaining all that I had written in the middle. Its timing was tragically apt.

While I was at breakfast in the morning the Home Office telephoned. Could I come in to see the Home Secretary? I went almost immediately. Reggie Maudling wanted to know whether there was more behind the leader – had we discussed the rundown of internment with anyone on the Republican side, and were we confident that something of the kind could work? I had to say that the initiative was our own, from within the *Guardian* office, and that unfortunately it was impossible to be confident that any particular course would succeed. But, even after yesterday's events in Derry, it still seemed to me to offer the best hope. He was extremely interested in the idea of progressive reductions of internment as a device to generate a better atmosphere.

The revulsion over the Bogside shootings was extreme, both in Dublin and in the Catholic North. Even John Hume, the sanest of the Ulster Opposition leaders, said that now it must be 'united Ireland or nothing'. In a leader that night – I had to write the first leader every night that week, always on Ireland – I asked whether John Hume had reckoned what 'nothing' really meant. It could only imply no talks, a prolonging of the crisis, further bloody confrontations, or conceivably a British withdrawal. The sequel to a British withdrawal was not pleasing to contemplate, I wrote: immediate burning of the Falls Road, most probably, to destroy any secure areas for the IRA in Belfast. It was neither a formula for peace nor would it lead to unity. The Catholic Opposition must be brought into talks soon, the leader said, and to achieve that they must be assured that internment would end soon, that Irish unity was not ruled out for ever, and that they would have an assured role in Ulster's government. Equally, the Protestants must be assured that nobody would try to force them into a united Ireland.

Conor Cruise O'Brien was in London. He had been a member of the Dail for the past three years and became Minister of Posts after the following year's election. He suggested that the British Government ought not to withdraw its troops now, as Lynch's Government in Dublin was demanding in its anger, but ought to set a date for eventual withdrawal. He thought that in reality Lynch's Cabinet would be scared stiff if Heath's Government showed any sign of pulling out at present, because they knew how bloody the action would be in the North and they knew that the Protestant forces would gain control of Belfast and much of the

North. I was attracted by his suggestion of setting a date, but John Cole shot it down on practical grounds.[6]

For the next Monday, a week after Bloody Sunday, I wrote another long leader setting out the various courses available to Britain. It was meant to be a neutral statement, though if possible of assistance towards negotiations. It is too long to quote here, but let me summarise the thorny alternatives:

1. Support Stormont and promote reform. This had been Labour's policy and the Conservatives'; and Mr Faulkner had done much to promote reform. But because of the Catholics' total distrust of Stormont, it must mean a prolonged military commitment in Northern Ireland. The momentum of events was working against this policy. It was bound to be costly, dangerous, and slow. Whether any alternative could be less costly, dangerous, or inadequate was open to question.

2. Cede the solidly Catholic areas. If Londonderry, Strabane, and the Newry district were ceded to the Republic, the worst security problems would be relieved. But it could only be seen by the IRA and in Dublin as the first stage in dismantling the whole of Northern Ireland – and many Unionists would see it the same way. As a permanent solution it could not survive, not even if everything west of the river Bann and Lough Neagh were ceded.

3. Nine-county Ulster. This was attractive at first sight, providing a better balance between Catholics and Protestants. It could be governed by a condominium of Great Britain and the Irish Republic. But again even if the Republic were to agree they could see it only as an interim solution, and again the Unionists would certainly not agree. It must be assumed that if the British Government started discussing it, the Unionists would fight.

4. United Ireland. By agreement, it was perhaps the ideal solution. But in this generation at least, the Northern majority would never agree to it. Nor could any British Government ever be expected to use force to bring it about.

5. Population transfer. This implied not only redrawing the border but making possible a movement northwards or southwards by anyone who wanted to move. But neither side was ready for such a proposal; the Catholics in Belfast would not leave voluntarily; and it was a prescription for perpetual hostility between two sectarian states.

6 Conor Cruise O'Brien, in his book *States of Ireland* (pp. 283–84), says that in his initial reaction to Bloody Sunday he 'over reacted' – to an extent disregarding the effect that a British announcement of a withdrawal date would have on the Protestant community, because he was responding to the mood of the Catholic community. The effect of setting a date, he says, 'might well be at least as dangerous as the feelings of the Catholic community about the continued presence of the troops'. The danger in the Catholic reaction, as he saw it, was that the actual presence of the British troops became 'a standing justification for the IRA, strengthening their hold on the ghettoes'.

6. *Shock treatment*. Let the British Government declare that its troops will be withdrawn by a given date, leaving Dublin and the Unionists six, twelve, or eighteen months in which to agree. But probably they would not agree, and civil war would then be inevitable. The British Government would be bitterly blamed, and the fighting might spill over into Clydeside and Merseyside.

John Cole responded next day with a signed article headed 'Will Ulster fight?' On the whole he discounted the risks of civil war – unless the Protestants came to believe that the British Army might be withdrawn, leaving them with no protection against the IRA. On the issue of exclusion from the United Kingdom and forcible inclusion in the Republic, he said, 'Protestants remain cohesive'. But he did not believe that a deal with the Catholics, giving them a fair deal at Stormont, would bring extensive Protestant violence. He also said that many moderate Ulstermen took literally the phrase 'full British citizenship'. Nothing would please them better than to live under the West Riding or Ayrshire county council without having to leave their homes and jobs. Weary of the mud thrown at them in the past three years, such people might peacefully accept the removal of Stormont provided it brought peace and was not a half-way house to losing their British link.

In mid-February there were strong indications that a British initiative was imminent, but it did not come for another month. The European Communities Bill had just gone before the Commons, where defeat would have meant a general election; the Maltese negotiations were at a delicate stage, and there were Rhodesian problems as well. On top of all that, the Prime Minister was having one of his confrontations with the miners, and electricity was rationed from February 10 to 18.

Maudling in his memoirs records that in February he put before the Cabinet a five-point memorandum:

1. Transfer law and order to Westminster.
2. A referendum on the border, to be repeated at intervals of fifteen years.
3. Minority representation in the Stormont Government, as in Parliament.
4. A Secretary of State for Northern Ireland, advised by a Northern Ireland Commission.
5. Progressive reduction of the numbers interned, until all internment was abolished.

He also records that Brian Faulkner, on hearing of these proposals, said that he was 'not prepared to be chairman of a county council'.[7]

Three weeks after Bloody Sunday, the IRA left a bomb outside the officers' mess at the Paras' barracks in Aldershot, killing seven people – five of them domestic kitchen staff, one a gardner, and one an RC padre. The 'officials', not the Provisionals, claimed to have left the bomb. In Ulster itself the violence continued.

7 Reginald Maudling, *Memoirs*, p. 187.

Ian Aitken reported at the beginning of March that the Government was about to ban the use of 'intensive interrogation' methods on internees, such as the black hoods and noise machines used to disorientate them. That ban came two days later. He also reported that the Government was now proposing a package of political reforms, among them periodic referenda on the unification of Ireland and some form of community government. But as the days passed no announcement came. Harold Wilson told me privately, having been himself in discussion with Ministers, that Heath had been outvoted in his own Cabinet. He had made the mistake of not including the Lord Chancellor, Hailsham, in the committee considering the proposals. Now he was having to water them down. That was giving Faulkner an advantage, since he could prepare his opposition. In leaders in the paper, without any reference to possible disagreements in the Cabinet, we said more than once a week that the sooner the Government got on with its new action in Ireland the better.

On March 22 Brian Faulkner came to Downing Street for the day, with his Deputy Prime Minister and his Cabinet Secretary. Both Ian Aitken and Simon Winchester reported a lack of harmony between Westminster and Stormont. Ian said that the British proposals included the phasing out of internment and British control over law and order. Both he and Simon said that the Stormont Ministers had no intention of yielding to the demands being made by Mr Heath, preferring wholesale resignation to acceptance.[8]

So it turned out. On the morning of Friday, March 24, the Prime Minister told the Commons about the rejection of his proposals by the Stormont Government, who had all resigned, and announced that the UK Government intended to seek powers of direct rule over the province. Mr Whitelaw was to become Secretary of State for Northern Ireland. Three proposals had been put to Mr Faulkner: periodic plebiscites on the border issue, to take it out of the day-to-day political scene; 'a start on phasing out internment'; and transfer of responsibility for law and order from Belfast to London. (Security was already controlled from London, but the boundary between security and law and order was sometimes hazy.) The third was the point on which no agreement could be reached. The Prime Minister renewed the assurance that British forces would stay in Northern Ireland as long as any faction was trying to terrorise or intimidate ordinary people.

8 Simon Winchester, in a letter to me in March 1981, says that only once during his time in Northern Ireland did I exercise a 'veto' over something he had written. That was shortly before Faulkner's visit to Downing Street. He wrote that the talks were bound to collapse: I argued that such a report, on the *Guardian*'s front page, could prevent the talks from ever taking place. At the time, Simon thought my judgement mistaken. On the morning of the Downing Street talks, his front-page report did in fact indicate that there was next to no chance of success.

It was some satisfaction to me that the phasing out of internment stood prominently in the Government's package. In practice Whitelaw moved faster than the Government had proposed – releasing more than one-third of the detainees or internees within two months of taking up his new office (377 out of 929) and nearly two-thirds by early July, so that only about 350 were still detained.[9] But the decision on individual cases was at the heart of the dispute with Brian Faulkner, because until direct rule the Stormont Government had the last word on arrests and releases. Part of Faulkner's case against Heath was that Stormont had offered 'joint decision' but Heath had rejected it. The Prime Minister told the Commons that the UK Government knew 'law and order' was a divisive issue in Northern Ireland and wished to take it out of Ulster's domestic politics. Control over police interrogation also came within 'law and order', though the Army also had its own interrogation centres. More generally, Faulkner said that the removal of law and order made Stormont 'a charade' in which he would have no part, and that the IRA would see it as 'a major step on the road to a terrorist victory'.

The Army was not too happy either, as David Fairhall reported the day after the announcement. Having taken much trouble to find and arrest the internees, it had reservations about seeing them freed to resume violent activity. But on the whole, David said, the Army was taking the change of policy in its stride – it had been expected for some time. The Army also knew that its previously friendly relations with most of the Protestant population were now in jeopardy. It was not until July, however, that any serious conflict with Protestant para-militaries came.

Craig's Vanguard movement called for a two-day general strike on the Monday and Tuesday after Heath's announcement, and that was widely observed, paralysing most transport and business on those days. The Northern Command of the Provisional IRA – the men in charge in Ulster – called for a month's cease-fire by the Provos: but that lasted only four days, until the Derry brigade decided to resume activity and others followed. Until July, however, the bombing and shooting were less frequent.

Simon Winchester attended Stormont's farewell session on March 29, which included Protestant denunciation of the UK Government. The leader of the Unionist backbenchers referred to 'Gauleiter Whitelaw'; and Brian Faulkner forbade any cooperation with Whitelaw's advisory committee – though in May seven reputable Protestants and four Catholics accepted membership.

Simon was called as a witness before the tribunal of inquiry into the events on Bloody Sunday – under the Lord Chief Justice, Lord Widgery – and was commended for the clarity of his evidence. Widgery's report found that there would have been no deaths if there had been no illegal

9 More than a hundred of those released in 1972 were detained again in 1973 or 1974.

march, nor if the Army had persisted in a 'low key' attitude instead of launching a large-scale operation to arrest hooligans.[10]

Of Maudling's five proposals, the Government had put four into effect. The fifth, minority representation in the Northern Ireland Government, had been overtaken by the suspension of Stormont but was to feature in future political negotiations. Power-sharing had been John Cole's idea, first explicitly put forward on August 16, 1971, immediately after the deployment of British troops in Londonderry and Belfast; the progressive phasing out of internment was mine, put forward the morning after Bloody Sunday. That phasing out was at the centre of the UK Government's new policy. Probably something like it would have been there anyway, but I should like to think that the *Guardian* contributed to bringing it about.

One nagging regret was that the release of internees was in the chain of causes leading to the sergeant's death in Andersonstown in June – and to the deaths of many others. Another is that in the next nine years, up to the date at which I am writing, the political negotiations led nowhere.

The Protestant wreckers

The Whitelaw initiative moved slowly forward – too slowly, we thought at first – but it nearly succeeded. Protestant barricades appeared in May and June, creating symbolic 'no-go' areas in Belfast to match the Republican 'no-go' areas in Derry. Army units handled a series of potentially dangerous situations in Protestant areas with quiet patience. The Provisionals called a truce at the end of June, to help negotiation, but it lasted barely two weeks – and was followed by Belfast's worst violence since the start of the crisis. In Derry at the end of July the Army used Centurion tanks to destroy the Provo barricades, ending the 'no-go' areas, and there was virtually no resistance.

Over the next year, while violence continued from both sides, Whitelaw negotiated. He had full backing from Harold Wilson and most of the Labour Opposition, and incidentally the *Guardian*'s fullest editorial support. At a conference near Darlington in September, agreement was reached on creation of an Assembly to prepare for a power-sharing Executive and a new Stormont Parliament – though the SDLP boycotted the conference because internment had not been ended, and Ian Paisley also stayed away. The first referendum was held in March 1973, but again boycotted by the SDLP. The voting was 57.4 per cent of the total electorate in favour of remaining part of the UK, and 0.63 per cent against; 31.9 per cent spoiled their papers or did not vote. In June elections were held for the Assembly: Faulkner's Unionists won 22 seats,

10 Lord Widgery's report published April 19, 1972. Simon Winchester noted that the Defence Ministry took care to brief defence correspondents before publication, telling them that the report 'cleared the army'. He was refused permission to attend the briefing.

other Unionists 13, Paisley's 'Democratic Unionists' 8, Craig's Vanguard 7, the SDLP 19, the Alliance Party 8, and NI Labour 1; 72 per cent of the electorate voted, in spite of a Provo boycott.

In October the Executive-Designate came into being, with Brian Faulkner at its head and Gerry Fitt (SDLP) as his deputy. No less notable, at a Sunningdale conference in December agreement was reached with the Dublin Government on creation of a Council of Ireland, with harmonising and consultative functions. The Sunningdale meeting was attended by the whole Executive-Designate, as well as the Prime Ministers and others from the UK and Irish Republican Governments. Although Whitelaw handed over to Francis Pym a few days before the conference, the agreement there represented the high point of Whitelaw's efforts.

But the Sunningdale agreement was soon torn down. Indeed the front-page headline on Simon Hoggart's report was 'A bargain – but Faulkner must sell it', and in the same issue from Belfast Derek Brown said that Faulkner must now face a Loyalist revolt. At the beginning of January (1974), while Heath was in confrontation with the miners, the Ulster Unionist Council rejected the agreement. Brian Faulkner resigned his party leadership, but for five more months tried to keep the Executive alive. At the end of January many of the Protestants withdrew from the Assembly, effectively killing it although it was not prorogued until the summer. The final blow came in May, when the Ulster Workers' Council called a general strike. This time it cut off most of the province's electricity and petrol supplies, and the paralysis was nearly complete. Overtly the UWC was protesting against the Sunningdale agreement, though in reality it was also against power sharing. When the strike was in its second week Harold Wilson, Prime Minister again, refused a request from Brian Faulkner to negotiate directly with the UWC. Faulkner then resigned, saying it was the saddest day of his life; Ian Paisley declared that it was a great victory. Direct rule, which had ended on January 1, returned on May 29. (Brian Faulkner tragically was killed in a riding accident in 1977.) Power-sharing was eclipsed.

The UWC victory caused some political confusion at Westminster. Some Labour MPs wanted Wilson to pull the British troops out. Others, including some well to the left, now wanted tanks used against the Protestants – having apparently learned nothing from the past five years. Wilson had no working majority in the Commons anyway and was not inclined towards any drastic course. John Cole wrote a bitter signed article, saying that the situation was right back to 1968. He acknowledged that a British withdrawal was now one of three or more possible sequels, and that if it happened either there would be a limited form of civil war or the Catholics might persuade the IRA to refrain from further aggressive action. His message was still that we ought to be patient. I wrote three leaders in that week, too, all saying that power-sharing was the only way

ONE CHURCH

to rebuild a civilised life in Ireland. But for the next year or two at least, it seemed to have disappeared beyond sight.

Back in the previous June, when I feared that Whitelaw's initiative was developing too slowly, I had spent three days in Northern Ireland and two in Dublin. Some conversations then were still relevant to policy after the breakdown. In Dublin it had been hard to find much official readiness to make union with the South attractive to the North. Censorship of books and publications, lack of a divorce law, the illegality of contraception, the primacy of the Roman Catholic Church entrenched in the Constitution: Irish society had to become more liberal before Northern Protestants could be expected to contemplate Irish unity. When I put this to Jack Lynch, then the Prime Minister, I received only what seemed weak excuses in reply. He questioned whether there was any social need for a divorce law and said the Northern Protestants were not asking for it. On contraception he said the law only prohibited the importing and sale of contraceptives, leaving doctors free to prescribe medical remedies if they wished. By June 1973 Lynch had been replaced as Taoiseach by Liam Cosgrave (after the February election) and the new Coalition Government was supposed to be more liberal. As yet, however, there was no evident movement towards constitutional and social change. A new climate in Ireland was not being fostered from the South.

Nor could peace and harmony come easily throughout the North. In Derry I had spent a congenial afternoon with John Hume, and he had taken me for a walk through the 'no-go' areas of Bogside and the Creggan. He wanted to show how peaceful they were, and how, since the Whitelaw initiative, people had started clearing the place up and painting their houses – a sign of hope. But around 4 pm as we walked downhill past the sandbags and barbed wire of the Bligh's Lane army post, a number of quite well-dressed secondary schoolboys were coming up the hill on their way home. Nearly all, as they passed the army post, picked up stones and hurled them over the double barbed wire to bang on the corrugated iron of the lookouts. John Hume said that that was really nothing, after all the explosions and shooting. True; but what an indication of the schoolboys' ingrained habits.

The most relevant conversation, however, was at Lisburn with the GOC, Sir Harry Tuzo. He said at that time that the UDA and other Protestants were ready to arm themselves quickly. It was disconcerting, he said, to go round the corner in a quiet Protestant district and meet men being drilled. He knew the arms existed and were a serious threat. The UDA differed from the IRA in that most of its members had jobs and therefore tended to be active only at weekends. But if events set them on a violent course, many UDA members would be given three or four weeks' paid leave by their employers.

The GOC had privately suggested some methods by which the Army could give Catholics – or Protestants – a 'slow handclap', by putting tight cordons round some areas of known activity. The object would be to remind them of the reasons why internment was being run down, of the requirement that violence must diminish, and of the urgency of political negotiation. Some of his ideas I had incorporated in leaders at the time, though without attribution. They were designed to strengthen Whitelaw's initiative and to force the pace towards a settlement, for General Tuzo believed that it had to come quickly or would fail. They came back to mind now, with the breakdown, though in the context of what the Army might soon have to handle. He had said then that his units had plenty of reserve available and could, for example, alter the situation in Bogside or the Creggan at any time – as they had successfully proved a month after our conversation. He said then that these were matters for political decision.

Thinking about the situation after the UWC strike, I knew that the choice must have lasting implications – keeping the troops in Northern Ireland for years ahead with a fairly low profile, or a tougher policy of military pressure on both sides, or pulling out and leaving the Irish to settle their own fate. The first course, staying with a low profile, was the easiest and most likely. A tougher military policy, on Israeli lines, would require greater resolution than any British Government was likely to show. The protests in Parliament and the press were likely to be too much for Wilson or Heath, and after Bloody Sunday any such course was psychologically unacceptable. And withdrawal? After years of trying to resolve the Northern Irish question, and after all the promises of the past, it appeared a betrayal of those many Protestants and Catholics who only wanted to live a peaceful life. Perhaps it might prove the shortest route to a settlement, but it was bound to be a terrifying gamble.

Simon Hoggart, in a valedictory article after living two years in Northern Ireland, had written that probably there was no solution. 'It could be,' he said, 'that like a misprinted newspaper puzzle the answer can never be found.' Harry Jackson at times seemed to share that pessimism. To abandon hope was against my own instinctive belief that, in the end, human solutions can always be found. But in Northern Ireland there may be no solution in this century.

13 Lib-Lab, Con-Lib-Lab, and Gnu

The approach to coalition or consensus politics evolved only gradually. Wadsworth had inherited a Liberal tradition with a friendly leaning towards Labour, and, because of the changing character of Parliament and public opinion, he developed the *MG*'s support for Labour while still encouraging the Liberals. In the 1951 election he nevertheless gave a reserved endorsement to the Conservatives, because of the Attlee Government's exhaustion, and in 1955 said that Labour was not yet ready to return to office. As recounted in Chapter 4, in 1959 I had no hesitation in advocating the return of Labour, under Gaitskell's leadership, though looking also for more Liberals in the Commons. In 1964 the *Guardian* worked for a Labour victory, after thirteen years of Conservative government, but wanted 'a solid block' of Liberals in the House.

Wilson's majority was three, dwindling to two in the summer of 1965 and then to one. In that period the *Guardian* tried hard to foster a working relationship between Labour and the Liberals. We did not propose any formal coalition but only an understanding on the main points of policy, where the two parties had much in common. Jo Grimond was willing, in spite of opposition in the Liberal ranks, and much of the initiative was his. Harold Wilson was ambivalent, playing for time until he could fight another election but trying not to alienate the Liberals in the Commons. In the *Guardian* we wanted a working relationship that would last beyond the next election – because I believed that if Labour's action was tempered by the Liberals it would avoid excesses in public ownership and social policy, and so reduce the risk that the Conservatives would swing too far the other way; and I believed that working together would improve Labour's prospects of staying in office. Although the *Guardian* succeeded in mellowing a few Labour Ministers by its line, and although personally I was instrumental in bringing Wilson and Grimond into private discussion in the summer of 1965, Wilson preferred to keep a free hand for Labour.

Thoughts of partnership grew again in 1973–74, though in a worse climate. Eventually Edward Heath became the advocate of a 'Government of National Unity', but at first on terms that others were unlikely to swallow. During both the 1974 elections a majority of the *Guardian*'s senior staff preferred straight support for Labour, in spite of disillusion with its performance in office; but a minority wanted again to foster Lib-Lab or Con-Lib-Lab agreement on the essentials of economic and social policy, and since I was one of the minority that was the line the paper took. My reasons will come later in this chapter – and I still believe that Britain could not and cannot afford to let its policy pendulum swing so far with changes of government. No other West European or Scandinavian country changes course so suddenly or sharply as Britain, and every other West European and Scandinavian country has lived successfully with coalition or consensus government. One-party rule has done mortal damage to Britain in the past twenty years.

The 'parallel lines' of 1964-66

In August 1965, buffeted by a half gale, I walked a fast nine miles along Orkney's Atlantic cliffs with Jo Grimond. Scenically it was spectacular and politically it was fascinating. We did it again next day, though this time on a circuit of one of Orkney's smaller islands. Jo and Laura also insisted on swimming after each walk, and I went in with slightly less enthusiasm; but that was not half as bad as a year or two later, on an autumn visit, when we again took to icy Atlantic water at Skaill Bay.

Jo had seen Harold, with no publicity, at the beginning of the month. That was partly the result of a considered campaign in the *Guardian* throughout the early summer for *rapprochement* between the two parties, which had helped to prepare the ground; and the actual meeting came about because I had persisted in private conversation with the Prime Minister in saying that the Government ought to be on closer terms with the Liberals. Eventually, a day or two after a conversation in late July and another leader, he sent a verbal message saying that he would talk to Jo before the recess; and I had gone to Orkney afterwards to try to find out what had come of it.

As we battled with the westerly wind, Jo said that the meeting had been interesting and friendly but had not achieved anything specific. He had not expected it to achieve much, for it was only a beginning, but he was doubtful whether Wilson seriously intended to follow it up. The discussion had been mainly about the economic situation, on which Wilson had said optimistically that by the winter Labour would be over the worst of its difficulties, which Jo thought improbable. They had discussed legislation for the coming session, but only in general terms, and Wilson had endeavoured to show that it would be acceptable to the Liberals. He had said that any of the Liberals would be welcome to talk to the Ministers concerned at any time, but, Jo said, 'We can do that anyway.' It was not consultation as Jo understood the term, and it did not look like being followed up.

He did not see how Wilson could avoid an election some time this autumn or winter, and it was now almost too late for a short-term agreement with the Government. Real consultation on coming legislation was essential. He would agree to keep the Government alive with the Liberals' ten votes only if satisfied that it was a genuinely reforming Government – that it was intent on securing industrial efficiency in spite of trade union conservatism; that it was going to stimulate competition, for example by abolishing the tariff on motor vehicles; and that Wilson

July 1966

had the courage to reconstruct his Cabinet (Callaghan being an instance of a good man in the wrong job, when Crosland or Jenkins ought to be at the Treasury). Though unimpressed by the Government's perform-ance, Jo thought it better than the Tory alternative, and if the Tories were to get back they could be in for another fifteen years. He mentioned a number of other specific objectives, such as stirring up the City of London which was supposed to be a citadel of free enterprise but was riddled with restrictive practices.

All this was in line with an interview which Jo Grimond had given to the *Guardian* in mid-June, which had been published as the front-page lead. There he had said the Liberals would consider joining a coalition in return for 'a serious agreement on long-term policies'. In that interview he had included electoral reform among his requirements. In a leader next day, while welcoming Grimond's initiative, we said that he was inconsistent in criticising Labour's extensive tax reforms and at the same time demanding electoral reform. Desirable though electoral reform was, it could not be among the 'top priorities' on which there had to be agreement. In August Grimond no longer included electoral reform among the immediate requirements; and the 'alternative vote' was now on the agenda of a Speaker's Committee anyway, with Wilson's concurrence.

The June interview had brought the *Guardian* more than one hundred letters in three days. Many were from Liberals saying that there must be no surrender of Liberal sovereignty, though some supported the Grimond view and favoured formation of a radical, non-socialist party of the left. Harold Wilson, in a private talk the week after the interview, said that the correspondence showed that Jo could not carry his party with him. Jo on the other hand was well pleased, because the massive mail he was receiving was mainly on his side and he was glad that the discussion had been opened out. In a further leader, 'Steering parallel courses', we said that while Wilson's determination to carry on was bold, parliamentary arithmetic and mortal frailty were likely to stop him unless he came to terms with the Liberals; and on their side the Liberals had fought the last election to achieve many of the things the Government was trying to bring about. On the most urgent issues the courses of the two parties, plotted in their election manifestos, ran parallel. Therefore, the leader said, they ought to work together.

That produced a lot more letters, many in support but some from Liberals who felt that they were being betrayed. Beyond doubt, though, the tide among those who wrote was now on our side; and I was encouraged also when Douglas Jay, a senior member of the Cabinet, told me that he was in favour of reconciliation in spite of the 'religious' obstacles on each side.

Conscious of the sensitivity among older Liberals, after the Orkney visit I had some fun reprinting as a 'historical footnote' to the controversy a series of extracts from the writing of C. P. Scott – beginning with a long leader of July 1912 which started: 'As a result of three-cornered contests it is quite possible that while Liberalism and Labour are snapping and snarling at each other the Conservative dog may run away with the bone.' C.P. had no doubt that 'the very life and temper of the only Liberalism worthy of the name' meant that in Labour 'they have here not possible enemies but real and trustworthy friends'. The Tories might shriek confiscation and parade the Socialist bogy, he said, but the working men of England were not Socialists in any revolutionary sense. A range of further quotations from 1921, 1924, 1926, and 1929 were apposite to the current situation, including one of the last leaders that C.P. had written for the paper which concluded: 'The time may not be very distant when real political affinities assert themselves and a great middle party may be formed out of the existing progressive forces of the country.'

On the opening day of the Liberal Assembly in late September, the paper carried an article by Mrs Shirley Williams, then Labour MP for Hitchin, which was both friendly and critical. The Government, she said, was producing many of the reforms that the Liberals said they wanted. First she put their demand for a Plan for Expansion and (a mildly Orwellian title, she said) a 'Ministry for Expansion': they had got the National Plan, published the previous week, as well as the DEA and

George Brown for good measure. They wanted an incomes policy relating incomes to productivity, a capital gains tax, a prices policy, and an attempt to end restrictive practices: to all of that the Government said Amen and had already done 'more than anyone thought possible.' Her list went through a series of other coinciding measures, ending with creation of the Highlands and Islands Development Board which, she said, might help to consolidate the Liberals in their Highland fortress.

It was a well-timed article, I felt (having commissioned it), and likely to help. Shirley Williams took up Jo's complaint of lack of a public response to his suggestions of a Lib-Lab agreement, saying that no party could put itself in the position of a rejected suitor. But the Government had to consider the risks of disaffection in its own ranks. 'The most we are likely to see in the new Parliament', she said, 'is a tacit and unarticulated consensus between the two radical parties to get the legislation that is of interest to both of them through the House.' She chided the Liberal party with not being sure what it wanted. Among the three million people who had voted Liberal at the last election were many who looked back to the days of Asquith and Lloyd George, and the Liberals could not 'deliver' their vote to a new radical alliance. There was no real Liberal identity, she concluded, though in the present parliamentary situation the Liberals had a new opportunity to find it.

At the Assembly in Scarborough, thanks to a forceful intervention by Jo Grimond at the start, there was little criticism of his proposal to seek a working partnership. Conservative and Labour philosophies came in for frequent condemnation, but the Liberals in Parliament were left with a free hand to decide their own course. In his closing speech Grimond derided the view that Mr Wilson could not come to terms with the Liberals lest he split his own party, saying that the Prime Minister must broaden his electoral appeal and that to antagonise the left wing would do him nothing but good. In a leader I supported Grimond's appeal for a 'broadly based progressive party' but said that tactically he was in an awkward position. The Government complacently believed that when it came to the point the Liberals would not destroy them. For Mr Grimond it must be a maddening situation. If he were to lean a little further away from them he could bring the Government down – at the cost of torpedoing what he himself was working for. But if he stood by them and kept them in office, he was likely to earn no thanks and no response.

At the start of the Labour conference in Blackpool the following week, the Prime Minister was barbed about the Liberals, thereby earning much applause, but not so barbed as to cause a breach. There had been no approach with a view to a pact, deal, or coalition, he said; and while Mr Grimond must show the fullest respect to those who had elected his ten members, Labour must show equal respect to the views of those who had elected their 300. (The disparity of votes compared with seats could hardly have been more marked: 300,000 to elect each Liberal, compared with 40,000 to elect each Labour MP.) He reminded the Liberals that in the Commons they had voted more often with the Conservatives than with Labour, and said in a ringing phrase that if effective government could not be carried on 'it will be an issue to be settled by the sovereign and independent decision of the British people'. In a broadcast that night, he said more circumspectly that he hoped Mr Grimond and his colleagues would continue to give the Government their support. On the national-isation of steel, the most contentious issue between the two parties, he said that there had been no decision yet on whether or not to proceed.

In practice steel nationalisation was shelved, and the Government managed to keep going through the winter, thanks partly to Liberal restraint. When Wilson called the election in March, the *Guardian* was caught in the very dilemma we had diagnosed for Grimond and the Liberals. Unanimously, the senior staff wanted Labour to have the op-portunity to carry on – but a fair number of us also wanted the Liberals reinforced and, if possible, in a position to keep Labour on a radical, non-socialist course. Leverage, however, was lacking. While we enjoyed de-flating extravagant claims from all the parties, including the Liberals, in the end we had to back Labour as our primary choice.

The main pre-election leader concluded by saying that there had been times in the past eighteen months when Mr Wilson seemed in danger of becoming the best Conservative Prime Minister in this century; but his social conscience had not been submerged, and given a five-year term he was likely to take us some way towards a more just and civilised Britain. And an eve-of-poll article by Peter Jenkins, while forecasting a clear Labour victory, said that Mr Heath's performance during the campaign could prove to have won him the next election – for the three weeks of electioneering had done as much to establish him as the 1959 campaign had done for Hugh Gaitskell.

The Labour party returned with an over-all majority of ninety-seven in the House of Commons. The Liberals had a net gain of two seats, though on a lower popular vote. Harold Wilson was comfortably in command, though the next great economic crisis was less than four months away. For the time being, Lib-Lab was a lost cause. There was no leverage and no interest in it among the triumphant Labour ranks. Jo Grimond, after ten years of herculean effort, handed over to Jeremy Thorpe; and the Liberal party began to drift slowly into the shadows. From time to time in the next three years the *Guardian* took a wistful look at the ideal of realignment on the non-Socialist left, but at that stage there was no longer any point in pursuing it actively.

Thorns, leeks, and thistles, 1967-73
U-turns were not invented by Ted Heath. Harold Wilson's 1966 Govern-ment practised them, and Wilson in Opposition after 1970 executed more. Stop-go was not eliminated, nor was collective bargaining left free; and

one of the biggest of all U-turns was Labour's on the Common Market. The Government's record on economic management between 1966 and 1970 (discussed in Chapter 9) sapped confidence in its competence, though by the time the 1970 election came Roy Jenkins's 'hard slog' was beginning to pay. Inevitably, however, the *Guardian* approached that election with severe reservations. John Cole, a steady Labour man in normal times, wrote a pre-election article on Labour's lost souls with a sorrowing reference to the negative nature of the choice ahead.

In the politics of Wales and Scotland there was a new element. The Nationalists were becoming a serious force. Gwynfor Evans had won Carmarthen for Plaid Cymru at a by-election in the summer of 1966, and another Plaid candidate came close to overturning a 16,900 Labour majority at Rhondda West in March 1967. In November 1967 Mrs Winnie Ewing won Hamilton for the Scottish National party, destroying a Labour majority of 16,500 in a vibrant campaign, and in Glasgow Gorbals in 1969 the Nationalist halved Labour's majority. In both countries the *Guardian* was served by reporters with sensitive political ears - Ann Clwyd* in Wales from 1966 and John Kerr* in Scotland from 1969, one being of Labour persuasion and the other more towards a Liberal-Conservative outlook, but both reporting at an early stage that the Nationalist tide was taking a strong hold in their countries.

Jo Grimond in 1969 tried to achieve a marriage of the SNP and the Scottish Liberals - though some of his colleagues feared that it was more likely to become a rape - but that, too, came to nothing. In the *Guardian*, as with his Lib-Lab endeavours, we encouraged his initiative and were sorry to see it fail. Scotland's relations with the UK were the breaking point, in addition to the resistance among cautious Liberals and firebrand Nationalists. After Hamilton the *Guardian* said that the force behind Mrs Ewing's victory was the wish of a majority of Scots to control their own affairs, but the idea of breaking away from the United Kingdom was a fantasy in which few Scots believed. Scotland's prosperity was inevitably and inextricably bound up with England's, that leader said, but Scots were well justified in wanting decisions about Scottish transport, industry, and social services to be taken in Scotland by people answerable to the Scottish electorate. John Mackintosh, Labour member for Berwick, had suggested that as a start the Scottish Grand Committee should meet for three or four weeks a year in Edinburgh; but the dour Secretary of State, William Ross, had dismissed that as impracticable. He was making a mistake, the leader said, and the Government ought to think again. That leader, which I wrote, was a plain expression of my own personal view - kept up to date by three or four visits a year to Scotland.

In May 1968 Edward Heath, in what became known as his 'Declaration of Perth', promised a constitutional committee to consider a Scottish Assembly. That month also the General Assembly of the Church of Scotland, half lay and half clerical in membership, overwhelmingly voted for 'an effective form of self-government' but within the UK framework. It called for a Royal Commission, which in October Harold Wilson established. That winter Jo Grimond went on a speaking campaign round Scotland, from Aberdeen to Galashiels and from Lerwick to Glasgow, calling for a unified Scottish home rule movement. He had the backing of the *Scotsman* and other Scottish newspapers, which in that context mattered much more than the *Guardian*'s. While in the north, I had a meeting with William Wolfe, chairman of the SNP, and quickly concluded that he was a level-headed man whose main concern was to get a better deal for a democratic Scotland. But the united front was never formed, chiefly because the SNP did not want to modify its separatist claim and because some of the Scottish Liberals were scared stiff. So Labour devolutionists, SNP, and Liberals fought each other in 1970 – except that that year the SNP put no candidate up against Jo Grimond.

Though Labour throughout the UK went into the 1970 election looking very shaky, it appeared to do well during the campaign. Pundits and polls alike by mid-June were forecasting a Labour victory. The *Guardian* was one of the few Fleet Street papers with no opinion poll of its own, contenting itself with reporting what polls in other papers said. In the last few days Marplan in the *Times* gave Labour an 8.7 per cent lead, while Gallup in the *Telegraph* put Labour 7 per cent ahead; NOP in the *Mail* gave a 4.1 per cent lead, while Harris in the *Express* said Labour was 2 per cent ahead. In the *Guardian* we said that Wilson looked like getting his third term, in spite of last-minute scares, and we hoped he would make better use of it than of the first two terms. But we did not discount Heath, as many other newspapers were doing. He had fought a better campaign than was always admitted by his colleagues or the press, our last but one leader before polling said, and he had sought to discuss the issues. He had gone down well when, late in the campaign, he had been allowed out to meet people. He had a quick mind and decisiveness, though at times something of Eden's hot temper. At Downing Street he could prove a capable Prime Minister, the leader said, and if he did not get that opportunity it would not be primarily his fault. That leader again was my own, written at the end of a campaign during which I had attended many of the party press conferences and some public meetings, in London and in Manchester.

The main leader summing up the paper's view had appeared, as was usual after 1959, on the Monday before polling. In it I stated our conclusions in these bare terms:

The *Guardian*'s view remains what it was: that candidates ought to be considered as much for their individual merits as for their party labels; that where a sound Liberal stands a fair chance of coming first or second he or she should be supported; that Mr Heath's Conservatism is, in the main, of a moderate and progressive character; but that Mr Wilson's Government, in spite of all its failings, deserves to be returned again. Labour ought to be given the opportunity to build on what it has already achieved – which means that it must have a clear working majority.

In this election we gave the Liberals less attention and less support than previously, though remaining friendly. I thought Jeremy Thorpe capable, but not in the same class as Jo Grimond and not a political pioneer. We accepted his view that the Liberals could not commit themselves in advance on what they would do if they were to hold the balance in the next Parliament, but we said that Mr Thorpe ought to be thinking about it. In the event, the need to concentrate his thoughts did not come until 1974.

Heath in fact did a Truman, confounding the prophets and the polls and finishing with an over-all majority of thirty-one. The Liberals fared poorly: though their popular vote was still above two million, only six members were elected in place of thirteen at the dissolution. For the Nationalists, Winnie Ewing and Gwynfor Evans both lost their seats but Donald Stewart came in from the Western Isles. Harold Wilson left Downing Street, shocked by his sudden defeat; Ted Heath came in, with some perilous election pledges to redeem.

He could not, of course, reduce the rise in prices 'at a stroke'. Nor could he cut spending 'in every single Ministry in Whitehall'. He could cut taxes, but Iain Macleod's death delayed action. He could and did begin the dismantling of nationalised industries, though luckily it did not go far. He could let 'lame ducks' die, and some did, but by 1972 prudence had brought moderation to that policy. He could and did start scrapping Labour's incomes and prices policies, returning to the free play of market forces, but on incomes he went dramatically into reverse in 1972. These matters have been discussed already in Chapter 9. What Heath could do above all, and triumphantly did, was to take Britain into the European Economic Community.

The great dilemma came late in 1973, when Heath seemed set on a largely sensible course but ran into conflict with the miners. Of that, more in a page or two. By then, to the consternation of one or two colleagues, I had started to ask whether conceivably we might support Heath in the next election.

In Scotland and Wales meanwhile, in spite of the partial setback in the 1970 election, the Nationalist momentum grew. Personally, I was glad to see it. The Labour party in Scotland needed a severe shaking, after thirty years of easy domination. It had become conservative, complacent, and in some areas corrupt. The quality of its candidates was sometimes deplorable. The Unionists, too, had sat too comfortably for too long in the richer seats. With three or four honourable exceptions on each side – John Mackintosh, Jim Sillars, and Alick Buchanan-Smith foremost among them – there was little new thought and little sensitivity to the changing Scottish scene. Members sitting for English seats often appeared more alert to Scottish and Welsh trends. The break-up of the old pattern of Scottish politics was a welcome stimulus. And, thanks to the jolt that the SNP gave the big parties, between 1974 and 1979 there was a marked improvement in the quality of Scottish MPs and candidates; but most of that period lies beyond this book.

There was, in all, a fascinating fluidity in the political scene by late 1973. There were also the fearsome effects of the Yom Kippur war and the escalation of oil prices. Did we or did we not want Wilson back? Was it time to revive ideas of coalition or consensus government?

The two elections of 1974

Round the table in the Gay Hussar's top-floor room, in mid-December 1973, twelve of the senior staff were gathered. The Arabs, the NUM, ASLEF, and some of the power workers were creating a variety of troubles; an announcement of severe electricity restrictions (in fact, the three-day week) was imminent, as was a supplementary Budget from Mr Barber. Because oil was no longer flowing freely from the Middle East, supplies to industry and to petrol pumps had been reduced. The miners, having had a generous settlement after their strike in 1972 and a further increase early in 1973, had now rejected the Coal Board's $16\frac{1}{2}$ per cent offer (inflation then being about 10 per cent) and banned overtime and weekend working. The railway drivers were demanding more than other railwaymen and looked like bringing most trains to a stop; and the power engineers were in their sixth week of an overtime and weekend ban. Nobody round our table disputed that the Government, after its 1972 experience, was prudent in preparing for a harsh emergency.

Beyond that, what? Edward Heath, so far as we knew, had not intended to call an election before the autumn. He might now have to bring it forward. Harold Wilson's shadow cabinet appeared ill-prepared. Whereas Heath and his Ministers had handled preparation of Stage 3 of their pay and prices policy with some diplomacy – through a series of consultations with the TUC and CBI, and with none of Heath's old abrasiveness – Wilson's team looked weak, without an alternative strategy, and the prisoners of the trade unions. The return of a Labour Government seemed certain to bring faster inflation. Hardly less troubling, Tony Benn was not only urging the miners and power workers on, unrestrained by Wilson, but was preparing a shopping list for further nationalisation. The proposed Public Enterprise Board (later the NEB) was welcome, but a random shopping list was not.

Two points emerged early in the round-table discussion. One was a common view that, regardless of the miners' action, the crisis brought on by the oil scarcity and the rise in world commodity prices was likely to be long. The other was that in the country generally this had not really sunk in. Keith Harper,* the *Guardian*'s labour correspondent, thought it was now understood by most of the union leaders and that consequently they were ready to live with Stage 3's terms. He said that Jack Jones was urging the T&G and other unions to 'go easy' in their attack on Stage 3, and he thought the miners' dispute could be settled for a '£5 package'. Others were less optimistic, believing that even a '£5 package' which went beyond Stage 3 was bound to lead to other inflationary settlements as in 1972; and recollection of the miners' fierce picketing then had also hardened feeling against making them a major exception this time. On a more cheerful note, we were reminded of BP's Alaskan oil reserves and of the North Sea, though the oil off Scotland was not likely to flow by the million barrels for another three years.

No strong political points were made at that gathering. A few days later Barber's mini-Budget left the better-off with virtually all that they had gained from his previous Budgets, which was no help in creating the right atmosphere for Stage 3 and national restraint. For New Year I wrote a leader broadly supporting Stage 3 and the Government's emergency measures to save energy, but saying that the Cabinet ought to think again about tax policy. Having previously lowered the standard rate of tax and extended surtax exemptions, all the Chancellor had now done was to put a small surcharge on surtax, effectively increasing the tax burden by 1 to 5 per cent for those in the top brackets. He ought in addition to lift the tax threshold immediately to relieve families with earnings below £30 a week, and later lift it further towards the national average industrial wage of £38, the leader said; and he should compensate by raising other rates by 5 per cent or thereabouts. Since everyone's living standards must now be cut, that would give a more equitable result. And as to Stage 3 or Stage 4, if the TUC were willing to determine priorities among union claims, that would be very welcome, but while the TUC was ineffectual the Government must persevere with its policy. Borrowing a Wilson aphorism, the leader recalled that one man's pay increase was another man's price increase.

Within the leader was a proposal that, during the emergency, personal incomes should have a ceiling of £9,999 a year. It was highlighted by the BBC's morning radio programme, and caused Peter Gibbings to ring me at home. He asked how far I intended to push the proposition. He thought it was mistaken, but that was not the point: he was seeking reassurance that, if we were going to make more of it, we should do so with some understanding of the worries in company boardrooms over the combined consequences of the oil shortage, oil prices, and the three-day week. When he had heard the BBC summary he had been disturbed; when he had read the leader he had found it exceptionally interesting, and although he believed he could shoot a lot of holes in it intellectually he accepted its general direction. He thought it important, nevertheless, that readers should be reassured that the *Guardian* understood the acute difficulties for managements as well as workers and that the paper was not taking a big lurch to the left.

In fact I had chosen £9,999 as a journalistic device, rather than £10,000 or some higher figure, and clearly that had worked. I told Peter that John Cole and two others had seen the draft, and two of the three thought it too mild. Because relations with Peter were easy, that call was no worry. He often commented as any intelligent reader might, and his perspective was useful. That morning he added that the *Guardian* and *MEN* must expect a drop in display advertising, because of the crisis and poor business prospects; though we were now closer to the balance we wanted between advertisement and sales revenues, that was probably about to be upset.

In January, with the three-day week injuring national output and individual earnings, expectations of an election grew – though in the paper we said that it would be better avoided. Tony Benn said that the three-day week was 'a fraud', but he did it on the basis of a miscalculation of the rate of rundown of coal stocks. The TUC tried to persuade the Government to treat the miners' case as exceptional, but Heath rejected this, rightly in the paper's view, because the TUC said nothing about preventing other unions from leap-frogging. At the end of January the miners went to a ballot on a national strike, and on February 4 an overwhelming vote for the strike was announced. Responding to a request from the Coal Board, the Government agreed to let the miners' claim be examined in the light of a 'relativities' report from the Pay Board – 'a thin plank to carry a heavy load,' we said in the paper, but 'worth trying'. The Prime Minister still said nothing about going to the country, and we still preferred reconciliation to an election.

Meanwhile, however, there had been another senior staff lunch – more combative than the detached discussion of December, and with the Labour faithful in a more aggressive mood now that voting seemed near. When I said that 'Who runs the country?' was bound to be a prime issue, even though the TUC was plainly in no position to run anything, John Cole objected to the implication that we were simply trying to pick the most reliable team of economic managers. The social purposes and power base of each party were as important, he said, and while the Conservatives' power base lay among the wealthy and the business world we ought to back Labour. He remained highly dissatisfied with Labour's stance on counter-inflation and he shared the reservations of others about Labour's competence, but he still adhered to a final choice of Wilson. Harry Jackson raised the European issue, which led to an inconclusive mêlée. Barber was savaged all round, but Whitelaw and Carr praised. Unluckily neither of our political correspondents, Ian Aitken and David McKie, could come so we missed their assessments. When I threw in the virtue of the Liberals holding the balance, it was derided by some and approved by others – about two to one against, I reckoned. None of us at that point guessed how important events were to make it.

When Heath announced the dissolution, allowing only three weeks for the campaign, I nevertheless headed the first long leader 'Do you sincerely want a moderate Government?' With inflation accelerating and growth gone, I wrote that the new Government's first task must be to prevent a deeper crisis, and I questioned whether either party was well placed to tackle it. The Conservatives were not preparing their followers for a tougher tax policy and were therefore bound to be confronted by the unions over their pay policy. But if Wilson gave in to the miners that must lead to a flood of inflationary claims, and in no time we should see prices spiralling faster upwards and the pound spiralling down. Labour would have to stay its hand on demolition of the Pay Board and Stage 3, and tone down its policy on public ownership. One outcome, however, could force the winning party to adopt a less partisan approach: a Parliament in which the Liberals held the balance.

Was I justified in taking a line that deviated from the consensus of the senior staff? I thought so: the regular consultation with them – with those whose advice I valued most – was something that I had instituted; and I ought not to be bound by it. Wadsworth's consultation with his colleagues was never systematic; he reached his decisions by a mysterious inner process, ruminating in private and talking either to nobody or as probably to someone from one of the universities as to anyone at Cross Street. At critical times he habitually set the line simply by writing a leader which no-one else saw until it was in type, when everyone in the leader writers' 'corridor' received a proof. I preferred to hear the views of others first, if time allowed. I never supposed that my political instincts were as acute as Wadsworth's, and I lacked his deep roots in the back streets of a Northern industrial town (Rochdale). Having heard the views of others, I felt free to make up my own mind.

A descant and cadenza to the main election theme came from the Nationalist challenges in Scotland and Wales. John Kerr was forecasting that the SNP would win between five and eight seats, to the disbelief of the news desk in London, and Ann Clwyd expected two or three Plaid Cymru gains. (She fought Gloucester for Labour only in October.) Jo Grimond had recently introduced a private member's Bill in the Commons, providing for Scottish and Welsh Parliaments along the lines recommended by the Crowther-Hunt and Kilbrandon Royal Commission – though adding extra powers over industry in Scotland. It was talked out by Conservative and Labour members; but I believed that it represented the right solution, keeping Scotland within the UK, and that in practice most of the SNP would accept it. The Conservatives, having promised in 1970 to table proposals for an elected Scottish Assembly, had tabled nothing; and Willie Ross remained adamantly anti-devolution. In the paper, therefore, I argued that votes for any candidate favouring moderate home rule could help to break up the political iceberg in the North – and could contribute to a third force in Parliament.

Polling was on February 28, and the results were not clear until the afternoon of March 1. They were a stalemate. The Conservatives were down from 322 seats to 296, Labour up from 287 to 301, the Liberals up from 11 (after by-election gains) to 14, the SNP from 2 to 7, and Plaid Cymru from nil to 2. There were also the thirteen Northern Ireland members – two of whom were likely to support Labour, ten were unpredictable United Ulster Unionists (anti-Faulkner and anti-power-sharing), and the thirteenth was the Rev. Ian Paisley. The Liberals had clocked up over six million votes, about 20 per cent of the total UK poll – thereby averaging 430,000 votes for each seat, or more than ten times the number needed by the big parties to elect one member.

'Lab-Lib-Nat is better than Con-Lib or going alone' was the heading on our first leader of March 2. Already it was clear that, since Wilson had no over-all majority, Heath was disinclined to depart. No statement had come from Downing Street on the Friday afternoon, nor had Jeremy Thorpe been invited to talk to either side. Before and during the campaign he had said that if the Liberals were to hold the balance they would work with either party to get the country on its feet but would prefer not to enter a coalition. The Liberals did not in fact hold the balance, because of the Nationalist and Ulster Loyalist numbers. But a Labour-Liberal-Nationalist alliance would have a working majority – and that was what the leader recommended, in spite of Harold Wilson's open hostility to inter-party arrangements. 'There need be nothing sinister, malign, or dishonourable' in such an arrangement, I wrote, and confidential talks 'ought to cover only the first priorities of economic policy'.

Since Labour had the largest vote, and since the Liberals could work more readily with Labour, a Lab-Lib-Nat alignment was the natural way to proceed. To satisfy the Liberals the package must mean shelving new public ownership, the leader said, and to satisfy the Nationalists it must mean agreement on how to handle offshore oil. It must also mean undertakings on Scottish and Welsh devolution; but I wrote that on those terms Plaid Cymru and the Scottish Nationalists were likely to behave reasonably and responsibly. Europe was the biggest obstacle, but that could be bypassed by stopping the clock on European renegotiation. And if there was to be no Lab-Lib-Nat alliance, then a Con-Lib package was preferable to no package at all.

Over the weekend Wilson sat tight, having made his public offer to form a minority Government, and believing that the others would not come to terms. On Saturday night and Sunday night, March 2 and 3, Jeremy Thorpe met the Prime Minister at Downing Street. By Sunday afternoon Ian Aitken had discovered enough to make clear that a Con-Lib package was highly improbable. Heath had said that Liberal membership of a coalition government was preferable to giving support from outside it, but he was prepared to offer only one Cabinet post – and that probably a minor one. On electoral reform he was ready to offer another

Speaker's Conference, but no assurance about the attitude of Conservative representatives at that conference.

With Ian's information in front of me, I wrote another leader on Sunday evening suggesting a 'Grand Coalition' of all three parties. That would represent the nearest approach to what the public appeared to want, I said, and it could govern on a programme of getting the country back to work and seeking industrial peace. The Treasury, as the most important single post, must be occupied by someone acceptable to all three parties. Unfortunately, I wrote, the hostility and distrust between Labour and Conservative backbenchers – as much as between their leaders – was probably too deep to permit such a sensible arrangement. But for good measure we published in Monday's paper nearly half a page of extracts from the economic, financial, and industrial section of the Liberal election manifesto, to show the degree of common ground that could be found there. (It had the additional merit, in my view, of rebutting the frequent Tory and Labour gibes that the Liberals had no policy.)

On Monday morning the Liberal MPs met at the Commons, and afterwards a letter went from Thorpe to Heath at Downing Street. The Conservative Cabinet met in the afternoon, and at 6.30 Heath handed his resignation to the Queen. Harold Wilson in turn went to the Palace soon afterwards. Though disappointed by the outcome, I wrote again saying that Wilson's minority Government should now be allowed to get on with its job – provided it postponed the contentious elements in its programme, which Wilson as a good tactician almost certainly intended. It would be welcome, however, if he took up electoral reform and devolution.

When Thorpe's letter to Heath was published it showed that the Liberals were not prepared to enter a Lib-Con coalition though they remained ready to support any minority Government 'on an agreed but limited programme'. As an alternative Thorpe proposed 'a Government of national unity' – the first time the phrase was used – to carry out a limited programme on priority matters. The Liberal MPs believed that there was enough common ground and goodwill to sustain such a Government. But it was rejected by Heath's Cabinet, partly because of the belief that Wilson would not join. Wilson's manoeuvre had succeeded; but I remained ready to commit the *Guardian* in future to support of inter-party alliances.

The New Cabinet included Callaghan as Foreign Secretary, Healey as Chancellor, Jenkins at the Home Office, Michael Foot (new to office) at Employment – and William Ross back at the Scottish Office. The last looked like an affront to those who wanted some measure of Scottish home rule, but we underestimated Harold Wilson's ability to make granite melt (helped by the trend of voting in Scotland). John Morris at the Welsh Office was a more congenial prospect. In fact there was some hearty arm-twisting the following summer, when diehards in Labour's Scottish Executive threw out the idea of an elected Scottish Assembly, and a special conference had to be called in August to reverse the decision. I went myself to that conference in Glasgow and enjoyed some of its ironies, with Willie Ross now shamelessly pretending to be the champion of devolution; its decision was never in doubt once Alex Kitson and Gavin Laird, from the T&G and the AUEW, had laid down a pro-devolution line. I went also to the Welsh National Eisteddfod in muddy fields at Carmarthen and found John Morris being amiably lobbied by home rulers, but he was mostly on their side anyway.

On electoral reform, one small *Guardian* enterprise after the February election was to commission a study from Nuffield College, Oxford – carried out by Philip Williams – on the effects of the 'Alternative Vote'. This was based on the Australian system instead of proportional representation; it kept single-member constituencies, with one party candidate in each seat, and ballot papers on which a voter registered a 1-2-3 order of preference. Using a number of assumptions which he explained, Philip Williams found that in the last four general elections the Alternative Vote would have helped the Liberals, hurt the Conservatives, and done little damage to Labour.[1] Looking at the detailed figures, I had no doubt that the Alternative Vote would prove a valuable reform; but the big parties were still likely to block it.

An autumn election was a near-certainty from the start of the 1974 Parliament, and in the early summer there were signs that the Conservatives, though not Labour, were overhauling their ideas about a coalition. In late June Jeremy Thorpe and David Steel announced the Liberals' readiness to consider taking part in a coalition, and a few days later Ted Heath dropped a broad hint, in a speech to a Fleet Street audience, of his willingness to have a 'middle way' coalition. His programme included a moratorium on using industry as a political football, a promise not to revive the Conservatives' Industrial Relations Act, and more serious measures to attack inflation.

At that point I asked Jo Grimond to write for the *Guardian*, bringing

---

1 The findings of Philip Williams were these. In 1964 the maximum effect of the AV system would have been to give Labour 316 seats instead of 317, the Conservatives 283 instead of 304, and the Liberals 31 instead of 9 – a result that would have been more comfortable for Harold Wilson. In 1966 Labour would still have had 363 seats, the Conservatives 240 instead of 253, and the Liberals 25 instead of 12 – a fairer result, and one that would have left Labour as strong as ever. In 1970 the Conservatives' 330 seats would have come down to 320, Labour's 287 to 280, the Liberals up from 12 to 25, and the Nationalists would have had 5 seats instead of none – but Heath would still have had his over-all majority. And in February 1974 Labour would have had 291 seats instead of 301, the Conservatives 213 instead of 296, the Liberals 98 instead of 14, the Nationalists 18 instead of 9, the UUUs 8 instead on 10, Faulkner's group 2 instead of none, and the SDLP 2 instead of 1. There would still have been a deadlocked Parliament, but with Wilson leading more obviously the largest group and with the Liberals unquestionably holding the balance.

his own thoughts on party alliances up to date. The result was some characteristic tail-twisting of his own party as well as others. He thought that the new popularity of coalitions 'covers a considerable sloth', and that to add Heath to Wilson was not a recipe for success. If the coalition was the lowest common denominator of Labour-Tory-Liberal policies 'it could finally bring us to our knees'. What he had wanted, he said, was a loose-knit social democratic movement faced by the Conservatives on one side and flanked perhaps by advanced Marxists on the other; but that had not come about. Now the leaders of our capitalist society showed the symptoms of a regime in decay.

They set no example of unselfishness [he wrote]. They cling to their perks. They still trumpet about growth and run to the Government when in trouble. I have no doubt that as the Gadarene swine approached the cliff they told each other that the great thing was to go faster and anyway that was what all the best pigs were doing.

Towards Labour, still cowed by the trade unions, he was no more kind.

The unions, indeed, which reject even the social contract of their own government. Unions which don't give a damn for inflation so long as it hurts someone else. Unions led by men who want to bust the system altogether.

He advised the Liberals to be chary of getting the coalition tag tied round their necks. A sense of national unity could be created only by cutting top earnings, curtailing perks, and using the State's financial powers to enforce the general interest; by an attack on nationalised monopolies and other restrictive groupings; by redirecting resources towards a programme of communal development and shared ownership; by devolution to Scotland and Wales; and by stopping 'mass legislation' for the next ten years. It was a rather different approach to the package of priority measures that the *Guardian* had been recommending.

As the election approached, the *Guardian*'s senior staff gathered as usual - with one lunch in Manchester just before the summer holidays, mainly to discuss counter-inflation (the rate then being nearly 20 per cent); and another in London in mid-September. At the London meeting I began by asking for opinions on what the Conservatives should do if, this time, they came out on top but without a working majority. Since this produced arguments in favour of consultation with other parties about a coalition - near unanimity on the point, indeed - I turned the question round and asked what Labour should do in the same situation. This produced less enthusiasm for negotiating a coalition. That was illogical, I thought, since Labour and the Liberals had more in common than either had with the Conservatives.

The 'Government of National Unity' became a central theme of the election from the day the Conservative manifesto appeared. That manifesto, or large parts of it, came out prematurely in the *Guardian*, *FT*, and *Daily Mirror*, after copies reached our offices on September 9. Tory headquarters had not intended to publish it until a week later. Its appearance in our pages led to a visit from a detective chief superintendent of the Sussex CID, who said he was investigating the theft of two copies from the printers. We had a delightfully civilised discussion on what the *Guardian* would or would not print if it received copies, then confidential, of drafts or proofs or unpublished documents – all very unlike the first appearance of 'Ginger' Hensley among us. Geoffrey Grimes and the CID man also had a technical debate on whether or not it was 'theft', in law, if there was no intention to deprive anyone of ownership.[2] The Conservatives were at first furious over the leak, but in the end it secured three days of publicity for the manifesto instead of one.

The key passage in the manifesto, printed at the beginning, said that the nation's crisis should transcend party differences. The Conservative party, 'free from dogma and free from dependence upon any single interest', was broadly based throughout the nation. While its objective was to win a clear majority in the House of Commons, it undertook to use that majority to unite the nation. 'After the election,' the manifesto declared, 'we will consult and confer with the leaders of other parties and with leaders of the great interests in the nation, in order to secure for the government's policies the consent and support of all men and women of good will.'

The Liberals unfortunately tied themselves in a nasty knot just after that manifesto, and it took all the persuasive talents of Jeremy Thorpe and David Steel to get them out of it. Their party conference had not been cancelled, since the dissolution had not yet come, and the Young Liberals called Thorpe a traitor for having mentioned the possibility of joining a coalition. A motion virtually rejecting both a Government of national unity and a two-party coalition went before the conference, leaving only the old alternative of support from outside a minority Government, but it was defeated. Since the Liberals were also demanding electoral reform, which was bound to mean the formation of a Government based on inter-party arrangements, that episode did much damage to their credibility. We dealt with them frankly in the paper, saying that they were heading for an illogical, contradictory, and absurd position. We welcomed Thorpe's rejoinder that he would listen to any proposition by any party leader, but we still regretted that, in fighting off the challenge from within his own ranks, he had committed himself not to join any two-party coalition.

2 Geoffrey Grimes, without admitting that there was any necessary connection between the copies said to be missing from the printers and the *Guardian*'s publication, argued that even if there were to be it was probably not an offence under the Theft Act. DCS Cornbill held that there were sections of the Act which covered this misuse of stolen property. Nobody mentioned the questions of copyright and conspiracy which had come up in the Morgan Phillips case sixteen years earlier.

Wilson, still imitating Tarzan, promised that with 'a strong mandate' Labour would unite Britain and take it safely through its worst crisis since the war. Coalitions were out, because they led to 'trimming' of policies and 'fudging' decisions. But much of the manifesto was nevertheless emollient in tone. So much so, that a few days later I wrote a leader which began by saying that, if the campaigners were to be believed, 'the choice now lies between Mr Wilson's non-Socialist Labour party, Mr Heath's non-Tory Conservatives, and Mr Thorpe's non-Coalition Liberals'. Were the non-Socialist and non-Tory images entirely true, I said, the choice would be more tolerable. But at least the threat of alternating and contradictory action and sudden U-turns had been lessened.

Since the *Guardian* was maintaining its support for an inter-party alignment, I decided that we should write a manifesto of our own. Having drafted it and accepted some proposed improvements, I put it into the paper as a 2,000-word leader one week before polling. It was offered for use either by a coalition or by a minority Government with agreed support from others. It was built with planks from each of the separate party platforms, but it said that each party must be ready to set aside some contentious measures of its own. The *Guardian*'s major points were these:

1. Incomes: give the social contract a chance. All parties agreed that the level of wage settlements must be kept within bounds. Labour regarded its social contract as the heart of its programme. It had kept its side of the bargain through its social policies, its tax policy, and pension increases. The unions now ought to honour their side, as a counter to inflation. The Conservatives had offered a 'national contract', which was the social contract wrapped in a Union Jack. Trade unionists doubted whether the Conservatives would honour the Government's side, particularly on personal taxation, wealth redistribution, and job opportunities. That was why a common policy must explicitly cover these points.

2. Public ownership: put new measures in cold storage. While the Conservatives and Liberals were asked to accept the social contract, Labour must modify its approach to public ownership. Labour was still committed to extending it 'into profitable manufacturing industry by acquisition, partly or wholly, of individual firms'; and the other parties regarded that as highly dangerous and divisive. It was also opposed strongly by the CBI. But this did not mean a total moratorium: where a particular case could be made – as perhaps with ports or shipbuilding – it could be accepted. Labour's ports proposal allowed well-managed centres to continue under licence. Nor should there be a bar to assistance such as Rolls-Royce had received.

3. Production and productivity: we must earn our way out of the crisis. Was it Henry VII, Elizabeth I, Walpole, Gladstone, or Disraeli who had first said that this is a trading nation? The home of the industrial revolution had built its prosperity on exports. What had happened to Mr Wilson's famous productivity crusade, and why was industrial production lower than at this time the previous year? A new programme of industrial investment was needed, to lead to a new export drive.

4. Whose wealth? The March tax measures must not be reversed. This referred to Healey's personal tax measures, not to his changes in corporation tax. Healey had freed $1\frac{1}{2}$ million people from income tax, at least until wage increases brought them back into the net. He had also promised a wealth tax and a capital transfer tax. These were not Socialist measures but broadly in line with Liberal thinking. Since the Conservative manifesto said that the tax system 'must be fair and be seen to be fair', was it too much to ask that they accept these changes?

5. *Industrial investment.* Companies must be able to make profits, to finance their own investment, and according to Harold Lever companies were now kicking at an open door. If so, there should be no difficulty here.

6. *Electoral reform, a Scottish Parliament, and a Welsh Assembly.* Electoral reform must come, and the Liberals were justified in insisting on this. A Speaker's conference followed by a free vote was the way. Elected Assemblies in Scotland and Wales had been promised by Labour, and the Conservatives were now moving in that direction. These promises ought to be fulfilled.

7. *Other priorities.* The renegotiation with Europe must be constructive rather than a confrontation. An agreement on pensions policy must be reached. So must an agreement on the public stake in offshore oil.

A programme such as this, the leader concluded, was more likely to bring prosperity than Mr Wilson's insistence on governing alone and on his own terms only.

The day that that leader appeared, we held the final senior staff lunch before polling. There was some good-natured sniping at the leader, mainly on the ground that it contained more points of Labour than Conservative policy, and that people like Margaret Thatcher and Keith Joseph would never stand for its tax proposals. I stuck to the view that if Heath was serious about a Government of National Unity he must make the kind of concessions for which the leader asked.

At the end of the lunch, because of John Cole's insistence that we ought to be giving stronger support to Labour, I went round the table not taking a vote but asking whether Labour ought nevertheless to be ready to enter a coalition. If the election left Labour in a minority, as it might, it was not inconceivable that Wilson might perform one of his great acts of statesmanship and call the other party leaders in for consultation. Ought we not to be doing all we could to prevail upon him to move this way?

John, Ian Aitken, Jean Stead, and Keith Harper stayed solidly with Labour and plainly preferred that the paper should be friendlier towards Wilson in the last few days before polling. Geoffrey Taylor,* reviving a rather subtle argument that he had put in mid-September, said that the Conservatives in opposition were less dangerous than Labour in opposition, which was a point in favour of the Cole-Aitken axis; but he was nevertheless content that the paper should stay on the course it had already taken. Peter Preston, while admitting to past adherence sometimes to the Liberals and sometimes to Labour, said that the leader was not sufficiently critical of Labour and failed to put forward the strong reforming programme that he thought essential; but he agreed that Wilson ought to be encouraged to come to terms with others. Brian Jones on the whole was in the Cole camp, and said that whatever else we said before polling we ought to discourage thoughts of a Lib-Con coalition. Harry Jackson also was generally in the Cole camp, but not strongly against the coalition line. David McKie, noting the high proportion of 'don't knows' still showing in the opinion polls, thought it quite probable that the election would leave nobody with an over-all majority and he agreed that that might force reappraisals; but he, too, would prefer to see Labour with a proper working mandate. There were only ten at that lunch, because of late cancellations.

Afterwards, walking back to Gray's Inn Road with John, I said I thought it was 7-3 in his favour. He disputed this (or so he recalls), reckoning it was $7\frac{1}{2}$-$2\frac{1}{2}$, with Peter Preston split between us. But if he was making that claim, which I surely did not concede, then I must have counter-claimed one quarter of David McKie and one quarter of Harry Jackson. John was always a friendly critic, except once or twice over Ireland; and part of his great value to me, in addition to his high qualities as a journalist, was that he gave plain and candid advice. He was important also because he knew more than I did about the way industrial workers lived and about the trade union movement, and he compensated for my more academic background. His criticism was sometimes a grindstone on which to sharpen and polish my opinion; but it was much more than that, for he was one of the major creative forces at work inside the *Guardian* office. Our differences over the 1974 elections were not painful.

The main leader on the Monday before polling recommended a vote for the Liberals, saying that the more Liberals there were in the new Parliament the stronger the hope of a sound and moderate Government. It noted the failures of economic management by Labour and Conservatives, and the impulse under a two-party system of each to reverse some of its predecessor's key measures. In the past five years the casualties had included the Industrial Reorganisation Corporation, the Prices and Incomes Board, the Pay Board, the Industrial Relations Court, pensions schemes, education schemes, and housing plans; and if the Conservatives were to win in this election the National Enterprise Board and the social contract would be added to the list. If Labour were to govern in a way consistent with its pledges on wealth redistribution and social welfare, but taming its nationalisers and expropriators, then it could be attractive. Yet a return to Ted Heath could be as attractive if he meant what he had been saying about inter-party talks and a broadly based Government, and about including industrial policy and social policy in those areas which, as he had said two days previously, 'can and should be protected from violent shifts'. The question was whether either of the big parties could be relied on to keep its promises of moderation; hence the attraction of voting Liberal, to help keep them to their words. And, the leader said, it was still possible for a moderate Government to be firm, progressive, and fair in dealing with the crisis.

The election gave Harold Wilson an over-all majority, but it was microscopic – only two or three, depending on whether you allow for the Speaker. Labour was up from 301 seats to 319, the Conservatives down from 297 to 277, the Liberals down from 14 to 13, the SNP up from 7 to 11 and Plaid Cymru up from 2 to 3, and the Northern Irish figures remained much the same. This was not the strong mandate for which Wilson had asked, but he deserved credit for having fought a shrewd campaign. As for Edward Heath, we said in the paper that although he was likely now to stand down from the Conservative leadership we hoped that he would stay in a senior post, perhaps as shadow Foreign Secretary. For the Liberals it was bitter disappointment, too, and there was now virtually no hope of electoral reform.

Through Callaghan to Thatcher

To speculate on what might have happened if Harold Wilson had responded to the *Guardian*'s advice would be about as profitable as trying to rewrite Barrie's *Dear Brutus*. Although Denis Healey proved, in my view, to be one of the best Chancellors in the whole post-war period, inflation roared ahead – at least until towards the end of Callaghan's term at 10 Downing Street. Wilson himself decided to resign less than eighteen months after the October election; and Jim Callaghan, as Prime Minister, comfortably lived up to his own self-caricature as the sound and steady leader. Lib-Lab latterly came into action in keeping him in office, and although electorally it did the Liberals no good David Steel handled his side of it responsibly and courageously. In 1979, after Mrs Thatcher's take-over, the country went through yet another sharp about-turn – most painfully in some of the industrial and social areas which Heath had promised to protect from violent shifts. Inflation again accelerated for many months, and her monetarism at first failed even to bring the money supply under control.

To speculate on what might have happened if Heath, not Wilson, had had a majority of three that October would be even more fascinating. Conceivably that could have produced the most effective Government since Attlee's of 1945-50. Much would have depended on whether Heath kept in check his occasionally aggressive temper and on relations with the trade unions (who failed to give Wilson the practical cooperation that he needed). From the standpoint of a left-of-centre newspaper, political realignment under moderate Labour leadership would have been preferable; but Heath had promised to try, and the experience of trying for an all-party consensus would have been politically educational for leaders and for followers. The flaw was the one touched on by Geoffrey Taylor at our October 3 lunch – that Labour was likely to behave less well in Opposition than in Government, and, if its supporting unions had not been frightened by the severity of the crisis, could have wrecked any search for an agreed economic and social policy.

The October election was my last as editor. From the start of the autumn campaign I knew that it was likely to be so. My retirement from the *Guardian* had to come in 1979 at latest. By then I would have had twenty-three years in charge of the paper, which I thought too long; I had already served almost twice as long as either of my two immediate predecessors, and longer than most editors survive in Fleet Street (whether physical or managerial forces remove them). For my own good and for the paper's, I thought I ought to go in 1976 or 1977. When an interesting appointment in Scotland was offered to me in 1975, with all the attractions of returning home and living within reach of the Highlands, I was happy to accept it.

Every election had been an enjoyment and a stimulus. What a newspaper recommends to its readers probably sways the votes of only a few; but its reporting and comment, before the campaign as much as during it, builds up much of a voter's basic information and sense of the political climate. Radio and television now play as great a part. But the democratic process cannot work without information and debate; and in the office a general election was always a time of stocktaking and decision. Had I become more conservative as the years passed? I am in no position to judge. Wadsworth used to advise young leader writers not to take themselves too seriously, for we were all intent on putting the world right – and he used to pinprick us by telling us that we lived too comfortably for our instincts to be radical. I hope that his teaching and guidance lasted until the end of my time as editor.

Four unusual episodes dominated my final months at the *Guardian*. Each lay outside the normal range of editorial work, but my part in each was unavoidable. Cumulatively, during periods of that winter, they made normal editorial duty impossible.

The first was a conflict with the NUJ's Central London branch – the *Guardian* chapel was in no way involved – which finished in the High Court in May. I could have taken substantial damages from the NUJ, which was nearly bankrupt, but I chose not to.

The second was Michael Foot's Trade Union Bill. As a former editor, Foot did not intend to undermine the independence of editors; but in Fleet Street and among non-metropolitan daily papers there was virtual unanimity on the threat implicit in his Bill. Through no wish of mine, I found myself acting as shop steward of the Fleet Street editors, and ultimately we secured partial amendment of the Bill.

The third directly concerned the *Guardian*'s own London and Manchester chapels. They revived an old proposal that the editorial staff should elect representatives to the parent Board or to the Scott Trust; they did it courteously, outside normal negotiations, but there were practical difficulties which prevented progress. The unique nature of the Scott Trust, crucial to the *Guardian*'s survival, was a barrier to the device the NUJ proposed. At the same time formal negotiations were taking place for the conversion of the *Guardian*'s printing – at last – to photocomposition and facsimile transmission. This was to coincide with the move to Farringdon Road in London, and it meant a reduction of editorial staff in Manchester: delicate matters for negotiation.

The fourth episode was the most serious and most nerve-racking. The Finance Bill, 1975, introducing the Capital Transfer Tax, included provision for periodic levies on trusts which did not distribute their income. The formula for calculating the payment implied demands – at seven, ten, or fifteen year intervals, starting in 1976 – of £2 millions or more from the Scott Trust. These would have crippled the *Guardian*, killing it within a few years. It fell to me to lead the negotiations with the Inland Revenue, the Treasury, and finally with the Chancellor himself to prevent this. Drafting an amendment that was not a loophole for tax-avoiding trusts proved exceedingly difficult; but a formula was found, Denis Healey accepted it, and the tax threat was lifted from the Scott Trust.

A gossip columnist's gossip

The first episode need not detain us long, but it was distasteful. A *Daily Mail* columnist, Nigel Dempster, brought a charge of professional misconduct against me in the NUJ's Central London branch. That followed a paragraph in July 1974 in the *Guardian*'s Miscellany, speculating about staff changes at the *Daily Express*. Nigel Dempster was mentioned as likely to move to the *Express*. I had a telephone call from Ian McColl, the *Express* editor whose departure from his post was implied, protesting about the paragraph and asking where it had come from.[1] McColl assumed that it had originated from Dempster. I neither confirmed nor denied this – though the terms of the paragraph made Dempster the obvious source. Dempster's move to the *Express* did not materialise, and he took to the Central London branch a complaint that, in breach of the union's code of conduct, I had revealed the story's source.

That did not bother me, but the branch set a hearing before a complaints committee for the Monday after polling in the October general election. It did so without asking whether I could attend and without giving me the fourteen days' notice required under the union's own rules. Remembering the events at the end of the February election, when the Heath–Thorpe talks spilled over to the Monday, I was not prepared to attend that day. So I wrote asking that the committee should either postpone its hearing or, if it preferred, in my absence find that there was no case to answer. McColl had written a letter confirming that I had not disclosed the source.

Incredibly, without hearing me and without having given proper notice of the occasion, the committee found against me. I knew that there were members of the branch who regarded anyone in authority as fair game – anyone from the second trombonist upwards, as a senior NUJ man had said – but a serious complaint could not be treated in this way. I therefore wrote to the union's general secretary, Ken Morgan, asking him to bring the matter to the attention of the National Executive. Ironically, when the union had abolished 'associate' status the previous year – a category designed for editors, exempting them from attending chapel meetings or being subject to chapel instructions in their own offices – I had elected to remain an NUJ member. Most other editors at that point had resigned from the union. But having first joined the union in 1946, I did not want to break my connection with it.

The NUJ National Executive in late November set aside the branch finding and ordered a rehearing. Then, still more incredibly, the January issue of the branch Bulletin published a highly tendentious account of the first hearing, with the plain implication that I was guilty. Since the Bulletin went to every NUJ member in Fleet Street, that was too much. A fair and impartial hearing now seemed exceedingly improbable. Lovell, White, and King, on my behalf, therefore took out a writ against the branch officials and Nigel Dempster to restrain them from holding a further hearing.

[1] Ian McColl was replaced soon afterwards by Alastair Burnet.

The case came to court on January 31, and by agreement was adjourned on an interim undertaking by the union not to hold a rehearing. Protracted negotiations between lawyers followed – triangular, because the branch officials were unwilling to accept what the NUJ's lawyers advised. Ken Morgan became extremely worried, because he knew that the NUJ's case was hopeless, that the union was in serious financial difficulties anyway, and that as the weeks dragged on I became increasingly reluctant to accept a simple staying of the proceedings. Counsel had advised that I could obtain substantial damages, and indeed had advised me that I ought to proceed in seeking them.

Eventually, thanks to the ingenuity of Ken Morgan and Geoffrey Grimes, a settlement was reached under which the union's National Executive could if it wished appoint a new complaints committee drawn from outside the Central London branch. I accepted £1,000 of damages and £500 of costs, but I agreed to waive payment in return for an undertaking that the union would contribute £1,500 to its own Widows' and Orphans' fund. (In fact the *Guardian* paid my costs, which were more than £1,500; and the NUJ was able to borrow the £1,500 back from its Widows' and Orphans' fund.) All this was reported in open court on May 22, before Mr Justice Oliver, who ordered a stay in proceedings.

That was not quite the end, however. The National Executive did not appoint a new complaints committee; and in August, having left active journalism, I resigned from the NUJ. The Central London branch, unbelievably, then said that I could not resign because there was a complaint outstanding against me. A gentle letter to the branch secretary dealt with that. Four years later, when I had again started writing and broadcasting, the Highland branch of the NUJ welcomed me as a member – with the knowledge and consent of the Central London branch.

Editors and the closed shop

The closed shop was the main issue over Michael Foot's Trade Union and Labour Relations (Amendment) Bill, but not the only one. The Bill was short, repealing the hated remnants of the 1971 Act, and thereby strengthening the hand of trade unions in forcing closed shop agreements on employers. The NUJ, by its abolition of 'associate' status for editors and by moves to prevent publication of work by non-NUJ journalists, had shown itself to be more militant than before 1971. In November 1974 the *Birmingham Post* stopped publication for a time because NUJ journalists refused to handle copy written by the paper's City editor – a member not of the NUJ but of the smaller Institute of Journalists. There was trouble also in Kent. Among the militants it was proposed that non-NUJ contributors should be restricted to two articles a year in newspapers and periodicals – and the names of Roy Jenkins, Clive Jenkins, Enoch Powell, and Conor Cruise O'Brien were among those cited in this context.

Small wonder that the reaction among editors – and among some non-executive journalists – was strong.

But the Bill went further than its ostensible purpose of restoring the pre-1971 position. It provided for the dismissal without compensation of anyone who, in a closed shop, refused to join a specified trade union or remain a member of it. Anyone losing his or her job under this provision lost the opportunity to make a claim against the employer or union for 'unfair' dismissal.[2] It meant that, where the employer agreed to a closed shop, an editor who refused to join the union or refused to accept union instructions or was thrown out of the union was liable to lose his job without compensation.

A further effect of the Bill – and Michael Foot himself at first seemed unable to understand this – was to curtail a union member's access to the courts if the union behaved irresponsibly or oppressively towards him or her. It was a point on which I was both sensitive and well informed, having just had the benefit of counsel's advice over my own small disagreement with the Central London branch of the NUJ. Foot by his own admission was trying to keep trade union cases out of the courts, which was reasonable. But to achieve that, he was trying to persuade the TUC to set up a voluntary appeals procedure of its own to deal with cases over union membership or union conduct. When the Bill became law, therefore, it was highly probable that the courts would be unwilling to deal with such cases until the voluntary procedures had been exhausted. The safeguard of an action based on breach of natural justice – as in my own case against the Central London branch – would become remote. That was not simply my opinion. It was the opinion of the QC briefed on my behalf, a specialist in this field. And how impartial would the TUC procedures prove when a union member and his union were in conflict?

The provincial editors were quicker to spot the danger than anyone in Fleet Street. They had an association – the Guild of British Newspaper Editors – and a secretariat. Soon after the October election they invited Harry Evans and me to an informal discussion, because they had been pursuing their own inquiries about the further Bill promised by Michael Foot. As a result of that meeting I offered to write to each of the Fleet Street editors, to find out whether they wanted to take a common stand. At first I was most reluctant to do so, remembering Haley's injunction against any collusion among the national newspaper editors.[3] But the case put by the Guild was so compelling that I agreed to do it. The *Guardian* was not in principle against the closed shop, and had said in leaders in the past that in many industries a closed shop could promote easier relations.

2 Although the Bill did not directly provide for this, it was the effect of repeal of a remaining subsection in Foot's Trade Union Act of the previous year.

3 See Chapter 11, p. 275, and footnote on that page.

But in this instance the threat to editorial independence was too great to be ignored.

The replies from all round Fleet Street surprised me by their unanimity. Every editor of every daily and Sunday newspaper felt that a protest ought to be made, and that included the Beaverbrook trio who normally stood aside. Meanwhile the extraordinary events in Birmingham in mid-November stimulated me into writing a vigorous leader in the *Guardian*, and it was followed two days later by similar warnings in the *Times* and *Financial Times*. The Guild had called on Albert Booth, Minister of State at the Department of Employment, but had made no progress whatever. Therefore, on behalf of the Fleet Street editors, I asked for a collective meeting with Michael Foot. That took place on November 19, in a large and ornate room at the Department at St James's Square which no doubt had been the scene of many high-level industrial consultations. We achieved a 100 per cent attendance of the Fleet Street editors, together with the editors-in-chief from the BBC and ITN.

Two propositions were put to Michael Foot, both of which he rejected. One was that the Bill should wholly exempt the editorial departments of newspapers, periodicals, radio, and television from its closed shop provisions. The alternative – with wording which I had worked out beforehand with Geoffrey Grimes, to ensure its legal precision – was a clause to protect senior editorial staffs from dismissal on grounds of refusal to take up trade union membership. Foot dismissed these, saying that he could not exempt 'editors and Jehovah's Witnesses'. (When the Bill was published three days later, effectively it did exempt Jehovah's Witnesses under its provision on religious conscience.) He turned down my alternative wording, without really studying it, on the ground that it would open up claims for exemption from many other groups. Albert Booth, sitting beside him and supporting him, mentioned the claims that might come from essential public services – for example, sewage. That caused Brian Roberts, from the *Sunday Telegraph*, to ask whether the Minister was equating the flow of sewage with the flow of news.

Moving the second reading of his Bill on December 5, Foot poked fun at the editors. He suggested that the threat to editors' independence lay not in the NUJ or the closed shop, but in proprietors and managements. He recalled his own days in Fleet Street and compared the appointment of editors with the coronation of the Czars 'in which the newly appointed autocrat would march in procession preceded by his father's murderers and followed by his own'. There was some truth in that, but it did not dispose of our case. He singled me out individually for special criticism, saying that there was 'not a word of truth' in my suggestion that the right of appeal to the courts (not only for editors but for any union member) against breaches of natural justice was being impaired. Plainly, he had still not grasped the point on that.

Rather than reply through a *Guardian* leader, since I had been singled

out individually, I replied through a signed article. I also sent him a
private letter, more fully to explain the legal advice that I had been given.
In the article I mentioned one new point, of which I had only just become
aware. It was that the TUC's appeals tribunal was not to be required to
give reasons for its decisions, which, I was advised, would make it virtually
impossible ever to take a case of injustice to court. That could be remedied,
however, by a simple amendment of the Bill to restore common law
rights.

That article ended by mentioning, with Ken Morgan's consent, discussions I had been holding with him on a possible compromise with the
NUJ. He had written to the Newspaper Publishers' Association, the
Newspaper Society, and other bodies suggesting a 'model clause' to be
included in all closed shop agreements. That seemed to me a useful
concept. Writing personally, I said that I would be prepared to recommend acceptance of a 100 per cent membership agreement in return for
seven conditions. Among these (they were set out more fully in the article)
were an appeals procedure that could go to a statutory tribunal or the
High Court; exemption from compulsory union membership for editors,
deputy editors, and others from time to time in charge of their publications; a declaration from the NUJ's National Executive that no restrictions
would be placed on contributions from non-union writers, subject to
some form of over-all financial quota; and safeguarding of the position of
existing members of the IoJ.[4]

On December 19 there was a further meeting of the Fleet Street group
with Michael Foot, but again without progress. Since some of the editors
were taking a harder line in their papers than I was taking in mine –
Freddy Fisher at the *FT* being against any compromise, and David Astor
at the *Observer* similarly inclined – I took the precaution of suggesting
that someone else should act as spokesman. I was more than willing to
hand over, but they asked me to carry on. Though our divergences
inevitably came out during the debate with the Secretary for Employment,
our concern was universal. He appeared to have given a commitment to
the TUC which he was most unwilling to modify.

In January, having long before committed myself to delivering a lecture
to the Royal Society of Arts, I used the occasion to explore the controversy
and to put forward a draft code or charter on press freedom. It was
designed to deal not only with pressures from trade unions (printers as
well as journalists) but with pressures from proprietors, managers, and
advertisers as well. I prefaced it by saying that, even if accepted by such

---

4 Nora Beloff, in her book *Freedom under Foot*, says that I wrote a personal article
because 'he had failed to carry his staff'. There was no dissent whatever from any of the
senior staff. I wrote a signed article because Foot had named me in the House and because
I wanted the latitude to mention my discussion with Ken Morgan, which would not have
been appropriate in a leader.

bodies as the NUJ and the publishers' associations, it could be no more than a general guide. It would be unenforceable, except to the extent that participants wanted to enforce it. The draft is printed at the end of this book, as Appendix 2. The lecture may sound dry and boring, but it was well received by a large audience. The topic was, of course, much in the headlines at the time. There was a stir, and correspondence afterwards, over that part of the draft which suggested that if staff wanted to share in policy decisions then employers were within their rights in seeking information about 'political affiliations and activities' of applicants. But I was unapologetic about that. If staff wanted influence, I felt entitled to find out where they stood. I knew I had four International Socialists on my staff, but two of them did their jobs well while two had disruptive tendencies.

Michael Foot did not get his Bill through as fast as he had hoped to. The Conservatives obstructed it in committee, with one magnificent filibuster by Leon Brittan in which he spoke for over an hour on an amendment, without repeating himself or straying to irrelevance, and often entertainingly. The Lords took a long time over it, too, with threats that they would throw it out altogether. Lord Houghton, after consultations with me and others, put forward an amendment for a code of practice to be agreed among the interested parties, laid before Parliament, and then to be available for citing in court proceedings although it would not be legally binding. Michael Foot was ready to accept that; so was the NUJ. But the union's annual delegate meeting threw it out entirely and demanded a campaign for a full closed shop with no exemptions for editors. Lord Goodman, at the same time, was fighting for full legal safeguards. And Michael Foot, for good measure, had spoken of my draft as 'a most admirable document'.

The conflict was still unresolved when the summer recess came, and after that I personally was off the scene. It continued in the autumn, and the Bill failed to complete its course before the end of the session. It had to be reintroduced in November and was finally passed at the end of March 1976. It contained provision for a voluntarily negotiated press charter but left the closed shop provisions more or less intact. So far as I know, that charter has never been negotiated; nor have many managements caved in to union demands for a full closed shop, as most editors feared. The long controversy, it seemed, had taught a number of lessons – though the fight is not over.

Workers on the board or Trust?

During the February election in 1974, I was aware of a move in the London NUJ chapel to demand a pro-Labour policy. That had been scotched by a majority in the chapel. But there was a more persistent move to try to secure some form of representation on the parent board or the Scott Trust. It had had its origins in the 1966 crisis, which had caught editorial and production staffs by surprise. Many members felt that they had been left in the dark until suddenly the crisis broke, and then their jobs, along with the paper, had been on the verge of disappearing without their knowing anything of the reasons. Distrust of the top management had been intense at that time. Although it had been overcome, and from 1967 or 1968 regular briefings were given to staff by Peter Gibbings, Gerry Taylor, and me, a residual demand to 'see the books' and have a voice at the top remained.

In 1970 the London chapel passed a resolution calling for two elected staff members, 'accountable to those who elect them', to join the parent board. The resolution also called for a staff veto over senior editorial appointments. After discussion with our management and the Trust, I had talked to the NUJ – both to the officials and to all the staff – at the usual half-yearly meetings in Manchester and London. In principle the trustees were sympathetic, though not to the proposal of a veto on appointments. But the practical difficulties were real, and, like Beaverbrook in another context, in discussion with our staff, 'I talked them out of it.'

It was no surprise, though, when in November 1974 Mick Downing – father of the London chapel – brought me a letter addressed to Richard Scott. This was simply to let the Trust know, as a matter of courtesy, that a proposal was about to be discussed in the London and Manchester chapels. It was an ingenious proposal, devised by a sub-editor, Laurence Dobie, who was also a playwright and novelist in his spare time. It called for two elected trustees – one elected by all journalists working for the *Guardian*, the *MEN*, and the *Weekly*, and the other elected by all other union members working permanently for the company's publications. It proposed a qualifying period of, say, one year before staff members could vote in electing these trustees. The proposal said further: 'The elected trustees would act rather like MPs; they would be open to questioning about matters connected with the company, but if they felt that there were certain confidential factors they could exercise their discretion in the matter.' It was a proposal neatly designed to overcome my main objections of 1970.

The first of these objections was that board members, as part of an executive body, must accept collective responsibility for all decisions and must take a broad view of company policy, not speaking only as departmental representatives. I therefore suggested the Trust, as a nonexecutive supervisory body – though there, too, the practical difficulties were great. My second objection had been on grounds of confidentiality, since board and Trust members must know about financial forecasts and commercial negotiations that could not be reported publicly, and must be able to debate policy in freedom and privacy. The third objection was that board members with executive responsibility could not be expected to refer back either to the full board or to others in the course of difficult negotiations, whether commercial or industrial, and that any other routine would lead to financial disaster. The fourth objection in 1970 was that a demand from *Guardian* journalists alone was bound to bring parallel demands from the *MEN* and production chapels.

Mick Downing's letter was well timed, because the Trust's half-yearly meeting was due a few days later. Francis Boyd was to retire from the Trust at the end of the year, having decided himself that he ought to be replaced by someone in closer contact with the staff. It was valuable that, this time, the NUJ proposal embraced all journalists, not only union members; though I thought the qualifying period would be better at two or three years rather than one. Another point, derived from experience when the company pension fund elected its officers, was that some departments tended to vote as a block. (We had tried more than once to secure election of a senior financial journalist, but we failed every time.) A fairer result was likely if the 'alternative vote' were to be used in these elections.

The Trust took a friendly view of the proposal. For legal reasons, to preserve continuity of the trust deed, newly elected members could join only by invitation of the existing members. Constitutionally that would have to be made clear. There was also a difficult question over the period of service – for if it was short a new trustee would hardly find his feet, and if it was long the 'electors' might feel left out. A term of five or six years was thought to be a possibility. Also, legally, Trust members were appointed for life and could not be forced to resign; but that was not likely to be a problem. The greatest risk was that any such scheme would founder on jealousies between unions or between *MEN* and *Guardian* staffs. Nevertheless Richard was asked to send a positive reply to the NUJ, with a view to further discussion, and to report back in the spring.

Since consideration of the proposal must take some time, involving the main and subsidiary boards as well as the unions, the Trust agreed to invite John Fairhall* to fill the vacancy left by Francis Boyd. John had been education correspondent since 1973, having been a general reporter for eleven years before that, and had done notable work for a time in East Africa. He was one of the journalists imprisoned by Idi Amin in Uganda and threatened with death, an experience about which he wrote with compassion towards his African fellow prisoners.

Exploration of the Dobie–Downing initiative went on for some months. In trying to meet *MEN* claims, the possibility of one trustee elected in the North and one in London was mooted, but that would have meant a dominant vote by the production departments in each centre. While it was thought that a well-chosen candidate from the production side could be an asset, it was also thought that the character of the Trust would begin to change and its continuity could be threatened.

During one informal exchange with some starry-eyed journalists – there are some – I had to remind them of my occasional sessions with the

Natsopa machine-room chapel in London. Those sessions were always stimulating and brought a policy perspective not normally encountered on the editorial floor. Most memorable to me was the visit of their chapel committee in July 1972, after the five-day Fleet Street stoppage in sympathy with the jailed dockers. They had asked to see me to say they were sorry to have been on strike, for they did not want to hurt the paper, but they had had to abide by union orders. They questioned me about the paper's view of the Industrial Relations Act and the imprisoning of the dockers, saying that the *Guardian*'s leaders were sometimes a bit too technical and too intellectual for them. When I had spoken for some minutes about the *Guardian*'s view that industrial relations were better kept out of the courts and about Wilson having the *Guardian* open in front of him on the despatch box during exchanges in the House earlier in the week, the chapel father interrupted me. All that was all very well, he said, but the chapel thought I'd got it wrong. The dockers, he said, were a rotten lot and ought to have been kept in prison. They were Communist wreckers; and as for the Industrial Relations Act, it ought to be made a lot tougher.

Thereafter the conversation became more lurid. They were less than complimentary about their own top union officials. But, they said, there was one point more than any that they wished to make. They knew it would hurt my feelings and they were sorry about that, but they had been asked to say it. It was that the *Guardian* was entirely wrong about immigration and the blacks. There were one million immigrants in this country and one million unemployed: hoof out the blacks and that would cure unemployment. The blacks had a bad effect on wages, too, and now they were trying to get into the printing unions. When I remonstrated that London Transport and the hospitals could not be kept going without them, the chapel men replied that that was a phoney argument. If London Transport and the hospitals paid proper wages, they would have no difficulty in recruiting staff. They went on to other issues, such as the purchase of council houses. They all wanted to buy their houses and were angry that they could not. They were also rather scornful about the *Guardian*'s views on social justice, saying that the workers ought to be able to look after themselves. Much of it would have gladdened hearts in the Conservative Central Office, though some of it would have scandalised that side of Smith Square; and the chapel did not think highly of Ted Heath.

Its relevance to the Dobie-Downing scheme, however, was that these men represented numerically one of the largest groups among the *Guardian*'s employees. They were a good lot, in that they showed greater loyalty towards the paper than most Fleet Street workers showed towards their employers. The *Guardian*, like others, had had some bad periods of guerrilla warfare on the production side; but generally relations were much more harmonious than in other offices. In that respect we were extremely fortunate, and I was far from suggesting that the Natsopa machine-room men ought not to be part of the proposed electorate. They ought to be; but, since the Trust among its duties was the ultimate guarantor of editorial standards and editorial independence, some care must be taken about the method by which even a minority of the trustees were elected.

The exploration, unfortunately, became stuck in soft sand. It coincided with a period when 'parity' of payment among various groups of employees was a sharply contested issue in union negotiations – an issue still not fully resolved, years later. To at least some on the union side and some among the management, the notion of a device for electing one or two trustees seemed secondary or irrelevant. In the end, therefore, it seemed prudent to shelve the proposal. But it remained, and remains, something that could be revived when the will exists.

While these discussions were taking place, there were also heavy demands on time for the planning and negotiation for the conversion next year (1976) to facsimile transmission. That entailed transfer from Manchester to London of most of the northern sub-editing (foreign, parliamentary, and others), and a diminution of staff in Manchester. Only the northern reporters, a residual but important part of the features department, the photographers, and a sports team were to be left there. At times the negotiation had painful echoes of the 1966-67 staff savings, but numerically it was not so severe. After the first phase of planning and briefing, the main burden fell not on me but on others, mainly Peter Preston – and the task was far from complete when I ceased activity in mid-July. The move to Farringdon Road was accomplished, however, leaving only the final stages of the London printing and publishing operation at Thomson House. The *Guardian*'s main departments were better housed, better equipped, and using more modern processes in their new home.

Almost the crack of doom

It was one of the most extraordinary meetings of my life. In Somerset House, under a high ceiling in an elegant room, one of HM Commissioners of Inland Revenue sat opposite to me. The table was pear-shaped, so that he and I were quite close, facing each other; somewhat behind each of us, round the broad bulges of the table, were our advisers. With me was only one – Stanley Porter, finance director of *G&MEN*. The Commissioner, Mr Barry Johnson, had a Treasury man and an Inland Revenue man on either side of him. The date was December 23, 1974 (four days after the second meeting of Fleet Street editors with Michael Foot).

Having sat down, we were briefly welcomed by the Commissioner. Then he said nothing more, but looked inquiringly at me. So I opened by saying that, so far as the *Guardian* could see, the Government and the Inland Revenue were about to put us out of business. Either we must reconstitute the Scott Trust, a process fraught with legal and financial hazards, or the new Capital Transfer Tax would mean periodic assess-ments which – on the expert advice that we had had – could start with a demand for £2 millions or more in 1978. If we were to reconstitute the Scott Trust there would be a CTT terminal assessment for very much more than £2 millions. On top of these, there was the Wealth Tax to come.

Mr Johnson questioned my calculation of £2 millions, for the periodic assessment. In fact our advisers had given a rather lower figure, but I did not mention that; instead I explained the method of calculation, based mainly on the full commercial value of the *Manchester Evening News* and disregarding the cost of maintaining the *Guardian* (a 'quixotic luxury', it had been called by the Inland Revenue in the thirties). Commissioner Johnson assented to my explanation, but said that they too had been looking at our figures, and he thought that £2 millions might prove to be on the low side. It could be as much as £3 millions.

He then turned to my date, 1978. The relevant date, he said, was the anniversary of the first transfer to the Scott Trust. This appeared to be 1936, so the first assessment would fall in 1976. (I checked by telephone to Manchester immediately afterwards, and the date was indeed June 10, 1936.) Mr Johnson then asked a number of questions about the Trust and its history, most of which I was able to answer. Next he asked about our reasons for not reconstituting the Trust: to the best of my ability, I told him about the advice received from counsel – primarily concerned with the complexity of proceedings to wind up the present Trust, in which the future generations of the Scott and Montague families must be repre-sented separately, even though an irrevocable renunciation of all family interests had been intended when the Trust was created. Its primary purpose had been to secure continuity for the *Guardian*.

Another road we could not take was to convert the Trust to one 'for the benefit of employees', a category to be exempted under the Finance Bill. If we were to do so it would be open to any group of employees to take the trustees to court, borrowing the old Inland Revenue case, and argue that the maintenance of the *Guardian* was a quixotic luxury. Nor could we convert to a charitable trust, because by law the Charity Com-missioners would then require us to make periodic distributions of profits instead of ploughing them back into the business.

Next I deployed the main part of our case. This we had submitted in October to the Treasury, the Inland Revenue, and the new Royal Com-mission on the Press.[5] The Government had invited representations on the newly proposed Wealth Tax, and we had linked this with the Chan-cellor's intentions on CTT. The *Guardian* editorially supported the prin-ciples behind both taxes – one being designed to create a more equitable

5 The third Royal Commission on the Press, appointed in 1974 under Sir Morris Finer. After the death of Sir Morris, Professor Oliver McGregor became chairman.

society by reducing great differences of wealth, and the other being designed to close offensive 'loopholes' in existing estate duty. But we were asking for exemption of newspaper trusts because we did not believe that there had been any intention to catch them. Commissioner Johnson said that the Chancellor was not contemplating any exception for newspaper trusts.

Continuing our case, I said that because of the unusual nature of the Scott Trust (though the same could apply to other newspaper trusts) we were caught twice over. In effect, the company was faced with having to pay a double tax which no commercially owned newspaper group carried. The new taxes would treat the Trust 'as though it were a small number of exceedingly rich individuals whose wealth ought to be eroded by redistribution'. In law, the Trust was legally prevented from accumulating funds. As a result the company would have to provide funds for payment of any assessment out of its *post-tax* profits (post Corporation Tax). This provision in turn must become subject to income tax at investment income surcharge rates, and the cumulative effect was very great. Even on an optimistic forecast, in many years it was bound to exceed the profits of the company, which were at present ploughed back. I then provided figures to show that in only two of the past ten years could the company have provided the sum required. Beyond doubt, the *Guardian* was going to be crippled in a very short time.

All this and much more I said to Commissioner Johnson. It was impossible to believe that the Government, in properly closing a tax loophole, had intended to kill a trust from which no individual ever received any financial benefit. That was why we were seeking exemption. He replied that, so far as he knew, having considered the matter the Chancellor did not intend to make special provision for newspaper trusts. To do so would be too difficult and too dangerous, because of the risk of opening new loopholes which others would use for tax avoidance. Others could let assets accumulate under the guise of public benefit although they would later be taken back into private benefit, and this would be wholly against the intention of the law on CTT. While not doubting the purpose or intentions of the Scott Trust, he could offer little or no hope that anything would be done to help us.

I had deployed all my arguments: he had yielded nothing. About twenty-five or thirty minutes had passed. I was stuck. Mercifully, at that moment a civil service tea-lady appeared – in smarter uniform than usual, and bearing china of a delicately non-institutional character. That gave me a minute or two to think. I could see no way forward, and the outlook for the *Guardian* was extremely bleak. So, I thought, I might as well start at the beginning again and go through the whole of my case once more.

That worked. This time some tiny shafts of light began to appear. One was that, depending on the debate in committee, the Finance Bill might be amended to extend the 'grace period' before first assessments applied.

Another was that two Finance Bills were likely in coming months, and the second could amend the first. A third point was that the Chancellor might take account of any recommendation made by the Royal Commission, to which we had put our case on the social value of newspaper trusts.

But these were no more than straws to a drowning man, and I was feeling desperate. So when Commissioner Johnson for the third time mentioned the probability of a controversial committee stage, I replied that the *Guardian*, however reluctantly, might have to brief the Conservatives on our problem. My recent experience with the committee stage of Foot's Trade Union Bill suggested that it would do us little good, since the Conservatives would probably treat this as ammunition to fire at the Chancellor. But what alternative was left to us?

That brought the Treasury man into action. Would I, he asked, refrain from saying anything to the Conservatives until the Chancellor had had an opportunity to write to me? He had discussed the position with the Chancellor the previous Friday (this being Monday), and he knew that Healey was about to write to me. He was sure that the letter would be in my hands before the end of the Christmas recess – that is, before the committee met. But the letter, he thought, would say no more than we had heard this morning.

Stanley Porter and I emerged from a side entrance and walked on to Waterloo Bridge for air. It was a freezing day, with a clear blue sky, but I was sweating. Stanley was shaken, too, though he had a good finance man's phlegm. Having compared notes, we decided that there was nothing more to be done immediately; he set off back to Manchester, and I to Gray's Inn Road to write a minute for Richard Scott (then in the South of France, where he lived on a small vineyard), Peter Gibbings (who would have been with us but had had to go to Manchester), and Lovell, White, and King.

The first week of January saw us back meeting tax advisers, counsel, and LW&K. We went over all the options once again, finishing close to where we had started. I rang the Treasury on the 8th and had a call back on the 9th: a letter was now on its way from the Chancellor, but it said no more than that we should meet when Healey returned from the United States in ten days' time. Peter Middleton, the Treasury man who had been at the Somerset House meeting, added that the Chancellor had also sent a note to the Inland Revenue saying that they must find a way to deal with our problem. They said it was extremely difficult, but he had said that he was not going to put the *Guardian* out of business. Peter Middleton said that the Treasury were not convinced by our view on reconstituting the Trust; I said that it was nevertheless held by extremely well-qualified counsel to be a hazardous course. He asked, meanwhile, that I should still say nothing to the Conservatives.

Since I was in touch with 10 Downing Street on another matter, and the Prime Minister was due to lunch with us the following week, I mentioned the tax issue. A message came back asking me to supply a short memorandum on the subject. Having cleared with Peter Middleton that this was not going to cause trouble with the Chancellor, I put together a crisp two pages. A copy was flown out to America, so that the Chancellor could read it on the plane coming home. It said once again that neither CTT nor the Wealth Tax had been intended to catch such a trust as ours, and that no public purpose would be served by imposing on the Scott Trust a levy which would force the end of publication of the *Guardian*.

The memorandum then set out five courses open to us. To form a trust 'for the benefit of employees' was impracticable for reasons that were summarised; so was reconstitution as a charitable trust. The best answer was that the Government should exempt newspaper trusts, just as they were exempting trusts for the benefit of employees. A fourth possibility was an extremely ingenious scheme devised by our lawyers, for reconstitution as 'a company limited by guarantee', but it was feasible only if the Inland Revenue in advance would assure us of tax clearances at certain stages; and I was extremely uneasy about it because of its sheer complexity and because it left uncertain the status of the trustees in matters of editorial conduct and editorial freedom. The fifth was the simplest, toughest, and now the most probable option. It was that we should carry on the business as at present until June 1976, then tell the Government that we had no money with which to meet the first CTT assessment, and invite them to consider what they wanted us to do. Since it was certain that the Industry Department would still be pouring millions out to lame ducks, while *G&MEN* until then would have been self-sufficient, it would be an ironic situation. Nevertheless that now looked like being our safest course. With that, the memorandum ended.

When Wilson came to lunch he had read it. He said little more than that it was a matter for the Chancellor, but we could be assured that his Government was not going to put the *Guardian* out of business. That was a good start. When Healey returned from the United States, he asked us to visit him. I went, together with Richard Scott and Peter Gibbings, and we took with us a new wording designed to block up any fresh loopholes. In fact we did not have to produce it, because Denis Healey, in an ebullient mood, said at once that he had decided to exempt newspaper trusts. He said that the method of doing it must be discussed further with the Inland Revenue and might involve an amendment of our trust deed. A public announcement would be made soon. He added that my two-page memorandum had been a great help in clearing his mind.

Though we were not out of difficulty, we went home that day (January 23) feeling a lot less worried. A letter confirming what he had said arrived by hand next day. The public announcement did not come until February 18, but that did not bother us because we had said nothing to anyone except the Royal Commission – not even to our own staff. The statement, made in the standing committee on the Finance Bill, said that complete exemption from CTT was to be given 'on newspaper trusts where no benefit can accrue to individuals in any way connected with the settlor'. But, it said, legislation would have to wait for the next Finance Bill.

That was excellent news, and I wrote a leader to explain what the fuss was about and why the news was so welcome to us. I had briefed the senior staff some days beforehand, but there were still many questions from others at Gray's Inn Road and in Manchester, and some suspicion that there must be more to it than we had explained.

The ending was still a long way off, though it was a happy one. A battery of further consultations had to take place at Somerset House, in counsel's chambers, and once on a bench in the law courts. By late June we were again becoming worried by the absence of an agreed formula, and I was supposed to go on long leave at the beginning of July – having handed over the editorship to Peter Preston, and preparatory to departing to Scotland. There was a long meeting at Somerset House on July 10, at which we thought the shape of a settlement was beginning to emerge, and a further session with counsel at Lincoln's Inn stretching until after the summer darkness had descended on July 11; and I was due to take my family on holiday to the Pyrenees, sailing with an early ferry from Southampton on July 12 – which I did, but too exhausted to enjoy myself much in the first few days.

The final formula was not reached until March 15, 1976, and was incorporated in the Finance Bill in April. For me it meant three special journeys from Scotland to attend the conclusive meetings; and, thank goodness, in the end the formula required of us no amendment of the Scott Trust and offered the prospect of continuity well into the next century. In the later stages we had a great deal of help from a new trustee, Hubert Monroe, who was himself a QC and a Special Commissioner of Inland Revenue; his appointment to the Trust at that juncture, when we were in turmoil over the tax question, was a fortunate coincidence for he had been invited to join before CTT became a bogy to us.

After all that, it may be of interest if I quote the relevant words from the Finance Act, 1976:

93. - (1) Paragraph 17 of Schedule 5 to the Finance Act 1975 shall be amended as follows.
    (2) After sub-paragraph (4) there shall be inserted – '(4a) Where any property to which this paragraph applies ceases to be compromised in a settlement and, either immediately or not more than one month later, the whole of it becomes comprised in another settlement, then, if this paragraph again applies to it when it becomes comprised in the second settlement, it shall be treated for all the purposes of this Part of this Act as if it had been comprised in the first settlement.'
94. - (1) The following paragraph shall be inserted after paragraph 17 of Schedule 5 to the Finance Act 1975 –
    '(2) This paragraph applies to a settlement if shares in a newspaper publishing

company or a newspaper holding company are the only or principal property comprised in the settlement.

'(3) In this paragraph –

"newspaper publishing company" means a company whose business consists wholly or mainly in the publication of newspapers in the United Kingdom; and ... [definition of a newspaper holding company].

and for the purposes of this paragraph shares shall be treated as the principal property comprised in a settlement or the principal asset of a company if the remaining property comprised in the settlement or the remaining assets of the company are such as may be reasonably required to enable the trustees or the company to secure the operation of the newspaper publishing company concerned.'

(2) This section shall be deemed to have come into force on 7th April 1976.

It was a far cry from writing leaders about the Korean war, General Franco, the Polish currency reform, and Truman's conflict with MacArthur, which was where I had begun with the *MG* nearly twenty-six years before; but negotiation of that formula was my last act as an executive member of the *Guardian*'s staff.

A farewell to Fleet Street

In 1966 the *Guardian* had been saved from a forced merger with the *Times* and then from extinction. In 1975 it had been saved again from unintended destruction by the Treasury and Inland Revenue. The Scott Trust, a feeble protector at first in the 1966 crisis, had recovered in the course of that crisis and lived up to its true purpose: for it was through the Trust that the *Guardian* was kept alive, and through the action of the company's new management between 1967 and 1970 that the paper was returned to health. Especially in the years between 1968 and 1975 – and onwards since 1975 – the paper has, I believe, lived up to all that C. P. Scott intended it to be. Of course I was too close to it to be a dispassionate judge of its performance; but as a passionately involved participant I thought it was a great paper.

By 1975, however, I was beginning to feel that it was time for a younger editor. Crozier died in the chair at the age of sixty-five, after twelve years as editor; Wadsworth's health collapsed also when he was sixty-five and still editor, after twelve years in charge. In 1975, though only fifty-five years old, I was about to enter my twentieth year as editor. The physical strain and mental tension were not lessening – though I could still beat most of the staff up the stairs to the composing room or on the one and a half mile walk back from Westminster, and I could write a sound leader or a front-page story as fast as anyone. But I wanted to stop editing while I was still fit, and if possible to return to Scotland while still capable of climbing.

That winter of 1974–75, with many weeks when I was diverted from the enjoyable side of editing – looking after the paper at night – strengthened the urge to move. (The following winter was very different, with snow climbing in the Highlands almost every weekend from January to late April.)

The chairman of the BBC, formerly Principal of Edinburgh University, knew of my wish to return north. When Michael Swann first asked whether I would run the BBC's Scottish operation, I was too deeply immersed in the Scott Trust's tax problem to consider it; but he came back, seeking an urgent decision, and the whole matter was settled in about five days. The announcement, published on March 14, said that the BBC's offer coincided with major changes in Scottish affairs and a new vitality in Scottish life, including the probable election of a Scottish Assembly and devolution of greater governmental authority from Westminster to Edinburgh. 'In this context,' it stated, 'the BBC has said that it intends to pursue a policy of giving greater autonomy to Scotland.' The terms of that announcement had been agreed with the BBC's Director-General, Sir Charles Curran. Regrettably, the BBC did not live up to its undertakings; but that is another story. The announcement said that for me the decision to leave had been difficult, for 'the editorship of the *Guardian* is in my view one of the best jobs in British journalism'. But a decision on the BBC's proposal could not be postponed.

The farewells included a lunch given by the Prime Minister at 10 Downing Street which Miranda attended, another given by Denis Healey at 11 Downing Street, one arranged by Denis Hamilton with all the Fleet Street editors, and a big *Guardian* staff party in the autumn. The board and the trustees, in addition to a dinner, presented me with a small and beautiful piece of sculpture. Miranda was there, too, but to my great sorrow had decided not to come to Scotland; she had patiently endured eighteen years of a life dominated by newspaper office demands, and she wished to make a career of her own. That I understood, though I would not have accepted the BBC offer if I had known that she might not come north.

I missed the *Guardian* greatly, as I knew I would. I missed the companionship of men and women of sharp intellect, political acumen, cheerful irreverence, and yet serious purpose. I missed the stimulus of news, of never knowing what topic would dominate the next day's work, and of getting the paper out every night. But the *Guardian*, I am sure, was better off with a fresh and younger editor. There was an awkward period of transition, with the switch to facsimile transmission. Since then the paper's quality and performance seem to me to have been stronger than ever. Financially it remains insecure, although thanks to sound management it is less insecure than many others in Fleet Street. It is still a friendly place to work and a powerful force for good.

Thanks

The warmest thanks to any and every reader who has persevered this far, or who has dipped in and enjoyed parts of this book.

And to all *Guardian* staff, past and present;
to all *Guardian* readers, past and present;
to Peter Gibbings and Peter Preston, for use of *Guardian* files and photographs;
to Bill Papas, for his admirable cartoons and drawings;
to Miranda Hetherington, and Tom, Alex, Lucy, and Mary, for a happy home in the years covered by this book;
to Sheila Hetherington, for research and valuable advice during the writing of the book, and for my new home since 1979;
to Nigel Bowles, at Nuffield College, Oxford, for reading the whole manuscript and proposing many improvements;
to the librarians at Nuffield College and at Glasgow University, for the use of their facilities;
to Frank Singleton and Ken Murphy, in the *Guardian*'s Manchester and London libraries, for their help;
and to Jeremy Lewis and Elizabeth Burke, at Chatto.

Alastair Hetherington

High Corrie
Isle of Arran
February 1981

Appendix A

TRADING RESULTS (£1,000s)

Year to March	The 'Guardian'	'MEN'	Other†	Group trading
1956	+59	+162	-	+211
1957	+24	+82	-	+105
1958	+38	+120	-	+158
1959	+26	+152	-	+184
1960	+66	+277	(44)	+377
1961	-3	+340	+a	+337
1962	-349	+158* (EC bought)	+a	-191
1963	-421	+174*	+a	-247
1964	-419	+481* (EN & EC merged)	+a	+62
1965	-635	+970*	+a	+335
1966	-601	+1,077*	+a	+476
1967	-777	(+1,000)*	?	+399
1968	-718	(+1,000)*	?	+273
1969	-936	+1,220*	-29	+261
1970	-1,155	+1,074* (Thomson share ceased)	-213	-185
1971	-1,206	+1,407	-293	-92
1972	-950	+1,432	-125	+357
1973	-769	+2,877	+343	+2,451
1974	-1,033	+3,360	+368	+2,695
1975	-1,261	+2,385	+227	+1,351

* Proportion paid to MG&EN (i.e. four-fifths of total).
a Anglia and other ancillary profit in each of those years. c £85,000 to £100,000.
† Apart from Anglia, which was profitable from an early stage, chiefly investments in property and buildings unconnected with newspaper publication.

Appendix B

January 20, 1975

ROUGH DRAFT OF AGREEMENT ON PRESS FREEDOM AND THE AVOIDANCE OF
IMPROPER PRESSURES

1 This declaration affirms the support of its adherents to the principle of the freedom of the press and other media to collect and publish information, whether written or visual, and to express comment and criticism.

2 We accept that the reputations of individuals must be protected by laws against defamation, though we believe that truth ought always to be a complete defence. We believe that news must not be distorted, suppressed, or censored and that comment ought to be fair and based on accurate facts. We accept that opinions and conjecture ought not to be presented as established fact and that it is wrong to falsify by selection or misrepresentation. We affirm that it is no less wrong for Governments, public authorities, corporate bodies, and individuals to issue misleading information or untrue denials. We believe that editors and journalists in all media must exercise due care and judgment in seeking to present true facts, in avoidance of either misleading their readers or of themselves being misled, and in endeavouring to be fair. We hold that editors and journalists, so long as they adhere to the principles stated here, ought to be protected from improper pressures, whether external or internal.

3 In particular we hold that managements must acknowledge the independence of editorial judgment and the ultimate responsibility of individual editors, in law and in practice, for the contents and conduct of their newspapers, periodicals, or broadcasting. We hold that neither editors nor individual journalists should be subject to instructions or directions from any trade union or association, whether their own or another, either on editorial policy or on their handling of specific reports, articles, pictures, or programmes; except that unions or associations may seek adherence by their members to their published professional codes of conduct, may give instructions to their members about agreed working hours and conditions, and may call upon members other than editors and their deputies to take industrial action at times of an official dispute.

4 We accept that the journalists of any newspaper, periodical, or broadcasting organisation have a right to be heard by their proprietors, managements, editors, or departmental heads on matters of editorial policy and conduct, on senior editorial appointments, and on the principles that may apply to other editorial appointments. At the same time we accept that the weight that may be given to their advice will depend on the knowledge, experience, and purposes of those who offer it. We acknowledge also that individual appointments are an area where discussion and negotiation must be confidential. We further accept that, to the extent that staff views may bear on the manner and conduct of a newspaper or broadcasting organisation, employers are within their rights in seeking information

about the political affiliations and activities of applicants for any journalistic job. In the whole field of staff involvement in helping to shape policy or reach executive decisions we recognise that informal consultation is likely to be at least as effective as a formal approach.

5 We acknowledge that, while normal newspaper work and the preparation of news broadcasts must be reserved for trained journalists, access to a newspaper's columns and to broadcasting time ought not to be barred to any citizen or group of citizens. Within the limits of space and time and the requirements of commercial viability, editors ought to give fair representation to opposing and minority points of view. While the NUJ and IoJ are entitled to protect their members' earnings, restraints must not be placed on the right of editors to publish contributions from a wide range of authors.

6 While recognising that the broad principles of press freedom are bound to be open to differing interpretations, we acknowledge the need for external and internal means of dealing with complaints and preventing abuses. The law and courts remain the final defence against defamation, obscenity, and contempt. The Press Council also stands as the primary forum through which an individual citizen or public body can secure investigation of a complaint. (What about broadcasting?) Within any office, informal discussion and reconciliation are generally the most expedient remedy. In addition, the NUJ and IoJ have their codes of conduct and any complaints by one journalist member against another journalist member can properly be considered through their disciplinary procedures; though it is of the highest importance that their procedures should be impartially administered and should respect natural justice.

7 Beyond these, we believe that it will also be beneficial if the Press Council accepts the need to investigate and report on any case where improper pressure is alleged to have been applied by a proprietor or management representative or trade union or group of workers or advertiser or Government body or other source of influence.

Possible parties: NUJ, NPA, NS, IoJ, Guild, SDNS, SNPA, ? Press Council ? Fleet Street editors individually

A. Hetherington
The *Guardian*

Biographical Notes

IAN AITKEN, political correspondent (one of two) from 1964 onwards. An Airdrie man and Oxford scholar; a factory inspector and then a trade union official, 1951-54 (approx.); with *Tribune*, *Reynolds News*, and the *Daily Express* between 1954-64, being one of the *Express* team in the US, 1958-61, and political editor of the *Express*, 1963-64. Tubby, convivial, and cheerful; a great asset to the *Guardian* because of his excellence as a political correspondent and the soundness of his advice. Married to a practising GP who was also a match for most of us in political argument.

J. R. L. ANDERSON, an assistant editor, 1948-67. An extraordinary man – thin, tense, moody, but an outstanding journalist. In 1944, only weeks after being invalided out of the Army, he returned to North-west Europe as one of the *MG*'s war correspondents. Chief correspondent in Berlin and West Germany, 1945-46; labour correspondent, 1946-48, and long remembered for his reporting of the first big strike in the nationalised coal industry – at Grimethorpe, in Yorkshire, where he went to live among the miners in order to write about their mood of frustration. An ardent yachtsman; he reconstructed the first Viking voyage to North America, sending radio messages to the *Guardian* two or three times a week as he navigated down the coast of Greenland and on to New England. Inherited property on the Thames and went to live there in 1967, writing books.

LEONARD BEATON: See Index.

FRANCIS BOYD, political correspondent 1946-71 (until 1964 we had only one political correspondent, but two thereafter). Joined *MG* as reporter 1934 from the *Leeds Mercury*; parliamentary sketch-writer 1937-39, then in Army; columnist and political editor, 1972-75. Knighted, along with his friend and rival, the *Telegraph*'s Harry Boyne, in 1976 after both had retired. Careful and thorough as a political correspondent, a reliable carthorse beside Ian Aitken's racehorse qualities – making them a good pair. A member of the Scott Trust from 1961 until retirement.

NEVILLE CARDUS, joined the *MG* in 1917, for 'semi-secretarial' duties under C. P. Scott, but soon became reporter and then cricket correspondent and music critic. He left in 1939 to go to Australia but returned to England in 1947 and continued contributing for a further quarter century. His *Autobiography* is on my short list of recommended reading for aspiring journalists.

LINDA CHRISTMAS, joined 1971 from *Times Educational Supplement*. Previously with Westminster Press at Swindon. Features writer, 1971-73; editor, 'Guardian Miscellany', 1973-75; prices and consumer affairs correspondent, 1975-77, and general features writer since 1977. A good source of ideas.

ANN CLWYD (Mrs A. C. Roberts), Welsh correspondent for ten years from about 1969; contested Denbigh for Labour in 1970 and Gloucester in 1974; Euro-MP for Mid and West Wales from 1979; vice-chairman of the Welsh Arts Council, 1975-79; member of the Royal Commission on the National Health Service, 1976-79. A fervent Welshwoman who wrote well.

JOHN COLE: See Index.

ALISTAIR COOKE, the *MG*'s UN correspondent, 1945-48, and chief American correspondent, 1948-70. At his peak, in the fifties, Cooke was one of the world's greatest journalists; his command of the English language was supreme, and his memory was so good that he needed no filing system. His coverage of the Hiss trial in 1949 was a classic of sustained reporting; and his work in the presidential campaigns of 1948, '52, and '56 was outstanding. He had a marvellous range of interests, from jazz and boxing to the physical geography of the American scene. But he had a slight blind spot about civil rights in the South, which was part cause of friction with Max Freedman; and latterly his involvement with television tended to distract his attention from *Guardian* work. The *Guardian*'s loss was television's gain, for he is a superb performer. Born in Lancashire and educated at Blackpool Grammar School before Cambridge; a naturalised American citizen.

WILLIAM DAVIS, financial editor, September 1965 to October 1968. He came from the *Evening Standard* and had the congenital optimism of a good Beaverbrook man. He was not a deep thinker, as Richard Fry had been and Hamish MacRae later proved, nor was he a deep investigator such as Charles Raw. But he was an excellent publicist, with a gift for imparting life to financial affairs, and he generated enthusiasm among his staff. He broadened the range of the City pages; and he left in 1968 to become editor of *Punch*. He had an ability to perceive simple truths - such as, in the sterling crisis of 1966, that foreign bankers studied the British press and the Government must say the same things at home and abroad, which even Harold Wilson until then had not absorbed.

CHRISTOPHER DRIVER, joined the *Guardian* from *Liverpool Post* in 1960; reporter until appointed features editor in 1964; freelance journalist and author from 1968, and editor of the *Good Food Guide*. Combined political, ecumenical-ecclesiastical, artistic, and gastronomic interests with great success.

JOHN FAIRHALL, joined 1962 as reporter. Previously with *Birmingham Dispatch*, *Smethwick Telephone* (three former *Telephone* men were on the *Guardian*), *Uganda Argus*, and the *Nation* (Nairobi). In Uganda for the *Guardian*, 1972; education correspondent from 1973. Brother of David Fairhall, defence correspondent. Both were yachtsmen.

DARSIE GILLIE, Paris correspondent, 1945-66; a huge teddy-bear of a man and probably the most learned of *Guardian* correspondents - a member of the Académie des Inscriptions, a classicist and archaeologist, and a first-class political journalist. Pre-war he served in Poland, Germany, and France with the *Morning Post* (merged with the *Telegraph*) and the *Times*. During the war he was in charge of the BBC's French service, and consequently in close touch with de Gaulle's team, some of whom became Ministers after the war but remained his friends. He was more at home with the *MG* than with his previous papers, for instead of being directed from London on what to cover he decided that for himself, and he was a non-conformist of *Guardian* character anyway. His coverage of French affairs was second to none; yet he once said to me that the only job he would prefer was that of professor of Greek at St Andrews, a post he could have filled with distinction. Sometimes he annoyed me by writing for the *Spectator* short and simple articles that I would have liked for the *Guardian*, but he called them 'boulevard journalism'. He was married to the BBC's representative in Paris, Cecilia Reeves.

HAROLD GRIFFITHS, joined *MG* from *Glasgow Herald*, 1955, as leader writer. Moved to London, 1962, and deputy financial editor, 1962-65; returned to leader writers' group, 1965, but left for the Treasury in 1967. For discussion of Common Market policy see Chapter 8, and for economic policy, Chapter 9. Harold was a son of James Griffiths, a member of Attlee's Cabinet and Harold Wilson's first Secretary of State for Wales.

KEITH HARPER, joined as reporter, 1961, from *Bristol Evening World*. Labour staff, 1968, until appointed labour correspondent, 1972.

ANTHONY HOWARD, reporter, 1959-61, specialising in politics; came from *Reynolds News*, went to the *New Statesman*, then *Sunday Times*, and then *Observer*. Editor of the *New Statesman*, 1972-78, and of the *Listener* from 1979. A short stay with the *Guardian* but a lively one. (He was a serving officer at Suez, as a platoon commander in the Royal Fusiliers.)

HARRY JACKSON, one of the few Londoners on the old *MG* staff, and now (1981) Washington correspondent. Joined about 1951; reporter in London, 1952-61; deputy news editor, 1961-65; special assignments at home and abroad, 1966-72; features editor, 1972-75 (to give him a rest after much travel, but it was no real rest). Tough, wiry, independent, and reliable. Appears a number of times in this book, especially in Arab-Israeli wars and in Ireland.

PETER JENKINS, joined 1960 as financial reporter (from *FT*); labour correspondent, 1963-67; political columnist from 1967 onwards, and also worked two years as Washington correspondent. Author of *The Battle of Downing Street* (1970), mentioned in Chapter 9. A notable columnist, though sometimes impatient with lesser mortals. Married to Polly Toynbee.

PATRICK KEATLEY, joined 1952 as reporter, from Vancouver; made his mark by exposure of maltreatment of horses being sold from Ireland for slaughter in France and Belgium. Specialist in African affairs; he kept in close touch with Kaunda, Nyerere, and Mboya from well before their countries' independence. Commonwealth correspondent from 1958 and diplomatic correspondent from 1967. Reputed to write his copy from Bush House, between World Service broadcasts, but that was an exaggeration; retained his youthful enthusiasm well into middle age. A source of many 'scoops'.

JOHN KERR, joined from *Glasgow Herald*, 1969, as Scottish correspondent; skier, mountaineer, and golfer as well as journalist; moved to BBC Scotland in 1977; member of the Clayson Committee on the licensing laws in Scotland, 1971-73. Rooted in Scotland but with a civilised knowledge of the world.

DAVID MARQUAND, recruited from post-graduate work at Oxford, 1959; leader writer until 1964, and occasional contributor thereafter. He stimulated senior common room exchanges in the leader writers' meetings. Labour MP for Ashfield, Derbyshire, 1966-77; adviser to Roy Jenkins at the European Commission, 1977-78; professor of politics at Salford since 1978.

PADDY MONKHOUSE: See Index.

JAMES/JAN MORRIS (James while with the *Guardian*), joined from the *Times* in 1958, having been *Times* correspondent on the first successful Everest expedition and having also spent much time in the United States and in the Middle East. Stayed five years with the *Guardian*, though under an arrangement which let him have a few months off each year for writing his books. Mostly wrote special features for us, but was also used for foreign emergencies – at one time transferring non-stop from Iceland (the fish war) to Algeria, where the civil war had taken an acute turn. Eventually took to full-time authorship, saying he was going to live in Montgomery because it was the only English or Welsh county with no traffic lights; in fact he went further west, to Lloyd George's Lleyn peninsula. Jan Morris from about 1973.

DAVID MCKIE, joined as a reporter in 1965, specialising in politics. Like Adam Raphael, he came from the Westminster Press, having served them in Keighley, Oxford, and London. Deputy features editor, 1968–70, under Peter Preston; deputy news editor, 1970–72, and prime organiser of 1970 general election coverage. Second political correspondent, with Ian Aitken, 1972–75; became deputy editor when Peter Preston took over as editor.

HELLA PICK, an indefatigable seeker of inside information and good at making economics intelligible. Austrian by birth; brought up in England; economist and linguist. Worked in West Africa, 1958–60 (until sacked from IPC by Cecil King personally); talked her way on to the *Guardian* staff, 1960, after freelance cover from Congo. Spells at UN and in Washington, 1961–66; Geneva base, 1967–70, with special interest in European integration; covered Common Market negotiations from London base, 1970–72; Washington, 1972–73; since then mainly covering East European politics and West European economics. For Hella on the Common Market, see Chapter 8; and on devaluation, see Chapter 9.

PETER PRESTON: See Index.

ADAM RAPHAEL, reporter. Joined in 1966, after training with Westminster Press at Swindon and Bath. Motoring correspondent as well as general reporter at first; in 1969 upset Dick Crossman but drew grudging admiration for the information he uncovered on Dick's pension and social security plans. (Dick said he would gladly pay Adam's one-way fare to Karachi to get rid of him.) To Washington, 1968–72. Joined *Observer* as political correspondent in 1976. The only member of the staff who regularly called me 'sir', in spite of discouragement, but could do so in a nicely insulting way.

BRIAN REDHEAD, reporter from 1954 (previously working in Newcastle, his home area); the *Guardian*'s first features editor, 1959–62; with BBC, 1962–64, with 'Tonight' team; planning correspondent, 1964–65; Northern editor, 1965–69, and important in maintaining morale among the Northern staff after the editorial headquarters moved south; editor of the *Manchester Evening News*, 1969–75. Freelance journalist and broadcaster thereafter. A fluent writer and talker.

NESTA ROBERTS, joined 1947, as reporter, from *Nottingham Journal* and *Evening News*. Previously she had had 'backpage' feature articles published in the *MG* from the age of nineteen onwards; first worked as a reporter with the *Barry and District News*. Deputy news editor, in Manchester, 1958–61; the first news editor in London (see Index), 1961–63. Health and welfare correspondent, 1963–66, and Paris correspondent, 1966–72. Continued as a freelance contributor from France, Italy, and the UK for some further years. A stylist.

JOHN ROSSELLI, son of the Italian Social Democrat leader Carlo Rosselli, who was murdered in France by Mussolini's agents; educated mainly in the United States, and post-graduate at Cambridge. Leader writer, 1951 onwards, also literary editor, 1953–56; deputy London editor, 1956–61, and occasional foreign correspondent; features editor, 1962–64.

CLYDE SANGER, joined as reporter in 1959 from *Central African Examiner*; staff correspondent in East and Central Africa, 1960–65, and at UN, 1965–67. With *Toronto Globe and Mail*, in Toronto, 1967–71, and *Guardian*'s correspondent in Canada since 1967, except 1977–79 when with Commonwealth Secretariat. Among many exploits in Africa was an escape from custody during troubles in Zanzibar, which involved swimming to secure an Arab dhow to carry a group of imprisoned journalists. Afterwards the chief African correspondent of *Newsweek*, John Nugent, wrote: 'I want you to know that of all the people locked up by the Zanzibar forces only Clyde Sanger consistently had the sense of awareness and good timing to keep all involved calm when the going got sticky. Were it not for his presence we might have been in a lot more trouble.'

LAURENCE SCOTT: See Index.

RICHARD SCOTT: See Index.

NORMAN SHRAPNEL, joined *MG* 1947. Reporter, feature writer, and drama critic until 1958, when he moved to Parliament as sketch-writer (or Parliamentary correspondent) – transferring, as he said, to a theatre with one of the best casts in the world. A shy and rather taciturn man, but good at getting other people to talk, as may be seen from items in successive *Bedside Guardians*. Retired early, about 1974, in order to have more time for his own writing and to live in the country.

JEAN STEAD: See Index.

MARY STOTT, joined 1957, from *Co-operative Press*; had previously been with *MEN* and other newspapers. Women's page editor, 1957–71. Married to Ken Stott, Northern editor of *News Chronicle*. See her autobiography, *Forgetting's No Excuse*, published by Virago.

GEOFFREY TAYLOR, joined *MG* 1947 as a sub-editor, and became chief foreign sub; away as editorial adviser to *Daily Times*, Lagos, 1956–59; foreign editor, 1960–69, also writing nearly all the African leaders in that period and later, and making a number of reporting journeys through Africa; Northern editor, 1969–72; to London as an assistant editor from 1973 onwards. A reserved man, good with his staff, and at home equally with writing-reporting and with editorial production. Contrived to live in remote rural locations, miles from anywhere or anything, but to get to the office on time. A writer of delightful light-hearted and leg-pulling leaders.

HARFORD THOMAS: See Index.

HARRY WHEWELL, one of the true Northerners. Reporter, 1950–57, and specialist in industrial affairs; Northern news editor, 1957–75; Northern editor from 1975. An agreeable touch of whimsy, in addition to straight reporting. Companionable. Married to story-line writer of 'Coronation Street'.

IAN WRIGHT, joined 1961, having been a community development officer in Kenya and then on the staff of Roy Thomson's *Timmins Daily Press*, in Canada. Started as news sub-editor; then to features, including work as film critic. In 1963, while on a facility trip (a tourist promotion) to Uganda, obtained a 'scoop' on refugees coming from fighting on southern Sudan; was sent back to the Horn of Africa and to Aden a number of times, 1964-66. To Vietnam, 1968-70, newly married (wife from FO's South-east Asia section, but became Saigon correspondent for *Economist* and others); covered everything from fighting in the northern provinces (the 'Scottish sector' because of its hills) to reconstruction in the delta. In August '70, on receiving cable asking him whether he would accept foreign editor's post living in Manchester, he replied at once 'Will exchange Saigon for anywhere stop booking on next flight'. Foreign editor, 1970-75; then to London as an assistant editor.

VICTOR ZORZA, our 'Kremlinologist' or commentator on Soviet affairs - intermittently from 1950 and regularly from 1953. By origin a Jew from eastern Poland; deported to Russia in 1939, aged fourteen, and sustained his family by black market operations; later escaped from a labour camp and made his way by the Middle East to England, where he joined the Polish air force; with BBC monitoring service after the war. An intense and complex mind, thriving on slivers of evidence that others might neglect. Journalist of the Year in 1968, after his accurate forecasting, a month before the event, of the virtual certainty of a Soviet invasion of Czechoslovakia - but, characteristically, he was furious with Harford Thomas for making his story the front-page lead and putting the point at the beginning, when by his careful process of logic he had left it to the middle of his article. (No less characteristically, he forgave Harford afterwards.) Most of his work was in analytical articles, sometimes rather turgid, but occasionally he wrote powerful first-hand reports - as from the Austrian border during the 1956 Hungarian rising. In some ways unworldly: I once found him in seclusion in a Lake District hotel, where he had gone to think - surrounded by some of the best food in England (for which the hotel was renowned) but eating next to nothing.

Index